P9-DWJ-771

OTHER WORKS BY WAYNE W. DYER

Your Erroneous Zones: Bold But Simple Techniques for Eliminating Unhealthy Behavior Patterns

Pulling Your Own Strings: Dynamic Techniques for Confidently Enjoying Your Life Your Way, Without Being Manipulated

Counseling Effectively in Groups (with John Vriend)

Counseling Techniques That Work: Applications to Individual and Group Counseling (with John Vriend)

Group Counseling for Personal Mastery: Everything You Need to Know to Lead Any Group in Any Setting (with John Vriend)

THE SKY'S

THE LIMIT

Dr. Wayne W. Dyer

SIMON AND SCHUSTER
NEW YORK

Published by Simon and Schuster
A Division of Gulf & Western Corporation
Simon & Schuster Building
Rockefeller Center
1230 Avenue of the Americas
New York, New York 10020

SIMON AND SCHUSTER and colophon are trademarks of Simon & Schuster
Designed by Eve Kirch
Manufactured in the United States of America

1 2 3 4 5 6 7 8 9 10

Library of Congress Cataloging in Publication Data

Dyer, Wayne W
  The sky's the limit.

  1. Self-actualization (Psychology) I. Title.
BF637.S4D89   158'.1   80-18616

ISBN 0-671-24989-4

To the memory of Abraham H. Maslow—the original pathfinder in the study of man's potential for greatness

To Cynthia Page Subby—who provided a special light for the creation of this book

Contents

Introduction

What's Your Limit?

Every once in a while you will hear somebody who's offered a third, fourth or fifth drink at a cocktail party say, "No, thanks, I've reached my limit."

That's a smart thing to say when you're drinking alcohol. Unless you are particularly fond of hangovers, or of abusing your body and your mind, it pays to know your own alcohol limit and respect it.

But too often, when we are offered a third, fourth or fifth drink from the cup of life (and life always offers, whether we realize it or not), we secretly say to ourselves, "Oh, no, I'd better not. I think I've reached my limit." As I once heard a babysitter yell after an exuberant child who was tearing around the house faster than she could follow, "Don't get too happy, now! Don't get too happy! You know every time you get too happy you fall down and hurt yourself!"

This book is about recognizing that, as far as your own potential for happiness, growth, creativity, constructiveness in society—whatever you as a human being value—is concerned, there are literally no limits to what you can attain.

Of course, if you want to do something that no human can—if

you want to be able to jump off a cliff (without a hang-glider) and fly—you are going to be out of luck. But this book is also about being able to become all that it is possible for a human to be—and, moreover, what *you* want to be, as opposed to what others or society as a whole demand that you be.

When I decided several years ago to give up writing textbooks which would be read by only a handful of professional people and to begin writing books for everyone, I had in mind a four-part program to help people achieve their own highest levels of happiness and fulfillment. I believed then, as I do today, that most people suffer unnecessary miseries in their lives because they don't know how to manage their emotions and have come to believe a lot of psychological nonsense, such as that "nobody's really psychologically healthy; everybody's at least a little bit neurotic," or "your personal problems are the products of deep-rooted character traits formed somewhere in your far-distant past, and digging them out will take years on the couch."

I wrote *Your Erroneous Zones* with the emphasis on how to rid yourself of self-defeating thinking and behavior, how to start thinking sensibly about making yourself "unneurotic," if you will. My second book, *Pulling Your Own Strings,* went on to show in a step-by-step fashion how to deal with other people who would manipulate or victimize you—people who may not have eliminated their own erroneous zones and who therefore may still feel they have to prove their self-worth by their ability to push you around.

Given that allowing yourself to fall into the victim traps of others is in its own way as much an erroneous zone as any of those dealt with in *Your Erroneous Zones,* we must combine the picture of the person who has eliminated his or her personal erroneous zones with that of the person who is pulling his or her own strings to form the picture of the total No Erroneous Zones, or *NEZ,* person.

Even when I began writing *Your Erroneous Zones,* however, I had in mind the ultimate book for the individual, which would teach how to go far beyond the NEZ state of being as defined in the first two books. There is far more to life than learning how to cope with your problems and how to deal with potential manipulators, how to manage your emotions and be assertive. Each person on this planet is inherently, intrinsically capable of attaining "dizzying heights" of happiness and fulfillment. The main barrier to most people's doing so seems to be fear, fear that the heights will make them dizzy instead of rooting their feet more firmly to the ground, which is actually what happens—as you will see in the pages to come.

There seems to be a widespread fear in our society of flying too close to the sun, of gaining too much and consequently losing it; of getting too happy and falling down. It infects not only individuals but the whole race. When we look at humanity's potentials for living in peace, harmony, productivity, even joy, and then look at the world as it is, the comparison is pathetic. And why has the human race gotten itself into this situation? For no other reason than that individuals have been blind to the limitlessness of their own potentials, and have spent their time striving to become average, to conform to what is "traditionally" expected of them, to fit into social structures that perpetuate the mess that much of the world is in.

"The sky's the limit" may be a cliché, and it certainly has been abused in recent years: "The sky's the limit on savings at Johnny's Used Car Lot." But the oldest clichés and stock phrases in our language usually contain the most truth, if we see them in their proper contexts; and if we really think about it, "The sky's the limit" turns out to be *most true* when applied to the potentials of human beings. If you think about it, the mysteries of the universe (how high is the sky?) are nothing compared to the mysteries of life.

Who is this living being who in the last few thousand years has crawled out of caves to create theories of relativity, to name the sky in the first place, to search the universe and even to prove that no machine designed according to any logical system—no human-designed computer—can ever match the mathematical creativity of the human mind?

So the next time you look at the sky in bewilderment and wonder, remember, you have within you far greater mysteries than this. The difference is that the sky cannot think about itself, cannot choose what it will be.

This book represents a turning point for me in many ways. I hope it also represents a turning point for you. It presents the how and the why for *total human development*, a program for learning how to think, feel and behave in ways that will enable you to transcend your "average" or "normal" self and evolve into a person you might never have dreamed of becoming until now. In these pages, I will encourage you to adopt humanistic values and a humanistic life style which will not only make your own life a joy to live each and every day, but will provide the world with the creative, imaginative leadership it needs to make it a more humane and more perfect place for all of us here, and those who will follow us.

To mark this turning point, to put a name to that person we can each become if we choose, I have coined a new term. I will call that person who transcends his or her "average" or "normal" self and fulfills his or her own greatest life potentials the No-Limit person, indicating that this person accepts no artificial or false limits.

The NEZ [No Erroneous Zones] person and the No-Limit person are really two sides of the same coin. You cannot become a No-Limit person without having eliminated your erroneous zones, and if you have eliminated them, if you are a NEZ person, you are already on the way to—or at least on the threshhold of—creating a life of full freedom for yourself. In this sense "NEZ" and "No-Limit" might be used interchangeably. But where I use "NEZ," it is usually to refer to "the bird before takeoff"—to the person who has eliminated her erroneous zones, but has not yet quite tested her new wings. Where I use "No-Limit," it is usually to refer to those who are already flying off into the limitless blue.

I hope you find this book excitingly *original*, not only in the sense that it says some new things, but in the greater sense that it is pregnant with thoughts that will strike responsive chords in you and help you to originate your own new way of looking at yourself and the world.

But if any book is to be truly original, it must be deeply rooted in what the author considers to be the most vital and seminal thought of the past.

Philosopher friends tell me it was Aristotle who first thought to define living things not in terms of what they happened to be at a given time, but in terms of their *potentials*, or what they naturally and *at their best* could become, which is the way I believe we should all see ourselves—while admitting that at any given time *we are actually the best we can be at that time!* (You're allowed to be perfect!)

Unfortunately the idea of exploring humanity's limitless potential for greatness has hardly been dominant in contemporary society, and so this book's "roots" lie deep in the work of a few extraordinary and "atypical" thinkers, rather than in the many writings of those in the "mainstream" of what today passes for psychology and philosophy.

Of the significant thinkers influencing my own development, by far the most important was the late Dr. Abraham Maslow, who devoted a large portion of his life to the study of what he called "self-actualization," or the very highest levels of being or evolution available to humanity. Maslow described the qualities that distinguish self-actualized people from others in an effort to create what he called a Psychology of Being. I have adopted or adapted a number of Maslow's "self-actualized" qualities in putting together my picture of the No-Limit person, and have dedicated this book to his memory because of my tremendous admiration for his pioneering spirit.

Maslow wanted to look at humanity from a different perspective. He believed in studying the great achievers and learning from their examples, rather than confining psychology to the study of sickness and low achievement, and ending up viewing humanity solely from the point of view of what can go wrong with the human psyche. Maslow believed in humanity's greatness. So do I.

My efforts in researching and writing this book have been directed toward making the work of Maslow and other kindred spirits in the humanistic sciences much more available and palatable to everyone. It is my belief that anyone can reach a high level of human development, can in fact become self-actualized, a No-Limit person, if he or she works at it. It boils down to the choices you are willing to make. No one is superior to anyone else by nature, and consequently anyone who wants to can make "great choices" and in fact become great as a human being.

In writing this book, I have emphasized the how as well as the why of becoming a No-Limit person. Too often, psychological researchers fall short when telling people precisely what they can do to attain their highest levels of human achievement and fulfillment. There is much speculation and philosophizing, but not enough specific *exploration,* in determining where we want to go and how to get there. I have tried to fill that "exploration gap" with this book. While I have learned a great deal from reading Maslow and others, and have in some ways tried to put what previous explorers have taught me into terminology for everyone, essentially I am presenting what I know to be true not because of what I've read, but because I have dedicated myself to *living it myself every day.* I have seen how to live *completely* in the present, and I know it works.

In many ways this book breaks the traditional boundaries of psychology and ventures into the realm of philosophy. Don't let that scare you, because I don't think of philosophy as that obscure jibberish spoken by academicians who call themselves philosophers nowadays. You can tell simply by the fact that you have never heard of a contemporary philosopher, that none has ever had anything to say to *you,* that academic philosophy must be a dead discipline—dead to the world, at least. The sad fact is that academic philosophy for the past thirty or forty years has been lost in the analysis of grammar and the construction of logical systems, concerned with technological and scientific issues to the exclusion of the humanistic search for wisdom that gave it birth in the first place. If "philosophers" fault a humanistic counselor like me for transgressing into their territory, they should look at themselves for neglecting the areas of that territory I'm trying to cultivate. For me "philosophy" retains its original meaning—it is the search for the ultimate human wisdom, and *somebody* has to do it. In fact, I think of myself first as a *practical philosopher* and only secondarily as a psychologist. Not since the great existentialists—Kierkegaard, Sartre, Heidegger—has anyone asked *what it is to be human,* and even the existentialists seldom looked at the greatest heights people can attain, focusing instead on pessimism and the absurdity of existence.

"Philosophers" today are so busy chopping logic or trying to prove that a tree exists or doesn't exist when nobody is looking at it, that they offer no help to the human being who must encounter the trees and forests of his own life.

This book is offered as a practical philosophy course in being fully human. At the core of my philosophy is the belief that you can motivate yourself and choose greatness even if you've never done so before. By avoiding academic psychological and philosophical jargon and replacing it with commonsense language, we can take the mystery out of understanding our own unique potential for becoming fully human and living happily on a daily basis. Just because some of the words and phrases that describe self-actualized people have defied "everyday-language" treatment by scholars, many of us everyday folks have come to believe that No-Limit living itself is beyond our reach.

If you have read *Your Erroneous Zones* and *Pulling Your Own Strings*, and have received help and enlightenment from them, I am sure you will see how this book naturally follows them and builds on their premises. It is not necessary to have read those books, however, to understand this one; where necessary, I have reintroduced themes and points from those books in order to develop them further here.

But in those two books and this one, I have written all that I have learned up until this point about living to your maximum potential, about gaining personal excitement and supreme ecstasy for yourself, combined with a genuine sense of purpose and mission which will give your life a meaning it may never have had before.

We are all grateful to those who make life throb to a swifter, stronger beat. I want to be one person who contributes to making your life, as well as my own, come *totally alive* each and every day. I want each person who reads my words, or listens to me talk, to be one step closer to his or her own full humanity. I want everyone to toss aside internal "psychological" barriers, and to see clearly what has been previously obscured: that *you can become all you choose for yourself.* If I can help you realize this for yourself, then my own sense of mission will be even more fulfilled.

I mentioned earlier that I had begun writing popular books with a *four-part program* for Total Human Development in mind. With *The Sky's the Limit,* my program for treating the adult individual as he or she relates to self, others and society is complete, but my program as a whole is only three-quarters finished. The "crucial last quarter" will consist of a book devoted to applying the principles of NEZ/No-Limit living to the raising of children.

It is indeed possible to raise children in such a way that they grow up to maximize their total humanity. They don't have to come down with the traditional "mind sicknesses" that most people inherit in our culture. Bringing up children to be fully functioning and creatively alive is a very real possibility, and the completion of a book which talks about how to do just that will be my next and final project in this series of books. Nothing can be more important to me or to us than the legacy of mental health and the belief in the limitless potential of human beings which we bequeath to the next and all future generations. But of course we cannot bequeath them until we have grasped them for ourselves.

Enjoy reading this book. I loved every minute I spent thinking about it, researching it, interviewing for it and writing it. If it infects you with the same enthusiasm for life that I have felt over these past months, we will all soon be flying together.

WAYNE DYER

When Alexander the Great visited Diogenes and asked whether he could do anything for the famed teacher, Diogenes replied, "Only stand out of my light." Perhaps some day we shall know how to heighten creativity. Until then, one of the best things we can do for creative men and women is to stand out of their light.

—JOHN W. GARDNER,
Self-Renewal

1 / NEZ to No Limits

YOU'RE ALLOWED TO BE PERFECT

Several years ago, while I was appearing on a national television show, a woman asked me a question that, judging from her demeaning tone, was intended to be a put-down. "Tell me," she said, "how does it feel to be perfect?"

This woman, like most other people, apparently feels that it is some kind of sin to think of yourself as perfect—that you should be dissatisfied with yourself and always be striving to try to fulfill somebody else's idea of what it is to be perfect, which of course always turns out to be unattainable. She probably also thinks that whatever is perfect has to stay forever as it is—that a "perfect" person would never change or grow. In fact, she probably thinks only God is perfect, which is why she thought it was a horrible sin of pride for me to admit that, in certain specific ways, I have concluded that you must allow yourself to think of yourself as perfect if you are ever to reach your full potential as a human being.

I remember telling this woman, "It's absolutely fine to think of yourself as perfect. It has nothing to do with being conceited, thinking you are peerless, or lacking motivation for future growth."

You know the ocean is perfect. So are flowers, the sky, your pet cat, and everything else in nature. They are as perfect as they can be even if they are always changing. The sky is different from what it was an hour ago, but it is still perfect. Your cat is always changing, and yet it isn't any less perfect. You can grow, change, and be different in a thousand ways, and still be a perfect creature. The essence of your perfection is in your own ability to look at yourself, accept what you see as perfect in the present moment, and then be able to grow into something quite different, *but still perfect.* It is ironic that we always think of animals as perfect, and yet we deny that same quality to ourselves.

You are as perfect a creature as is capable of being created on this planet—make no mistake about that. You are the result of billions and billions of years of evolution, God's handiwork, and all the other influences that have shaped your arrival here. Physically, you can't get any better than you are. Your body and your mind—if you want to distinguish between them—are nature's most perfect models to date for ensuring the survival and perfection of a living species on earth. You should marvel at your own potentials every day.

Being perfect means viewing yourself with new eyes. It means letting yourself *arrive fully into life,* rather than always hanging around the edges, thinking you're not quite good enough yet to get into the Big Game. It means being in awe of your own humanity and your limitless potential as a human being. It means *granting yourself permission to grow and achieve up to the highest levels you can imagine.* In this sense, you are capable of being perfect. You can think of yourself as a finished creation—without having to boast to others or prove anything to anyone else—if you cultivate the kind of stability, confidence and sense of inner pride that I will be talking about in these pages, while giving yourself a pass to total human fulfillment.

SICKNESS, HEALTH AND SUPERHEALTH: THE MEDICAL MODEL

If you take the medical model for the treatment of illness in our culture, you will find that most medical practitioners operate between point A and point B on the continuum below.

A	B	C
Illness	"Normal Health"	"Superhealth"
Medical Treatment	Preventive Medicine	Individual Initiative

Point A represents illness requiring medical treatment—which will result in the individual's recovery to normal health, or in chronic illness, or in death. Point B represents an absence of symptoms of illness, or what we call "normal health."

Virtually all the medical practice in our culture focuses on the treatment and elimination of sickness. Between points A and B you will find all the illnesses that plague mankind, and some kind of program to treat each of them. We are obsessed with devising ways to make sickness disappear, with getting people to point B.

Between point B and point C, which I have called "Superhealth," lies the fertile territory for "preventive medicine," which ranges all the way from giving people vaccinations and getting them to brush their teeth, encouraging regular exercise and proper nutrition, to keeping workers from inhaling asbestos or coal dust, to environmental considerations such as pollution or the depletion of the earth's ozone layer.

There are, of course, many sound medical practitioners and others who advocate or practice preventive medicine, and a small but hopefully growing minority who want to expand the scope of the field to include all aspects of our lives that contribute to ill-health, from physical to mental to environmental factors. There are a few who are beginning to look seriously at the prospects for behavioral medicine and methods for teaching people to think, feel and behave in healthy ways, from the very beginning of their lives. But even those who want to expand preventive medicine are rare and somewhat scorned by the powers that be. Tranquilizers, antidepressants and drugs of every kind are the general means of medical practice today. The abuse of some of these drugs has been cited in United States government reports and given wide publicity by the media. Yet the prescriptions continue to pour out of medical practices to the tune of hundreds of millions of orders each year. The amount of unnecessary surgery performed is alarming and well documented. Yet the practice of medical treatment between points A and B goes on and on, and it will continue to go on and on until people begin to object in large numbers.

Almost nobody has thought of operating between points B and C to the extent of studying people who are extremely healthy, vigorous, happy, fulfilled, devoid of chemical dependencies, and so on, and finding what their characteristics are, what their "secrets for superhealth" may be.

This may be largely because "superhealth" is a matter of individual choice and initiative. If you have started jogging, swimming, playing tennis or whatever because your doctor has warned you to lose weight or take care of your heart or build up your lung capacity, that is one thing—preventive medicine to maintain normal health. You may still resent the time necessary for your daily exercise-chore and spend most of it worrying that you really should be doing something else.

But if you "just naturally" get exercise every day because you love it, love being in touch with your body and *its* amazing capacities to return a well-hit tennis shot or run ten miles, wouldn't miss it for anything, that is a different matter entirely. What is a chore for someone else is a joy for you, and you are not going to give it up even temporarily just because you think your "normal health" is now assured. The difference between joyful, conflict-free exercise and "chore" exercise when it comes to your physical health is hard to estimate, but when it comes to your mental health (and who knows where physical health leaves off and mental health begins?) it's the difference between the "Normal" and the "No-Limit" person.

When enough people reach the stage where they think for themselves and don't want physicians simply to write them prescriptions for drugs to control "anxiety attacks," then "A to B and back again" will cease to be the norm for physical health in our culture. A NEZ person already knows that he, not a pill, can cure his anxiety, and consequently he will look inward rather than outward for the solutions to his anxiety. The excitement of practicing medicine between points B and C involves having doctors who want people to stop thinking and living in sickly ways. It means teaching patients to want to be superhealthy, to be in charge of their bodies, rather than reinforcing their illnesses by using external means, such as drugs, as the exclusive treatment method.

PSYCHOLOGY AS MEDICINE: THE PATHOLOGICAL APPROACH

The field of psychology, which has traditionally been viewed primarily as an adjunct to the "treatment" branch of medicine, also operates between points A and B on its own continuum, which looks like this:

A		B		C
Mental Illness		**"Normality"**		**NEZ to No Limits**
Psychosis; danger to self or others.	Debilitating neuroses; partly functional but "below average."	"Neurotic" but mostly functional; "average."	Mental health; no erroneous zones and pulling own strings; "above average."	Mental superhealth. The Sky's the Limit!
Intensive treatment; drugs, institution-alization.	Psychotherapy or other treatment; drugs, etc.	Psychotherapy "recommended" for everyone.	Self-control; no treatment necessary, but "recommended."	Self-actualization; no treatment wanted.
Panic	Inertia	Striving	Coping	Mastery

Virtually all research on human behavior has been accumulated by studying people who have symptoms between points A and B which make them function below the average, or "normal," level of their societies. With the notable exception of some "rebels" like Maslow, psychologists have traditionally focused on neurotic symptoms, on depression and on the absence of clinical psychological sickness as an indication of "normality." They have written extensively about mental ill-health, but very little about attaining mental health. They have written a lot about striving, but almost nothing about ever arriving anywhere. They see people as always having to improve rather than accepting them as healthy the way they are.

The profession, like the whole society, seems obsessed with the future and planning for it. No attention is given to the present or how to enjoy it. All the emphasis is on being "well adjusted" to the way things are, being "normal" or "average." Virtually no attention is paid to the inborn capacity of *every* human individual for greatness! Psychology studies those who have the most symptoms, and then creates a theory about why people behave as they do based on *an absence of those clinical symptoms* as the ideal goal for everyone. Psychologists look at those who manage to get along, who don't get into trouble, and who are functioning (although they may have no inner peace), and use them as models for everyone to emulate.

There are other, more exciting and more significant dimensions to the study of human beings. Why not look at those who are happiest, the highest achievers, creative, constructive and the most productive among us and see what we can learn about *them* before we make generalizations about what is possible for any one of us? Their examples could not help but provide fertile suggestions for everyone to follow. This would be the positive approach to psychology, and yet there seems to be wholesale resistance to such thinking. Maslow used the study of greatness in his research on self-actualization, but while he made some major contributions, his suggestions are largely ignored in psychological practice today, partly because there are no "hard statistical data" to support his findings. But the fact is that there *can be no "hard statistical data"* relevant to the study of human greatness. It is in principle impossible to predict where or tell how genius, imagination or creativity will erupt in the world. There *can be no formula* for arriving at original theories or creating original works of art. It would be absurd to try to apply scientific measuring instruments and calculations to the study of human potential in the first place. To be sure, one can generalize about what kind of upbringing, education and environment cultivates NEZ people, what kinds of influences, attitudes and *choices* create No-Limit people. But those judgments are deeply *subjective,* resting as they do on the attempt to understand the internal workings of "great minds," and Maslow went about it in the only legitimate way possible, using his best "common sense" to interpret what he read and heard and felt and saw —the same approach I am taking in this book.

Still, the "social scientists" of today are seldom willing to venture beyond areas of study where "findings" can be *quantified,* where numbers can be assigned to everything, charts and graphs drawn. So they go on taking their surveys, filling in blanks on their yes-or-no questionnaires, getting their funding and writing their research projects and putting them into academic journals for other researchers to read. If all people are unique, and if they are constantly changing each and every day, then all one can say about any social-research finding is that it applied to that group of people on that given day, and given the propensity of humans to be different and to change, then it is unlikely that one would get the same results if one were to repeat the study. These "scientists" are not helping people change and grow into more happy and effective people. Instead they, like many of their medical counterparts, wallow around forever between points A and B, hardly daring to believe there might really be a point C.

You need not fall into the trap of charting your "progress in life" solely between "normality" and something worse. If you are psychologically "normal," that is, coping with life as well as the next person, why not see yourself *between* points B and C, and forget about whether or not you are sicker today than yesterday, or how you stack up against all the other people who choose to be unhappy and neurotic? You can begin to look at yourself in new ways even if the professions which deal with human behavior never stop studying exclusively what they observe as sickness in others, never begin to focus on *what is possible for humanity at best,* and even if the "science of human behavior" never does anything to help you. You need not wait for the bureaucrats within the profession to catch up. You can start to look at yourself and your life in exciting, original ways that will make your every moment on this planet more than worth living.

FROM PANIC TO MASTERY—AND WHAT'S IN BETWEEN

Across the bottom of the chart presented in the last section, you will note:

Panic	Inertia	Striving	Coping	Mastery

There are many ways to assess your current "growth status." One is to estimate your level of readiness to handle problems or situations arising in daily life—from the ordinary to the potentially pleasant or joyful to the tragic. The scale above is a well-known measure of mental health. It is essentially a five-rung ladder on which you can plot how you typically react to the whole range of situations in your life.

Panic

Panic strikes people when they are confronted with problems and feel they have no ability to resolve them. Panic means to run about aimlessly, to have no confidence as to how you will react in a given situation; to be unpredictable, untrustworthy to yourself.

Perhaps you are confronted with a flat tire at night in the middle of nowhere, and you've never changed a tire before. Your initial reaction might be one of panic. Perhaps you just cry, or get out of the car and walk around, first in one direction, then the other. You might get hysterical, scream obscenities out into the darkness, at your tire or at the nail in the road. You are expending a lot of energy, but all of it in anger, frustration, confusion and conflict, none of it in solving the problem.

Soldiers in battle who panic sometimes stand up and walk into a stream of bullets. Most people who are placed in mental institutions for protection are there because their psychic lives are in a state of total panic and they cannot be trusted not to hurt themselves or others. Their behavior is uncontrollable and unpredictable.

All of us experience panic at one time or another in our lives, particularly when we are confronted with alien surroundings and problems we have no experience in solving. They key to whether we become completely immobilized is the length of time we are at *panic* and how often it occurs.

If you stub your toe in the middle of the night, flail out with screams and hop around the house on one foot for a few minutes, perhaps even pound the walls, this approximates panic, but is not serious (in fact, it is a natural response) because you are not immobilized in the face of a problem requiring action. You can't unstub your toe; all you can do is wait for the pain to go away.

If, on the other hand, you are still screaming uncontrollably three weeks later, are accusing your family of deliberately moving the furniture so that you would stub your toe, are still flailing away at objects and people long after the pain has subsided, then you are a candidate for institutionalization, because your panic has lasted too long and has taken on extreme qualities.

Some people spend their lives feeling a sense of panic about their jobs, their relationships, their financial plight and many other concerns. They flounder around from one problem to another, never quite knowing what to do or how they are going to react, with their insides churning around like a whirlpool. If you find yourself on this bottom rung, then you know you can move only in one direction—up!

Inertia

Inertia describes a state of being in which you are unable to move yourself, incapable of action. In this state you will either be motionless or be carried along "the way you were going before" or the way others direct or push you. In terms of problem-solving, inertia often follows a spasm of panic. Emotionally it is usually associated with depression and/or boredom. If the depression is chronic and deep, or the boredom is "existential"—that is, it is not boredom with this or that situation or activity, but with all of life—it can lead to psychosis and/or suicide. Sören Kierkegaard captured the essence of existential boredom in *Either/Or:*

> I do not care for anything. I do not care to ride, for the exercise is too violent. I do not care to walk, walking is too strenuous. I do not care to lie down, for I should either have to remain lying, and I do not care to do that, or I should have to get up again, and I do not care to do that either. *Summa summarum:* I do not care at all.

Depression and boredom result in a lack of initiative about everything, in passive behavior such as staying in bed or at home doing nothing but feeling sorry for yourself. Many relationships as well as individuals suffer from inertia. In the extreme, a couple that has had vicious, screaming fights every day for twenty years will stay together because both parties are afraid to do anything, because at least there is "security" (in the form of predictability) in knowing there will be a fight at three-thirty this afternoon, and the world as a whole has come to look so bleak that they can't imagine any change that might make a real difference. They cannot imagine living at a higher level.

Inertia is far more dangerous and painful than panic to the average or "normal" person. When you are without action, you are a candidate for the most depressing kind of life style imaginable. You vegetate and deteriorate. Perhaps the greatest cause of tension and stress on the human organism comes not from changing jobs or locations, or from divorces, or even from deaths, but instead from *living day to day in unresolved relationships,* not knowing where you are going but feeling chronic depression about your life. The inertia makes you churn inside. It casts a gray pall over the whole world.

If you are in a state of inertia, any step, any action you can take will help alleviate the turmoil. Going back to the flat tire in the middle of nowhere: after you have screamed, kicked the car, cursed the nail in the road and vented your anger, you may spend some time at inertia. Perhaps you'll just sit on the ground and mumble to yourself. Maybe you'll get back into the car and brood for a while about your misfortune. If the inertia lasts too long, of course, the tire will never get fixed—but you also know that staying inert is not going to work, so you get on to the next level of mental health on the five-rung ladder.

Striving

To strive means either to struggle in opposition to someone or something or to devote serious effort or energy to something. Either way, striving involves having some direction and goal orientation. It means trying to do something, whether it is to eliminate your erroneous zones or to gain financial security. Striving is not success, but at least action is being taken, which is far superior to being in panic or inertia.

On the other hand, many people for whom struggling is the dominant mode of being spend their entire lives striving but never arriving. Chronic or compulsive striving implies chasing and being future-oriented virtually all the time. It is likely to leave you always flitting from one task to another, never able to enjoy the present because you are constantly looking toward the next objective, still spending a large portion of your life being unfulfilled. Many adults and young adults suffer from compulsive striving, or "Hurry Sickness," in a serious way. It is "What Makes Sammy Run," and it represents chasing after *something that will always elude you.*

There must come regular times in your life when you are here, arrived, and capable of enjoying the moment. But for some, this is impossible. Some strivers can't even enjoy a vacation; they are too busy thinking about what they left behind, or what they must do when they return, so that they can get back and plan for the next vacation a year from now.

Going back to the flat tire in the wilderness: perhaps you have tired of brooding and have wandered back to the trunk. You open it up and find the spare tire and the jack, but you don't know how to work the jack or take a tire off. You walk a few hundred yards looking for a house or someone to help you, and then you turn back because there are no houses or lights in sight and you don't like talking to strangers anyway. You might not find a house or a telephone in that direction for ten miles. You try the other direction. Nothing that way either.

You go back to the car. Perhaps you fall back into panic or inertia. Perhaps you pull the jack and the spare tire out and briefly consider trying to make sense out of the directions, then give up because suppose you put the jack in the wrong place, put the tire on wrong. You are striving—not solving, but striving, and it is a good step, although an insufficient one, to be sure. Striving can be transformed into coping, even into mastery, or it can lapse back into inertia or panic, or it can become a way of life itself. The choice is up to you.

Coping

"Coping" means just getting along, not letting things immobilize you, and becoming a "well-adjusted" person, which seems to be the goal of most parents and teachers in the world. But "coping" has a second association even more relevant for our purposes, with which those who know what a coping saw is will be familiar. A coping saw is "a saw of ribbon shape under tension in a U-shaped frame used for cutting intricate patterns of wood," and here "to cope" means "to shape . . . to conform to the shape of another member"—to *fit into* some shape already given, or *to fit a pattern already established.* In the psychological field, "coping" has always meant *adjusting to the status quo*—shaping yourself to the image of what you should be that is presented to you by "average" or "normal" society. If this means cutting off some of your hopes, dreams, secret aspirations, if it means *resigning yourself to having some favorite pieces of yourself lopped off in the process,* that is taken as "just the way life is," the price you must pay for conventional "success."

You see it on their report cards over and over again: "Sally is a well-adjusted little girl. She fits in nicely with her peer group. She copes with her studies and she adjusts well to the other children." In other words, "She is learning to be just like everyone else and to be a follower who will never be a problem to anyone else."

Going back once more to you and the flat tire: if you cope with the situation you may not end up getting your tire fixed right away, but at least you won't be immobilized or overly upset about it.

You may spend some time in panic, inertia or fruitless striving, or you may decide to start coping immediately. In the first few minutes you may already have reasoned, "Well, there's nobody nearby, this is such a deserted road that nobody's likely to come along for quite a few hours, and if I just read the directions on the jack and proceed carefully, chances are that I'll figure it out myself before anyone shows up to help me." Or maybe you decide, "The risks of my doing this wrong are too high; I'll just put on the hazard lights and wait patiently until somebody comes along to help. I'll sleep all night in the car if I have to." Or maybe you decide to take off in one direction or the other and just not stop until you find help, even if you have to walk twenty miles.

Whatever you decide, if you are "just coping," your decision will probably be in line with what "normal" society would expect of you in such a situation. If you are a young man who just has never changed a tire before, you may consider it a matter of pride not to go for help, to figure it out for yourself. If help is offered, you may even turn it down. If you are a woman who has always considered tire-changing a man's job, you will probably not even consider trying to solve the problem yourself; you will go for male help or wait until a man comes along (and perhaps be frightened that the *wrong* man will come along).

You may be such a good coper that essentially you have no erroneous zones with regard to this situation. If someone offers constructive help you will accept it gratefully and graciously; otherwise you will figure out, through reading the directions and some trial and error, how to do the job yourself. Or you may decide, "I'm not in any hurry, I'm tired, it's a nice night—I'll go to sleep in the car for a while, and deal with this later if nobody comes along soon."

I am not against learning how to cope, but I do not see coping as the highest or best possible level of being for any human.

All too often coping is thought of as the top of the human-potential ladder, when in fact it is still miles and miles from the "very top"—if there is a "top" at all.

Over and over you have heard about learning *how to cope.* The psychologists of America for the most part talk endlessly about teaching people how to *cope with* their problems—which means "get around them according to conventional ways of coping." While it is certainly better to cope than not to cope, just plain coping is a long way from mastery of, or true control over, yourself and your life situations, and still farther from true fulfillment, which entails change, not adjustment.

In the larger psychological sense which includes your whole life, why should you merely learn how to adjust to, or cope with, the problems or sicknesses of the world? Coping means just getting along, not letting things immobilize you, and becoming a "well-adjusted" person, which seems to be the goal most parents, teachers, political leaders and other authority figures in our world have for the rest of us.

Even if you are a terrific coper, far superior to anyone who is stuck in panic, inertia or striving, even if you are the President of the United States, General Motors or Harvard, there is a much nicer place on the horizon, a place where you can be every day if you seek it out and believe you are capable of being there.

Mastery

Ladies and gentlemen, this is the place. Mastery means being master of your own fate—being the one person who decides how you are going to live, react and feel in virtually every situation that life presents to you.

Mastery is what this book is all about: the transition from NEZ to No-Limit living. When you have read this book entirely, and have mastered its contents in a way that makes its philosophy applicable to *your own life,* you should be spending a lot of time at the top rung of the ladder.

I am not saying that anyone is always at mastery, or at any other level of the ladder presented here, in all areas of life. During the courses of our lives we all shift around between panic and mastery innumerable times, and the world's best carpenter or wood sculptor may be a terrible father, while "the greatest father in the world" may privately be in a state of chronic desperation about his vocation, marriage or anything else. But depending on our given problem or promise areas, we are higher or lower in our abilities to deal with them effectively. Being a NEZ to No-Limit person means spending more time at mastery, less time at any of the lower rungs on the ladder, in more areas of your life. Total No-Limit people would then be complete masters of their own emotional worlds. According to Maslow, such people are few and far between, but they *do exist.* Maslow thought that the self-actualized person, or in my thought the NEZ/No-Limit person, *had to be rare* on our planet. He believed, in effect, that "many are called but few are chosen"; that only a *special breed of person* could attain what I have called *total mastery* of life.

In this I disagree with Maslow. I believe *anyone* can refuse to accept immobilizing reactions to situations or problems. And that they, not some mystical force of heredity, astrological sun-sign or personal psychology, are in charge of how they think, and consequently how they feel.

One more trip back to the flat-tire scene reveals you at mastery. Even if you have never had a flat tire before, you do not feel this is a reason why you cannot change a tire now. You know you will figure it out. Although it will involve a little trial and error, it can also involve excitement and adventure teaching yourself how to do something new, something you would like to know how to do right away the next time you get a flat tire.

You are full of confidence that you can master this situation, because you have a strong belief in yourself. There is no time for self-pity or low-level expectations that you can't handle this situation. You know there is an owner's manual in the glove compartment, with diagrams and step-by-step instructions. You are on your way.

Challenges are the stuff of life. They are to be welcomed with open arms. Of course a No-Limit person is not going to say, "Whoopee, I got a flat tire, and now I have a fun challenge." If someone who knows how to change a tire comes along and offers to help, nobody is going to say, "Go away, I want to figure this out for myself." The NEZ person will accept the help with graciousness and thanks. So will the No-Limit person. The difference is that the NEZ or coping person may drive away saying, "Well, wasn't that nice, I could have been in a real jam," having perhaps sat by the roadside paying little attention while the stranger changed the tire, chatting as pleasantly as possible—while the No-Limit person will either have asked the stranger to *show him how to change the tire* or have watched every step so closely that he *knows he can do it himself the next time.*

Mastery is the level of being at which you are to your life, your destiny, the way a master craftsman, artisan—no, a *master artist*—is to his creation.

Mastery is a level all of us can enjoy a great deal more of the time than we've ever imagined. This book is about achieving mastery in your own world, rather than settling for anything less. It is about going after what you really want and feel inside yourself, instead of hanging on to the familiar or routine and staying at those lower rungs on the ladder. It is about trusting yourself and taking risks. It is about achieving success in the only way that a No-Limit person can do it—by pursuing what is important for you.

Henry David Thoreau put it this way: "If one advances confidently, in the direction of his own dreams and endeavors, to lead the life which he has imagined, he will meet with a success unexpected in common hours."

WHO CAN BE A NO-LIMIT PERSON?

Many leaders in the field of human behavior have used their own terminologies to describe the highest levels of human emotional evolution, among them the man in my profession whom I most admire, Abraham H. Maslow. Maslow used the term "self-actualization" to describe those he considered most highly evolved in terms of mental health. Carl Rogers talked about "fully functioning" people; Eric Fromm's conception was of the "autonomous person." David Riesman talked of the "inner-directed man" and Carl Jung about the "individuated person." There is much overlap in the characteristics each of these scholars attributes to what I have called the No-Limit person, but there is also a lack of agreement about specifics and still less hint in their writings as to *how an individual can attain these heights.*

As I mentioned earlier, my primary disagreement with Maslow's conception of the human greatness of the "self-actualized person" concerns just *who* can achieve these upper rungs of the human ladder. Maslow implies that being "completely evolved" is reserved for a very special category of elite people. My experience in my own life, as well as my "helping" profession, has shown me that any person is capable of reaching his own "highest level of evolution." I am convinced that if you really want to achieve a superior state of living each and every day, you can very systematically set about it, and there is no reason in the world why you can't succeed. You *do not* have to be a "special person" with the good fortune of having inherited "self-actualizing genes" in order to be a NEZ or No-Limit person. I firmly believe that each person who resides on this planet has the innate capability to live his life in a rewarding and spontaneously exciting way. Anyone can rid himself of self-defeating thinking and behavior and grow into a human being who lives fully day by day. In sum, *a high level of mental and physical health is available for anyone who is willing to go after it,* and no one has any better chance of becoming more self-actualized or more fully functioning than anyone else.

You do not have to say to yourself that you just can't do anything about the way you are because you've "always been that way." You don't have to tell yourself that you can't really change or that it is next to impossible for you to achieve a higher state of existence because you are so fixed in your ways. You *can go after* what you want for yourself by deciding to work, one day at a time, on adopting a *philosophy of life* that is going to bring you the greatest amount of fulfillment and happiness, regardless of your circumstances or the problems that you've encountered until today.

WHY BE HERE IN THE FIRST PLACE?

Somehow we got it all screwed up! We have convinced ourselves that the real purpose of life is to try to outdo everyone else and to chase endlessly after goals that always elude us. Everywhere you see people pushing, striving, worrying and making life a game of acquiring possessions or social status rather than inner satisfaction. The purpose of life in contemporary society appears to be setting future-oriented goals, externally determined—pleasing Mommy and Daddy or getting good grades on report cards, diplomas from "the right" universities, job titles and promotions, awards, money, three cars, two televisions, electric can-openers, and finally a retirement nest egg. No one ever seems to *arrive.* We all are so busy chasing after external objects of one kind or another that we have no time left for enjoying our lives.

Why be here in the first place? That is the first question you have to ask yourself if you are going after a philosophy of life that will really change the way you live.

Remember, you do not have to be here! As countless suicides have proved, if you want to check out right now, no authority, no "law against suicide," no preacher rattling on about the sanctity of life, can possibly stop you. "To be or not to be, that is the question," and whether you realize it or not, you answer it in one way every day simply by not killing yourself.

But: ". . . I have set before you life and death, blessing and curse; therefore choose life. . . ." (Deuteronomy 30:19) To me this means far more than "Don't kill yourself" or "Be a survivor." It means choosing life in all its glorious richness and limitless potential, choosing it for *what it really is,* the most incredible miracle of the universe.

"Therefore choose life. . . ." It has an intoxicating illogic to it. If someone said to you, "I have set before you carrots and spinach; therefore choose carrots," you might say, "That hardly follows," and you would be right. The argument is missing a "minor premise"—something to the effect that carrots are better than spinach, which you would have to accept before accepting the conclusion.

But suppose instead you were told, "I have set before you carrots sautéed in butter and spinach boiled in gasoline." At that point the waitress would hardly need to tell you, "I recommend the carrots," but if she said, "Therefore choose carrots," you might say, "*You're not kidding!*"

And so it is with "therefore choose life." A living being only has to know the difference between life and death, which *only adult humans seem capable of forgetting,* to know which one is better. The real import of the Biblical passage to me is that *only adult humans are presented the choice* between life and death. We are the only beings on earth capable of saying to ourselves, "Some lives just aren't worth living; mine is one of them; therefore, I choose death."

But with this added liability to adult human consciousness comes an even greater dividend, because *a dimension has been added to our potential for appreciating life.* The deepest meaning of the Biblical passage may be "Only you are capable of fathoming the full difference between life and death, because only you have an inkling of the full potentials of life. *The future of all life on earth has been placed in your hands.* Therefore, choose life."

Relatively few people in the world commit physical suicide directly, consciously, "purposely." Those are the ones who, whether psychotic or not and for whatever reasons (some of which may sometimes be legitimate, it seems to me), have asked themselves, "Why be here in the first place?" and have come up with the answer "For me, there's no longer any good reason at all."

But just as you are uniquely capable of answering, "No reason at all," you are equally capable of answering, "Every reason in the world!"—and of *finding more reasons to choose life than any other being in the universe* (that I know of). So if you are *slowly killing yourself* or know in your guts that you are *not really living* (you feel like "one of the walking dead"), you may not be "choosing death" in any direct sense, but *neither are you truly choosing life.* That is, you're "hung up" like a ship on a reef, somewhere between panic and coping, and the next time the tide rises you don't know whether you'll float or sink.

Why be here in the first place? If you choose to be creative about it, you could list an infinite number of reasons. But since you've already chosen life (considering that you're still here), let's start with a simple philosophy—the simplest version of my proposed philosophy of life that I can offer. Let's pretend that the real purpose of being here in the first place is to journey through life with a maximum of enjoyment, victimizing no one and undertaking tasks that will make this planet a better place to be on for everyone now living here and those who will live here after we leave.

That may sound like a tall order, but as a philosophy of life I think it is not "too ambitious" for *any* human being, and the key to it is that it starts with your *taking joy in your own life.* A distinguished educator, Nevitt Sanford, put it this way: "In terms of balancing human values, I would give the enjoyment of life first priority and justify that on the grounds that if you don't know how to enjoy life, you're going to be a burden to other people."

NEZ, ZEN AND *MUGA*: THE ART OF LIVING NOW

Futurizing: That Vicious Circle

If you are really going to go from a NEZ to a No-Limit state of being in your life, you must carefully revaluate how you are spending the limited number of your days. If you are chasing endlessly after the symbols, counters or markers that "normal" people use to evaluate "success" in life (the prime symbol being $), forever postponing your gratification with life *as it is given now* and expecting "really to live" some time in the future, there *will never be a present in which you really live!*

"Futurizing" can become the most destructive of habits. The present is always used up in planning for the future, which never quite comes. If you are trying to acquire enough wealth so that you can be happy forever, you will never achieve happiness. The pursuit itself will become the purpose of life. If the chase is what really motivates you, when you reach one monetary plateau you will simply up the ante on your expectations and feel that you need more money.

If you have bought as the purpose of life prestige, money, awards, recognition or any of the multitude of what I call "external" rewards that society constantly tries to sell you, you are stuck on the treadmill of always chasing after "success"—which, practically speaking, entails all of the modern "neurotic" ailments, including high anxiety, stress, hypertension, ulcers, depressions, worries, headaches, cramps, twitches, heart disease, and emotional traumas such as unsatisfying family relationships, a flabby life style, a lack of love in your life, and so on *ad nauseam.*

Futurizing is really one of those massive social erroneous zones that infect our culture. There are several things a NEZ person can do to transcend it and begin living now. The first is to recognize fully that *now is the only time you ever really have.* This little bit of truth seems so basic, so simple, yet very few people know how to live in the present. Unless and until the "time machines" of science fiction are invented, no one will ever really be able to escape the present and live in any other time, but if you constantly let your mind wander all over the "map of time," now regretting or feeling guilty about the past, now anxious about the future, you can literally live your entire life *in absentia*—absent, even alienated from the only time in which you can ever "really be living."

Henry David Thoreau said, "The mass of men live their lives in quiet desperation." This may be even truer of the late twentieth century than it was of the nineteenth. If so, this means that the vicious circle that causes it, called the I.F.D. (Idealization, Frustration, Demoralization) Disease by Wendell Johnson in *People in Quandaries,* is on the rise among us—and so is our need to understand how it operates and how to break out of it.

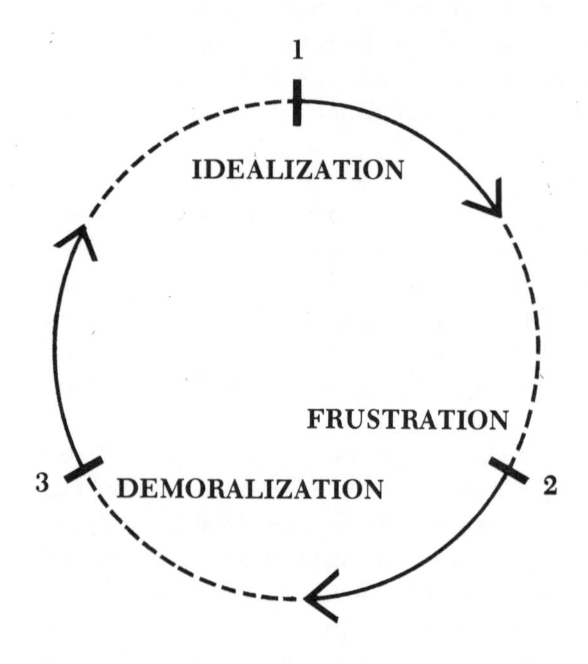

At point 1 on the circle is the inclination to *idealize* the future; to believe that when this or that happens, the future will suddenly be so much different and so much better than the present. "Things will be great when I get to the dance next Friday; when I graduate; when I get married; when I get that promotion; when we have our first child; when we get our new house; when I get that bonus; when the holidays finally get here; when our friends arrive from out of town; when they leave; when I pass my examinations; when the divorce finally comes through"; and on and on, always anticipating something in the future and using up the present moment planning, figuring, hoping, wishing, dreaming of a "golden future time."

As the circle continues to point 2, the predictable result is *frustration*. The future can never quite come up to your idealizations. As soon as it becomes the present, therefore, it is "ruined." "The dance wasn't really that great; graduation was a bore; the honeymoon was over right after the wedding ceremony; I spent the bonus even before I got it; the holidays were tiresome and I couldn't wait for them to end."

The third point on the circle is the *demoralization* you feel every time the future becomes the present and "lets you down." It may result in prolonged and serious depression, or, if you have become accustomed enough to dealing with disappointment, you may quickly "resign yourself" and try to tell yourself not to expect so much from life in the future. Either way, what do you do next? You idealize the future again and start the process all over. You end up fitting neatly into a life of quiet desperation. The only way out of this trap, which immobilizes countless millions of people, is to straighten out that circle and begin living your life fully, TODAY.

Transcending Your Past

While it may seem too painfully obvious to mention, the fact is that *the past is over,* and, whatever may have happened "then," it will never come again, and you can never get it back. Any time you find yourself using up your present moments being immobilized because of something that occurred in the past, you are victimizing yourself unnecessarily. The first step in transcending your past is to *surrender* the attitudes toward it that immobilize you now. This involves changing your attitudes about the present, rather than trying artificially to erase anything from your real past.

If you have decided to use up the present by wallowing around in your past, regretting its lost opportunities or reminiscing about the "good old days," bewailing the fact that "the times they are a-changin'," or wishing you could relive your earlier years, you will consistently be killing your present. But if you decide to surrender the past whenever it inhibits you from thinking, feeling or behaving effectively in the present, "your past" will rapidly come into the NEZ/No-Limit perspective.

I want to emphasize that "surrendering" does not mean giving up your memories, or that you should forget anything you have learned that can make you more happy and effective in the present. I have already cited bits of wisdom—philosophy and poetry—from humanity's near and far-distant past which I think are eminently worth preserving because they contain truths which can illuminate the potential beauty in our present lives. But I *am* talking about ridding yourself *immediately* of those learned attitudes which inhibit you from functioning effectively and happily today.

For example, if a loved one has just died, your temporary feelings of grief are natural. As unspeakably agonizing as the loss may be, the world is reminding you of the unfathomable difference between life and death, and it is a message you cannot ignore. You are bound at this time to endure this pain; not to feel it would be inhuman, not to express it would be psychologically catastrophic for you.

But if you were to hang on to this grief indefinitely, if you *never* allowed yourself to let it go and get on with living now, then you would be condemning yourself to live forever in the past—a compulsively self-defeating response. Your grief cannot bring your loved one back; it can only purge your sorrow at that person's loss, and at best lead you to rededicate yourself even more deeply to life.

Likewise, if you recognize that you have behaved badly in a certain situation, that you have carelessly or needlessly hurt another person, you can surely apologize, express your feelings of sorrow about having behaved that way. But if you let continuous regret, remorse, self-persecution keep you from functioning NOW, if you persist indefinitely in feeling guilty and upset over something that is over, then you are behaving in a nonproductive manner. Feeling guilty is not going to make your life any better. You can learn from your mistakes, vow to avoid repeating them, and get on with living now.

Packing Your Bags

Your own life history can be a strong force for good in your life, or it can get in your way and keep you from living fully in the present: it depends entirely on how you decide to *use it now.*

The sad fact is that psychology since Freud has seen people's pasts almost exclusively in terms of destructive influences. A therapist may spend months or years with a patient trying to dredge up forgotten traumas, to identify what his parents did to him during his childhood to get him so screwed up, and so on. Of course, there may be a great deal of validity to this approach for many people, although one might wish psychologists were as good at helping people overcome the destructive influences of their pasts as they are at pointing them out.

But, as so often with the "medical model" of psychological treatment, this approach only uncovers half the story. Suppose it turns out that your father was rigid, domineering, overly strict, and you can trace some of your present "erroneous zones" to his influence. Obviously you have to eliminate those zones from your consciousness. But do you end up resenting your father for having "done this to you"—blaming him for not having been "flawless"? Do you end up holding *him* responsible for things that only *you* can change? Your resentment can become an erroneous zone in itself—a reservoir of blame and bad feeling that victimizes you *and* him.

And, equally important but almost *never* mentioned, *what have you received of real value from your father?* Perhaps he took you fishing a lot, taught you how to fish, and you love fishing to this day. Do you remember your father with love and appreciation when you are tramping happily around along backwoods streams?

Perhaps his "rigidity" extended to a completely uncompromising devotion to personal honesty, and he "pounded that into you." Some of your childhood friends may be in jail today because they fell victim to the temptation to cut this legal corner a little too close or fudge that set of numbers just a little bit, but you *know* that will never "happen to you," because for some reason such temptations never even cross your mind. Your fundamental honesty is the pride of your life; you would pay any price to preserve it, and God help anybody who questions or attacks it, because they are going to run head on into a stone fortress.

Well, who showed you how to build this fortress, anyway?

Looking back at your past *has to involve gathering up and cherishing all the wisdom, truth and beauty, all the sources of inspiration, that your own life history has bequeathed to you, if you are truly to become a No-Limit person.* Where are you going to get a creative, inspiring philosophy of life if not from the pool of wisdom you have accumulated during your own life experience?

Transcending your past may start with admitting that what's done is done and surrendering those "fixations" which have kept you mired "back then" and alienated from NOW, but it culminates when you "pack your bags"—gather up from your past everything you really feel like taking with you. From "packing your bags" it is only a short bus ride to the present.

NEZ, Zen and Muga

The art of full present-moment living is rarely seen in our culture. In fact, we do not even have a common word or descriptive phrase for the art of living completely in the present. Existentialist philosophers have used Kierkegaard's concept of *immediacy* to describe the state in which you are *in direct contact with your present*—a childlike state in which *nothing interferes with* your appreciation of the present moment, nothing (from regrets about your past to idealistic expectations about the future) "mediates" between you and the now in which you live. But too often this "immediacy" is associated with a *childish* state in which you remain unaware of the larger world around you. It is thought that when you pass from childhood to adulthood you have forever lost this "innocent" state, this childlike joy of "immediacy," and can never really regain it.

If we believe that we can all be "living now" and determine to look for concrete examples of how to cultivate such an art, we must turn to other cultures which have studied this matter more deeply than we have. For the person who is ready to live now, a short diversion into Zen can become a ready bridge to living now.

It is appropriate that NEZ happens to spell Zen *backwards*, because the NEZ person will attain the inner peace sought by the Zen student from exactly the opposite direction. While Zen depends on mind-to-mind instruction from *master to student* in order to achieve satori, "awakening" (or total present-moment awareness), NEZ approaches the same goal without relying on any master other than yourself to show you the way.

Zen is supposed to result in absolute mental tranquility for the individual. Some time ago an article in *Newsweek* magazine, "Japan's Art of the Moment," discussed an example of that culture's way of cultivating complete present-moment living: the ancient tea ceremony, called *chanoyu*.

> For a moment, there is nothing in life except the sensation of the bowl and the tea. What the tea drinker is in fact feeling is summed up in the timeless Japanese word *mu*. In its literal sense, *mu* means "nothingness" or "zero," but it connotes far more—a fixed and intense concentration on the immediate task or pleasure. All distractions are shut out. In this "zero state," the mind focuses only on what is at hand. It is precisely this ability to focus, to make every second, every inch, every stroke of the brush or pen count, which characterizes the Japanese achievement in all the arts.

Abraham Maslow described the Japanese Zen-based culture as far more highly evolved in the art of present-moment living than Western cultures. He used the Japanese word *Muga* to describe total present-moment awareness, and he has defined *Muga* in this way:

> This [*muga*] is the state in which you are doing whatever you are doing with a total wholeheartedness, without thinking of anything else, without any hesitation, without any criticism or doubt or inhibition of any kind whatsoever. It is a pure and perfect and total spontaneous acting without any blocks of any kind. This is possible only when the self is transcended or forgotten.*

Achieving a *Muga* state in any human activity will provide you with a level of internal peace and personal satisfaction you may never have experienced before. If you can learn to concentrate all your present thought on a tennis match, a long-distance run, a sexual experience, a concert, a creative undertaking, or your life's work, you will find yourself experiencing a joy, an ecstasy ("standing outside yourself") that you may never have imagined possible.

Muga, total present-moment living, does not involve playing any fancy mental trick on yourself, nor does it require specialized training in Zen or any other discipline. It involves only giving up the self-defeating attitudes and behaviors that have kept you from enjoying your present moments *for a few of those moments every day.* The entire process of getting into the present begins with giving up the past and the future in favor of the now, for as many of your life experiences as you possibly can.

LIVING NOW

Survival: Forced Back to Now

Our lives are very fragile. Whether we so choose or not, they can come to an abrupt end at any time without a second's warning. Thousands of people are killed every year in automobile accidents. You probably have friends or acquaintances who have suddenly collapsed and died from heart attacks, or who have terminal diseases and "have been given" six months to live. You may have seen the bitter irony of death coming to people who seemed to have long and promising lives ahead of them.

If anything can give us an appreciation of *living now, when life is really offered to us,* it is the comparison between the *fragility of individual life* as described above and the *genius for survival that*

* Maslow, *The Farther Reaches of Human Nature* (Viking Press, 1971), p. 243.

seems to inspire our species as a whole. As it turns out, *the capacity for survival of the human race seems to depend on the ability of some individuals to live totally in the present moment when their lives are threatened.*

Terrence des Près wrote in *The Survivor: An Anatomy of Life in the Death Camps,* about some of the most horrible experiences ever visited upon human beings—the experiences of Jews in the Nazi extermination camps of World War II. While our everyday problems may be very real to us, we are not usually subjected to physical torture or moral obscenities designed to make us abandon all hope for ourselves. But we do have the capacity to learn something about living now from those brave souls who survived in conditions that killed almost everyone who entered those camps.

Des Près's conclusion on how *a few survived* is:

> Only a radical and defiant return to elemental life could keep them going in a dark, dead universe; minute by minute, day by day, month by month, year by year. Time ceased (menstrual cycles stopped); place lost significance; the mind closed down in self-defense.

When it comes to your ability to sustain your own life, your natural, spontaneous reaction is to negotiate the situation one day, one minute or one second at a time. The past and the future vanish. The present is the only basis of your survival. Des Près writes eloquently about those who survived the Holocaust, about human beings who were shuttled about like cattle on their way to the slaughter, who were subjected to years of torture:

> The survivor survived because he had a capacity for life. Reduced to incoherent protozoa, he struggled from the sea. He endured because, thrown back radically upon the biological basis of life, he found life good. He lived from moment to moment in a state of elemental struggle, focusing upon whatever infinitesimally small item of existence was before him: a helping hand when someone fell, the gift of a coat from someone who had two, a fish head, a bowl of bean soup, a morning fleck of sunlight upon a spear of grass glimpsed during roll call, a bowel movement, the fag end of a cigarette, a minute's rest at the side of the road. These were not fancy consolations, nor were they some sort of Survivors' Zen. They were milliseconds of sanity in a long madness. They were points of light in a long darkness.

It seems that those who did not survive as long as they still had a chance were those who were unable to retreat into the total primitiveness of the present, and therefore were unable to find life good or to continue to choose it.

Normality: Living Now Sometimes

If you really want to remember what it is to live in the present, totally absorbed in what is going on in this particular time, then find some small children to watch. A small child can follow a bug for ten minutes, oblivious to anything but the fascinating shape, color and movements of that bug. When he is tired of chasing the bug, he may move on to playing a teasing game with a playmate, and then to throwing stones at a tree. Whatever he does, he is completely lost in the present. This same fascination for being in the present is possible for all of us because each of us has both a child and a survivor deep within us.

We have all experienced what we call "magic moments" in our adult lives—moments we remember as being ecstatic, blissful, rapturous, glorious, perfect; states of total involvement in the present. Some people's "magic moments" may usually come in erotic encounters; others may find magic in musical concerts, lectures, or athletic experiences. Others may have their peak experiences in building a new recreation room, in wandering through the woods or in conversations with stimulating people. Some women have told me they have had their most intense Muga experiences in childbirth, or in holding their newborn infants for the first time. Artists have told me of painting for hours with the single-minded fascination of being totally lost in their work. Others with well-established creative outlets tell how they can spend twelve hours at a sewing machine working on a new article of clothing, or in writing a poem or a book.

Each of us has had some experience of becoming so involved in what we are doing that we lose our sense of date, time, place and any other quantitative measure of "where we are." We transcend time for a while. A typical reaction to a Muga experience is that when we look back at the length of time we "really" spent we are amazed that we had *no sense of the time passing.* Hours passed in what seemed like minutes. We were so lost in our present that we literally transcended time and space.

We all know what it is to return to total involvement in the present. The trouble is that while all of us have experienced "living now sometimes," most of us have had these experiences all too rarely in our adult lives. The transition from NEZ to No-Limit living means (a) cultivating the art of living now to the point where we can enter the Muga state *whenever we choose,* and (b) entering it more and more often, for longer and longer periods.

I want to emphasize that "living now" does not imply refusing to plan for the future, although it may imply planning as little as possible, or eliminating all the "planning" that is really idle anticipation or "futurizing." You can have a *Muga* experience *now* in planning a vacation, a work project or literally anything you genuinely look forward to doing. As long as you do not "get your heart set" on the future's yielding some predetermined or idealized experience, and instead enjoy your tentative planning (looking through travel brochures, learning about all kinds of new places, finding some that seem best suited to you) for what it is—an *experience now,* and not some "bet" you are anxiously placing on the future with time you resent spending now—even planning can become a present-moment pleasure.

But for most people, learning how to enter a *Muga* state when they choose to and maximizing *Muga* experiences in their lives will require a major effort at self-retraining, a major retooling of thoughts and attitudes.

Engagement

The final stage of present-moment living involves putting it into practice or engagement. The French existentialists had a word for it: *engagé.* It means to be engaged in something that has such deep meaning for you that the more deeply you allow yourself to dedicate yourself to it, the more creative you allow yourself to be in the pursuit of it, the more of your inner resources you muster in "working on it," the more you are *living now.*

In my own life I have found that *my work*—my counseling, my books, my lectures, my personal appearances on behalf of what I believe to be the ultimate in mental health—has been the most constant force, the "prime mover," in my own personal drive to become a No-Limit person.

I will be talking more later on about the importance of meaning and purpose in the No-Limit life. But right now I want to emphasize that "living now" in your work, career, vocation, "calling," or whatever you want to term the way you spend the heart of every day, is *usually* (not always) central to your attainment of a No-Limit level of being. That is, if you haven't found a way to be satisfied with your vocation, you are likely to become bored, frustrated, depressed. You may have found a way to "make up for" the lack of meaning in your nine-to-five job by finding purpose, meaning and *engagement* in the roles you play in off hours—in an *avocation,* which is some activity apart from your vocation that takes you away from your primary job and gives you enjoyment or satisfaction, such as a hobby, volunteer part-time work or whatever. Robert Frost, one of the great No-Limit poets of this century, expressed the ideal of uniting what one loves with what one "works at" as well as I have ever seen it written.

> But yield who will to their separation,
> My object in living is to unite
> *My avocation and my vocation*
> As my two eyes make one in sight.
> Only where love and need are one,
> And the work is play for mortal stakes,
> Is the deed every really done
> For Heaven and the future's sakes.*

Now, obviously, not everyone can be lucky enough to get exactly the job he or she wants. You may love animals and want to get a job helping a veterinarian, but all the veterinarians for fifty miles around may already have all the help they need. You may have to "settle" for something else, at least temporarily. If you do, can you afford to sit around at your job resenting it and futurizing about getting the job you *really* want someday?

Of course not—but fortunately the union of vocation and avocation and the achievement of engagement in your work depend as much on your ability to love what you do as they do on your ability to do what you love: if you have sufficiently cultivated the art of living now, you can *find* meaning, fascination and fulfillment in *any* job.

Why is that one garbage man is surly, bangs the cans around as hard as he can, and leaves trash scattered in the gutter, while an-

* "Two Tramps in Mud Time" (emphasis added).

other one is always pleasant, neat and tells you, "It's fascinating what people throw away; the archaeologist who excavates the dumps in a thousand years is really going to have fun trying to figure out what all this stuff is," or tells you, "You know, there's a new recycling center for cans and bottles opening up a few blocks away"? The garbage, the trucks, the boss and the pay are the same for both of them, so I leave it to you to judge why one of them is happy and constructive and the other is miserable and destructive.

While engagement in our vocations may be central to the art of living now for most of us, and has led many over the ages to create our greatest works of art, make our greatest scientific discoveries, become our leading humanitarians, the No-Limit person is capable of engaging totally in virtually *everything* he or she may do, from getting shoes repaired to landing on the moon.

I said earlier that NEZ approaches "living now" from one direction and Zen from the opposite. In part, this is because the NEZ person relies on no "master" to show the way, but rather creates his own way for himself. But perhaps even more significantly, Zen relies on periodic *escapes from the world* to attain Muga states, while the No-Limit person will look for *more total engagement in the world* to attain those same states.

This is not to say that the refreshment, strength and inner peace that come from Zen meditation cannot be brought back to the world; they can be and are, with very healthful results. It may be that if the *Muga* experience as I've explained it doesn't make sense to you, and if you have a hard time imagining (or remembering) what it is to live now, then trying out Zen, Yoga or other Eastern arts of *Muga* cultivation can provide the insights and feelings you need to cross the bridge to No-Limit living. But in my thought, Zen is only one possible bridge to living now, and as a philosophy it is far from where we want to end up—back in the world again, in all its glory.

Engagement: The richness of the concept extends from the thought of the existentialists to the phenomenon of childbirth.

A critical point in the final stage of human pregnancy is known as "engagement," the point at which the baby stops floating around all over the womb and its head wedges down into the mother's pelvis in the delivery position. The midwife knows that now life is on its way out into the world.

That is the way I really think of "engagement": you stop floating around all over the womb and get your head into a position to live in a whole new world which is about to open up all around you. You prepare to meet that world with the wide-eyed wonder of the infant and the accumulated wisdom of your adulthood. Engagement means that you will be *living now before you know it.*

To point out the practical power of engagement in everyday life: have you ever had a cold that had you coughing, sneezing, your nose running, but at the same time you had something very important to do? What happened?

Your body put your cold on hold while you fulfilled your engagement. Perhaps you had to give an important speech. Maybe you were going scuba diving for the first time, or you had an exam that just couldn't be rescheduled. After your engagement ended, the cold continued. The nose ran, the eyes watered, and so on. But while you were heavily engaged in your activity, no symptoms of a cold. Why?

Have you ever noticed how tired you get when you have something unpleasant to do, and how you aren't even aware of fatigue when you are vitally involved in an exciting project? You can go for days on end with very little sleep when you are redecorating your home, writing an important book, learning to fly an airplane, or traveling in a new and exciting place. And yet you can become exhausted when you have to face a project that is boring to you. Why?

I think the answer is quite basic: when you are creatively involved in your life, you have no time for illness or tiredness. Similarly, when you are busy, active and living your present moments, time seems to pass too quickly; there clearly is no time for depression or anxiety. You are trouble-free even though the "background" of your life may still be just as real. Inevitably when I encounter a person in counseling who is suffering from depression, I find the antidote is some kind of fulfilling activity. The ultimate resolution does not lie in rehashing the person's childhood, in blaming his parents or anyone else for his problems, but in helping him find the way to greater involvement in life. Busy people seldom have time for inhibiting emotional problems. Of course, being *too* busy can become a sickness in itself, but the essential message here is that being alive in the present is the most powerful antidote to emotional turmoil or depression ever invented, and *the ability to live in the present is essentially an attitudinal skill,* which has to be cultivated during the course of your everyday life.

For example, if you are waiting in a gasoline line, fuming about the fuel shortages and getting madder and madder about the sheiks in the Middle East, the oil-company conspiracies and the bungling bureaucracies in Washington, then you have *elected* to use up this present moment in a wasteful, self-defeating way. You are still going to sit in the gas line if that is your choice, but *how you decide to do it* is completely up to you. Could you use the time productively, to write letters, read a novel, talk to others in the line about working out alternative life styles so you could no longer be held hostage by the oil executives of the world? Can't you find *any* way to make the situation work *for* you rather than against you?

In my personal campaign to cultivate the art of living now, I have found that increasing the frequency of my own Muga experiences in recent years has depended largely on my becoming more willing to abandon the traditional ways in which others have thought I should live my life. I have found that the more freedom I allow myself to experience what is important for me, the more extended my Muga periods have become.

In sports, I am far more able to concentrate completely on what I am doing if I put everything else totally out of my mind—the office, the book, the client I am to see in the morning. To spend hours in a hotly contested tennis match on a hot summer afternoon without caring about the "blistering" temperature, the humidity, my sweating, fatigue or any other interferences, it has been necessary for me to say to myself, "I don't care *who* thinks I should be in the office at two P.M. on Thursday, August third, just because it's a 'business day.' " The more I allow myself the freedom to play hard and be totally in the game, the more I transcend time and space and live totally in the present, the more I know that I am learning to live now.

By the same token, when the next person comes through my office door, I will be better able to put the tennis match out of my mind and lose myself completely in his or her situation without saying to myself in the back of my mind, "If only I hadn't slipped on that one shot, I could have won that second set," or "I bet I can beat that guy next time."

And when it comes time to do some writing, I can likewise count on my ability to sit at the typewriter for a full day, completely unaware of the passage of time, with no sense of fatigue, hunger, boredom or any other distraction; to allow myself simply to write what I feel is important for me to say.

The more I give myself permission to live in the moment and

enjoy it without feeling guilty or judgmental about any other time, the better I feel about the quality of all my work. I am not concerned with how critics view my work, and because I write, first, to please myself and, second, with the chance of pleasing some readers, I am totally satisfied. I know inside myself, for instance, that even if no one else ever reads what I write, what I am saying is important enough for me to justify formulating and preserving it for myself. The exhilaration I get from writing for hours on end is its own reward. Being paid to write books, having readers improve the quality of their lives because of what I've written, being on a best-seller list and so on are spin-offs—"accidents that happen" as a result of my living present moments in the ways that seem significant to me.

In fact, the way the title of this book was decided on was the result of one of the most immediate Muga experiences of my own life.

Some time ago I took a ride in a hot-air balloon. Two hours passed in what seemed like five minutes as we floated up off the earth and the winds blew us wherever they were going. Between the infinity of the sky above us, all around us, and the solidity of the good green earth below us, sharing this experience with a person I love, I found myself more fully in the present than I had ever been.

Months later, when I was considering final titles and themes for this book, from "You're Allowed to be Perfect" to "Winning One Hundred Percent of the Time," and a friend suggested "The Sky's the Limit," I fell in love with it—I'm sure because it captured the "living now" inspiration of that balloon.

I hope you are now ready to take your own balloon ride, to *live now:* to accept the fact that mastery of life has always been and is still in your hands.

2 / False Masters

It may be something of a shock to you to jump from the concept of mastery to that of *false mastery* or *authoritarianism*, but my studies of the road to self-actualization and my own experiences on the roads of life have taught me that the most persistent barrier between normality and No-Limit living is the authoritarianism which is so rampant in contemporary society.

Most of us probably think we know pretty well what kind of person an authoritarian is. The stereotype is of a domineering sort, usually male, who expects blind obedience from anyone he can bully into accepting his authority; an aggressive, impatient, arrogant type, opinionated, narrow-minded, unreasonable. We might think of someone like Hitler as the archetypal authoritarian.

There is truth in this stereotype, but it is just the surface and only a small part of the story. The dictionary definition of "authoritarian" is (1) relating to or favoring blind submission to authority; (2) relating to or favoring a concentration of power in a leader or an elite not constitutionally responsible to the people.

From this it is clear that the "authoritarian-father" type described above is only a true authoritarian if he takes his own values, opinions and "directions" *from an authority he in turn accepts as higher than himself,* to which *he* gives blind obedience—whether it is the President, the General, the Church, the Boss, or just the ruling norms of society. So, however much noise the "authoritarian-father" type may make about the self-evident; undeniable correctness of his opinions, however much he may pretend to be the master of himself, the master of the house, or of anything else, he really hangs his identity outside himself, on the Great Unquestionable Authority to which he has pledged his total allegiance.

Such false mastery can be relatively innocuous, or it can be extremely dangerous. In Hitler's Germany, Hitler was not the authoritarian at all: the authoritarians were those Germans who blindly followed him and made totalitarianism possible in the first place. Thus the "authoritarian-father" type is just the opposite of what he seems; he is a person with no real self-confidence, with a weak ego, and with perhaps a touch of paranoia, who clings to *his* authority figure as a helpless infant clings to its mother.

And the "authoritarian father," or the "active authoritarian," is obviously only half—or less than half—of the picture. *He is nothing without those who blindly follow him*—the passive, submissive and (until recently, at least) stereotypically female counterpart, those who take all his orders and never question what he "thinks," the children or employees or acquaintances whose thoughts he can command. The "authoritarian mother," the "traditional wife," she who in the most authoritarian societies may even be regarded as her husband's property, may seem in her submissiveness the direct opposite of the authoritarian father, but that does not make her any less authoritarian in any important sense. It takes two to tango, and it takes many links to make an authoritarian chain.

From all this it should be clear that an "authoritarian" person is not necessarily a person who has authority. In fact, a person may be authoritarian just because he has no real authority over himself—because he accepts artificial limits placed on him by society and lets his frustration out on others. "Authoritarian" is generally accepted as a bad thing to be because it restricts, stifles, dominates others. Less often noticed is that it has the same effects on "the original authoritarian," and that all participants in restriction, stifling or domination are equally authoritarian.

I said earlier that I consider rampant authoritarianism to be the most persistent barrier to No-Limit living in our society. Anyone who is an alert observer of society can plainly see how few people think for themselves, but some social scientists have estimated that *as many as seventy-seven percent of the people in our culture* (Western civilization) *manifest more authoritarian qualities than nonauthoritarian* on a daily basis.

This is not surprising in view of parallel statistics showing us generally to be in abysmal states of mental health. I believe that our tremendously increased incidences of chronic depressions, "nervous breakdowns," family breakups, suicides, alcoholism, chemical dependencies, ulcers, hypertension, stress and other mentally related illnesses are due in large part to the internal frustration and boredom that authoritarianism breeds. As a human being, you were built to think for yourself. Your mind is going to rebel with anxiety, your emotions will be ruled by the weight of mental chains, if you don't allow yourself the freedom to think up to your full, limitless capacity. You will end up blaming others when things go wrong. By the irony of fate that makes us quickest to recognize our own faults in others, you will quickly blame other people's authoritarianism (allegiance to different Great Unquestionable Authorities) for the world's troubles—and you will not know how to relate to a truly free-thinking person if you meet one.

In fact, it is the free and serious thinker you may be the quickest to condemn as authoritarian, because he has the audacity, conceit or whatever to rest his position in life fundamentally on his own judgment. (On what authority do you think that? *Just your own?* Well, that doesn't mean much!)

If authoritarianism is as huge a social erroneous zone as I think it is, we are going to have to transcend it before we can shape a NEZ society, before we can even begin to fulfill our greatest potentials as human beings on any large scale. But as always, the solution starts with you, the individual, and in order to help you assess your own degree of authoritarianism it will pay to look a little more deeply into the psychology of authoritarians of all stripes.

Back in the 1940s, a group of seven social scientists headed by T. W. Adorno completed a monumental study on the psychology of authoritarianism. The results were published in 1950 in two volumes entitled *The Authoritarian Personality,* with almost one thousand pages of research, questionnaires and statistical tables, and a multitude of technical conclusions describing personality traits the researchers found to be associated with authoritarianism, which they defined pretty much as I have above. Reading this huge collection of information is generally restricted to academic sociology courses, but the content is so important that I feel it should be made more available to all of us common folks, so I am going to summarize and interpret it here.

What is important as you read about authoritarianism is for you to see how often you display authoritarian traits, and to ask yourself whether authoritarianism is in fact the predominant element of your personality. It may also be instructive for you to use the following descriptions of the authoritarian personality as a kind of guide to help you define what it is about yourself that you would like to change, and what you really have to change if you are going to become a No-Limit person.

CHARACTERISTICS OF AUTHORITARIAN PERSONALITIES

In summarizing more than a thousand pages of in-depth research on authoritarian personalities from T. W. Adorno and other authors, and coupling their findings with my own observations, I find that the following qualities are most indicative of an authoritarian personality.

Intolerance of Ambiguity

One of the key traits of authoritarians is the need to have things spelled out specifically before they can be comfortable. Unless there is a yes or no answer to every question, no matter how complex the question may be, they show signs of anxiety. As a result, the authoritarian has little tolerance for people who are working in intrinsically ambiguous areas—philosophers, artists, social or political thinkers. They insist on knowing precisely where they are going in life and when, and are threatened by the mysterious, the unknown and the unknowable. They often cling to the security of habit, and are often afraid to quit a job or to end a relationship, not because it wouldn't be in their best interest, but because it would leave them in a state of uncertainty too threatening to endure.

Since being intolerant of ambiguity implies an overwhelming need for certainty, whether false or not, it leads people to be superorganized about their lives, and to demand that others run their lives the same way. Authoritarians tend to think of themselves as *perfectionists,* but this is true only in the trivial sense that they have to have things done one way, and not in the greater sense that they are helping create a better way for everybody to live. Thus authoritarians are easily upset, and in fact often immobilized, when things don't go exactly "their way," which is the way "their authority" (whoever it may be) says they are supposed to go. One of the favorite sayings of authoritarians is likely to be "A place for everything, and everything in its place." They cannot adjust to the idea that in this life few things or people will stay where they want them to be for long.

Intolerance of ambiguity manifests itself in the family when the active authoritarian, usually the father, insists on everyone's obeying his rules all the time. If the family is playing a game "just for fun," the authoritarian typically interrupts to point out the tiniest infractions of the rules as he understands them, and most of the "game time" is spent looking things up in the rule book.

In parent/child relationships, parents who are intolerant of ambiguity often impose unrealistic expectations on their children, asking them, "What are you going to be when you grow up?" when the children are five years old. Countless fights erupt about keeping the house (and especially "your room") clean, because anything that is messy or out of place constitutes an ambiguity that cannot be tolerated. After all, there is only one way a house should be, and when it isn't that way, that is an occasion for reacting with hostility.

Parents with this authoritarian bent often demand "perfection" from their children in school, and their children often learn to demand it from themselves, but "perfection" only means obeying teachers to the letter and getting A's on all the tests, and not asking teachers difficult or challenging questions, reading novels under the desk when the class gets too boring or repetitive, or questioning why so much of school has to be unexciting in the first place. Those same children then learn to impose equally unreasonable demands on themselves, their parents and other family members, and eventually their own children.

Those who are high on the intolerance-of-ambiguity scale often must plan out everything, including vacations, financial budgets down to the last penny, and how the underwear is placed in the drawer. A vacation without reservations, or without a well-detailed itinerary, creates internal havoc that is ulcer-breeding if it is not resolved. Authoritarians must know in advance what they are going to do, and it must be confirmed at all costs. Moreover, they soon impose these kinds of needs for certainty on everyone around them, and to those who are more tolerant of ambiguity they are constantly saying things like "Why don't you plan your life better? If you put everything where it belongs, you'd know exactly where to find things when you want them. You'll be sorry if you don't get more organized."

From dressing and grooming in "perfectionistic" style to a home that is organized down to the last pin and needle, from standards of "order" imposed on everyone to a need always to have a plan, authoritarians almost all have the "accountant-bookkeeper" mentality, applied to everyday living. They see life's "record book" not as a diary filled with memories of rich experiences, but as a ledger with straight-ruled columns for assets and liabilities. The purpose of life is to end up on the assets side of the ledger in terms of conventional social values, and to avoid any mistakes that might put you in the liabilities column. While authoritarianism makes for "orderly" homes, vacations, schools, lives, jobs, retirements and so on, it leaves very little room for enjoying the things you have while you actually have them. It also rules out healthy adventurousness, exploration and spontaneity.

Sex is a good example: authoritarians see it as a preprogrammed act with a precise script to be followed, rather than as a way of expressing love. They are seldom interested in foreplay, or in affectionate embraces after "the act" is completed. They are typically orgasm-oriented (especially males), and they also tend to be fastidious about "cleanliness," sometimes to the extent of showers before and after. They may see no reason to make sex into anything other than "what it was intended to be"—a means of reproducing the species, or perhaps for the release of "unneeded" sexual energy.

On the job, intolerance of ambiguity shows up when authoritarians encounter others who are less in need of constant "certainty" than they are. They demand to know exactly what their co-workers are doing, what their goals are and how they propose to attain them. They can be horrible busybodies, and very adamant about their "advice" to others. More extreme authoritarians may have their own personal goals charted out in five- or ten-year intervals. They have to pretend or try to be sure where they'll be at ages twenty-five, thirty-five, forty-five and so on. They are thrown into a dither whenever they are unable to meet their own timetables, and the idea of simply not caring where they'll be in so many years is just plain incomprehensible to them.

One afternoon I was walking along the beach and a man passing by recognized me from a television appearance. He said hello and asked where I was going. I told him I wasn't going anywhere. I was just walking on the beach.

"But how far are you going to walk?" he asked.

"I don't know," I told him. "I'll walk until I don't feel like walking anymore."

"But you must have some idea that you're going to walk down to the pier or someplace," he insisted.

"No idea at all," I said.

He was perplexed, as though the idea of an open-ended walk on the beach made no sense to him and I had to be kidding him. How could you take a walk without any idea of where you were going, how long it would take you, or what your score on the walking meter for that day would be? He really thought I was putting him on, trying to give him a hard time, instead of trying to tell him frankly what I was (or wasn't) doing. He refused to understand that it is all right sometimes not to have any goals at all, that sometimes just doing something for the real enjoyment of it is far healthier than planning everything out to the last detail, keeping track of your "progress" every step of the way, and ceaselessly comparing your "achievements" with past attempts in such areas as beach walking, reading, swimming or sex.

Dichotomous Thinking

A dichotomy is basically a division of some group of things into two mutually exclusive sets: the division of a school class into the boys and the girls, of a group of animals into the sheep and the goats, of a group of whole numbers into the odd and the even, and so on. Obviously the proper use of dichotomics is essential to thought and language: without them we would be completely incapable of reasoning. Less obviously, the abuse or *improper* use of dichotomies, which is characteristic of authoritarians, is one of the greatest dangers to real thought, meaningful communication and mutual understanding in our culture.

It is this systematic abuse, *the compulsion to divide everything and everyone into mutually exclusive groups*—good/bad, right/wrong, friend/enemy—and "let it go at that," without taking into account the subtleties, qualifications or even downright mistakes that may be involved, which I have labeled "dichotomous thinking."

By this I mean that the authoritarian *lets his thinking be ruled by the need to dichotomize at all costs,* instead of using a dichotomy as a tool of thought which is suited only to certain specific jobs.

"Dichotomous thinking" may be seen as an outgrowth of intolerance of ambiguity. Where people and complex human questions are concerned, dichotomous thinking represents a "rush to judgment" which at once cuts off the authoritarian's chances of increasing his own wisdom and knowledge and alienates those he has placed in opposition to himself.

An example of dichotomous thinking would be: if you believe homosexuality is a perfectly legitimate life style for consenting adults who choose to practice it, the authoritarian is likely to jump to the conclusion that you are trying to promote homosexuality for everyone. You are either for it or against it; the authoritarian will not allow you any qualifications or "middle ground." The authoritarian generally reserves the right to tell you in no uncertain terms what you "really think" or stand for, and nothing you say will alter his determination to put you in one camp or the other.

Authoritarians are generally hardest on those closest to them. If someone in the family wonders whether there might be certain advantages to liberalizing abortion laws or softening some drug laws, for example, the authoritarian may well react with "You are either for or against abortion; which is it?" or "If you want them to make marijuana legal, then you must support the legalization of heroin and all hard drugs as well."

The bottom line is that authoritarians have no room in their internal circuitry for middle positions, for operating in the gray areas where almost all human activities occur.

Similarly, you will hear authoritarians saying things like these: all Jews are good businessmen; all blacks have rhythm; all Asians are cunning; all teenagers are rowdy; this generation is going to the dogs; all women are wily; all men are only after sex.

It is really absurd to label "all" people in any grouping as being either one way or the other. If you typically engage in dichotomous thinking and try to force it on others, you had best look to the authoritarianism "in your own house."

Rigidity of thought

Authoritarians are not only intolerant of ambiguity and often dichotomous in their thinking, but they are also exceedingly rigid in the way they perceive the world, and thus their expectations for themselves and others. In this sense, authoritarians have very strong resistances to change, and are threatened by any disruptions of things as they are accustomed to experiencing them.

"Rigidity of thought" has many meanings, but for authoritarians it generally implies an unwillingness to entertain any thoughts that conflict with their own preconceived ideas. If someone approaches the authoritarian—especially the "active" or typically male "authoritarian-father" type—with a point of view that is in contrast to his own, he is likely to become loud, indignant, incredulous, scornful. He may shout and try to intimidate. The last thing he will do is listen, evaluate and be prepared to change his position if it seems warranted. It is virtually impossible for him ever to admit having been wrong or having learned anything from anyone else; that would be an admission of his own weak ego and lack of real self-confidence. You will never hear the "authoritarian-father" type say, "Well, you may have a point there." He will immediately go on the defensive with something like "I really can't believe you think that way. For someone who is supposedly intelligent . . ."

Rigidity of thought may lead the authoritarian as far as resorting to personal insults, ridicule and even physical violence. With authoritarians of any type, rational and constructive discussion is virtually impossible. Dialogue is never a pleasant or stimulating chance to learn something new or experience a different way of seeing things. It is never a *cooperative effort to reach agreement,* beginning with mutual respect on each side. It is usually as perfunctory and abrupt as "authoritarian sex" —a wham-bam-thank-you-ma'am approach to which you, if you are smart, will say no-thank-you-ma'am and retreat.

To the NEZ person, the most frustrating thing about authoritarians is their inaccessibility: *most of the time, there is literally no way to reach them.* I know of countless families in which children will say, "My dad's a great guy in his own way, but I just can't talk to him about politics," or "My mom's a terrific woman, but if I try to talk to her about sex—forget it."

Whole regions of thought become taboo when an authoritarian is involved. A rational person has only to be abused, intimidated or scorned once to say, "I don't need this. Let sleeping dogs lie." Thus *the only way* authoritarians are ever going to be "reached," the only way they can *ever* change or grow, is if they recognize their own problems and take their own steps toward correcting them.

Some time ago a young girl came to me in hysterics because her father had labeled her a whore. I asked the father to come in and discuss the matter with me and his daughter. He arrived full of resentment at the idea that there was anything to discuss, and I found it was impossible to reason with him while his daughter was present. It seems she had received a phone call from a young man whom her father had labeled "a troublemaker." He absolutely insisted that his daughter was not to associate with "that kind," even though he had never even met the young man to make his own judgment. Whether he was relying on rumors about the boy, or acting out of paranoia for his daughter's "purity," or exploding for some other reason, I couldn't tell at the time, because he was so adamant that anyone who even questioned his position was a supporter of teenage prostitution, child abuse, pornography, venereal disease and dozens of other evils.

I had already seen that the daughter was as far from being a whore as I am. I also saw that the father's idea of whom his daughter should date was so rigid that he felt no remorse at calling her a whore and reducing her to tears just because the boy didn't fit perfectly with *his* preconceived image. Finally I asked the girl to leave. The father settled down somewhat, but his rigid thinking was so overpowering that I found it impossible to make any progress with him. My conclusion was that he could not even *hear* his daughter's or anyone else's opinons on anything; that he was "selectively deaf," an arch-authoritarian, and that the only way to help the daughter was to teach her how to avoid being upset over ugly labels that other people chose for her, even if the labeler was as significant a person as her own father.

The ironic aftermath of this case history was that three years later the girl left home at the age of nineteen and married the "troublemaker," who by then had graduated from college with honors and was going on to graduate school. It turned out that the father's original condemnation of the boy had been based on solely religious and ethnic prejudice. The girl's family was "Christian"; the boy was Jewish. To this day the father refuses to talk to his son-in-law or his own daughter.

Rigidity in most authoritarians extends from "thought" deeply into habits and behavior. They will typically read only one kind of editorial in a newspaper, one expressing opinions with which they already agree. They subscribe to the same magazines year after year, never even entertaining the idea of reading periodicals that air viewpoints opposed to theirs. They will often return to the same restaurant over and over again, ordering the same meal at the same table night after night. They may never have tried Greek, Oriental, Mexican or any other kind of "ethnic" cooking, because it is "foreign" and they know they wouldn't like it.

Rigidity of routine usually extends into authoritarians' sex lives as well: they tend to have intercourse at the same time in the same way forever, or until it becomes so boring that they simply do without it.

The rigidity of authoritarians is *threatened by change in any form.* Authoritarians almost always vote for incumbents, and become "incumbents" in their own lives as well. They hesitate to move to new parts of the country because they "wouldn't know what to expect." They often stay in the same jobs, even though their work may have become little more than a daily drill for them, because they are afraid of the changes involved with a promotion, a geographical shift or even a completely new vocational choice. They often hate their work, and rather than looking inward at their own attitudes they blame the boss, other workers, the corporation, the new generation or any other convenient scapegoat. They are as susceptible to boredom as anybody else, but they hang on anyway, waiting for the gold watch and hoping that retirement will give them some relief.

Of course "retired authoritarians" may be even more obnoxious than working ones, because they tend to become angry at everyone else who is responsible, as they see it, for their lack of money, motivation, excitement or enjoyment as older people. They may get mad at the kids for not wanting to visit them, even though a visit may seem to the kids like spending several weeks in a tomb with a pushy encyclopedia salesman. They are angry at the younger generation for ignoring them, when their own rigidity drives everyone, young or old, away in a hurry. And they never seem to realize that their own rigid thinking is the source of their misery. They may thrive on being grumpy and actually look forward to their frustrations. They may look for things to complain about, "be happy" when a disaster strikes or an energy crisis surfaces to give them more fuel for their cherished antagonisms.

The rigidity of authoritarians is a disease that begins with thought and spreads to all aspects of their lives. It infects them and all those around them with boredom, anxiety, depression. Authoritarians must live with routine, and yet they essentially hate the sameness of it all. They won't take risks to break the boredom because they fear change, yet they blame the world for not changing to conform to their old, stale ideas of what it should be like.

Anti-Intellectualism

In line with their typical intolerance of ambiguity, dichotomous thought and rigidity, authoritarians usually distrust "intellectuals," particularly those who actually make their living as thinkers. Authoritarians are often skeptical of anything they cannot "see with their own eyes," and downright intimidated by philosophers, psychologists, artists, professors or others who make their livings working primarily with their minds.

Authoritarians are typically quick to put down people who read professional journals, go to lectures, plays or operas, or tune in to discussion shows on television. A typical authoritarian remark would be "Oh, those professors, they're all a bunch of Commies (bleeding-heart liberals, eggheads, bookworms). They don't know what the hell they're talking about when it comes to the real world."

When authoritarians are honest with others, when they feel unthreatened—for instance, in interview situations—they often admit to secret admiration for those who have "book learning." Authoritarian parents almost always want their children to go to college, but almost never want the children to come home and begin acting as though they knew more about anything than their parents (even though that is supposedly why the parents sent them to college in the first place). It is quite common for authoritarian parents to brag about the academic or intellectual accomplishments of their children, but only when those achievements indicate conventional "success" in the established rat race ("my daughter was first in her class in law school") and never when rebelliousness against established order is involved.

Since artistic pursuits are viewed as "risky" from a practical, career point of view, and *art naturally involves a high degree of ambiguity,* you will seldom hear an authoritarian parent saying, "I'm so happy, my daughter has decided she wants to be a painter (writer, sculptor, film-maker, rock-music artist, etc.)."

Putting aside the riskiness of artistic careers for a moment, let's look a little more closely at the connection between the authoritarian's intolerance of ambiguity as discussed earlier, his anti-intellectualism, and his discomfort with art and artistic career pursuits.

Authoritarians' intolerance of ambiguity means that they compulsively want every piece of language they hear or read to *mean just one thing* which is clear and readily identifiable. Remembering the bookkeeper mentality, "$12,500 in the savings account" means just one thing. But consider the beauty of such poetry as Shakespeare's "To be or not to be, that is the question . . ." or Keats's "Beauty is truth, truth beauty, that is all/ Ye know on earth, and all ye need to know." The truth *and* the beauty of this language lie precisely in the fact that these poems *mean something different every time they are read!* They contain such universal truths, or so much "concentrated wisdom," that they are true in an *infinite* number of ways. A trillion different people over countless generations in the most different conceivable situations can gain enlightenment from such poetry. A single person can read such simple words again and again and gain new inspiration, new insights into life. Compare the prospect of reading the world's most inspiring poems over and over again with the idea of reading an accountant's ledger over and over again and you will see what I mean.

So the *artistic use of language* depends on the *fertility of its ambiguity*—that is, its ability to reveal some truth, show some beauty, in lots of different ways to all kinds of different people.

The same is true of a great painting, photograph, symphony, building or any other work of art, and also, at least according to many thinkers, of great works of philosophy and other intellectual disciplines. Martin Heidegger, for instance, says that

> multiplicity of meanings is the element in which all thought must move in order to be strict thought. To use an image: to a fish, the depths and expanses of its waters, the currents and quiet pools, warm and cold layers are the element of its multiple mobility. If the fish is deprived of the fullness of its element, if it is dragged on the dry sand, then it can only wriggle, twitch, and die. Therefore, we always must seek out thinking, and its burden of thought, in the element of its multiple meanings, else everything will remain closed to us.*

But if art and thought depend on the *fertility of ambiguity*, as described above, and the rigid, dichotomous-thinking authoritarian

* Heidegger, *What Is Called Thinking*, Fred D. Wieck and J. Glenn Gray, trans. (Harper & Row Torchbooks, 1968), p. 71.

is compulsively *intolerant of ambiguity*, it is no wonder that he does not know what to make of original thought *or* art. In sum, the authoritarian, doubting his own judgment, tends to mistrust anyone who ventures into the subtle and complex fertility of art or intellectualism.

The typical authoritarian response to someone who is intellectual or highly educated is avoidance. Of course, there may be legitimate reasons for avoidance of some "intellectuals" by rational people: there are plenty of authoritarians among academics and others with fancy degrees and titles. Not only are authoritarians of this stripe seldom real leaders in their fields—they are usually devoted members of some "school of thought," blindly following what some "great man" has taught—but they are prone to one of the most obnoxious of authoritarian diseases, intellectual snobbery. Intellectual snobs are really so insecure about their own personal worth that they have to *hide behind* degrees and titles, to pretend that college graduates, "bookish people" or "scholars" are *more intelligent* than anyone who earns a living by other means.

Of course this is absurd. A person who can figure out how to repair a radio, or how to fix an engine, or rotate crops, or breed cattle, or any of thousands of occupations, can be every bit as intelligent as someone who can solve quadratic equations or recite from the classics. "Book learning" is meant to cultivate only one kind of intelligence, and to me the greatest "intellectuals" have been those who learned primarily by *doing*.

Of course they had to be steeped in the literature of their fields before they could "stand on the shoulders" of previous generations and advance the "state of the art" in their areas, but No-Limit types, like Ralph Waldo Emerson, Henry David Thoreau, Albert Einstein and George Bernard Shaw, *transcend* all who had gone before them by *going out into the world and trying out their ideas.* They were workers as well as thinkers, and they were brilliant because they had overcome the dichotomous thinking that says a person has to be either a worker *or* an intellectual. Whatever your work, you can be brilliant at it only if you think about it, but having a Ph.D. degree doesn't prove a person is capable of thinking *at all*, nor does the lack of a high-school education prevent you one tiny bit from thinking "brilliantly."

Viewed from this perspective, the authoritarian with three academic degrees is as anti-intellectual as the authoritarian who never went past the third grade.

Anti-Introspection

In addition to being anti-intellectual, authoritarians tend to be anti-introspective: to resist looking inward into their own motivations for their behavior. They do not believe in asking themselves why they are really doing anything, and typically dismiss out of hand any avenues toward self-improvement that might lead them to learn more about themselves. They are apt to see psychotherapy, meditation, Yoga, and other ways of approaching and facing themselves as not only a waste of time, but perhaps a conspiracy by some sort of "cult" to brainwash the entire population. They are so unsure of themselves that they don't dare risk exposing themselves to the influences of "the shrink," the Yoga teacher or any of those other "weirdos."

What they are really afraid of is changing their minds, admitting that they have not always been right about everything (or, rather, their chosen Great Unquestionable Authority hasn't). They secretly know they submitted once, and don't trust themselves not to submit again.

Anti-introspection is another of those authoritarian "blind spots"—in this case, it involves the refusal ever to look in the mirror, psychologically speaking. Authoritarians reject looking inward because they have come to rely so strongly on external support systems to convince them of their value as humans. They really believe that their worth comes from their accomplishments and accumulations, and that the only way to increase their worth is to accomplish and accumulate more. While they may often say they want to get out of the rat races that their lives have become, they refuse to believe that *the only exit door opens inward,* that the first step toward getting out is to face the inner turmoil and fear that keep them from taking the risks that are necessary to get out of the routines they despise so much. They know they are not happy doing what they are doing, that living in relationships based on emotional outbursts and absence of affection is unpleasant, but they won't take the inner road to make it change. They continue to place all hope and blame for everything on externals, using anyone or anything as an excuse for their feelings of entrapment. Until an authoritarian starts to question himself, and see what it is about him that keeps him locked into an authoritarian life style, he stands no chance of changing.

Conformity and Submissiveness

It is particularly ironic that people who exhibit classical authoritarian behavior rate consistently high in the areas of submissiveness and conformity. According to Adorno, "Conformity is one of the major expressions of lack of an internal focus." By this he means that authoritarian people are motivated, virtually governed, by opinions and social forces external to themselves; they are weak when it comes to relying on their own independent sets of values, beliefs, instincts. They find it easier and more comforting to adjust to imposed standards than to look inward for the keys to guiding their own lives. Consequently it seems natural to these people to be submissive to established authority and conventional modes of behavior. While authoritarians can certainly make a lot of noise about many issues, they rarely stray from established, prepackaged "lines" on any subject, and they use tradition and "the way we've always done things" as rationales for their conformity. "Well," they reason, "if you try to create your own life style, not only will you be taking a chance because you're experimenting with what's never been tried before (the unknown), but you will have all of conventional society against you." Too often part of the excuse authoritarians use to make others conform to "tradition" is that so many other people are so authoritarian that they will make life practically unbearable for the innovator, who will be sorry he ever tried to buck the system in the first place. When it comes down to action, or, as psychologists call it, "behavior," the authoritarian is typically quite submissive to authority, and quite suggestible and gullible, particularly to propaganda and hype, in contrast to the more autonomous individual who challenges authority and refuses to accept things as they are simply because an authority figure or institution decrees they should be so.

Conformity and submissiveness are first seen in the attitudes of authoritarians toward their own parents. Among authoritarians the concept of the parent as absolute authority figure is sacred. So it is that authoritarians find it difficult to express criticism or resentment toward their own parents in any kind of way that could lead to healthy readjustment of parent/child relationships, and they are equally intolerant of receiving such feedback from their own children. The authority of the parent is seen as a one-way street, in which the parent deserves respect just because he or she is an authority figure, and authority figures must be unchallengeable because any challenge to any authority is seen as a challenge to all authority, order and "civilization." The authoritarian relationship between children and their parents never matures to friendship, mutual respect and tolerance, but remains a constant struggle between a would-be subordinate and a dictator.

This totalitarian view of parenting carries well beyond childhood. Even fully grown, ostensibly mature adults often have difficulty honestly expressing their feelings toward their parents. The schism exists for a lifetime in authoritarian people because, as they see it, the key to the role between parents and their children is one of conformity. The unresolvable question, of course, is, "To what set of values should we conform?"

Authoritarians tend to refer to authority figures a great deal in discussions or explanations of why they "think" as they do, and they are generally submissive to authority figures in everyday dealings with them. For instance, an authoritarian janitor will accept what a doctor tells him about medicine—whether he believes or understands it or not—just as he expects anyone to accept what he says about his job, whether they believe or understand it or not.

I have worked with many clients for whom conformity and submissiveness are dominant ways of life. Many women have been taught by authoritarian parents that the only way for them to behave is to go along with what the male segment of the population, particularly the husband and father, tell them. Women who resist this stereotype are often classified as somehow neurotic—aggressive, feminist reactionary, "butch" or "castrating"—by male authoritarians. As long as a woman is content to "go along" and be submissive, she "gets along" with authoritarian males. In counseling, I always think it is important to help anyone to resist automatic conformity to anything, because it detracts seriously from a person's basic human dignity by elevating other authority to a level higher than one's own. This is true for dominated children, wives, husbands, employees or anyone else: if you can't think for yourself, if you are unable to be other than conforming and submissive, then you are always going to remain gullible, a slave to whatever any authority figure dictates.

There is no such thing as *always having to obey the law.* When the laws are immoral, they must be challenged and disobeyed. Likewise, when authority figures are abusing you, you are not obliged to follow their dictates. If anyone insists that you must be just like everyone else to be a good member of your family or your society, it is absolutely vital for you to refuse to conform and to establish yourself as a person with your own dignity and self-respect.

I once had a discussion with a police officer in New Mexico whose job it was to give out speeding tickets to drivers who were exceeding the speed limit by a few miles an hour in the middle of the desert, where nobody lived for fifty miles around and you might see another car every fifteen minutes. He agreed that no one's life was being jeopardized by the five- or six-mile-an-hour "speeders" he ticketed, that it was a stupid law, that he was really victimizing people rather than enforcing safe driving, and that it was a shabby practice: the state was just employing him to man a speed trap where profits could be made on out-of-state "visitors" by enforcing a ridiculously low speed limit. Still, every day he would "go to work" and wait at the bottom of a hill where most drivers would not bother to slam on the brakes just so they could conform to the small sign that suddenly and for no reason said "Speed Limit 50 mph."

When I suggested that the officer refuse to take such an assignment, or that he try to have the law changed, or that he complain to the powers that be, he smiled and said that he was just doing his job, that it wasn't up to *him* to write the laws or decide how they would be enforced. He was submitting to an unjust law and he knew it, but he couldn't imagine questioning it, challenging it or refusing to enforce it on others.

You can be a man or woman, child or adult, black or white, rich or poor, or anything in between, and easily fall into conformity and submissiveness to authority as a life choice. No one has a monopoly on throwing away his basic human freedom. In fact, all of us, at one time or another, make conforming and submissive choices in our lives. The important thing is for you to recognize it when you are doing it, to ask yourself if it is what you really want and, if not, to adopt some new strategies to rid yourself of the *habit* of conforming and submitting, which is perhaps the central hallmark of the authoritarian.

Christian Bovee, the nineteenth-century American author and editor, once wrote, *"There is no tyrant like custom, and no freedom where its edicts are not resisted."* If you must rely on conformity and submissiveness as your primary resource for stability, then you are indeed the slave to a tyrant that dwells within you, and you will be inhibiting the freedom of those you claim to be your loved ones and crushing any chance you may have for your own independence.

Sexual Repression

Authoritarians are typically uncomfortable about their own sexuality. Just because they are so uptight about it, they see "dirty sex" almost everywhere. As I have already noted, they have superficial attitudes toward sex: performance- or orgasm-oriented attitudes that lead them to want to "do it" as fast as possible to "get it over with." They are constantly feeling that there is *too much sex* in today's world, too much emphasis on sexuality. They may be extremely critical of sex-education programs in schools, but in snide and snipping covert ways they talk about sex all the time. They often pursue sexual "outlets" very selfishly, using the "partner" as a tool or victim.

There are deep contradictions in the sexual attitudes and behavior of authoritarians. The "authoritarian father," while always threatened if his daughter is "subjected to" sexual advances, and extremely "protective" of her, is likely to feel that his son is supposed to "go out and get laid now and then" because it will help him to become *a man*. Authoritarian males tend to have numerous extramarital affairs themselves, but with as little affection toward the "other women" as they display in their own marriage—and they would never allow their wives the same "freedom" they steal for themselves (hence the term "cheating on your wife/husband"), primarily, I think, because they are secretly so aware of their wives' dissatisfaction with their sexual "performance" that they are scared to death that their wives will leave them for the first man who can *perform* better in bed than they can.

The authoritarian male may cultivate a highly macho image, and be concerned above all about how others rate him on the traditional masculinity scale based upon his sexual prowess, about which he may boast incessantly. But his boasts are all about sexual *conquests*, marks on the scorecard of women he has conquered—all to cover up the fact that he doesn't get any real enjoyment from his sexual activities at all.

The topic of sex rarely leaves the authoritarian's mind. From male or female you will hear endless innuendos, sexual double entendres, and silly references demeaning sex creeping into everyday conversations. Then you will hear the contradictions: they are outraged at how sex seems to be infiltrating television, advertising, movies, books and everything else.

Authoritarians habitually see sex where it is not. If someone of the opposite sex is friendly to them they jump to the conclusion that they are being "propositioned." They always know the "hidden reasons" for anyone's actions, which are of course always sexual. They imagine that anyone who is friendly with someone of the opposite sex is sleeping with that person, or is about to, or wants to.

"Authoritarian-father" types will be among the first to lecture you on how immoral pornography is, but also the first to sneak off to the porno flicks or to get some hot homemade movies for a stag gathering.

The extreme effects of the "authoritarian father's" sexual repression were illustrated in the movie *Joe,* made in the early seventies, when the Woodstock Generation was still in rebellion. Joe was obsessed with the perversions of the younger "potheads" of that generation, especially with their orgies, their wild sexual experiences. As so often happens with repressed and repressive authoritarian fathers, he was rewarded with a teenage daughter who ran away to join "the opposition." But as the movie developed, it turned out that Joe was primarily obsessed with getting in on the forbidden sexual freedoms. His underlying disgust was not really with the younger, sexually promiscuous generation, but with himself because he was missing out on what they found enjoyable. Joe's typical authoritarian male-chauvinistic sexism led him first into a "forbidden orgy" with his daughter's peers. Then, driven insane by his own guilt at having transgressed the sacred boundaries of "standard" sexual morality, and determined to wipe "that threatening, foreign culture" from the face of the earth forever, he picked up his shotgun and went blasting into a nearby hippie commune. Among the bodies he finally found the corpse of his own daughter. The story is as old as time: the man killed his fiancé out of jealousy, the general had to wipe out the village to save it. But any time a young daughter has to be "wiped out" to preserve her "purity," you can bet that an authoritarian type (be it male or female) is holding the gun, and that his own sexual repression and/or guilt, combined with his ability to blame everyone but himself for the "wild sexual immorality" of the world, is pulling the trigger.

Ethnocentrism

This fancy sociological term means being centered on prejudice toward your own ethnic group or culture, and implies a strong tendency to evaluate and label others in terms of your own group values, rather than granting them their own rights to be uniquely themselves or to have their own ethnic or cultural values. All the research on the authoritarian personality points to ethnocentrism as the most common quality among those who scored highest on the authoritarianism scale, and it is also in many ways the most dangerous of the authoritarian qualities, because it is the most capable of leading to violence between individuals, between ethnic, cultural or racial groups, or between whole nations.

In everyday life you will constantly hear authoritarians putting other people down not on the basis of how they behave or perform in given areas, but purely because "they are not like us." Authoritarians are loaded with ethnocentric prejudgments about almost everyone and everything that is not of "their group." There are as many slurs and demeaning categories as there are other groups to judge: chink, wop, spic, nigger, honky—the list is endless. People who have different skin colors, religious beliefs, tastes in food, customs of dress or anything else are judged not on the basis of how their behavior and customs serve them, but in strict comparison terms, and results are always the same: "those other people" are crazy, immoral, stupid, lazy, greedy, weird, inferior. And the reverse is also true: anyone of the authoritarians' own group is automatically okay, to be accepted and defended at all costs, first to be hired, last to be fired, and so on, regardless of his or her own personal merits.

When we prejudge other cultures in terms of how they measure up to ours, set ourselves up as the standard-bearers of civilization, we are inclined to send out "missionaries" to make the infidels more like us—or to use their "inferiority" as an excuse to dominate them, exploit them, even conquer them, which is what happened to the American Indians. You will hear authoritarians saying things like "Those people in Africa are all uncivilized and lacking in motivation to improve themselves. Just look at their culture! They have no industrialization, no technology—they are living back in the fifteenth century." This type of authoritarian would never look at the benefits that accrue to nations that are not industrialized, would never consider that perhaps these people enjoy being close to the earth, or notice that schizophrenia, anxiety, pollution, cancer, carnage of the highways and many other destructive aspects of our "great industrialized culture" are not even a part of these people's lives. Instead authoritarians may conclude that these backward savages don't appreciate their diamonds, aluminum, ostriches or trees enough, and that what they really need is an American company to take over for them and "show them how it's done"—i.e., mine their diamonds and aluminum, kill all their ostriches for feathers, and cut down all their trees for furniture.

Within families the most obvious forms of ethnocentrism occur when parents try to make their children conform to "the way our family has always done things," or the way things were done in the Old Country, or the way Catholics, Protestants, Jews, Moslems, etc., are supposed to do things, or the way Italians, Lithuanians, Irish, Japanese, etc., are supposed to do things. There is certainly no harm in a certain amount of ethnic pride, in finding your heritage fascinating and in wanting to learn about it and preserve what you find good in it. But the stories of what rigid parental ethnocentrism can do to a child or a family are too numerous and often too horrifying to ignore. A typical one appeared in the papers several years ago, when a teenage girl and her boy friend jumped to their deaths from the top of a New York City tenement building because the girl's parents, acting out of some rigid tradition (I forget which, but it doesn't matter), refused to let her date—even though all her friends were dating—because that wasn't the way it was done in the Old Country. They virtually kept her imprisoned in her room until it drove her crazy.

The effects of parental ethnocentrism are seldom so extreme, but we all know of families in which a child has decided she wanted to marry someone from a different ethnic, religious or sometimes even geographical or political background and her authoritarian parents have disowned her, refused to talk to their "loved one" ever again. Or they have been so strident and threatening, and she has been so vulnerable, that they have managed to bully her into rejecting her true love and marrying someone from "her own group."

Less often noticed is that children, adolescents and young adults are also capable of being highly ethnocentric in their own ways. If a teenage girl, for example, expects her parents to "get modern" and be "with it," meaning "act more like the kids in *my* subculture"—get into rock music, learn to disco dance, get themselves some blue jeans, etc.—and heaps scorn on her parents for their "stodgy, fuddy-duddy" values, beliefs and life styles, it can create as much havoc and alienation as if the ethnocentrism were coming from the parents. Young people can be incredibly authoritarian, whether their parents are or not—which is hardly surprising, because, with authoritarianism so rampant in our society, they can "learn it" just about anywhere. And, like all authoritarians, they can be almost impossible to reach or reason with, especially for their own parents. Perhaps they will "grow out of it," although the odds for that don't seem so good—unless more adults grow out of it, and especially out of their ethnocentrism, and give *everybody's* children some more tolerant examples to follow.

In American society in general, racism has obviously been the most widespread, pervasive and destructive form of ethnocentrism, and I would hope its effects, from the days of slavery to the present, are well enough known to all of us that I do not need to go into detail in recounting them here. What I want to dwell on for a moment is the way ethnocentrism in general and racism in particular tie in with the larger phenomenon of *anti-minority thinking and behavior,* a disease in our culture that promotes alienation between all kinds of "minorities" and "majorities."

This is not simply a racial issue by any means. Political minorities, for instance, have a great deal of difficulty being recognized in this country. Unless you are a Democrat, a Republican or a so-called Independent (uncommitted)—if you are a member of a small party, or are trying to start a new "third party"—authoritarians, whose primary cultural group has become not their ethnic or racial group but simply the Great (Silent) American Majority, will react to you in a typically ethnocentric way: you're a kook, a Commie, a reactionary or whatever other label comes most quickly to mind. The most usual way to dismiss minority political opinions is to label them ultra-"conservative" or -"radical," "far right" or "far left," and to label the holders of those opinions "another Hitler," which immediately gives the authoritarian majority the excuse not only to ignore whatever merit the minority opinion may contain and to exclude the minority from the political process, but also to attack minority thinkers personally, sometimes to the point of harassment or outright violence.

This is only one example; you will see anti-minority stances by authoritarians in virtually every area of human experience. And even though every single opinion now held by the Great Majority once originated with a minority—for instance, the idea that the United States should declare independence from Britain and write its own constitution—authoritarians never come over to the side of a minority until a vast number of others do so first.

In the early and middle 1960s majority opinion was strongly in favor of the Vietnam War; the "authoritarian opinion" was that any good American would blindly support the actions of the U.S. government. But as the sixties turned to the seventies and the long, grueling efforts of the antiwar minority paid off, it became fashionable to be against the war, and to see the folly of a Western nation trying to force its way on a country so completely different from its own. Then the authoritarians crowded onto the bandwagon, and even applauded the antiwar books and films which showed the horrible truth about that insane *ethnocentric* intervention. At present it is hard to find anyone who doesn't claim he was against the war all along, just as it is hard to find anyone in France who was alive during the German occupation of World War II who was not a member of the Resistance (although huge numbers of French citizens collaborated with the invaders). And that is another thing about authoritarians for whom the Great American Majority has replaced the strictly ethnic group as the focus of ethnocentrism: they are apt to develop very convenient memories. This is partly a function of another authoritarian trait, the *inability to admit you have been wrong about something,* or the knack of *covering up the fact that you are not flawless.*

It is easy to be for something when everyone but a tiny "fringe group" or minority is for it, and the authoritarian takes the easy way out in even the most trivial of things. For example, when long hair began to be worn by a few young people in the sixties, authoritarians were uniformly vocal in ridiculing this "sissy look." Ten years later, when long hair for males came into vogue among the majority, those same authoritarians were suddenly growing their hair longer and longer, and paying fifteen dollars a haircut to get what had once been a "sissy look" styled to the same perfection their wives had once demanded.

The inclination to stay with the majority on virtually everything is of course a measure of the low esteem most authoritarians have for themselves. It is admittedly risky in "practical terms" to challenge the established norms of society and strike out in a new direction, and anyone who lacks self-confidence will hang back and wait to see which way most of the herd is running, taking great care to stay in the *center,* where the view might not be so great and you might get jostled or have your toes stepped on regularly, but at least you are in the safest possible place. Unless, of course, the herd gets spooked and most of it gets pushed by "the masses" off a cliff, in which case only those who have been on the fringes are likely to survive—to become the leaders of the next generation.

Take the great events of recent American history: the civil-rights movement, the antiwar movement, the women's-rights movement or any other struggle in which minority opinion was mocked by the majority in the earliest stages. Authoritarians' anti-minority prejudices and consequent pro-majority compulsions are expressions of the mentalities of their "followers." They are against abortion if most people are; they do not support local political reform unless their neighbors do; they want to know what everyone else thinks before they commit themselves to tax reform, nuclear energy, the Equal Rights Amendment or anything else.

In light of what has been said up to now about the authoritarian personality, it is not surprising that ethnocentrism, whether the traditional kind, as in whites throwing out all blacks from the "sacred center" of society or vice versa, depending on which race is in power, or the modern kind, where "the majority" has become the central ethnic group for so many, which results in society throwing out *all* minority opinions, has its roots in the customs of *whatever society the ethnocentric person chooses to identify with.* In fact, the Greek root of the word is *ethnos,* one of whose definitions is "a group of kindred in clan and tribal organization;—contrasted with *demos.*" If one looks up *demos,* one finds the root of "democracy," to which authoritarians pay such blind lip service: ". . . the common people, the populace," meaning pretty much the strange ideal that all people are created equal, and that you shouldn't judge anybody for any superficial, ethnocentric reason.

There is no doubt about it: in this free country it is your constitutional right to refuse to think at all if you want to. You can sit back and stay "safely" with the majority, maybe even smugly, while berating those who voice unpopular minority opinions. But the world will be improved only by those who are willing to follow their own consciences, even when it is unpopular to do so.

In the late twentieth century, it is time for us to rid ourselves of the authoritarian rule of the *ethnos*—the tribal social rule that dictates that there be one chief with twenty ranks or classes of society under him—and to take the *demos* as the center of a No-Limit society; to accept the idea that all of us common people were meant to find a way to live together peacefully and prosperously on this earth, but that the only way we can do that is if all of us allow the ethnocentric scales to fall from our own eyes.

Remember, "witch" burning, slavery, gladiators, executions of the mentally ill, human sacrifice and many other practices which we have abolished today were once carried on because they were acceptable, approved by the majority. It wasn't the authoritarian personalities of the world who led us away from such evils. We were led into humanitarian paths because a few No-Limit people were willing to take unwelcome stances and start minority groups that ultimately made this a better world for all of us.

Paranoia

Perhaps because they harbor so many illusions of superiority over others and secretly feel that others must view them the same way, authoritarians tend to be paranoid—to suffer from delusions of persecution. They find it very difficult to trust other people and typically have low opinions of humanity in general, believing that everyone is really out to get everyone else, that "you always have to watch out for yourself and get the other guy before he gets you."

Authoritarians' basic distrust of themselves and everyone else makes them suspicious about every human encounter, afraid of anyone who seems to be trying to influence them. Their first question is, "What is this person trying to get out of this?" But their paranoia, based as it is on their overactive imaginations and not on reality, and creating needless anxiety, obviously cannot help them to be more effective in protecting their own interests. In fact, it may lead them to be more gullible in some situations, since people who really *are* out to get them and recognize their low self-esteem can often find ways to exploit it and victimize them—specifically, flattering them into falling for scams. Realizing that they have been "screwed again" (but not realizing why), they become increasingly paranoid—a vicious circle which in extreme cases can result in panic, hallucinations or even clinical psychosis.

More often, however, when paranoia leads to psychosis it is because authoritarians cannot admit that they are "to blame" or responsible for *anything* that has not worked out or that has gone wrong in their lives, and therefore must blame someone else. The lesson drawn from this each time is that one should be less trusting in the future, which means more suspicion, more paranoia; and so it can go all the way to the mental hospital.

Even to support the relatively mild paranoia of the majority of authoritarians, however, it is necessary for them to imagine multitudes of enemies out there, all kinds of conspiracies. Social protest groups are secretly funded by the Russians; there are spies everywhere; the big oil companies have a conspiracy with the Arab sheiks to rip us off; the black family that wants to move in down the street is working for some huge corporate blockbuster; and on and on. Of course the authoritarian's own feelings of persecution never lead him to greater sympathy with or support for others who really are being persecuted, or toward eradicating persecution completely; they simply lead to withdrawal ever deeper into ever-tightening spirals of paranoia.

Authoritarians who are high on the paranoia scale will constantly warn their friends and family members to "be careful," which is the opposite of spontaneous and natural. They teach their children to be distrustful of everyone, and they instill paranoia in their families with stories about the terrible things that can happen if you allow yourself to be open, or trust anyone you don't know.

A paranoid picture of the world is not going to help us make the world a better place to live in. Certainly we can all have better locks on our doors, a closed-mouth approach to everyone we don't really know, and perhaps we'll protect ourselves to some degree from some disaster—but if we accept the "better locks" philosophy of life, in the end we'll simply be breeding more distrust for each other.

If you feel that everyone out there is a potential enemy, you are closing yourself off from the vast majority of people who are sincere, trustworthy and exciting people to know. If you learn how to spot and deal effectively with real potential victimizers, you will then trust yourself to be open to new people and new ideas. My experience has been that when you carry yourself with dignity and simply refuse to be taken in by the few fast talkers or con artists who run across your life's path, and when you deal straightforwardly with these kinds of people, they tend to go away and seek out meeker victims.

But the huge majority of people I encounter are not in the least interested in ripping me off or abusing me in any way, and that must be true of the vast majority of people you encounter, too. So if you find yourself always suspicious of the motives of others, if you believe that there are "disease germs" everywhere, and that the world is a hostile, unfriendly place, *you yourself are assuring that your worst expectations will almost always be confirmed,* and the only thing you'll get for your paranoia will be more hostile reactions from others, more paranoid feelings in yourself, and a lifetime of skepticism and irrational fear. The choice, as always, is yours to make.

Anti-Weakness

As indicated in the last section, authoritarians seldom take responsibility for their own mistakes—but, by an ironic twist of psychology, they will be among the first to hold others responsible for everything that happens to them, no matter whether the others are really responsible or not.

> Jesus replied, "A man was going down from Jerusalem to Jericho, and he fell among robbers, who stripped him and beat him, and left him half dead. Now by chance a priest was going down that road; and when he saw him he passed by on the other side. So likewise a Levite, when he came to the place and saw him, passed by on the other side. But a Samaritan, as he journeyed, came to where he was; and when he saw him, he had compassion, and went to him and bound up his wounds, pouring on oil and wine. . . ."*

In terms of this parable, the authoritarian is the priest or Levite, who is thinking, "That guy is just playing possum; if I go over there he'll probably jump up and rob me" (paranoia) or "Would *he* stop to help *me* if I were hurt?" or "I'm not a doctor; suppose I do something wrong and the guy ends up suing me for everything I'm worth," or any number of other unneighborly excuses for passing by on the other side. This attitude reduces to the "every man for himself" philosophy of life—the "survival of the fittest" philosophy known as Social Darwinism, which basically says, "Those who can't make it on their own in this competitive world shouldn't be coddled and protected; their failures are nature's way of weeding out the weakest links in the human evolutionary chain."

Authoritarians tend to oppose all forms of social welfare—to be

* Luke 10:30–34.

indignant about anyone being "on the dole" just because they are handicapped or otherwise unable to work or cannot find jobs. They may hear that a "recession" is here, that unemployment has risen to such-and-such a percent of the work force, but still they will not admit that because of economic conditions beyond any one person's control, and beyond the control of the government, there are no jobs available for eight, ten, twelve percent of the work force.

It is only the compulsive "anti-weakness" mentality of the authoritarian, the capacity for self-deception, that allows him to condemn all the unemployed as being *unwilling* to work, and sometimes to go so far as pretending that those who are unable to find work would really *prefer* to be on the dole, rather than to have some meaningful way to contribute to society and feel that they are pulling their own weight. Again: there are some "welfare cheaters" among us, just as there are a few white-collar con artists among corporate executives. But ninety-nine times out of a hundred, the beaten, bleeding person on the other side of the road really has been victimized in some way and deserves a helping hand.

Nevertheless, the anti-weakness authoritarian persists in blaming inflation, high taxes, high oil prices, dirty streets and every other imaginable social evil on the social-welfare system he sees as so omnipresent in our culture. "People shouldn't be given something for nothing from tax money; people who can't work should be supported by their families, or they should be able to find some way to support themselves," are typical authoritarian anti-weakness comments.

Taking this anti-weakness tendency to extremes, authoritarians can be highly critical of using educational funds to provide programs for the retarded or mentally ill; they tend to see special education, vocational rehabilitation for the seriously handicapped, or welfare in any form, as a "ripoff-handout" they shouldn't have to pay for. They may be opposed to the use of tax funds to help the elderly, even though the elderly may have worked hard all their lives to contribute to the society as a whole.

Authoritarians tend not to support help for the weak because they *equate weakness with evil;* the outcasts of society are responsible for their own situations—for not having made it to the center of the herd—and are dangerous because they may be desperate (may have been driven to desperation just because they are outcasts).

The anti-weakness mentality carries over into the homes of the authoritarians, where the "weak" son who is not athletic, who studies too much or writes poetry, or who pursues similar "sissy" interests, is scorned by the authoritarian father. A son is expected to "stand up and fight" for his macho image; to prove himself a man on the battleground of life. The "contact sports," such as football or hockey, are preferred over gentler sports like tennis, even though they are far more likely to result in injuries that will prove troublesome in later life, and the authoritarian father is the one you see "screaming for blood" on the sidelines, or, if his nine-year-old sustains a painful injury in a Little League baseball game and starts to cry, the one who is more concerned with shutting him up than with how serious his injury is. Of course, girls are expected to be "strong" in their own ways, but since authoritarians tend to cling rigidly to traditional sexual stereotypes, most of the anti-weakness pressure tends to fall on the boys.

A most destructive aspect of prejudice for the strong can be seen in the way children's sports have been taken over by authoritarian parents who not only have regimented the life out of them but have used them to impose their anti-weakness mentality on the young participants.

At one time, before the imposition of so many formal Little League programs, children met in a schoolyard or a vacant lot, chose up sides, and the game was under way. It was understood that everyone who showed up got to play. Nobody said, "Oh, Jimmy, you're not good enough. Go home." If "too many" children showed up, they would bend "the rules" and have ten or eleven on a baseball team, or take turns rotating in and out every few plays in a touch-football game. Of course, there was an argument on every other play, and then an argument about whether they were going to argue all day or play ball, but the children resolved it themselves, and learned some valuable things about reaching agreement among themselves, with no adult to step in and "settle their hash" for them.

When the game was over, everyone would go home and forget the score. The next day they'd come back and start playing a whole new ball game, with no supervision, with the evenness of the teams and the fun of the game assured by the choosing-up-sides process. The weakest players would naturally be chosen last and might have to play right field, but if they improved enough they would be chosen *next* to last the next time (quite a thrill), and *they were always chosen.* They were never told they were inferior just because they weren't as talented as some of the others, or were maturing more slowly, or whatever.

Then along came the authoritarian parents and ruined the whole thing. The children don't choose up teams every day anymore. The adults assign them permanently to teams, with expensive uniforms and fancy equipment. They are put through drills and coached (or screamed at) unmercifully. There are no arguments among the kids: everything is decided by the referee or the umpire, and if you argue with him you're out of the game. The adults keep track of the won/lost records, and now the kids are reminded that they've lost fourteen times already this season, and are in last place, and winning isn't everything, it's the *only* thing, and so on. They have "standings" to remind them how they stack up against everyone else, and the implication is, if you are a "weak team" you should be ashamed.

The players labeled the weakest by the adult coaches now no longer get to play. They may get uniforms as a consolation for coming to practice, and they may get into a game or two for an inning or a play or two if the game is already safely won or hopelessly lost, but they either ride the bench and get to feel inferior all the time, or they get to be the "manager" or the "water boy," or they don't "make" any team at all and are completely ostracized from the sport and the society of their friends. If they dare show their faces at a league game, they can be treated to the spectacle of the authoritarian parents (who have given one another all kinds of awards for all they've done to improve children's sports) showing their real class, screaming at the opponents, hurling obscenities at the refs, putting the screws to their little "stars" to "hang tough" or "get in there and make me proud."

A person interviewed for this book recently told me, "The day I didn't make *any* Little League baseball team was one of the most miserable of my childhood. I had no illusions about being a great baseball player," he continued. "I matured slowly, and wasn't much of an athlete at the age of ten, but I liked to play, and all my friends were there. It was the year the Little League was first started in our town, and I guess I didn't know what had hit me until all the coaches read all the lists and my name wasn't on any of them. I walked home in a daze, leaving behind all the kids who had made it and were laughing and slapping each other on the back in the dugouts, knowing that my summer was ruined, that somehow they were in and I was out.

"I cried for hours. Fortunately my parents understood what I was going through, and they were really indignant that *anybody* should be left out of children's sports (and my father was a college football and wrestling coach!). They said, 'Look, if those adults have taken it over and they're going to run it like that, you're better off out of it.' I thought they were just trying to make me feel better. I didn't know until years later how right they really were."

An interesting note is that this ten-year-old non-athlete was eight years later an All-American swimmer, captain of his prep-school lacrosse team and goalie on the soccer team. "But," he says, "for years after that I hated baseball."

Somehow it seemed so much more sensible when we left the children to run their own games. They knew enough to include everyone, not to brood over past losses, to play hard and then forget it when it was over, and not to judge their peers solely by how well they played. The girl you chose last for the kickball team still cracked the best jokes, or was the first to find a fair settlement to an argument. ("Oh, just do it over! Nobody really saw it that well.") She was also the most loudly cheered when one day she finally kicked the ball clean out of the lot.

Children seem instinctively to know that being "weak" in one way or another is perfectly okay, and that if you let someone play, work and try to improve, he will naturally gain new skills and confidence, which go hand in hand. They know (until it is "beaten out of them") that no one should have to ride the bench, that you don't need a lot of coaching and fancy uniforms and equipment to have a good time. They know these things, and you can let them prove it by taking your anti-weakness mentality and putting it where it belongs, which is "out of the game"—yours *and* theirs.

The truest measure of the conscience of any country is how it treats those who are less fortunate than "the majority," unable to "make the team" without some extra help. If we adopt an overall authoritarian anti-weakness mentality, all our potential greatness as a nation goes out the window.

It is certainly *much more helpful* and advisable to help people learn to help themselves than it is to adopt programs designed to foster everlasting dependency on money that is not earned, if only because (I believe) doing meaningful work, being a *contributing member of the culture,* is a basic human need; no mentally healthy person is truly happy unless he or she is really "on the team," and, by the same token, kicking a person out of "the league" is a wonderful way to promote mental illness.

Everybody can do something, and even though it may take tens of thousands of dollars to care for and equip a severely handicapped man to do what he can, or to support a single mother raising small children (perhaps by supporting day care centers so she can go to work when it's appropriate—and if she can find a job), it is worth it to know that we have not "passed by on the other side."

Power Worship

The other side of the anti-weakness coin is the authoritarian's typical worship of power, regardless of how the power is being used. For instance, some authoritarians are likely to have (or want) big, powerful cars, even though they can't legally go over fifty-five miles an hour on any road in the country and the machines are certified gas hogs. Or if they are more inclined (as most seem to be) to worship *money* as the basic measure of power in our society (which it may be), they want the most expensive, most luxurious status symbol of a car, to signify that they are worth a lot of money. If they cannot have a Rolls Royce or a Cadillac, they will tell you how much their current car cost, what a good deal they got on it, how comfortable it is, how good the gas mileage is, or anything else you really don't want to know about it.

An authoritarian visiting the Hoover Dam will be more interested in how much concrete went into it, how thick and high it is, how many tons of water it holds back, and how many kilowatts of electricity it generates, than in the beautiful patterns made by the water flowing over it, the flowers that grow under it, or the fish swimming around in the lake behind it. He will be more impressed by the fact that a politician got eighty-seven percent of the vote in an election than by anything he stands for, and more impressed by the fact that his brother-in-law is worth $2.3 million than by the fact that he's just been indicted for income tax evasion.

The focus on *money as power* in the minds of authoritarians is not surprising, considering that they are what I have called "externally motivated," compulsively looking to measures outside themselves to validate their own worth—and what more visible and measurable commodity could there be to use for measuring your worth than money?

"This painting cost four hundred dollars," the authoritarian is likely to tell you before you even ask. "That rug is worth a fortune, but I got it at a real bargain. We spent two thousand on our vacation, but it was worth it because the neighbors spent four thousand and they didn't even get a tour guide! See that kid over there, our daughter Jenny? Her education cost us twenty thousand, but she'll earn that back her first year out of college."

"Dollar value" references can be applied to almost nothing or almost everything, but high esteem for dollars and wealth are sure signs that you are talking to an authoritarian who places low value on internal gratification and a maximum value on gold, dollars or anything else whose value is ultimately determined by forces originating outside himself.

Authoritarian worship of power often extends to the idolization of "strong" historical figures, often "military men." Alexander the Great, Napoleon Bonaparte, George Patton and, sometimes, even Adolf Hitler are rated among those most admired by "arch-authoritarians." The military and the police are often considered the most important elements in society by authoritarians, who typically will tell you that the police are being "handcuffed" and the military constrained too much by civilian branches of the government. The emphasis on the sanctity of power extends even to elected government leaders. Authoritarians are apt to believe that a good citizen should *always* respect *the power* of those in office—the governor, the President, or whoever. This reflects the authoritarian's tendency toward conformity and submissiveness in general.

The role of police and military in society may be idolized by authoritarians, but the real focus of the authoritarian's devotion is the locus of power that the military represents. Authoritarians worship the power of guns and ammunition, and, in line with their paranoia, they strongly support the right of all citizens to arm themselves. As a result, they typically oppose the control of handguns or any kinds of firearms. They support the use of any and all weapons in war. They are first to advocate the use of nuclear weapons ("Singe the treetops" in Vietnam, "Nuke the Ayatollah"), and the first to cry for the increase of military budgets at the expense of domestic or humanistic priorities. They often revel in war stories, whether from books or films or from their own lives, when they may have participated in war as combat troops or in any other way. To the authoritarian, the glorification of war as evidence of a nation's power is more important than denouncing war as evidence of humanity's having reached its lowest possible level in its efforts toward resolving its disputes.

Authoritarians are also typically in awe of historical figures like Andrew Carnegie and John D. Rockefeller, who gained fame for accumulating great wealth and power, who were able to climb to the very top of the establishment and to enforce their will on so many others. Seldom willing to take the risks necessary to accumulate great influence or power themselves, authoritarians fantasize about the powerful and wealthy as one of their most universal characteristics.

No human being ought to be considered better than any other simply because he has accumulated wealth or authority. World history has shown again and again that it is dangerous for a society to have individuals with too much power. I am sure the main reason that no dictator or militarist has been able to come to power in the United States is that we have such strong traditions as a nation of individuals who refuse to worship power for its own sake, and because our Constitution provides for the separation and balance of powers as a guarantee against any one person or branch of the government becoming too powerful. But we cannot be reminded too often that our freedom depends on our preserving these traditions at all costs; that some threat to them arises in every generation; and that if we lose them we will have nobody to blame but ourselves. If, as I believe, authoritarianism is on the rise in our society, accompanied by an increase in the blind worship of power, the greatest current threat to our freedom comes not from foreign powers or domestic political minorities, but from the dangers of excessive power-worship among a majority of us.

We are all human! No one on this planet is endowed with any supernatural power that ought to elevate him in importance above you or anyone else—no four-star general, no President, no wealthy financier, no show-business superstar.

Over the past few years, during appearances on numerous national television and radio programs, I have met hundreds of those people we label "superstars" in all fields, especially in show business. While I have always believed that no one is any better than anyone else, coming into direct contact with superstars confirmed it in a pretty dramatic way. Every superstar has his or her share of hangups, twitches, pimples, insecurities, fears, anxieties, worries, problems and everything else that all human beings face on a daily basis. Movie or TV screens, just like the wide screens of history and all our media, tend to make the "superstars" look bigger than life, but in person the wealthiest and most powerful are no different from you or me in how they look, how they think, what they say or how they react to life. While some delude themselves that they are better than the rest of us because they wear expensive clothes, drive fancy cars, live in mansions, can hire and fire hundreds of people at will, control a newspaper chain or make U.S. foreign policy, they cannot hide their very real humanity. In person, without the makeup and the carefully placed lights, off the stages of history or of TV or movie sets, without the wide-angle lenses and other aids, they are people, plain and simple, just like the rest of us. Some are more authoritarian themselves, others less—on some days, in some situations. Keep that in mind, and you'll be on your way to ridding yourself of whatever insidious power-worshiping may have gotten hold of you.

Superpatriotic Totalitarianism

Everything that has been said in this chapter points in one way or another to *totalitarianism* as the ultimate social evil that authoritarianism is capable of breeding.

In fact, totalitarianism is not possible without enough authoritarians in the population to form sufficient binding ties ("authoritarian-submissiveness chains") of domination from a central political ruler (or rulers) to the people to allow the ruler(s) to govern the nation.

In the case of classical political totalitarianism, as represented in modern times by fascistic dictatorships and in ancient times by absolute monarchies, the totalitarian ruler claims to be the representative or even the incarnation of some god or "national spirit" greater than himself. Whether or not totalitarian rulers believe their own myths, the idea that the human(s) whom authoritarians take as their Great Unquestioned Authorities are themselves representative of something far greater than "mere humans" is intrinsically appealing to authoritarians. Being fully human is not enough for them; the "disorganization" of not having a central authority and a clear place for everyone in a social hierarchy is upsetting, while to believe that you are linked to being "superhuman" or "immortal" in some small way because of your relative closeness to the Central Authority is comforting.

In modern times and in our culture, *superpatriotism* has been both a dominant trait of individuals who rate high on other scales of authoritarian characteristics and, I believe, the bridge for increasing numbers of people from individual authoritarianism to political totalitarianism. As such, superpatrotism may be the greatest threat to our freedom we will face in coming years. The would-be despot can as easily deify himself as the incarnation of democracy, of the national interest or national defense, as he can pretend that he is the offspring of the Sun God. But nowadays you find that most "arch-authoritarians" (those who rate highest on all authoritarian scales in the most areas of their lives) tend to be the strongest believers in "My country right or wrong"—the essence of superpatriotism. Even though this concept is dangerous, and has led many people to their deaths fighting unjust wars in countries around the world since the beginning of time, the authoritarian who sees no room for questioning the authority of the government (especially in times of "national crisis") will label anyone who disagrees with the government as subversive and *unpatriotic*—against or not caring about his country! People who challenge authority by exercising their constitutional rights to demonstrate in public—students who march on Washington to protest wars or drafts, women who want equal rights, minorities who "don't know their place"—are never credited with *caring enough* about their country to get involved and perhaps take some risks to try to make it better. To authoritarians, any attempt to change the country is an attempt to destroy it, and a citizen's duty is to obey the authority figures, without ever asking whether they are lying, stealing, trampling on people's rights or otherwise abusing their positions. One simply never challenges people in "higher positions," not because they don't sometimes *need* to be challenged if they are to do their jobs properly, but because it is not within authoritarians' "programs" to break away from their conformism and submissive internal circuitry. Just as the "authoritarian husband" will not believe that his wife really loves him unless she allows him to be the absolute monarch of the house, so the authoritarian does not believe that anyone *really loves his country* unless he blindly follows the dictates of its leaders. *Real* love of country is shown by singing the National Anthem the loudest, flying the flag the highest, putting "foreign" countries down the lowest, and being ready to rush off to war on a moment's notice to defend the flag and the Republic for which it stands, "the land of the free and the home of the brave."

But notice: the National Anthem that authoritarians sing the loudest *ends with a question.* It does not say, "That star-spangled banner still waves o'er the land of the free and the home of the brave." It really asks all future generations of true patriots two philosophical questions pregnant with hope; questions we should all as "good citizens" ask ourselves: What is freedom? What is bravery?

In Nazi Germany, supposedly a citadel of higher learning and advanced civilization, a whole nation got drunk on the idea that the Führer was their divine link to becoming a super-race. The Germans then should have been able to say, and perhaps some did, "We're doing this for the personal benefit of Adolf Hitler—you know, that guy who used to be a house painter—because we all decided he was the one person in the country we wanted to make powerful and famous. So we're giving up all our rights to him and making him omnipotent tomorrow." But they weren't thoughtful enough to avoid shouting deliriously that they were all doing this for the *Fatherland,* for *its* glory and greatness—for *patriotic* reasons which the Führer just happened to embody.

So it was that questioning the authority of Adolf the house painter became tantamount to treason, and hundreds of thousands of highly civilized people were marshaled into behaving in the most obscene and immoral way ever recorded by history. And when the Nuremberg Trials were conducted, the same old tired excuses for murder were given over and over: "I was just following orders."

In the U.S.A. in the early 1980s we seem to have relatively few outright Nazis or fascists among us, and a strong enough democratic heritage that we are not likely to fall into outright totalitarianism, at least in the near future. But the insidious thing about totalitarianism is that it can be very hard to see, especially in your own country, and, of course, it can be present in greater or lesser degrees, and in many different ways. But if its rise is dependent, as I believe, on the rise of across-the-board authoritarianism in individuals (more people showing more of the authoritarian traits I have listed more strongly), you can do your share to combat it *by eliminating authoritarianism in yourself.*

The mistake most people have to make in order for a totalitarian society to overwhelm a democratic one is *always to see threats of totalitarianism coming from outside*—threats of having it imposed by some foreign power or a coup by a "minority group." By a trick of authoritarian psychology which should be familiar by now, *the arch-authoritarian will be the first to see threats he labels "totalitarian" everywhere but in himself,* the first to exhibit patriotic (a type of ethnocentric) paranoia and point the finger at the Russians, the Cubans, the Chinese (before they became our allies), the Ayatollah or whoever else can conveniently be labeled "the greatest [or only] threat to our freedom at present."

The way this can actually lead to the growth of totalitarianism from within should be evident. If the external threats are not real, or are exaggerated, which is a direct effect of paranoia, some people are going to start saying so. Authoritarians will then label them unpatriotic, subversive and so on. If there is enough authoritarianism in the society as a whole to discredit or suppress the criticism—which must mean the denial or erosion of the individual rights of the critics—then totalitarianism has taken a "great leap forward."

This syndrome was clearly displayed in this country's closest brush with outright totalitarianism to date, the rise of McCarthyism in the 1950s. Senator Joe McCarthy's paranoia (which, as paranoia often does, included delusions of personal grandeur) led him to see Communist spies everywhere, and anyone who questioned his vicious attacks on innocent people of course immediately came under suspicion himself. People's constitutional rights were trampled right and left; their privacy was invaded; they were hauled before witch-hunt tribunals to be confronted by witnesses who lied or stretched the truth because they had been intimidated by the threat that they would be next if they didn't cooperate. Innocent people, many good and great Americans, lost their jobs, were blacklisted from their professions, and McCarthy's personal power rose to frightening dimensions.

Fortunately there came a day when the bubble burst. McCarthy's paranoia ran away with him. He started making charges so ludicrous against people so obviously above reproach that almost nobody could miss what was happening: someone was a Communist spy if and only if he challenged the personal power of Joe McCarthy. The brave people who had tried to challenge him all along were in principle vindicated when Congress censured him and the "reign of terror" subsided, although many of their lives had been irreparably damaged.

McCarthyism would not have been possible if enough Americans had been slower to credit the threat of totalitarianism's being imposed on them from halfway around the world, and quicker to recognize signs of their own blind submission to the call of superpatriotism and the domination of a man who pretended to embody it.

By the same token, totalitarianism is far less likely ever to be imposed on us from *outside* if we are democratically strong *inside*, for the simple reason that even most dictators have the sense not to try to conquer nations they know they can't govern, and recognize that the hardest people to govern will be those with the strongest devotion to democracy and the least authoritarianism in their populations.

For a nation that is highly authoritarian to begin with, it may be sufficient to run the government off, seize "the palace"—the capital—and convince enough of the previous authority-hierarchy to collaborate. But for a nation short on built-in authoritarian-submissiveness chains, a would-be conquerer must expect massive resistance: general strikes, riots, industrial sabotage, incessant attacks on the "occupation troops," and generally a conquest that is more trouble than it's worth.

Taking a potential conquerer's look at the U.S.A., a huge country with more than 200 million people and a highly complex economy in which disruption of one or more sectors—agriculture, industry, mining, transportation, communications, energy supply, etc.—would throw a monkey wrench into the whole works, *what other nation could possibly govern this one if we all simply refused to be governed by anyone but ourselves?*

The flat answer is "none," and if we keep it that way and each of us resolves to eliminate authoritarianism from his *own* thinking and behavior, to adopt the philosophy that *the sky's the limit* on the freedom we can *all* share, we will be doing far more to assure our national security and independence than we can ever do by building bigger and better bombs.

If we can set an example for the world of the heights that a democratic nation dedicated to "life, liberty, and the pursuit of happiness" can attain, if we really show other peoples how it can be done (while learning all we can from the attempts of other nations to do the same thing), we will be doing far more for world peace and prosperity than we can ever do by sending troops anywhere.

But to do this we must not lapse into inertia by assuming, as the authoritarian superpatriot does, that the United States of America as it is today is *by definition* "the freest nation in the world," that it *already* represents the most freedom any people can ever get, and that our only job is to defend the citadel against all those "foreigners," "Commies," or whomever else we automatically see as trying to tear it down.

Remember that even if we want to think of our country as "perfect now" in the sense I outlined in Chapter 1, it is like a living thing—its nature is to change, evolve, hopefully to *grow* so as to cultivate the highest human potentials of *all* its citizens. If we insist on seeing it as a rock or any other inanimate thing which is supposed to stay the same unless external forces "attack" it, we are going to end up reacting with authoritarian paranoia whenever change "threatens," and we will be all the more likely to fall prey to totalitarianism.

Hopefully you have been asking yourself some questions as to the amount of authoritarian thinking and behavior in your own personality while you've read this chapter. Perhaps you've tried to rate yourself on each of the traits I've mentioned. If so, you've probably recognized that you strongly exhibit some, partly exhibit others, and don't exhibit others much at all; that you typically exhibit some in certain situations and relationships but not in others, and so on. As you've read, you probably also have recognized portraits or snapshots of people you know, and said to yourself, "Jane and John are just like that, but Mary and Sam are more like this," and so on.

If you now think your primary task is to eliminate authoritarianism in yourself, and are prepared to go back through this chapter if necessary to see where *you* stand on the authoritarian scale, you have understood my message. If you are content to say, "Yeah, those other people are just like that, but I'm not at all," you have missed or rejected my point, and as far as your own personal drive to become a No-Limit person is concerned, you are unlikely to even begin the process.

ARCHIE BUNKER: THE AUTHORITARIAN MODEL

To what extent are Americans in general prepared to recognize and condemn authoritarianism when they see it in others or themselves? Fortunately, the answer seems to be: to a pretty great extent, if it is presented so as to creatively reveal it for the false mastery it really represents.

In this media age, the *democratic quality* of our "mass art," or of the art-form products that reach most of us through the mass media—television, radio, movies, mass-market magazines and books—is a good measure of where we as a people stand on the totalitarian–democratic balance scale.

Probably you can identify much mass-media "programming" as promoting authoritarianism in many ways. But there are some bright spots, and among them are TV shows that tend to combat authoritarianism by *showing authoritarians for what they are*—often through the medium of ridiculing extremes of authoritarianism in situation comedy.

Probably the most popular character in the history of American television to date has been Archie Bunker. The writers of "All in the Family" and "Archie Bunker's Place" have revealed the continuing ability of Americans to laugh at a caricature of the arch-authoritarian ("Archie") by creating one comic character who embraces virtually all the authoritarian personality traits described above. Since authoritarianism is such a widespread phenomenon in our culture, and most Americans can still recognize it when it is portrayed in a "fictitious" character, using Archie Bunker to satirize contemporary American authoritarianism was a stroke of genius as great as Charlie Chaplin's ridiculing Hitler.

Archie Bunker is the authoritarian personified. He has appeared on multitudes of television screens in America for a decade or more, and people have tuned in to laugh in unprecedented numbers because there are so many folks out there who either are just like him or are living with people who display his attitudes. While Archie the Arch-Authoritarian is funny and the show is meant to deliver a satirical look at a bigot, Archie's popularity lies primarily in the fact that there is so much truth in what is being written and acted out.

Archie Bunker has had hundreds of episodes written for him to show a multitude of authoritarian personality traits. One week he is showing racism or ethnocentrism against the Jews, the blacks, the Puerto Ricans, the Italians, some other minority group. The next week he is railing against the welfare system or "those Commies" who are trying to get us all. The week after that he is lecturing his daughter about artists, who are all "fairies," or waving the flag in front of his son-in-law. He doesn't trust anyone, particularly intellectuals. He loves movies about war, he stereotypes everyone he meets, and he is about as rigid and as blind to his own faults as any person can be. He idolizes power, especially the military. Of course he is always looking for a scheme to get rich, and is always bilked out of his money because of his greed.

Archie Bunker is portrayed as being just about as intolerant, as dichotomous and rigid in his thinking, as ethnocentric, sexually repressed, paranoid and superpatriotic as a person can be. He is forever putting other cultures down and evaluating people in terms of his own authoritarian standards. People who disagree with him are immediately "meatheads," "dingbats" or "dummies." His wife is usually seen as a doting scatterbrain who is always trying to please Archie, but when push comes to shove—if anything threatens her simple, basic honesty and humanitarian sense of justice—Edith always manages to assert herself and win out over the follies of poor old Archie.

As the Archie Bunker shows are presented, everyone can laugh at Archie—his ignorance, his basic stupidity, his malapropisms of language, his ridiculous prejudices. But we can afford to keep laughing only for as long as Edith, Michael, Gloria, Louise Jefferson or whomever else "poor old Archie" happens to be trying to manipulate and exploit at the moment continues to triumph at the end of every show—for as long as we continue to be capable of "laughing away" authoritarianism for the ridiculous travesty of human potential it is. The background message of the Archie Bunker shows is a question to all viewers: How many authoritarians, Archie types or others, stop laughing at the caricature long enough to ask themselves whether they aren't just like him, just as laughable in certain areas of their lives or certain situations? How many Archie-type authoritarians sit in their chairs in front of their televisions doubled up with laughter and telling their wives or husbands, "Joe is just like that"? How many get the message that you are really supposed to be laughing *at yourself* whenever you *see yourself* in this show?

There's no doubt that television shows like "All in the Family" have anti-authoritarian social effects, if only because they convey the impression that racism, for example, is no longer in fashion among the authorities—in this case, the writers, directors, actors and television network that produced the program. Most authoritarians, hearing the unanimous laughter of live or canned audiences at the comic excesses of these caricatures, begin to get the message that while it was once "in" to ridicule "the niggers" in most social circles, now it is "out," and in public they don't do it anymore, for fear of being ostracized.

But only if all of us vow to go beyond merely responding to social pressures and take our own independent and principled stands against authoritarianism *based on our own individual philosophies of life* will the message of "All in the Family" and other real works of democratic art be fully understood.

Finally, let us remember that precisely because the character of Archie Bunker is funny to us and Archie himself is portrayed as perpetually oblivious, self-satisfied and "happy as a pig in mud," and because we don't have to imagine any real threat of totalitarianism from *his* kind (just because he is so ludicrously ineffectual), we are likely to skim over the serious bedrock content of the Archie shows as they apply to us as individuals. We are likely to overlook the fact that Archie is still a serious distillation of the authoritarian attitudes or biases that so many people seem to have adopted as their *de facto* philosophies of life. We are also likely to forget that authoritarians, for all their pretensions to mastery, tend inwardly to be chronically depressed and unhappy people, suffering from an almost total lack of real human fulfillment, secretly aware that they are bumbling through life chasing some unknown, inhuman thing, being tolerated but never really respected by others, and suffering from blind, inert acceptance of their fates.

I do not believe that *anyone* has to suffer under the blind submissiveness of authoritarianism. I believe that *anyone's* adopting an authoritarian philosophy is the result of that person's choice. While I hail Abraham Maslow for his pioneering work on human greatness, I disagree with him where he implies that there is little hope or choice left for authoritarians, that they are pretty much doomed to remain the way they are. In *The Farther Reaches of Human Nature,* Maslow writes:

> These people [obsessive and authoritarian] *have* to be this way. They have no choice. This is the only way in which such a person can achieve safety, order, lack of threat, lack of anxiety, that is, via orderliness, predictability, control and mastery. . . . The new is threatening for such a person, but nothing new can happen to him if he can order it

to his past experience, if he can freeze the world of flux, that is if he can make believe nothing is changing.

I believe anyone is capable of changing if he is willing to take the necessary risks and give up the ghosts of the past. I have seen people as far gone on authoritarianism as Archie Bunker turn themselves around because the right ideas hit them at the right time in their lives, just when they had become really tired of being the same old, dull authoritarians.

3 Transcending Authoritarian Thinking

Thought is an attribute that belongs to me;
it alone is inseparable from my nature.
—René Descartes,
Meditations on First Philosophy (1641)

While I recognize that most people remain fixed at plateaus far below the heights that No-Limit people achieve, I simply cannot admit to myself that it is because some humans are more "blessed" than others by the good fortunes of heredity. To me, it is quite simply a matter of choice, and *how* you decide to think is one of your most important choices to make in life. Some people are unwilling to admit that they have an alternative in their lives, and so they settle for living at an "emotional subsistence level." This lower level allows them to function well enough to avoid being immobilized, and to get through their days with a minimum of trauma, and for most people this is acceptable. It is living at the "coping" level, presented in Chapter 1. The No-Limit person is quite different in this regard.

While No-Limit people can generally solve most of the problems that confront them without being immobilized, like most ordinary folks, they go way beyond a simple acceptance of life as it is handed to them. The No-Limit person believes very firmly that he has choices which can elevate him beyond being "normal" or like most other people. No-Limit people look at life in a unique way, and because of this "different" vision they can see things very clearly in terms of choices which they can make, rather than seeing themselves as being trapped or otherwise unable to exercise control over their life situations.

No-Limit people are operating at higher levels of enjoyment, happiness and fulfillment, because they have learned to think and make choices which most people simply refuse to make. You can become a human being who lives at higher fulfillment altitudes if you are willing to give up your commitment to thinking ordinarily, or behaving as a coper, and instead opt for personal mastery in your own life circumstances. You can become the creator of what you are, rather than the result of what others have programmed for you. You can have an absence of anxiety in favor of inner peace, when you are willing to make the choices that will bring it about. You can decide to be at peace with yourself, to be happy and content by giving up the opposite choices that you have been making up until now. The entire process begins with your own willingness to *look at your personal thinking habits* and to work at transcending any authoritarian thinking which gets in the way of your becoming a No-Limit person.

In the last chapter, the first four characteristics of authoritarians —intolerance of ambiguity, dichotomous thinking, rigidity of thought, and anti-intellectualism—all dealt with individual ways of *thinking*, and the fifth, anti-introspection, indicated the authoritarian choice *not to think about oneself.* The last, superpatriotic totalitarianism, treated certain widespread *diseases of thought* among individuals that can lead to disastrous social consequences. In fact, all the characteristics of authoritarians really *reflect their refusal to think for themselves,* their insistence on letting "higher authorities" do their thinking for them, and thus their tendency to divide the world into those who are "with them" and those who are "against them."

The ability to *think for yourself* is therefore essential to No-Limit living: to avoiding the authoritarian anxiety, paranoia or panic that results when you categorize so many of your fellow human beings as being fundamentally "against you," to going on to enjoy your own independent thinking capacity at its highest.

Many philosophers have considered thinking to be the very essence of what *makes us human.* Several centuries ago René Descartes, often considered the founder of modern philosophy, said, *cogito, ergo sum:* "I think; therefore I am." By this, I take it he meant that it is the fundamental nature of the human being to think, to wonder about things, to question, to try out different possible answers to questions; and to question, reformulate or reject those answers in the ongoing process of evolving a *body of thought* that guides each human along his life course for as long as he may live. In other words, it is in the nature of every human being to think toward building a *philosophy of life,* the accumulation of a store of wisdom-for-self-guidance which is automatically called upon *every time you do anything.* In this sense, every human being already has a philosophy of life, and the only real question is whether that body of thought, opinion, belief and values by which you guide your life is growing in a way that makes you more excited every day about life and its limitless possibilities, or whether it is stagnating in a way that leaves you open to boredom, depression and despair.

Perhaps the central premise of this book is that *you are responsible for the thoughts you have in your head at any given time.* You have the capacity to *think whatever you choose,* and *virtually all your self-defeating attitudes and behaviors originate in the way you choose to think*—as will your self-fulfilling attitudes and behaviors, once you learn to think "like a No-Limit human."

Your thoughts are your very own personal creation and responsibility. Once you accept your thoughts as a fundamental key to your total humanity, you will be on the way toward changing anything about yourself that is keeping you from the mastery of your life. But to transcend authoritarian thinking toward No-Limit thinking, you have to accept that human emotions don't "just happen," human actions don't simply "take place." All your feelings and behaviors are preceded by those mysterious mental phenomena we call thoughts, and no one, nothing, no force in the world, can make you think something you don't want to think. Your inalienable corner of freedom, even if others are forcibly enslaving you, remains in your ability to choose the thoughts you have within your own mind. Once you understand that all your emotions and behaviors come directly from your thoughts, you will simultaneously understand that the way to attack any personal or psychological problem is to attack the thoughts that support your negative emotions and self-defeating behaviors.

If you truly believe that you alone can control your own thoughts, and accept that the road to No-Limit living lies through your learning *now* how to think in new and different ways rather than those in which you have thought before, if you can make sense out of the statement that your *attitudes,* the ways you approach the world, are nothing more than reflections of your thoughts, and remind yourself that you can choose any attitude you would like to have under virtually any circumstances, then you will have taken the first step on the bridge of thought that leads to No-Limit thinking.

DICHOTOMOUS THINKING

If authoritarianism is fundamentally the result of a disease of thinking that results in the *decay of the thinking process,* or in people *just not thinking* for themselves, I would say that *dichotomous thinking,* the compulsion always to divide everything and everyone in the world into neat little categories, and to defend the rigidity of your divisions at all costs, is the root cause of the disease. Therefore, the ability to transcend this kind of thinking is indispensable to becoming a fully functioning person.

You will remember from Chapter 2 that if you are a dichotomous thinker the first thing you will do on meeting new people will be to put them into a number of categories: conservative or liberal, young or old, good or bad, traitorous or patriotic, religious or atheistic, selfish or unselfish, and so on. Next you will use your labels as convenient excuses for avoiding or condemning people who are different from you. Likewise, the first thing you will do upon hearing of a war in some obscure corner of the world will be to ask, "Which side are *we* on?" If you think "*we*" are the American people as represented by our government, you will know immediately, for example, that we are for the "rebels" and against the Soviets in Afghanistan. You will then "root for our side," perhaps support U.S. aid to or intervention (overt or covert) on behalf of our side. You will pick up "reasons" for "your position" from the mass media, the President or some other source. But you will never bother to go to the library and pick up a few histories of the country or countries involved, written from as many different perspectives as you can find, survey what magazines of radically different persuasions have to say about it, nail down as many hard facts as you can, determine who is lying and when, consult your own sense of justice, and determine whether you really do support the official government position wholeheartedly or whether you really think it should be changed. Essentially, you will ignore all the historical complexities that lead to the outbreak of *any* war, and the corresponding complexities of attempts to resolve armed conflicts short of one side's totally annihilating or overrunning the other (which is what *you* will be rooting for—the total victory of "our side" in what you see as a win-or-lose dichotomy, although it is questionable whether anybody really ever has won a war).

Nor, if you are a dichotomous thinker, will you ever say what the NEZ person would say if he just didn't have time to investigate the situation independently: "I just don't know enough about it to make a judgment." You will rush to take "our side's" position, and then be forced to pretend to know what you are talking about.

Dichotomous thinking requires *less thinking* because it gives you a ready cop-out when you are confronted with situations that really *call for* creative thinking if you are to make fully human responses. The rush to dichotomize keeps you from really seeing or hearing the people you are judging, because in your mind you have just shoved them into some bin labeled "bad," "enemy" or "reject" and decided that there is no profit in paying any attention to them. Consequently you forgo being open and creative and having to use your intellectual equipment in dialogues with yourself or anyone else.

Dichotomous thinking is the basis of nonunderstanding between peoples, fighting and warring, stereotyping and social injustice. But the real personal damage of dichotomous thinking is that it keeps you, as a single individual, from growing and becoming a more fully alive and creative human being. A fixed or rigid dichotomy is really a barrier against further thought, exploration and investigation, and the more barriers you erect within yourself, the more you restrict your own individual ability to be living at your highest possible level. All the dichotomies that you use to place people and ideas immediately into rigid categories are impediments to your own growth and development as a human being.

When you compartmentalize others, you do the same thing to yourself. Every time you divide the world on any level in an either/or subdivision and say, "That's the end of it, that's just the way it is," you are also subdividing yourself and consequently limiting your own ability to be open to new and growth-producing experiences. But, most important, when you divide the people or ideas of the world into rigid either/or categories, you are viewing the world not as it is but *as you see it,* now and forever. You are blinding yourself to its wonders, to the excitement of all its open questions. Before long you will have suspended your natural curiosity and openness about the world; you will have *stopped thinking.* Rather than questioning, seeking and exploring, you will fall ever deeper into the compulsion to dichotomize according to set patterns, and your mental and emotional growth will be inhibited.

Not exercising your thought is as bad for you as not exercising your body, or worse. Dichotomizing is nothing more than a convenient way to escape really thinking through any problem or set of conditions. It leads you to go straight to the quick, simplistic answer, to want to find someone or something outside yourself to blame for your troubles. For instance, during the energy crisis that has gripped our economy for the past decade, you have heard many people prattling on about how "the oil companies are at fault; the bureaucrats are doing it to us; the OPEC nations are responsible; the President is indecisive." These have been the lines of most politicians as well as of the grumbling public; the tendency is to want convenient scapegoats, rather than to investigate and think through the intricacies involved in trying to build a cohesive energy policy that will be satisfactory to everyone.

Clearly, this kind of dichotomous thinking goes nowhere toward resolving the tremendous energy crises that face our world; it simply puts people into categories and leaves the resolution of all our problems to someone else. Those who must take responsibility for *doing* something about the energy crisis may be trying desperately to deal effectively with all the various grumbling segments of our culture, and to maintain some kind of sane approach to the utilization of energy; but hard as they may try, they will never please those who are determined to do nothing but complain, who insist on looking right past the real problems that call for thinking. They may be among the first to respond to the call of their country if it comes to invading the Persian Gulf to protect our oil supplies, but they will be among the last to respond when the country's situation calls for constructive, creative thinking on how to use less oil or develop alternative energy sources.

What I am suggesting is that a world which discourages dichotomous thinking in the first place, in which more people see the gray between black and white divisions and see that every side of every question that calls for thinking has some "right" and some "wrong" in it, and that the resolution lies in some give and take, some negotiation—a world which recognizes the individual's right to be listened to (instead of being dictated to)—will progress toward a culture we can all be proud of. But transcending dichotomous thinking and getting on with real thinking can start only with the individual. That means you! Once you and enough other individuals begin to be more open to differing points of view, to be less inclined to dichotomize, our social structures (which are all comprised of individuals) will cease to victimize anybody.

Compulsively thinking in dichotomies will poison your own psyche in many ways, primarily by giving you endless opportunities to be unnecessarily upset and immobilized. It actually leads you to use other people's differences from you to victimize yourself. For example, if you just can't understand the way children are nowadays, if all children seem hopelessly insolent to you, and therefore you go out of your way to avoid all children, you will find, if you think about it, that those very children you despise so much are actually in control of your emotional life. Whenever you see a child acting in what you consider an insolent way, you will become angry, upset, unable to "think straight" or function as well as you would otherwise. Your very act of putting "all children" into one category labeled "insolent" gives them power over you that keeps you from being as happy as you would like to be. Similarly, if you decide to hate all people in any group, you give those people quite a bit of emotional control over you. Whether they want or ever use that power you've given them or not, you secretly know you have given away some of your control over your own destiny, and you resent it.

Instead of labeling any group as a collective to hate, you can shift your approach to begin looking at and listening to individuals in that group instead. Males, Americans, whites, Jews, blacks, Asians, mechanics, attorneys, children, alcoholics, Communists—each of these groups is comprised of individuals, all of whom are as different from one another as they are from you. Once you label them all with any one stereotype, you are setting yourself up to be upset by what you expect them to do, rather than by anything any of them is really likely to do, and cutting yourself off from learning more about people who genuinely think differently from you. The more barriers you construct to prevent real, constructive dialogue with "different others," the more you restrict yourself from reaching your own full potential.

I hope you now understand why the dichotomous thinker has very little chance for inner peace. He is too busy putting all the people and ideas of the world into this or that compartment ever to have time or motivation for self-development. The very act of dichotomizing is an externally directed activity that places the locus of control for your own life on someone or something outside yourself—the socially dictated rules that tell you how to separate the patriots from the subversives (or any convenient dichotomy) and the bewildering varieties of people in the world who seem to need classification by you. Obviously you can have no inner peace as long as the controls of your life are located outside yourself. The point is, you will cripple your own life mission of being happy and creatively alive if you become a compulsively dichotomizing thinker, but if you learn how to go beyond dichotomous thinking, to transcend that black-and-white stereotyping that so infects our own personal lives as well as the very fabric of our society, and if others follow suit, we will be creating a society that can ultimately make this world truly work at its highest potential. But first, and before anything else, you must take responsibility for doing that in yourself, and then in helping others to do it as well. This is *my* mission in life right now: to go beyond black-and-white thinking in myself, and to help others do the same. Before long, we can all help create a world of people who think openly, with flexibility, who listen to one another's questions and answers for what they should be, in honest efforts to create a world that is more humane to all of us. But we can do that only by starting with ourselves.

HOLISTIC THINKING

The No-Limit person understands fully that dichotomies exist only in the minds of individuals. They are only tools of thought we have invented in order to make some sense of and to control certain parts of our worlds. But in reality dichotomies are always used to divide up something which was one in the first place. We are all *combinations* of opposites. We are whole people who have infinities of different qualities and potentials that are always shifting around within us according to the ebb and flow of our thoughts and feelings. To transcend dichotomous thinking toward real human thinking, we must see behind the veils we have interposed between ourselves and the real world. We must remember the *whole world,* which was "out there" long before we divided it up with our endless categories. We must heal the rifts in our own bodies of thought that we have created by our attempts to classify everything and everyone with this or that label. In sum, we must *get back to holistic thinking.* We must remember that before there were sheep or goats, boys or girls, before anyone thought up the idea of odd or even numbers or thought to call their societies "civilization," *there was life.* We must appreciate that all humans who lived on this earth before us shared the same sun, looked up into the same sky, fished in the same oceans, hunted for the same food. We may even be inspired to stop and realize for a moment how we and all other humans are *the embodiment of human life now,* and how each of us has some fish, some ape, some genius, some fool, some strength, some weakness, some richness, some poverty in us as "parts" of our existence. Each of us is at once a whole person, one organic representation of all life, and a tiny slice of life as a whole.

The idea of being a member of a culture is not a goal for those who think holistically. In fact, theirs is quite the opposite point of view. The important thing for holistic thinkers is to see themselves as part of humanity rather than any special subgroupings, be they nations, ethnic groupings or cultural cliques. They scorn identification within any artificially contrived borders, and feel that the boundaries so many people pay eternal allegiance to are in fact causes of strife and unrest.

The holistic-thinking person sees the world in a global way, as all of humanity, having concerns which must be addressed and resolved. The fact that someone is unemployed in India, or starving in Biafra, is a concern for all of humanity, not a problem that must be solved by the individual governments involved. We must all band together and treat people as dignified, and any efforts to divide people by class, nations, religions or any other boundaries is strongly resisted by those who think in holistic ways.

Humanistic thinking has to start with the holistic approach, with an entire view of the universe and how you as one human individual fit into the spectrum of all life, past and present; by recognizing that all of us are in this thing called *life* together.

Holistic thinking involves learning to *suspend,* to put aside for a moment, all those categories by which we have been conditioned to "file and forget" so many people, ideas, things and possible experiences before we even consider them, and to see ourselves and our worlds in their original, irreducible wholeness. It means admitting that we have been so busy listing all the differences that might separate us from others that we have tragically neglected to see all the common natures, hopes, dreams, times, places and situations that unite us. We have been too busy dissecting humanity to imagine what a joy it might be to get our act together.

Holistic thinking sometimes means just sitting back and appreciating the way the trees "just happen" to create oxygen, which we humans breathe, or the miracles of nature's ecology in general, or the way all of human society is inextricably interconnected, and the fact that all theories of sociology and human behavior are just our best guesses right now as to the way it all works. It means recognizing that the forest is not just the sum of its trees; that however we may classify, dissect or atomize things in our thought, we are still left with the ultimately mysterious nature of "the whole"—whether it be the whole universe or the whole of humanity or the whole of each individual.

NO-LIMIT THINKING

What I call No-Limit thinking begins with a holistic view of the world, and from there on it requires constructive work on your part. Real No-Limit thinking is perhaps the highest art of which the human being is capable. While No-Limit people are generally perceived to be functioning at higher levels in their lives, it is important here to describe the thinking qualities which separate them from other individuals, without making it sound as though everyone who is not a No-Limit person is somehow inferior or neurotic. People who display No-Limit characteristics seem to look at the world differently. They see everything in the world as an opportunity, rather than as something to be feared or avoided. They look at any experience as a potential for excitement and growth, and they are very much interested in novelty, newness and the mysterious. To No-Limit people, the world is a miracle, and they go through their days in awe of the universe. They are easily touched by things that ordinary people see as routine. They can walk along a beach for an entire day, lost in the excitement of the ocean, the sand, the birds, winds, seashells, never growing tired of the experience. Each day seems to be a whole new world for No-Limit people, and they can become engrossed in the beauty of something that they've done many times before without feeling it is boring or repetitious.

People who choose No-Limit thinking are basically gratified human beings. They feel that they belong in the universe and they are satisfied in all areas of their lives. They feel loved and are capable of giving love without qualification or agony. They are rooted in the *present* in their relationships, not obsessed with where their relationships are going or where they have been, or wondering how things are going to work out. They can completely accept other human beings for what they are, and refuse to judge, or otherwise condemn others, be they strangers or close intimates. Their strong feelings of belongingness lead them to adopt attitudes that are quite different from most people's. Because they feel at peace with the world, they are not interested in changing others. Instead, they find it easy to accept others as being different, because they have a model for doing so; that is, they have learned to accept themselves as whole and complete.

Largely because of this accepting attitude, the No-Limit person is not burdened with anxiety. He has chosen to think in self-respecting ways, and no one else can ever convince him that he is less than worthy. This all-pervasive self-respect permits him to function at the highest levels both for himself and in the service of others. Because his own self-worth is intact, and because the source of that self-worth is internal, he and people like him are free from the crippling effects of other people's opinions, both positive and negative. They do not decide how they are going to think or behave because of what others think. Somehow they have managed to consult themselves about how they should be functioning, and this sense of self-confidence permits them to operate quite independently of the opinions of other people.

No-Limit people think from a perspective of *mastery* rather than *coping* in their lives. That is, they feel that they are determiners of their own fate, rather than always adjusting to life's circumstances. They are able to think naturally and behave spontaneously in most life situations, and this is largely due to their lack of anxiety about how they are going to be judged. Why are they free from being anxious about being judged? Because they do not think as judges themselves. These are people who are going to express precisely what is on their minds, and they are going to pursue their goals even when others around them are displeased with them for doing so. They are not attempting to alienate others; they simply don't worry about what others are going to say, since they know that they will receive a thousand different opinions if they are confronted by a thousand different people.

No-Limit people often have a notion of their own fate and feel a sense of mission about their own lives. This sense of mission is acted out with a determination and zeal that most ordinary people never understand. They want to get things accomplished in their own chosen field, and the areas of work and inquiry are unlimited. The important point to understand about No-Limit people is that they are vitally involved in projects and undertakings, and that their involvement transcends their own personal worlds. They can be dispassionate about their behavior, and they are unaffected by other people's not understanding their commitment and enthusiasm for what is often their own life's mission. If others are perplexed by their work, they don't spend a lot of energy trying to justify the rightness of their position. Instead they proceed, because they feel it from within. Contrary to authoritarian persons, No-Limit persons are not motivated by a need to assess, or judge others in a negative fashion. They trust their inner selves, while authoritarians rely almost exclusively on external signals to determine how to think and behave.

While authoritarian people are intolerant of ambiguity, No-Limit people welcome it. No-Limit people find themselves most comfortable in situations in which the outcome is uncertain, and spend a large part of their lives exploring unfamiliar territory. The idea of meeting someone from another culture or going to a new city or trying a new ethnic restaurant is a source of excitement and something actively to pursue in their lives. Rather than avoiding new experiences, No-Limit people welcome them.

No-Limit people are living their lives at a higher level, mostly because they have learned how to think in terms of appreciation rather than criticism in life. To No-Limit people, criticism is largely a waste of time. They are doers, and they are so involved in the process of doing that they just don't have any time or energy left over to look over their shoulders to evaluate their own happiness. In fact, they don't even engage in the practice of evaluation; instead they are experiencers. They don't take the time to wonder if they are having a good time; they simply have a good time and leave the wondering to others.

No-Limit people are not "sickly thinking" people, and they have little time or patience for those who want to spend their lives discussing their various ailments and states of immobility. They don't think "sick"; instead, they become so involved in life that they treat their bodies in a healthy fashion. They are not prone to abuse their bodies, and they are deeply tuned in to the importance of having a healthy body which is capable of fighting off diseases. They respect their physiology, and consequently they are able to fuse a positive attitude with a positive body health as well. Certainly No-Limit people can become ill, but their internal mind-set of not thinking sick, and not focusing on sickness and complaining to everyone about the various disease processes that are currently infecting their bodies, gives them a whole, healthy perspective on life. Because they are not interested in hanging on to their illnesses, and because they believe strongly in their own capacity to heal themselves, they simply are not as "sickness-oriented" as others. They live healthy lives, they keep in shape, they are extremely physical and they are not complainers.

What I want to emphasize is that No-Limit people are not different because of some biological nature they possess, but because they have *chosen* to think and behave in more self-enhancing and self-fulfilling ways in their lives. While it may appear to the researcher or casual observer that No-Limit people are simply stronger and more independent people, the truth is that they have really decided for themselves that they are not going to be weak or manipulated by others. In addition, they have a full awareness of their own limitless potential, and a commonsense approach to life that keeps them operating at such levels. They know that they cannot get everyone to agree with them about everything they do, so they don't make that their life goal. They know that worrying about approval, or being anxious about disapproval, is a waste of time and emotional energy, so they simply refuse to do it. They know that the past is over, and that the future is promised to no one, so they work at living in the present and being grateful for what they have. They know that having to do unpleasant things, such as washing dishes or taking out the garbage or anything else, is a necessary condition of being alive. But they choose their thoughts, and their thoughts about doing dishes are positive: that having to do dishes means having enjoyed food eaten from those dishes; that having to empty garbage represents having had ample meals, whereas people in some parts of the world have neither surplus nor dishes. They are, in fact, in charge of their thinking and consequently their attitudes, and they choose attitudes that keep small things in perspective and that serve them rather than make their lives miserable.

THE TRANSITION TO NO-LIMIT THINKING: FUSING THE DICHOTOMIES

As always, the best way to grasp an abstract concept like No-Limit thinking is to see how it can be made to work in concrete terms in your own life. Here are some examples of the most common kinds of dichotomies that are habitually misapplied with destructive effects, along with some reflections on the wholes that lie behind them, and specific suggestions as to how you can transcend the authoritarian abuse of them toward a No-Limit perspective on life. As you read through them, ask yourself, "How have I victimized myself or others and stunted the growth of my own philosophy of life by dichotomizing along these lines?" You will find many other examples of dichotomies which could be added to the list, and you'll soon "get the knack" of how to transcend them.

Rather than thinking in dichotomies or divisions, it is much more helpful and effective to begin thinking in terms of fusion, melting, or fading the splitting process. When you learn to view the most common dichotomies in *holistic-fusion-melting-bringing-together terms,* you will have given yourself a dose of personal freedom unlike anything that you've ever experienced before. You will be free because you will see the people of the world for what they are, rather than how you think they should be compartmentalized.

Masculine/Feminine

There's no question about it: it's a girl or it's a boy. In the delivery room or on the birth certificate, there's not too much reason for saying, "It is dominantly female as evidenced by the nature of its sexual organs, but let us remember that it also has hormones conventionally labeled 'male.' "

But no sooner is the child out of the delivery room than the trouble starts. The girl is supposed to be "feminine," the boy "masculine." The girl is wrapped in pink, the boy in blue, because with infants it is generally impossible to tell the difference without peeking inside the diaper, and few adults are willing to do that just to find out how they're supposed to react. With a little boy they are supposed to say, "My, aren't you a handsome fellow! You're going to be big and strong like your daddy!" With a girl they are supposed to say, "My, aren't you pretty! Look at those gorgeous eyes! I bet you got those from your mommy."

From there on it is all downhill, with boys going down one side of the hill and girls down the other. At first they simply don't understand when they're told, "Girls can cry, but boys can't; boys fight, but girls don't; girls cook and sew, but boys don't." But after they're told enough times that boys are supposed to be "masculine" and girls "feminine," and memorize all the arbitrary lists of what each of those categories means they can and can't do, they dutifully break their little necks trying to conform to the stereotypes that have been laid on them, and go around enforcing them on each other with a vengeance ("Sarah, you look like a boy in those clothes!" "Jimmy, you run just like a girl!").

To see just how absurd and arbitrary this dichotomy is, we have only to look at the way the psychological community has devised tests to show whether you are more masculine or feminine. In formulating the tests, questioners typically asked males and females a series of questions. If most males said they preferred showers to baths, and most women said they preferred baths, showers were considered masculine and baths feminine. If most males preferred athletics to reading, and most females preferred reading, reading was considered feminine, and athletics got to be masculine. The psychological community has perpetuated this nonsense by standardizing it into tests that stereotype people by scoring their masculine/feminine behavior. The typically male qualities are regarded as dominant, aggressive, outdoorsy, power-seeking, achievement-oriented, desiring leadership, interested in science and math, and competitive. The "healthy" female was described in *Psychology Review* by a team of researchers as: "more submissive, less independent, less adventurous, more easily influenced, less aggressive, less competitive, more easily excitable in minor crises, more easily hurt, more emotional, more conceited about her appearance, less objective, and less interested in math and science."*

Even the father of psychoanalysis, Sigmund Freud, has been described as having viewed a healthy woman as one who ". . . must be passive, resigned to her inferiority, and hopeful of achieving fulfillment by bearing a child."†

* *Psychology Review*, 1968, No. 75, pp. 23–50.

† Hilary M. Lops and N. L. Colwell, *The Psychology of Sex Differences* (Prentice Hall, 1978), p. 47.

This dichotomizing practice has taken hold so deeply that many people have come to believe that there are actually male and female types of activities, which makes about as much sense as thinking there are male and female kinds of rocks. But still, on this basis, anyone who strays from his assigned sexual role is classified as deviate and in need of treatment.

It should be obvious that if you buy into this dichotomy, you cut your potential for human experiences in half, and if you decide that you like only supermasculine men and superfeminine women, you are going to be cutting yourself off from a lot of people.

All you have to do is look objectively at yourself to see that we are all amalgams of male and female to begin with. As a man you have female hormones, breasts, soft skin and virtually everything that a woman has, with the exception of female reproductive organs. As a woman you have male hormones and the same features as a man with the exception of male reproductive organs. If you are a woman you may be taller than a lot of men or even most men, even though it is supposedly masculine to be tall and feminine to be shorter than "your man." You can do virtually everything a man can do except produce sperm, and he can do just about anything you can do except bear children.

So what's the big deal? How did we ever even *get* to the point of splitting up human activities into masculine and feminine?

Some would say male chauvinism is to blame. Others would say it is just easier for people to dichotomize and adopt strict social rules governing their behavior than to face the bewildering ambiguity of admitting that we can all be whatever we choose. But to transcend the masculine/feminine dichotomy means giving yourself permission to be *whatever you elect for yourself, without giving thought to what sexual-role stereotype you are fitting.*

A woman who waits for a man to initiate a sexual encounter when she would really like to initiate one herself, who holds back just because "a woman isn't supposed to do that," is choosing to continue to live by the dichotomy that has been imposed by a chauvinistic culture. Similarly, for a man to avoid such activity because he fears he would appear "too feminine" in it is for him to allow the same chauvinistic culture to dictate what *his* life can and ought to be.

For a man to be interested in sewing is not "deviate" unless you decide to let statistical charts dictate your moral judgments. A woman who wants to lift weights or become a truck driver is not displaying neurotic behavior induced by traumas in her childhood. People who do not conform to rigid masculine/feminine categories are not sick, except insofar as the rest of us make them sick by condemning them for what they find natural to do.

We need not place any limits on our abilities to undertake any activity that interests us. Each of us can enjoy whole new realms of human experience previously forbidden to us and reserved for the opposite sex. Men, when they bring themselves to be honest, can admit that they really enjoy softness, flowers, a tender embrace, cooking a meal, taking care of a baby, or any of the multitude of experiences that authoritarian-thinking people have come to label as feminine, as much as they enjoy any of their "masculine" experiences. Similarly, women can enjoy their femininity and still love to play ball, chop wood, go hunting, running, hiking, race-car driving, or anything else that has come to be labeled as masculine.

Once you begin to see yourself first in the holistic sense of just being human and *then* in terms of what kind of human you want to be, completely disregarding sex-role dictates drawn by the artificial masculine/feminine dichotomy, you can heal the split in your head that has placed such strict limits on what you imagine you can enjoy, and see yourself as completely whole—the way you were when you first came out of the delivery room.

Strong/Weak

As you may have gathered from my treatment of authoritarian anti-weakness, I do not think any one person is simply "strong" or "weak," and if you tend to categorize people in these terms you are doing so on the basis of some single criterion for strength or weakness in yourself or others that has nothing to do with reality.

What is real strength, what is real weakness? That is a philosophical question.

Who was stronger—Martin Luther King or the man who assassinated him? Adolf Hitler or Albert Schweitzer? The world's weight-lifting champion or the woman who lifted a car off her son (and broke her own back in the process)?

After you have thought through what *you* believe *real human strength* could be *at its best,* and assessed yourself according to *your own* criteria, you may well find that you are quite strong in dealing with your family, but you turn into a coward when you confront your boss or co-workers. You may feel powerless on Monday, but like Wonder Woman on Tuesday. In fact you are a composite of all kinds of strengths and weaknesses, and the way to holistic No-Limit thinking here is to fuse all those dichotomies and see each individual piece of your behavior as a whole which you can interpret as containing elements of strength and weakness, if you choose to think in such terms.

Look at your own past. When you have operated from what you now consider to have been real strength, you may have been trembling, feeling very weak inside. And sometimes when you've been cockiest, felt the strongest, like the biggest kid on the block, you may have behaved like a bully, in a way that was indicative of fear and trembling deep inside.

Every time you see someone behaving in a way that leads you to categorize him as strong or weak, keep in mind that there are always some strengths behind the weaknesses and some weaknesses behind the strengths. The holistic view of life will enable you to accept yourself as a human who was born long before anybody had the idea that he should downgrade himself because he thought of himself as weak.

When you determine your own fate according to your own best thoughts, you are transcending your weaknesses and taking charge of your life course as best you can. You become the commander of your own ship, rather than a passenger in transit for others to command. But this will happen only if you accept yourself and others *as humans,* as originally and always strong and weak at the same time.

Childish/Mature

You hear it all the time. "Stop being so immature! You are such a child. Why are you always acting like a baby?"

This dichotomy is used almost exclusively to put others down, and is virtually never used by people who have real confidence in themselves as independently thinking adults. In fact, in our culture it is usually used by adolescents to put other adolescents down. From one man interviewed for this book:

"In our school in the fifth, sixth, seventh grades, the girls who considered themselves the most mature, the ones who caked on the makeup and got padded bras and suddenly forgot how to run, were of course the ones who rated all the boys as 'mature' or 'childish.' For several years they couldn't think of anything but rating people on their 'maturity.' 'Immature' was the worst insult they could hurl at you. And whom did they pick to label 'mature'? The best fighters; the biggest, the tallest, the cockiest, the most authoritarian, and most *superficially* mature boys.

"And by the same token, the boys who put on the biggest macho airs, who were the first to bully others physically weaker than they, to prove what 'big men' they were, agreed that the girls who wore the most makeup and acted in subservient, almost slavish ways to their 'men' were the *most mature.*"

Anyone can have an immature idea of what human maturity really is, especially if he has never really thought through what he might mean by "maturity" at its best or highest.

Who is more mature—the child who tries to mimic the way adults act, becomes solemn and restrained, and cuts himself off from the "childish" games and fantasies that his more "immature" peers are enjoying, *who refuses to accept himself as a child,* or is it the child who thinks, "Of course I act in immature ways sometimes! What do you want from me, anyway? I'm only ten years old! The difference between you and me is that I know I've got a lot of growing up to do, and I intend to take my time and enjoy it. There's no sense trying to rush it. Besides, you seem to think there *is* such a thing as 'growing up, period'! You do it once and then you're done. *I guess you think you've already done it, and you don't have to think about it anymore.* Well you are never going to grow any more that way. I hope I am still growing when I'm seventy years old!"

To my mind, the first step toward real maturity, the only kind of maturity worth pursuing, is to recognize that no one person is ever all child or all adult, and it would be a sad thing if anybody were. The person who acts whimsically, silly and "immaturely" at some times is quite capable of reacting very seriously and "responsibly" under the appropriate circumstances. The adult who is controlled, organized, proper and thorough on the job should also be capable of just letting go, acting zany, and being like a little child under "the proper" circumstances. That anyone would encourage others to act in certain rigid ways arbitrarily labeled "mature" all the time, or that he would demand the same closed life style of himself, is evidence of shallow, dichotomous thinking that ignores the holistic phenomenon of each of us as originally and always part child and part adult, partly mature and partly immature, for our whole lives. Sticking yourself in one behavioral mode you call "mature" is very limiting; it will keep you from trying out new and exciting things, and, most important, it will stop you from wondering further what real human growth is, from seeing its open-ended nature, from constantly revising and expanding your philosophy about what kind of person *you* want to be, and ultimately from growing at all.

Civilized/Uncivilized

To label people who are more like us as civilized and those who are less like us as uncivilized is an example of ethnocentric dichotomizing of the most destructive kind. Every culture on earth has its own idea of what it is to be "most highly civilized," but if by that we mean creating the happiest, most fulfilling and creative lives possible for everyone, it is obvious that no one culture has a monopoly on wisdom in this area, and that we have a lot to learn from other cultures, past and present.

The more we open our minds to the study of other cultures, the more we see that the ones we have always labeled "most civilized" have also carried on "barbaric" practices which we would never call civilized. Ancient Greece may have given us democracy, philosophy, timeless art like the Parthenon or the plays of Aeschylus, Sophocles, Euripedes and Aristophanes. It may have given us mathematics, physics, the Olympics, the *Illiad*, the *Odyssey* and other legacies too rich for us ever fully to appreciate. But it was still a culture of slavery and exclusive male suffrage, still one where in some cities unwanted or "weak" infants were left out on hillsides to die, still the culture that killed Socrates because he asked too many questions.

How do we really measure the level of civilization in our own culture? Do we really think about it at all? Or do we just say, "Our culture is the ultimate in civilization, and anything different is just less civilized"? If we do the latter, we surely cut off any hope for improving our culture along humanistic lines—just as surely as does an individual who considers himself already completely mature, thereby cutting himself off from his own potential for personal growth.

Transcending this dichotomy involves asking yourself a few questions. Would you say that dropping nuclear weapons on huge populations is civilized? How about the use of napalm or chemical defoliants in war? How do we explain why so many inner-city children get out of high school without learning to read, or the high rates of hunger, poverty and anxiety in our "civilized" culture? Is our level of civilization ready to be judged by the number of tape recorders we own, or by how many of our houses have indoor plumbing?

People in less industrialized nations may not wear designer blue jeans. They may drive camels instead of Cadillacs. They may have critical shortages of skyscrapers, color televisions, automobiles, hair dryers, nuclear power plants, plastics, fast-food chains and three-martini business lunches. But they may also have critical shortages of cancer, depression, Valium, smog, traffic jams and accidents, rapes and muggings, murders and suicides, environmental pollution, energy crises, empty days and sleepless nights. Their survival techniques may be a marvel for those in the so-called developed nations to behold. If we look at them objectively, we will find that they are civilized by some criteria and uncivilized by others, just as our culture should always appear to us.

Once you open yourself to asking questions like these of yourself and your own culture, you will immediately be open to the holistic approach to "civilization," which is to take the entire realm of human experience, past and present, into your view as you ask yourself what *you* really think "civilization at its best" might be. Once you come up with some tentative answers that provide you with an equitable way of evaluating all cultures, your own included —as "objective" a set of standards as you can get—you will immediately see how "uncivilized," narrow-minded and ethnocentric most of our judgments of who is civilized and who is not have become, and how much more civilized the whole world could become if we all stopped calling one another uncivilized.

Body/Mind

You are one whole human being. Your body and your mind were born together long before you were ever taught to distinguish between them. If you have come to believe that your body and mind really are two separate and independent entities, you have fallen prey to one of the most self-alienating of dichotomies, which can lead to a constant struggle for dominance between your "mental" and your "physical" needs.

Do you ever think to yourself, "I may not be coordinated, but I'm smart," and neglect enjoyment of your body, or even abuse it, to pursue strictly intellectual or "mental" activities? Do you see your body as your "weak card" and *discard* it in favor of "your ace," which is your mind?

Or do you, instead, think of your body as your ace? Do you take great pride in your physical appearance, your ability to lift more weights or hit a golf ball farther than anyone else, but think of yourself as "not too brainy," or even as *dumb,* and discard your mind on the basis of this stereotype you have imposed on yourself?

A holistic approach to your humanity will help you to transcend this dichotomy and become more complete as a human being. If you want to hit a baseball with a bat, you will have to train your entire body-and-mind to complete the job. You cannot just stand there and watch the pitch curve across the outside corner of the plate without thinking, "That looks like a strike. The count is three–two, I've got to swing." Your mind has to command your body, and your body has to work in conjunction with your mind. "Step into it now," you think. "Don't swing as hard as you can; leave some flexibility in your wrists in case that curve breaks sharply as it crosses the plate. Just try to meet the ball and punch it into right field. You don't need a home run, all you need is a base hit to drive in the go-ahead run. . . ."

The pitch does break sharply down and out, but you are ahead of it. At the last instant your wrists snap and the head of the bat smacks solidly into the ball.

You don't even have to think now. You are off and running for first base before you even notice whether the ball is going to drop into right field for a hit or be caught.

As you run down the first baseline for all you're worth—as you run to work or run around the park—you might stop and wonder, "Is my body doing this, or is my mind?" And you might ask yourself the same thing when you are writing a letter, moving a sofa or driving to work.

There is no real split between your body and your mind. There is only the split that some people have invented to distinguish between "mental" and "physical" activities. You can transcend this dichotomy by recognizing that body-and-mind are involved in every single human action.

Your body and your mind—you can't have one without the other. When you die, even if your brain, or your mind, were willing and able to go on, they can't if your body checks out on them.

Holistic, No-Limit living means you must train and exercise your entire self, body-and-mind, together. Your mind needs to be challenged and exercised as regularly as your body, and vice versa. If you can grasp their fundamental unity, you will be well on the way to holistic, No-Limit thinking.

Conscious/Unconscious

This is a dichotomy that may be familiar only to those who have bought into traditional or Freudian psychoanalytic theorizing, but it has played a tremendous role in promoting a kind of dichotomous approach to life which has become increasingly widespread in our culture.

Some psychiatrists will tell you that our psyches (souls or minds) are divided into three parts: the id, the ego, and the superego. According to this Freudian theorizing, the pie of your mind is divided approximately like this:

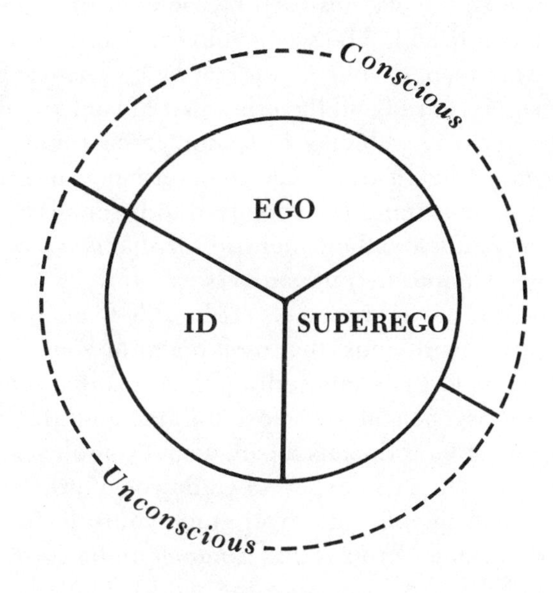

As you can see, your mind is said to be fundamentally divided between its "conscious" and "unconscious" halves, basically *the half you know about* and *the half you don't know about* (which therefore is *unpredictable,* or *untrustworthy*). But the picture is complicated by the fact that according to this theory, the *central* or *basic* pie of your mind is divided into *three* roughly equal sections, the id, the ego and the superego, with the id and about half the superego on the "unconscious" side of the basic dichotomy, the ego and the other half of the superego on the "conscious" side.

People who subscribe to Freudian ideas will tell you that *your id* is something like "the undifferentiated source of your animal energy," portraying it as some dark, primitive, uncivilized, *unconscious* force within you that would destroy you and all those you love if it were to be let loose.

But fortunately they will also tell you that your id is civilized by *your ego* and *your superego.*

Your ego is then defined as that *conscious* part of you that has been "derived from the id through contacts with reality, and mediates the demands of the id, the superego, and external reality."

Your superego is then said to be "a major sector of the psyche that is only partly conscious and that *aids in character formation by reflecting parental conscience and the rules of society.*"

In other words, the classical psychiatric view of you is that you are forever caught in a bind between your *conscious*—your ego and part of your superego, *of which you can be aware*—and your *unconscious,* that is, your id and the other part of your superego, your animal urges and the influences of your parents and society, *of which you cannot be aware.* Since the conscious and the unconscious halves of your mind are supposed to be about *equal determiners of your behavior,* the conclusion is that *you can be aware of or control only about half of yourself.*

To be sure, you are supposed also to be able to uncover a certain amount of your unconscious, that dark realm of your psyche from which mysterious forces supposedly pull so many of your strings, by consulting a psychoanalyst, whose training and highly detailed "theories" of what your dreams mean, what "complexes" lie down there, and so on enable this expert to guide you a little way into the jungle far better than you could ever guide yourself. But, still, you are supposed to think of yourself as *fundamentally split,* as though your psyche really did come into the world divided, much as a pizza pie comes to your table already cut up, and there will always be that "pure-animal" id down there which you never can trust. You just never know when the savages are going to come screaming out of the jungle and overrun that little encampment called "your conscious mind."

To my mind, the whole pizza pie that psychoanalysis has tried to sell you is a huge fraud that has been perpetrated on the public.

The unconscious as an entity simply does not exist! You are being sold half a pie at full price.

At best, the psychoanalyst has a few hunches about what resides deep within anyone else. Certainly you have thoughts and leftover reactions from your childhood, and you have dreams in which your mind operates quite differently from the way it does while you are awake. But to assign responsibility for your behavior to something which, by definition, you cannot be aware of or control is to give yourself an instant cop-out every time you want to avoid responsibility for anything you are doing. Further, you are to believe that you need a psychiatrist to guide you into your own psyche with a lot of rigid theoretical categories and arcane jargon. This, of course, puts off and squelches your own potential for looking into yourself in the terms and with the philosophy of life that make the most sense to *you*.

Why should you accept that you have a "sick" and a "healthy" side, and that deep within you resides an ugly monster who will gobble you up if it goes unchecked? I do not believe that for a minute. I believe that deep within you lies a fully human, highly evolved and functionally happy person, if you are willing to let it out. It is a myth to believe we have evolved into creatures who have fundamentally sick cores. This whole dichotomy is the result of speculation left over from the earliest days of psychoanalysis, and it has no validity for your life unless you choose to think of yourself in this way.

The way to transcend the conscious/unconscious dichotomy is to forget about dividing your psyche into parts as Freud and others did for the purposes of research, and to view yourself as a complete whole. As Maslow said in 1971, "Only now are we becoming quite sure that the integrated person, the fully evolved human, the fully matured person, must be available to himself at both these levels, simultaneously. Certainly it is obsolete to stigmatize this unconscious side of human nature as sick rather than healthy. That's the way Freud thought of it orginally but we are learning different now."*

When you view yourself in a holistic way, you will no longer need to divide yourself into your "conscious" and "unconscious" halves. You will be able to think, instead, that you have a truly human, important person deep within you, and that your real na-

* Maslow, *The Farther Reaches of Human Nature*, p. 88.

ture lies in wanting to be happy and fulfilled. And *why not* look at yourself this way, instead of from some silly sick/healthy, conscious/unconscious perspective? Why place needless, artificial, theoretical barriers of thought between yourself and No-Limit living?

Secure/Insecure

This is one of those "popular-psychology" dichotomies which has come over into common usage as a convenient way to file and forget others, or even yourself.

How often have you found yourself saying, "He's just the way he is because he's insecure," and felt very secure in your own superiority to the person you have labeled this way? How deeply do you really believe that anyone (yourself included) is either an *insecure person* or a *secure person*? Is there no room in your thought for everyone being in the middle—that is, a combination of both?

Virtually everything you do entails some security and some insecurity for you. If you stand up to an insolent clerk one day, you may outwardly be full of confidence, but you may be shaking inside. If you are stopped by a policeman for what you consider no good reason at all, you may appear to be quaking and shriveling on the outside, but inside, knowing you have done nothing wrong, you may have all the security in the world.

All of us have moments of relative security and insecurity, so any dichotomy that labels any of us as being either one or the other is a waste of time. Furthermore, if you label yourself as "secure" or "insecure," it will keep you from trying to change what you've described yourself as being. If you call yourself insecure, you may well find yourself leaning on others constantly to do things for you that you don't have the confidence to do for yourself: "George, will you take my car to the garage for me? You know how insecure I am around mechanics." At this rate you are never going to get over your hangups about mechanics, and it will be solely because you have "filed and forgotten" yourself under "insecure" (around mechanics, at least).

To be insecure is obviously not a good thing, if it means you are like somebody clinging to a precarious hold which, if it gives way, will send you plunging down the mountainside, into panic. But neither is being *too secure* a good thing, if it means valuing your security too much. Too great an emphasis on "security" can lead to inertia, boredom and depression as quickly as too little true security can lead to panic, ceaseless striving or other miseries associated with insecurity.

To transcend the secure/insecure dichotomy, you must recognize that you have to risk some feelings of insecurity if you are ever going to learn to walk a tightrope, water-ski, become a writer, start a new business, try out a new recipe or do anything that requires learning. You have to expect the No-Limit life to lead you into situations that most people would call quite precarious, and you have to expect others to say of you, "He's just acting that way because he's insecure." In any situation, however, what matters is how you see yourself, and when you do get those feelings of "insecurity" ask yourself whether you have them because you really do feel *internally insecure* (as though your mind is about to plunge into panic), or whether you just feel insecure because you have come to think of yourself that way in this kind of situation. You will be surprised how often your insecurity comes from your own and/or others' stereotypes of you, and how often a little calm thought about your situation can get you out of your panic if you just stop worrying about how "insecure" you are.

By the same token, you must recognize that No-Limit thinking requires you to *decide for yourself what kind of security you want in your life,* what kind of life (no matter what the conventional "insecurity risks" might be) will give you the most inner peace and the most confidence to go on and take new "risks" in forging your own destiny.

The questions to be asking yourself in any situation are not "Am I secure or insecure now? What can I do to make myself more secure?" but "Is my behavior right now effective in making me happy, no matter how others might label it or how I might have labeled it yesterday?" If you are happy now, you have all the security you need! If not, no amount of worrying about whether you or others are "secure" or "insecure" is going to make you any happier.

Think for a moment about a few areas of your life in which you or others have labeled you "very insecure," and a few in which you would be rated "very secure." Then think up all the ways you can in which you are or *can make yourself* internally secure in those areas you have categorized as "insecure." This exercise should not only show you how absurd the "secure/insecure" dichotomy can become, but should also show you the way around it. For example, if you have started with

VERY SECURE	*VERY INSECURE*
Cooking for the family	Dealing with auto mechanics

you may next have thought, about "Cooking for the family," "I am getting sort of tired of having to cook all the meals. I'd rather spend a few afternoons a week doing something besides preparing dinner, and when I do cook I'd like to try some new recipes." About "Dealing with auto mechanics," you may have thought, "I am at least secure in knowing that I can afford the costs of any repairs the car needs. I am insecure because I've never dealt with mechanics before, I don't understand cars too well, and I'm intimidated by people who can talk about them knowledgeably. That's why I've always asked George to take the car to the garage for me. But I can make myself internally secure in that area simply by taking the car myself the next time and learning more about cars from the mechanics." In other words, insecurities are eliminated by actions, not by merely labeling yourself insecure.

If you now go back and consider what you can do about the "insecurity" (unhappiness, boredom, depression) you have associated with "cooking for the family," you will find that your solutions to "too much security" bear a striking resemblance to those you have thought up as cures for your *insecurity* about auto mechanics, or whatever other insecurity problems you have uncovered. You may have thought something like "I can have more fun cooking if I ask George to cook a few times a week or bring some of our favorite take-out food home, so that I can get out of my cooking rut, forget cooking some afternoons, and have time to consider new recipes and shop for special ingredients."

The similarity between these two solutions to "opposite" problems lies in the fact that in both cases you have thought about what *you can do* about the problems, have invented some *strategies for action.* This is what I call No-Limit thinking at its best: you have forgotten the dichotomy and responded to the call of questioning-and-answering, of problem-solving, of *creative thinking,* as your own life has presented it to you now.

Regardless of how you view it, there is really no such thing as a completely secure or insecure person. Learning to fuse this dichotomy and to view others and yourself as limitless combinations of securities and insecurities which you can work on each day will lead you in the direction of true No-Limit living.

Teacher/Student

This dichotomy, along with parent/child, boss/underling, master/apprentice, and numerous others which have been invented through the ages to indicate that one person is supposed to be taught or trained by another, is fundamentally one that older people or people of conventionally "dominant status" use on children or other "apprentice people" to keep them in positions of inferiority. It begins with a simple enough truth—for instance, that your history teacher has been around longer than you have, at least in studying history, and therefore should be able to help you learn more about history. The trouble starts, however, when it is assumed that the teacher is the "active" one in the relationship and the student is the "passive" one, so that the teacher is basically "operating on" the student, rather the way a doctor operates on a patient, and "imparts" or "implants" knowledge rather the way a doctor puts in a pacemaker or transplants a kidney. Next the student is supposed to "sit still" for the operation, leave it to the teacher to decide how it is to be performed, and if it is a success the teacher gets to walk out of the operating room to the congratulations of all for his teaching brilliance, while the student gets a pat on the back for having sat still so well, and a promotion to the next operating room. Wham-bam, another authoritarian-submissiveness chain has been forged.

The holistic truth that lies behind this dichotomy is that every teacher in the world *should also be* a student, whether he is five years old and teaching a three-year-old how to draw with a pencil or sixty-five and a distinguished history professor. And, furthermore, *no one can really teach anyone else anything*, in the sense of implanting knowledge or skills in a passive student. The learner must decide to investigate, think about or practice something for himself, or no amount of teaching can make any kind of knowledge "sink in"; so the responsibility for learning anything is in the learner, who must first decide to become his own teacher before any other teacher can help him.

You know that no child is going to learn anything he refuses to become engaged in, regardless of how hard you try to teach him what you want him to know. You may *condition* the child not to cross the street alone, for instance by spanking him, but conditioning is not teaching or learning in any significant sense. You also know, if you've ever tried to teach anyone anything, that all your teaching has been a combination of your experimenting with or *being a student in* the teaching process and your *demonstrating* what you are trying to help your "student" master.

Take the example of teaching a child how to ride a bicycle. Maybe the child has been riding a tricycle for years, but now he has his first two-wheeler. You may put training wheels on it for a while to let him get the feel of the bigger bike, but when the time comes to take the training wheels off and let him see whether he can keep himself up on two wheels, no amount of running behind him and holding the bike up, coaching him on "how to keep his balance" or pretending that you are not going to let go and then sneakily letting go when he isn't looking is going to help. Either the child will get the knack by trial and error or he won't and the training wheels will go back on for a while. The effective teacher may *demonstrate* a few things, like how to push off with enough momentum and step down hard enough on one pedal to have a chance of staying up, how to put a foot back on the ground and lean the bike sideways to catch yourself without falling if you are losing your balance, but he will encourage the "student" to hold the bike himself, try pushing off and staying up for as long as he can, and then try again. He will not shout streams of confusing directions, interrupting as the child is trying to concentrate. If he feels the child is too self-conscious with him around to concentrate completely he will go away and leave the learner to his own teaching; meanwhile reflecting on what his own trial-and-error in helping someone learn to ride a bicycle has taught him this time about how to help someone better next time.

The more that self-reliance is cultivated in the learning process, the more effective the teaching. Conversely, the less self-reliance involved, the more the "teaching" degenerates into mere authoritarian "conditioning." So where is the dichotomy? The whole purpose of teaching, of education, should be to help students become their own best teachers, take full control over and responsibility for their own learning. The teacher who learns how to help students take control of themselves also learns more about teaching with every effort, and learns from his students.

Every time I taught a course as a college professor, I learned as much about the subject matter and about how human beings think and behave from my students as they did from me, and I became more aware of how silly the teacher/student dichotomy fundamentally is. After all, perhaps the most important thing a teacher can do is to demonstrate how to be a student. And, likewise, *the most important thing a parent can do is to demonstrate to children how to be their own parents;* the best thing a boss can do is to demonstrate to employees how to be their own bosses; and so on for masters, apprentices and everyone else. Transcending the authoritarian tendency to think that all these kinds of relationships are one-way streets requiring dominance/submissiveness or implying superiority/inferiority simply requires that you take an inventory of all the relationships in your own life that have been given "teacher/student" or similar labels, *reverse the labels* and see all the ways in which it is true that your students are your teachers (or your teachers are your students), your children are your parents or vice versa, and so on. As you do this, you will feel your thoughts changing, the whole "body of your thought" shifting, your attitudes mellowing as the tension generated by your former need to play so many artificial roles of dominance or submissiveness melts away. Your behavior in these relationships will adjust itself to fit your new conceptions. Anxiety will be replaced by a sense of humor; competition or conflict will be replaced by a sense of cooperation, and authoritarian-submissiveness chains will be replaced by a network of true No-Limit relationships. Keep in mind that everything you know, you decided to learn, and that no teacher, however talented, could force you to learn something you chose not to. We are *all* at once teachers and learners in every encounter of our lives.

Work/Play

This dichotomy is one of the most pervasive and destructive in our culture. In many ways, transcending it represents the essence of No-Limit thinking, perhaps the single most far-reaching step you can take toward No-Limit living.

How many times, in how many ways, have you heard or said it: "All work and no play makes Jack a dull boy"; "Work hard, play hard"; "All I do is work, work, work"; "All right, the fun's over, let's get back to work"; "We are members of the working class, they are members of the leisure class"; "You've got it easy now, but wait until you grow up and have to go to work"?

Specifically, how rigidly do you divide your own time between those fun things you classify as play and the miserable drudgery you think of as work? How much do you look on your primary work, your employment or vocation—whether it's plumber, housewife, advertising executive, student or anything else—as something *you're forced into doing* because you have to make a living, or something you desperately want to succeed at so that you can get rich and retire early and you *won't have to work anymore?*

How much do you consider yourself *a slave to work,* whether it's washing the dishes, mowing the lawn, building a bridge or writing a newspaper story? How deeply have you bought into the idea that *play is a reward for finishing your work,* whether you're a grade-school student being threatened with being kept in during play period for not finishing your homework or a businessman who *works hard* fifty weeks out of the year, partly for his two-week vacation? Ultimately, how deeply do you believe that what is work cannot be play, and what is play cannot be work?

Changing your attitudes about work/play involves more than simply labeling what you enjoy as play and what you dislike as work. In fact, changing the way you use words won't help if that's *all* you do, but considering *whether any activity can be called work at its best or highest unless it can also be called play* may just lead you to the point of transcending this dichotomy.

Consider what it might mean to *do your best work.* You may immediately think, "Doing my best work is when I write the best report I've ever written, one my boss and the clients agree is exactly what they needed," or something similar. You may also think, "That has nothing to do with whether I had fun or suffered like hell while I was writing it."

Think again. You may have made an assumption: that "your work" is the product you produce (the service you perform, or whatever) *and not* the activity of working! Now, surely *part* of what you mean by "my best work" may be "the best poem I've ever written," or anything else. But the *meaning of the whole word* as you apply it to your life must include your evaluation of *how good a time you had working,* or *how much your work was also play.* This is the sense in which you say, "The best job I ever had, really, was . . . [whatever it was], because I enjoyed *the work,* loved the people, got really good at it, and found it exciting and challenging."

If you agree that "your work" must mean *both* the activity and the product, then you can immediately see that work at its best or highest *must* be a combination of work and play. You can call any kind of drudgery or activity that you are resigned to hating "work" if you want to, as long as you resolve either to find some way to enjoy that work or to give it up. What is crucial is that you *not see any activity as drudgery just because you or others have labeled it work,* and resign yourself to being miserable while doing it because of the label that has been assigned to it. If you are truly interested in a No-Limit life, you have to accept that *the only kind of work you are interested in is work at its best or highest in all senses,* and that *your ability to make all your work-activities into play has to come first.*

And how did this absurd dichotomy originate in the first place? How did some people come to accept that there is work and there is play, and that you have to spend most of your time working so that you can enjoy the rest of your time (as much as you can afford) playing, that play is the reward for "hard work," and so on?

I imagine that for most of us it started in school, with parents who insisted that their children had to start early to "work" around the house, assigned them numerous "jobs," all the while conveying what a horror it was to wash the dishes or cut the grass. Perhaps they told the children if they wanted to live in the family they had to put in their share of the work, justifying their policies on the basis that they were really just getting their children ready for the way school, or life, "really is." But for most of us it very likely started with school, with teachers calling certain times "play periods" and making certain we knew that when class was in session the teacher was the boss again, and that there was no reason for us to expect to enjoy ourselves, because this was *work time*—time to be conditioned to the idea that work and play were very, very different.

Now, what is the authoritarian advantage of this kind of dichotomy (which authoritarian students and teachers alike accept and/or promote)? I think it is precisely that *if play (fun) can be separated from work* so that *your fun is made dependent on how well you perform in the hierarchy's judgment,* then *the hierarchy has gained another external reward it can grant or withhold from you at will, and has gained yet one more way to manipulate you!* That is, the hierarchy gets to tell you when you have earned the right to play.

The key to transcending this dichotomy is to recognize that *your ability to fuse work and play in everything you do is something that nobody can take from you unless you thoughtlessly give it away.*

Going back to the section on "Engagement" in Chapter 1, in which I mentioned the union of vocation and avocation—another form of the work/play dichotomy—it will not hurt us to read Frost once more:

> *But yield who will to their separation,*
> My object in living is to unite
> My vocation and my avocation. . . .

What the poet here says is that *vocation-and-avocation were originally one,* at least in his mind, and that *some people have yielded to their separation,* or have given in to the (authoritarian) idea that, for the "mature adult," work and play must really be separate, even mutually exclusive activities! Frost wants to emphasize that for those who have lost the vision of the fundamental unity of "work" and "play" at their highest, *it requires creative thinking and courageous life choices to transcend this dichotomy now.* It does not matter whether you remember when work and play were one in your own life history, although you may if you remember all the work you put into building that tree hut or making that beautiful sand castle, and how you were lost, *engaged* in pleasure, for every second of it. What matters now is that you *go ahead* to make everything you label "work" and everything you label "play" into the whole of work-and-play in your life history *from this moment on.* You do not have to do anything to your play to "make it" into work in the sense I am talking about. All you have to do is recognize how you always work when you are really playing.

For example, if you are totally engaged in a game of tennis, how are you working as a whole person? You are running here and there, your body and your racquet are playing the ball to the ultimate of their coordination with your mind; you are learning and strengthening yourself and "your game" every instant (as long as you are thinking and not worrying about the game). In what sense are you *not working?* You are certainly not "broken," like a clock that's stopped, of which you say, "It's not working. I have to get it fixed." On the other hand, you are exerting yourself both physically and mentally (if you want to distinguish between them) to the maximum. Afterward you may even say, "What a workout!" During this activity you have been conditioned to call "play," you have been doing everything that anyone can associate with work!

By the same token, when you have found a way to make your everyday work, or your vocation, into play (whether your work requires a lot of physical activity or not), you are obviously doing everything characteristic of both work and play at the same time.

You will remember my having said, in connection with "Engagement," that fortunately the union of vocation/avocation, or work/play, does not depend on your ability to get the job you love, but on your ability to love the job you get. Of course, you want to go after the job you think you will love! What better way to assure your ability to love the job you get? But as to those jobs *you have chosen to do* (and even with the dirty dishes, you chose to wash them when you used them; you *could* have eaten out of the pans, or bought TV dinners), *why not* be as creative as you can about making those jobs into play for yourself? Why accept the idea that nine-to-five *has* to be a drudge because that's work, and play is for later? Why go in to work every day with the prejudice that fun time is over now? Why be the surly garbage man who bangs the cans around as hard as he can and leaves trash scattered in the gutter because he can't make his work into play? *Why not* be the garbage man who is always pleasant and neat, finds fascination in what people throw away and what archaeologists of the future will make of it, who tells you about the new recycling center?

Whatever you now think of as work "in the negative sense"—whether it's cutting the grass, washing the dishes, getting the report in on time, sitting behind the movie projector for eight hours at a stretch with "nothing else to do" but change reels every half hour—you can find a way to become totally engaged in it and fascinated by it for the whole time you are doing it.

So washing the dishes, taking out the garbage, going to work every day are necessary conditions in your life. *So what?* Does that automatically make them work-and-not-fun? Not on your life! If you choose your own attitudes toward them without any intervention by artificial work/play dichotomies, you will know that washing dishes can easily be "play period"; a time to remember how much you enjoyed the food you ate from those dishes; to engage in your own private thoughts and reflections as you watch the water flow and your hands and the dishcloth getting those good old dishes clean again for tomorrow's meal; to listen to your favorite music, chat with your family, just plain meditate, or anything else that constitutes recreation (another word for play-and-work at their highest, meaning *self-re-creation*).

The beauty of a renewed holistic attitude toward work-and-play will turn out to be that the more you learn how to play at your work (your vocation especially), the better the products of your work will naturally be *without your worrying about your work at all.* That is, your book report as a product can't possibly be worse and, I think, inevitably will be better in the eyes of others, if you allow yourself to play with it, to enjoy writing it. Your two weeks off will be all the better if you do not feel you have sacrificed a year of hard, onerous work for them, and that all the pressure is on you now to cram in a full year's worth of play.

Of course, you may occasionally have to reject some so-called work *or* play activities that others have tried illegitimately to force on you. Maybe your boss *is* a hopeless authoritarian who will never give you any room for growth and will seem to do his best to make your life miserable; maybe you really don't want to play tennis this afternoon, as much as someone else is trying to drag you out onto the court. In that case you have to reject the activity; quit your job no matter what the risks, or say, "Hell, no, I *won't* go play tennis this afternoon." But whatever your choice in a specific situation, if you want to enjoy No-Limit work and No-Limit play at *their highest,* you have to remember that you can't have one without the other, and that *when you've got one you've also got the other.*

Robert Frost himself exemplified what he was saying in "Two Tramps in Mud Time." His vocation was "poet." His avocation was writing poetry. It was only, I think, because he had grasped the fundamental unity of play-and-work for himself, in his own life, had *created it for himself,* that the entire body of his poetry, his legacy of beautiful and true thoughts, rings so deeply in the ears of so many thoughtful people. To parody another No-Limit poet: Work is play, play is work. That is all you know on earth, and all you need to know.

Love/Hate

Authoritarians have a strong tendency to divide the world into things and people they love and those they hate, despise or condemn. "I love my country; I hate these creeps who take everything the country gives them and then refuse to defend it when the chips are down, these kids who are against the draft." "I love my family.

I hate that guy Jones down the block." "I love the old buildings downtown, but I hate those new ones they're putting up." "I love working in the garden, but I hate cleaning the basement." This tendency reflects the authoritarian's intolerance of ambiguity and need to dichotomize at all costs, but its result is likely to be shallow love and blind hatred, which, if it is not outright dangerous, at least fills the authoritarian with conflict and often makes him look like a fool.

Suppose you say, "I love my family, but I hate these kids who take everything the country gives them and then refuse to defend it." What happens when your teenage son, whom up to now you have been very proud of, and who is attending a very good college, decides he is against the draft? You have said so often how much you hate "his kind" that now you are committed to hating him as a person, withdrawing all your love from him, unless you can *make him change his mind.* You may try to bludgeon him out of his position, tell him you won't pay any more of his tuition if he doesn't come to his senses, but you don't stand a snowball's chance in hell of succeeding. Your categorical hatred attacks him in a very personal and emotional way, and if you won't listen to his reasons, why should he listen to your ranting? Furthermore, if he gives in on what he believes because of your threats, are you then supposed to be proud of him?

Your categorical hatred has put you into a box. You can't say, "Well, I hate all those creeps *except* my own son" and be consistent. The only consistent or holistic way out is to get rid of your categorical hatred and be satisfied with disagreeing strongly with your son, trying to *reason with* him as best you can, *rethinking* the rights-and-wrongs of the draft as best you can together, ultimately trying your best to reach mutual agreement. Even if it takes ten years, you can still have fun trying!

But if you are an arch-authoritarian to begin with, you will be more afraid of possibly changing your present position than you are of breaking up the family that you said you loved. You will disown your son, force him to leave the college you were so proud of him for getting into, and probably cause tremendous anguish for your spouse and other family members, who may come to feel that your love for the family is pretty shallow if it can turn so easily to automatic hatred and banishment of one of the members.

It is precisely to avoid this kind of love/hate trap that wise parents make it clear to their children that "I will always love you, even if I hate some of the things you do." By making their love *unconditional,* they leave themselves room to express strong disagreement or even hatred of their children's actions. ("You lied to me about why you were late getting home from school. I detest that behavior"—which is *not* to say, "I detest you.") It is certainly possible to love the person and hate his behavior at the same time.

In my experience, only those families that have adopted some version of this fundamental attitude, this fusion or resolution of the love/hate dichotomy, have stayed together. Those families in which it was understood that if you hated a person's behavior at a given time you also hated (withdrew love from) that person at that time have long since scattered like chaff before the wind.

Thinking a little more about the nature of hatred, it should become obvious that it is futile ever to hate anybody, and probably equally futile even to hate anybody's actions, for the simple reason that hatred in itself is an emotion of *reaction* (and not an inspiration to constructive action) whose main effect is to throw the hater into emotional turmoil, anger, rage, immobilization and either the quiet fuming that goes with inertia or the completely ineffectual blithering that goes with panic.

Without doubt, the best Allied soldiers in World War II were not those who were obsessed with hatred for "all Germans" but those who said, "There is a horrible political disease in Germany, so horrible that I will die fighting it if I have to and kill Germans who are fighting to spread it if I must, but I do not hate all Germans, or even all Nazis. My mission is as much to save Germany from this disease as to save the rest of us, and, really, I am fighting on the side of those Germans who have tried to resist it one way or another and failed, those who stand for the principles I love." They were the ones who could go out and get the job done without having their judgment or efficiency fouled up by the internal "static" that hatred breeds; those who were too busy fighting the disease *or* the people who had it.

The same principle of loving your family members unconditionally *as people,* even though you may have to stand *unconditionally opposed* to some of their actions at a given time, has been extended by many great religious thinkers to the idea of loving *all other humans* unconditionally as people (as though they were members of your family), whether or not you may have to stand mortally opposed to what they are doing at a given time. This is the essence of holistic thinking.

The logic is simple: if you have hope for yourself, a vision of how great life really can be for you, why not have equal hope for everybody else? How can humanity ever reach its full potential for common happiness if people not only give up hope for each other but at the same time give up hope for themselves, which you do in part every time you give up hope for any other person? How are you ever going to help anyone (yourself included) by grouping some of them into those you hate and others into those you love? Isn't *everybody* you say you love bound to do something you "hate" sooner or later? Aren't you equally bound to do something that those who love you hate? Would you want them to hate you for what you did? At this rate, everybody in the world would end up hating everybody else in short order; not only would all our own personal relationships (and therefore our own lives) be poisoned, but dictators and tyrants would have a field day manipulating people's blind hatreds for one another, and all human freedom would be smothered in favor of endless conflicts of hatred. In fact, pushing the love/hate dichotomy as far as it can go along authoritarian lines could easily lead to the total extermination of humanity.

This is why the Apostle Paul said, for instance:

> Love is patient and kind; love is not jealous or boastful; it is not arrogant or rude. Love does not insist on its own way; it is not irritable or resentful; it does not rejoice at wrong, but rejoices in the right. Love bears all things, believes all things, hopes all things, endures all things.
>
> Love never ends; as for prophecies, they will pass away; as for tongues, they will cease; as for knowledge, it will pass away. For our knowledge is imperfect and our prophecy is imperfect; but when the perfect comes, the imperfect will pass away.*

If you are to accept yourself as *perfect now* in the ways I urged in the first chapter, you will "let the perfect" (the whole or the complete *you*) come *right now*, and *forget your self-immobilizing hatred for anyone, yourself included.* You will let the "imperfect," the love/hate categories into which you have placed so many things and people, "pass away," simply by establishing the proper relationship between what you love and want to nurture and cultivate and what you may hate, what you want to eradicate in the world, in your own mind. To me the proper relationship is, "I may hate what

* I Corinthians 13: 1–9.

people do, but I need never hate another person; therefore, *love and hate are never really in conflict at all as far as other people are concerned.* I accept that everybody, myself included, will naturally do things I disapprove of at one time or another, and that sometimes I will have to stand in the way of their behavior. But that will not keep me from fundamentally loving, or *having hope for,* everybody—including myself—*all the time.*"

If there is one thing that virtually all religious thinkers have stressed, it is overcoming the love/hate dichotomy *in your own life.* "You shall love your neighbor as yourself." As with all great philosophy and poetry, it can shed new light on the meaning of love every time it is read. But for now I interpret it as meaning "If you cannot love your neighbor unconditionally (no matter how much you may have to oppose what he does), you cannot love yourself unconditionally." That is, *you are destined* to love your neighbor *just as much as* you love yourself, *no matter how much or how little that is.* If you hate your neighbor and behave in a way that is destructive to his life, that is the perfect measure of how much you hate yourself and are self-destructive in your own life.

The bottom line is: the choice is yours. You can continue to divide as many people, activities, events, ideas or whatever as possible into those you hate and those you love, or you can transcend this ceaseless dichotomizing in favor of the holistic, No-Limit approach, by simply deciding to love yourself and all other people as much as you can, by refusing to be upset or immobilized by hatred of them or their actions.

Good/Bad

This is perhaps one of the most frequently used dichotomies in our language, and because it represents such a categorical *judgment* on the part of whoever uses it, it is subject to a very wide range of abuses.

You hear it all the time. "He is a bad boy." "You are being bad." "That's a good girl." The assumption behind these proclamations is that people can be neatly separated into the categories of good and bad, and that those people who are bad are not deserving of credit, while those who are good are to be complimented. In reality, however, there is no such thing as a bad person. The concept of *bad* is a moral judgment, and one person's *bad* behavior is another person's *good* behavior, and vice versa; therefore circumstances often will dictate what is judged to be good or bad. In wartime it is bad to avoid killing your enemy, while in peacetime it is good to avoid killing at all costs. Despite the fact that the act of killing is still the same, the judgments of good or bad are always changing, depending upon the context of the behavior. So that, depending on the justness of the laws and legal authorities in the jurisdiction in question, you as a juror, for example, may end up concluding, "Yes, technically it was murder, because the laws of this country forbid killing Gestapo agents under any circumstances, and this man premeditatedly killed that agent who was coming to drag his family away to a concentration camp. But I cannot condemn this man for having done that, so I am going to have to forget that technical definition and vote my conscience: not guilty."

One fundamental abuse of the good/bad dichotomy, and a very pervasive one, is thoughtlessly allowing external laws and social conventions to make your moral judgments for you according to fixed rules. Our jury system is designed as well as possible to prevent this by providing that a juror can vote however he wants, without having to justify his vote to anybody and with no possibility of being called to account or being punished for it, but, still, many jurors and "judges" in all areas of life are basically unaware of this, and vote guilty just because technically the defendant has broken the law. Thus, no matter what the extenuating circumstances may have been, they feel that "the laws" have to be defended at all costs, with no regard to possible gross injustices to individuals. To transcend this particular abuse of the good/bad dichotomy, you should remember that each person has a combination of good and bad behaviors as they are generally defined in our culture. In fact, each piece of behavior has a combination of what we call good and bad built right into it, and learning to transcend the simple dichotomy and to look for the context of the behavior is a far greater way of thinking. You transcend the dichotomy when you can see good and bad as being the same thing in many ways. A criminal who has been arrested for burglary will most likely be labeled as a "bad" person. But the context of the burglary needs to be examined. This is not to say that the act ought to go unpunished, but simply that it may be essential to examine the robber in order to judge the crime, as in Victor Hugo's *Les Miserables,* in which the culprit stole a loaf of bread in order to feed his hungry family. Would you say that the refugees who sneak across borders in order to survive are all bad when they are trying to preserve their own lives and better themselves? If you were in their shoes how would you behave? Weren't the Pilgrims simply refugees who entered another country (the American Indians') illegally? Were they bad or good?

The point of transcending the dichotomy is to give yourself the kind of open vision that refuses to stereotype people and, instead, gives you the ammunition to do something constructive about what needs to be corrected in our culture. Rather than simply judging people and things to be bad, it is far more effective to look at all sides and then set about taking constructive action. The actual practice of providing good/bad labels does nothing but help to keep conditions exactly as they are and create neat little categories of good and bad where everyone can be nicely slotted. There is a combination of good and bad in virtually all human behaviors, and the most effective thing that you can do is avoid judgments and say to yourself, "Well, I could be wrong, and I'll keep an open mind about that."

Examples of good/bad judgments that make absolutely no sense are: "The weather is really bad today," or "That was a really great football game, but the one last week was lousy," or similar observations when you are simply projecting judgments onto things that in themselves are not good or bad at all. The weather is just the weather, and no amount of dichotomizing about it is going to change it, so when you say it's bad you are merely voicing your personal choice to get upset about it, to let *it* bother *you*. Why not see the storm as beautiful, take the holistic view that if all days were sunny this would be a barren planet, and enjoy the weather for what it is? Likewise, you may have thought the football game last week was lousy because it was a 0–0 tie with no "spectacular" plays, while the one this week was good because it was a 28–24 victory for your side, won with a seventy-yard touchdown pass with three seconds to play. By saying last week's game was lousy you are saying, "I chose not to enjoy what I *could* appreciate in last week's game"—the hard line play, the way one line seemed to dominate the other for a while, the way the other line "came back" and dominated for a while, the fact that neither side could break the game open, the suspense of knowing that even a field goal or a safety could win the game at any moment. Whenever you find yourself making a good/bad judgment of this type, ask yourself what you are choosing not to enjoy, or to be upset about, at the instant you make that judgment, and how you could "turn the game around" and enjoy your *time now* by seeing the good in what you've labeled bad.

Finally, and most importantly, you often hear people saying, "Jane's a bad girl," "John is a good man," or similarly labeling *people* categorically good or bad. This is parallel to the judgment of people instead of actions or behavior discussed in the last section on the love/hate dichotomy. At the risk of doing some dichotomizing myself (and you will remember my having said earlier that the proper use of dichotomies is essential to thought and language; it is the authoritarian abuse of them we have to look out for), I would say such categorizations of people as totally good or bad is *never* necessary or justified, and the way to transcend this abuse of the good/bad dichotomy is simply never to label the people themselves, but only their behavior insofar as you have to (remembering that all behavior is bound to have some good and some bad in it). For instance, suppose you say, "Jane's a bad girl" because she is irrepressible in school, a habitual discipline problem *for her teachers*. If you think about it, that same quality of irrepressibility may make her a great leader or a creative "genius" someday, if only people will stop trying to destroy it by labeling it categorically "bad" and, instead, try to help her see how she can "make it good." It may also be what you enjoy most about Jane now in certain circumstances, if you think about it. Maybe you felt you had to discipline her when she sassed back at that supercilious uncle who's always putting her and you down, but you may well have been saying inside, "Way to go, Jane! I wish I'd had the guts to do that myself."

If you look carefully at all your good/bad, right/wrong and other such categorical judgments, you will be able to transcend the abuse of all of them by throwing some out as completely senseless and throwing others out because you have no real need or excuse for making them.

Patriotic/Unpatriotic

As you will recall from my comments on the superpatriotic/totalitarian trait of authoritarians, this particular dichtomy is capable of leading to horrendous social consequences of national or international scope. The fundamental difference between this and other dichotomies like good/bad and right/wrong is that, while the latter have some legitimate uses, as when, practically speaking, you have to make a moral judgment, it is very hard to see any legitimate use at all for the patriotic/unpatriotic dichotomy. The truth is that the dichotomy is an artificial one. An individual may love his country passionately and still not feel that it is being just in its treatment of its citizens. An individual might refuse to kill others and still love his country, or quite the reverse—go off to war and kill the enemy and still be a traitor to his country's cause. In fact, the decision to be patriotic or not is a choice, and no one ought to be condemned for disagreeing vehemently with the conduct of his country's leaders.

Countries themselves are not immutable. They are comprised of individual leaders and citizens, who are capable of being both sound and outright immoral at the same time. The concept "my country, right or wrong" has no place in the framework of a No-Limit person. Only you can answer for yourself what real patriotism or love of your country means to you, and it is every person's inalienable right to decide that matter for himself. Therefore, what patriotic purpose could possibly be served by labeling another's attitudes patriotic or unpatriotic? By doing so you will deny or abridge his democratic rights to his own opinions, to isolate him from the political process *as a whole*, to discredit him *as a person* for thinking the way he does, and to prejudice others against him, so that you can further the dominance of whatever authoritarian-submissiveness chain you have subscribed to.

To overcome this dichotomy, the simplest tactic is, just don't ever use it—unless you can find some use for it which you really think is legitimate in any situation, but I will be surprised if you can.

In this connection, it might help you to wonder whether the nationalistic way most Americans currently divide *the whole world* up in their minds is really of any practical use to humanity at all, Americans included.

The idea of pariotism, or *love of your country* as a positive value, is dependent on your recognizing *your country*, the particular geographical area in which you live, its political, economic and social system, as being a terribly important entity in the first place. By accepting "American," for example, as a "primary identification" for yourself, you are immediately tempted to see yourself as an American *as opposed to* a German, a Russian or a Japanese.

There may be no harm in this if you merely mean that the

opposition is an inconsequential difference of some interest. That perhaps you have a certain cultural heritage different from that of many Russians, or even if you see the U.S. engaged in a "game" with the Soviet Union, for instance, to see whether our "dominant" political philosophy is capable of producing better lives for Americans than theirs is for Russians.

But if your fundamental identity as an American means to you that "we've got to beat those Russians *at all costs,*" if you basically come to see yourself as part of a nation whose obligation is to extend the domain of the "free world" as defined by American territories and spheres of influence, if you define your patriotism as love of your country *and* hatred of other countries or their peoples, then you resign yourself to the idea that our whole planet and all the people on it, yourself included, are just huge pawns in what one songwriter called "the patriot game," about the horrible carnage wrought in Ireland by blind patriotism:

> Come all you young rebels, and list while I sing;
> The love of one's country is a terrible thing.
> It banishes fear with the speed of a flame
> And it makes you all part of the patriot's game. . . .
>
> And now I am lying, my body all holes.
> I think of those traitors who bargained and sold.
> I'm sorry my rifle has not done the same
> To the traitors who've sold out the patriot's game.*

This song of bitter irony calls upon all of us always to wonder, what *is* the game of the *self-styled "patriot"*? Is it not to make us forget that before there were nations there were people, *there was life,* and, instead, to accept that now we people over here in the "free world" and those people over there in the "underworld" are really representatives of the dichotomized forces of good and evil in the whole world, just destined to battle it out until "our countries" overcome theirs, or vice versa?

The natural extension of the tendency to identify yourself with your country in any primary way at all is the tendency arbitrarily to dichotomize the whole world along "battle lines," and to oppose

* "The Patriot Game" by Dominic Behan, first and last verses, as sung by Judy Collins, *Whales and Nightingales.*

yourself *in your own mind* to huge masses of the rest of humanity on what, as far as I can see, is absolutely no real basis at all.

Therefore, to call yourself patriotic is just as bad as to call someone else unpatriotic, insofar as it sets you against millions or billions of people you have never met, just because they live in different countries. You may be stuck on the idea that your country and its "ideals" should dominate the world that *you assume everybody else is the same as you are.* You assume that the truly patriotic Russian will be as much out to gain world dominance for the Soviet Union and its ideals as you are out to gain world dominance for the U.S.A. and *its* ideals. You assume that people of "foreign" countries are "out to get you" all the time.

All great revolutions, including our own American Revolution, were originated by traitors to their own mother country. The concept of traitor depends clearly on who is doing the labeling. Certainly George Washington and Thomas Jefferson were traitors and patriots at the same time. As with all dichotomies, it turns out upon close examination that there is some truth in both extremes and that the dichotomy must be fused in order to see it properly. A NEZ person feels a sense of commitment to inner truths and is never internally limited to the man-made boundaries that lead to the dichotomy of patriot/traitor.

To transcend the patriotic/unpatriotic dichotomy, therefore, I think the best way is to forget it, just never to use it, and, furthermore, to forget the heavy emphasis you have placed on being an American (or whatever you consider yourself) *as opposed to* a member of another nation or culture. Just think of yourself as a human among all the other billions of humans on this planet—a global No-Limit person, if you will.

We/They

This final dichotomy really represents the end result of all authoritarian dichotomizing, which is to divide the world into all those people you categorize as "with you" and all those who are "against you." Whether you have chosen to categorize others as "weak" while you think of yourself as "strong," or vice versa; whether you have chosen to think of yourself as "mature" while you categorize others as "childish"; or whether you have chosen to consider others "uncivilized" while you credit yourself with being "civilized"; the effect of every act of *dichotomizing humanity* is to segregate the group you love from the group you hate. It places those you label as "good" against those you label "bad," and generally creates all kinds of artificial and unnecessary, often dangerous, divisions between yourself and those other human beings who occupy this planet with you. In sum, the more authoritarian your thinking has become, the more you will have listed groups of people under negative, "they" categories.

When you opt for the we/they dichotomy you begin to think like this, with all the obviously inherent prejudices that go with it.

I am spontaneous	*You* are unorganized	*They* are shiftless
I am gentle	*You* are passive	*They* are shy
I am assertive	*You* are aggressive	*They* are pushy
I am a naturalist	*You* are uncivilized	*They* are naked savages

You can see how the flavor changes when you think in terms of dichotomies. You simply come up with a more unflattering concept to describe the same piece of behavior. But the dichotomy produces a we/they kind of division that separates people rather than bringing them together.

You can transcend the we/they dichotomy by *seeing everyone as WE*, by admitting the simple fact that all of us are equal parts of *life now together*, by coming to see that the beggars in the streets of New Delhi, the boat people in Malaysia, the royalty in Buckingham Palace, the factory worker in Detroit, and *you* (whoever you are) are *equal parts of humanity now*.

All of the dichotomies listed here, and others that may come to mind as you work at eliminating this divisive kind of thinking, are tendencies that bring about separateness rather than togetherness, splitting rather than holistic integration, and feuding rather than resolution of differences. The world is not easily divided into opposite black and white divisions, and those who try to make it that way seldom do anything to make this place a better home for all of us. The world is in the gray virtually all of the time, and if you are always coming down squarely on *either* black *or* white, you are simply deluding yourself.

To transcend authoritarian, dichotomous thinking toward holistic, No-Limit thinking in your own life, you have primarily to realize that a rigid dichotomy is nothing more than an artificial human contrivance. These dichotomies are used by authoritarians to bring about conflict between individuals and societies, or between individuals and themselves, *to further the aims of a given authoritarian society,* or a specific authoritarian-submissiveness chain. The more dichotomies you can think up for yourself to transcend, and the more ways you can think of for yourself to transcend them, the more individual steps you will have taken on the road to No-Limit thinking and the No-Limit life.

4 First Be a Good Animal

From the high art of No-Limit thinking, let's take a break and run around on the ground awhile, maybe climb a tree, go for a swim or play with the baby. If I have made my point about how to be a NEZ/No-Limit thinker, it should be an easy step for you to consider the natural joy that is available for you every day just because of your status as an animal among animals on this planet—despite the fact that many of us have come to look down on "the animal side" of our natures.

To become as fully human as it is possible for you to be, you cannot avoid looking at your own relationship to your body and your basic human biology. Are you at peace with your body, knowing no shame about your "animal" qualities, and in fact welcoming that part of yourself that is closest to nature? Or are you riddled with shame and guilt about your body, preoccupied with trying to hide this part of your basic humanity? Do you believe in a fundamental split between your intellectual or reasoning side and your more basic biological, animalistic side that keeps you from seeing yourself primarily as one single, unified human being, accepting and enjoying *all* the ingredients that constitute your humanity?

The widespread alienation of people from their own animal natures that has led so many of us to neglect or abuse our bodies, or at least to miss out on so many physical pleasures, seems to have begun with intellectual speculations about what "sets men above beasts." Some claim that humans' ability to reason and think sets them in a class apart from all other animals. Others see spirituality as the unique claim to superiority over all other living things. Sophisticated academic journals are replete with references to the human's ability to transcend instincts, citing the size of the brain, the ability to invent and the capacity to use tools or to build highly "advanced" and complex societies as key factors that have given us dominion over the earth.

Such speculations may be valid and interesting in their proper places. But they are often made in the context of trying to prove how much *better than animals* we all are—as though we are so uncertain of our own worth that we have to write down all the reasons why we are "superior" to dogs, frogs or amoebas. Their main social effect has been to split people in two, psychologically speaking, to make them repress the simple fact that no matter what kind of animals we are, we are still animals, and must respect and enjoy that undeniable fact.

Look at it this way: if a horse could write, or think as well as you believe you do, can you imagine it writing down all its attributes under the title "Why I Am Better Than a Dog"? If you'll pardon the pun, surely a horse would have more sense.

And the very fact that we seem so anxious to deny our basic animal natures, and that this denial leads to so much human conflict and unhappiness, should make us ask whether in many ways we aren't just a little bit denser than other animals; whether maybe we can learn more from our dog than it can ever learn from us.

In all my years of counseling, I've never had a dog as a client, not that some people wouldn't drag their dogs to therapists if dogs could make themselves neurotic. But I've never seen a dog have difficulty accepting itself as a dog—and, furthermore, just the kind of dog it is. I've never seen a German shepherd puppy trying to make itself up to look like a three-year-old greyhound. I have never heard of a dog evaluating itself poorly on its barking performance, or getting depressed because the dog down the street barks with more resonance than it does. A dog won't enroll in barking school and tear its hair out if it doesn't get an A in barking.

Of course, dogs are not the only unneurotic animals. I have

never known a cat to feel ashamed of itself because it failed to catch a mouse. The cat learns from each attempt, gets a little quicker, and moves on to the next attempt, without crying over missed mice. Antelopes, bears, ants and whales don't seem to be in much conflict about themselves, either. Parakeets and snakes don't seem to have identity crises.

In fact, human beings seem to be the only animals capable of making themselves neurotic by fighting the fact that they are animals in the first place—and it seems that it is always those who are regarded as the most "sophisticated" in our culture who are most anxious to divorce us from being animals by suggesting that we should be ashamed of our basic biological natures; that we should never admit we have anything in common with those beasts we see in zoos or depicted on "Wild Kingdom."

To me this is all nonsense. We are all animals, and if we need proof of that, we have only to observe that we all do some very basic animal things every single day. We hunt, we sleep, we copulate, we smell, we fight, we groom, we make nests, we defecate and urinate, we run, we lick, we suck, we look for shady places on sunny days. In fact, we do virtually everything that all animals do. To be sure, we do some things differently from other animals—but mainly we try very hard to pretend that we are really above all those groveling "animal" creatures with whom we share this earth.

Our conflicts with our animal natures can be seen in our dualistic attitudes toward animals. You will often hear people saying things like "He is so base, just like an animal," or "They are disgusting, they act like animals." Then the same people will use comparisons with animals to express the ultimate in human capability: quick as a cat, runs like a deer, strong as a bull, memory of an elephant, wise as an owl, eyes of an eagle, free as a bird.

I suggest that all of our conflicts with the "animal side" of our natures can be resolved if we just drop the first half of this dualistic attitude, stop short whenever we find ourselves denigrating our own natures as animals, placing all other animals below us (even lower than we place ourselves), and turning our backs on what we can really learn from other animals about the best ways to be ourselves.

Walt Whitman summed up my feelings in *Leaves of Grass:*

> I think I could turn and live with animals,
> they are so placid and self-contained. . . .

Not one is respectable or unhappy over
the whole earth.

As far as your "animal nature" is concerned, you have nothing to be ashamed about, but much to rejoice in. Everything you do to keep yourself alive and healthy is something that virtually all other animals do every day—and it is hard to deny that most animals are more in harmony with their basic natures than humans are.

The more you stop to observe and learn from animals, the healthier a philosophy of life you are likely to have. Samuel Butler said it this way: "*All the animals except man know that the principal business of life is to enjoy it.*" If you could just get that sentiment firmly etched on your consciousness, you would be a much happier person every single day for the rest of your life. If you stopped the worry, anger, fear, anxiety, planning, procrastination, comparisons and all the other *exclusively human* neuroses with which this society has burdened you, and instead adopted a more *enjoyable* approach toward your purpose in being here in the first place, choosing to *learn from the animals,* you would be much better off in every regard.

At times you may enjoy debating about the real essence of humanity, trying to determine the relative roles of heredity and environment as they shape individual people, comparing your reasoning versus your instinctive powers. But at other times you will be much better off by simply forgetting all those academic arguments and accepting yourself for what you are: an animal on this earth whose earthbound being rests in your body.

If you honestly assess your situation in this life, what else can you be on this earth but your body? It's a sure thing that you are nothing without your body (beyond what legacy you leave to future generations after you die), and that your very essence is in your biology, in that organism that is *you* wherever you go *here* and *now*. Even if your "real self" *were* your mind, your spirituality or your mental process, then that real self would still be pretty damned dependent on your "unreal self" (that is, your body) for survival, because when your body is unhealthy, deteriorating, dying, then, regardless of how healthy the rest of your "real self" may be, you are still on your way to being very dead.

We need not make the issue of your "basic reality" into a religious or metaphysical one. It is just plain common sense. For the period of time that you are here on this planet, you *are* your body and all that it encompasses.

To be sure, your body includes that magnificent, incomprehensible organ, *your brain*. As a human being, you have unfathomable reasoning capabilities and spiritual dimensions. But your real self is that wonderfully perfect, fully evolved organism called *your body*, which is your brain, your heart, your feet, your fingers and everything else.

Your body is not just a suitcase in which you carry your brain around. Rather, your brain is a nerve center, the cockpit from which that mysterious actor known as *you* pilots the body, on the basis of your basic needs as a human being, the data coming in from your senses, and your thoughts on where you want to fly today.

If you learn how to take care of your body, how to use all its glorious qualities, you will be a much more effective, productive and happy person while you live on this earth. After your body dies, who can say what is possible? Your spirit may in fact evolve further (this is my belief). You may transcend your animality (I believe this as well). Your total beingness may be quite different from anything we know about in this world.

But for your tenure here, with all of the rest of us, your real self is one with your own body, your constitution, your membership in a species; yes, one with your full animal self.

TRUST YOUR ANIMAL INSTINCTS

If you stop to consider your basic animal nature, you will recognize that every moment of every day your animal instincts are pushing or pulling you in one direction or another. The question for the NEZ person is: Can you harmonize your life with your animal instincts in such a way that you can attain "true peace" with those instincts, and go on to live a happy life with them—in other words, attain true No-Limit living?

Before we can answer this question, we must ask another: What *are* our instincts? And how are we to recognize them when we feel them?

Instincts are responses to environmental or external stimuli that are hereditary and unalterable, that do not involve reason. They are immediate responses of your body *to relieve bodily tension* created by those life situations that call for basic animal reactions.

In other words, if someone throws a punch at you, and you respond through your instincts, your arm will fly up to block it, or you will duck this way or that, without your having to think about it. If you see someone you find very attractive sexually, your body is again going to respond immediately.

To be sure, not all animal instincts are present in human beings. We do not possess the strong inborn circuitry that permits geese, without pilot training, to fly in perfect formation with other geese, or bees, without architectural degrees, to build perfect hives every time. But we do have very strong biological inclinations and urges that were present in humans long before they learned anything through formal training methods, and we are certainly capable of getting back in touch with those urges and biological hunches if we have a mind to. But we must remember that not only are our instincts weaker than those in other animals, but we are capable of suppressing them as other animals are not. (We can stand there and take the punch if that's what we've decided to do.) Further, our instincts are systematically suppressed by cultural pressures, by learning experiences and ultimately by our own defensiveness toward them.

Your leftover animal instincts, weak as they may be right now, are not bad, are nothing to be ashamed about. On the contrary, people who rely heavily on their instincts for survival, for problem-resolving and life expansion, who regard the deep urges within human beings not as "the sick part of us," as many in the field of mental health, particularly psychoanalysis, would have us believe, but as the potentially promising and virtually limitless parts of our natures—such people are generally coping with or even mastering their lives.

As I emphasized earlier in connection with the conscious/unconscious dichotomy, if you probe deeply into yourself, you are not going to encounter a wild, "uncivilized" beast without any culture. You are not fundamentally a veneer of a human being who, if left fully to explore your deepest animal instincts, will come upon a severely disturbed schizophrenic, rapist, killer or some unrestrainable nonhuman. In fact, I believe you will find just the opposite. Deep within you lies a survivor, an organism that can function effectively in practically any environment and is capable of the highest levels of achievement. Deep within you are natural attitudes, capabilities and potentials that will aid you in every operational area of your life. But to tap them you must let yourself trust that reservoir of animal instincts you have kept deeply guarded within you, and rely more on your natural human abilities than on all the cultural rules for behavior that you have learned.

I use the word "instinct" broadly throughout this book, to refer to all those very special qualities that permit you to behave in ways that are basic to your own survival without your having to think about your actions in advance, including what we call urges, drives, inclinations or human predispositions. Whatever they are called, they are there, we all have them, and what I am interested in is helping you to be able to call them up more effectively, to get back in touch with them for the resources for human strength, peace and growth that they really represent.

The nature of your instincts is such that you do not have to *do anything*—learn any new skills, acquire any new knowledge or get promoted to any new position—in order to get back in touch with them. All you have to do is stop blocking them out of your mind, stop arguing with them, overriding them and putting them down.

Learning to trust your instincts does not start with *trying* to do anything, in the sense of striving. If you are *trying* to get back in touch with your instincts, in essence you are putting needless pressure on yourself to do things that your body already knows how to do—run, play, copulate, breathe, bask in the sun. By the same token, when you try to force your body to do anything it doesn't want to do, such as sit still for ten hours at a stretch or smoke cigarettes, it will resist.

Your body is perfect! It knows how to be a body, how to do all the things that bodies are capable of doing. It knows how to walk, sweat, sleep, ejaculate, be hungry, cry. It is also a very good learner. You can teach it to swim, drive a car, write a letter, play a guitar, cut a diamond or climb a mountain. But while you are teaching it a new skill, it needs to be allowed to do it according to its own instincts, rather than to be rushed by artificial programs, pressured and castigated for not doing it exactly the way "the book" says it is supposed to go.

For instance, just about all skiing accidents that result in broken legs or arms or other serious injuries are the result of people overriding their instincts and attempting hills too steep for their bodies to handle without more practice and training. As they hurtle down these hills, the unprepared amateurs are getting all kinds of warning signals. Their instincts are telling them, "You're going too fast, the trail is too narrow and winding, your body doesn't know how to handle this, how to stop you now without falling down, but if you keep going you'll just keep picking up speed, and if you hit those trees going this fast you are going to be pretty busted up."

The NEZ person at this point just takes the most graceful fall he can, no matter how much snow he gets up his sleeves. When his more expert partners stop and ask what happened, he will say, "This turned out to be more hill than I'm prepared to handle, and the only way I could stop safely was to take a fall. I guess I'll take the skis off, trek over to the intermediate slope, and meet you at the bottom."

What he has done to keep his body from being injured has been to heed all the instincts that in that crucial split second were telling him, "Hit the dirt!"

On the other hand, those who repress their instincts are those who in that crucial split second say, "No, I don't want snow up my sleeves, the indignity of taking a fall in front of all these experts, the hassle of trekking over to another slope. . . ."

That split-second mistrusting of their instincts is what leads skiers to take falls at higher speeds than their bodies can handle, and to break bones—or at best to make it down the hill somehow, with their pride intact but their bodies saying, "God, that was a stupid thing to do. You could have got us killed!"

Trusting your instincts simply means letting it happen, permitting your body to do what it knows how to do. It means relaxing, easing up, forgetting about pressure and about judging your body's performance by anybody else's standards. It means *really trusting your body* to go ahead and perform all its wondrous instinctive miracles without your *trying too hard,* without letting the "performance evaluation" side of your mental processes take over. If you find yourself reprimanding your body for not doing something as well as you had demanded, you have adopted an attitude toward it which actually gets in the way of your functioning smoothly and naturally in virtually any situation that life may present to you.

Ralph Waldo Emerson had this to say about trusting your instincts: "All our progress is an unfolding like the vegetable bud. You have first an instinct, then an opinion, then a knowledge, as the plant has root, bud, and fruit. Trust the instinct to the end, though you can render no reason."

When it comes to the question of when or whether you are

going to trust your animal instincts, you have to ask yourself, "When can my instincts be wrong about what is best for me?"

To answer that question, we take examples from our own lives. My favorite example of genuine instinctive behavior will be familiar to anyone who has ever had children. It dates back to 1967, two months after our daughter Tracy was born. It was about three o'clock in the morning. I was sitting in bed studying for an exam I had to take the next day. My wife was sound asleep next to me, undisturbed by my rustling pages or moving blankets, or by the bright light shining in her eyes. Tracy's bedroom was downstairs at quite a distance from ours.

Tracy coughed. I barely heard that cough, and I was wide awake. But my wife awoke immediately from a comalike sleep at that tiny sound. She was surprised that I was still awake. "Could you check Tracy?" she asked. "I heard her coughing."

My wife was not displaying any superhuman talents. She was simply open to her basic maternal instincts, which had turned off all sounds and lights and images while she slept except for the cries or coughs of her daughter. So instinctively connected was the mother to the particular sounds of her daughter that she heard a tiny cough from a far-off section of the house. It led her to awaken briefly out of a sound sleep, analyze the situation ("Wayne is awake, he can take care of it"), ask a question, satisfying herself that the safety of her daughter was assured, and go peacefully back to sleep.

Just as mothers have very special links with their infants that no amount of reasoning can dismiss, and that can be broken only by the mothers getting stone drunk or the mental equivalent, *you know that you have a limitless store of infallible animal instincts within you.* They aren't learned, they aren't environmentally determined. They are born with you, and the mother cat who knows instantly when one of her kittens needs help is no different from the human mother who awakens to a faraway cough in the night.

When can your instincts be wrong about what is best for you and those you love?

Let us consider another set of case studies in instinctive behavior that is offered by the experiences of *survivors*—those who, as discussed in Chapter 1, survive physical trials in which others just give up and die.

In Chapter 1, the ability of the survivor to "retreat" into total present-moment living was stressed. By this time it should be evident that being able to *live now* is vital to, almost equivalent to, being able to trust your basic animal instincts, or to being a good animal.

The survivor is above all a person who really knows how to trust his basic animal instincts. When ordinary people are suddenly thrown into life-threating situations, case after case has shown that those who are able to abandon their judgments and rely totally on their instincts make it through the ordeals alive, while others do not.

Erich Maria Remarque, in one of the most brilliant novels of war ever written, *All Quiet on the Western Front,* describes the daily horror of life in the trenches in World War I. His protagonist, after surviving for years under the most awful circumstances, explains how he becomes afraid that his instinct for life may be deserting him: "We scatter and fling ourselves down on the ground, but at that moment I feel the instinctive alertness leave me which hitherto has always made me do unconsciously the right thing under fire." He recounts how injuries usually came to those who abandoned their instincts, and how the finest soldiers were those who relied totally on what their bodies told them to do in times of crisis.

An example even more applicable to you and me was provided by those people who survived the famous Andes plane crash. They were not specially trained or equipped to survive subzero temperatures. They were normal folks just like you and me, and the lesson from their experience was simple: those who relied on their instincts made it, while those who let their culturally inherited superstitions overrule their instincts did not. The real essence of that story was how the survivors went back to their instinctive basics in order to emerge alive. But what did the big press stories dwell on? The "cannibalism" to which the survivors had to revert: that "horrible animal behavior" they indulged in when their instincts told them, "Those other people who are already dead—their bodies are the only nourishment for us on this mountain; we must eat them."

Did they behave like animals? Certainly! But like *good animals.*

Whom else did those survivors hurt? Certainly not the dead comrades whose bodies they ate. Can you imagine one of those unlucky fatalities coming back from the dead and saying, "Don't eat that body—I may have left it, I may not need it anymore, but I want you to starve to death so it can rot where it lies or maybe be found and flown back to be buried in my home-town cemetery"?

The dead certainly did not care. In fact, they probably would have said, "Sure, eat it! I don't need it anymore."

To choose not to do that "horrible, cannibalistic thing" in those circumstances was to choose death. It was to let *what you thought* the reactions of people then in warm, comfortable homes many thousands of miles away would be to your situation *dictate what you should do*; to let the ordinary standards of society ("Well, we didn't eat Grandpa when he died last year") override your best animal instincts for survival, and kill you.

Taking examples of instinctive behavior like this and others you can cite from your own experience, you might come to the same conclusion I have as to when your animal instincts can be wrong about what is best for you or those you love. I think the answer is, *never, when you respect them, cultivate them and heed them "like a good animal."* Your instincts can only be "wrong," can only become a threat to you or anyone else, when you screw them up or frustrate them by repressing, denigrating or ignoring them. Then and only then are they likely to turn on you with a vengeance, visiting anxiety, fear, internal conflict, as a result of the bodily tension which *they* knew how to resolve in the most creative and constructive way possible but which you refused to let them resolve in their own way. Then and only then do the natural, dynamic tensions whose rise and fall, whose *interplay* makes up your life, stagnate, back up, and turn into *stress*, that destructive pressure-on-yourself that is indicative of a body-and-mind in panic or inertia.

The solution to this situation is obvious. You must trust your body to take care of you even when you doubt that it is possible for it to do so. You must never forget that this thing called your body is a wonder of wonders, and that if you try to deny its perfections and circumvent its instincts, you only talk yourself into being sick. Your inner biology will see you through virtually any circumstance with your safety and health intact, if only you will permit it to function. The essence of becoming a good animal is learning to trust your body, and all of its marvelous inborn instincts, to guide you through life with a maximum of pleasure and a minimum of pain and suffering.

Consider, then, how far we have gone away from our basic animal instincts concerning pain, for instance. Pain is a warning, and all animals but humans will inevitably do everything they can to avoid it. But along comes your cultural upbringing to tell you that not only are you supposed to expect a certain amount of unnecessary pain in your life, but under certain circumstances you are actually supposed to welcome the chance to suffer completely gratuitous pain and inflict it on others!

One of the most clear-cut and horrible examples of this kind of attitude can be seen in what has happened to the so-called sport of professional hockey.

Any child who has ever played hockey on a pond can tell you it is possible to have a great game without anybody getting hurt, except for the minor bumps and bruises that come from any contact sport. Anyone who watched the 1980 United States hockey team run away with the Olympic title knows that perhaps the greatest hockey games ever played did not require blood on the ice. Just the opposite: Olympic rules and the Olympic spirit simply do not allow for ridiculous fights that have nothing to do with the game.

But what has "professional" hockey become? Not a sport, but a mandatory series of brawls in which it is a "crummy game" unless somebody has his nose broken, somebody else has his head split open, and most of the time is spent with the players groveling on the ice punching viciously at one another, or even climbing up in the stands to punch hostile fans. Here the measure of a good hockey player is not so much his skill in scoring or defending against goals, but how downright vicious he can be in inflicting pain on others, and how "strong and silent" he can be when his own bones are fractured.

And what do people who are appalled by this say about these players? Naturally, "They are animals!"

Nonsense! There are no wild animals on earth that choose pain when they can avoid it, or that inflict more pain on other animals than is necessary to ensure their own survival. Predators kill as swiftly and cleanly as possible, and they do it instinctively. The tiger sinks its fangs into the neck of the antelope and, with one swift shake of the head, breaks the antelope's neck. It is over in an instant. Perhaps the domestic cat who catches a mouse will play with it longer than necessary, but that is a different story: her instincts have already been interfered with, confused; she no longer knows quite why she is doing this, anyway. But let her go hungry for a few days and see how she treats the next mouse she catches.

What does the professional hockey player who goes out onto the ice knowing that he is likely to suffer completely unnecessary pain think? He may thrill to the idea of building up his macho image before the crowds. Or perhaps he is just resigned to the idea that this is what the crowd expects, this is really what brings people in through the gates. Perhaps he even curses the crowds because they cheer more loudly when he gets into a fight than when he scores his most beautiful goals, and he calls the *crowds* the animals. But whatever he thinks, he is unlikely to recognize that every time he skates out onto the ice to participate in one of these travesties of sport he is violating the most basic of his animal instincts. He is unlikely to speculate that when he "sees red," loses his temper and begins punching and slashing at one of his fellow "professionals," his body is really rebelling against the violation of its instincts that made this whole inhuman show mandatory in the first place. He is not first of all fighting with anyone else; he is first of all engaged in a vicious battle with his own natural, animal instincts against suffering unnecessary pain himself or inflicting it on others.

A similar perversion of instincts occurs with regard to the natural animal inclination to seek pleasure. How many birds do you know that, when they've finished a busy few hours of nest-building, will tell themselves, "I can't stop now, I've got to build three more nests, or build this nest three times as big as the next sparrow's, to establish myself as the *really successful* sparrow on the block"?

The bird, of course, does not think of nest-building as onerous work it must drudge through in order to earn the luxuries of a bath, a song, a worm, a playful flight with her mate and friends. In sum, birds do not suffer from work/play dichotomies, and have no capacity to restrict their natural desires for pleasure in all things.

Only humans are able to inflict on themselves and others the strange idea that seeking pleasure for its own sake is bad, is hedonistic, and you shouldn't do it. Of course this goes against everything your body knows. But you listen to those fools out there, and find yourself unhappy.

Even a rosebush knows enough to grow upward and toward sunlight. Of all the varieties of roses, there never has been one that sent all its branches into the darkest, dankest corner available, or buried all its buds in the ground. The plant's instincts aren't perverted to say, "Sunlight is bad because it feels good. You should be ashamed of yourself for wanting that sunlight. I know it feels good and it helps you to grow and be healthy, but it is very selfish of you to keep going after the sunlight every single day."

Only humans are capable of telling themselves, "Wait until your old age, save for more sunlight in twenty years, but for now suffer in silence and stretch toward darkness, even if it kills you."

This is obviously absurd! Your instincts tell you to behave in healthy ways, and learning to listen to them can only help you be more effective in every single thing you do in your life. I mean every single thing!

NINE WAYS TO BE A GOOD ANIMAL

All of us human animals have basic needs, and instincts or natural drives that tell us how to fulfill these needs. If we listen to our bodies, we are perfectly capable of eating exactly what we need without consulting a nutritionist. We know how to sleep without going to sleeping school. We know how to find or make shelters, how to obtain oxygen by breathing, how to defecate, urinate, menstruate, have orgasms, reproduce ourselves. Our most basic needs and our instinctive ways of meeting them are nothing we could change if we wanted to; they are given to us as nature's way of ensuring the survival of our species, and our relation to them is simple: if we respect our animal needs and heed our animal instincts, we live. If not, we die, in one way or another.

Here are nine of our most basic human needs, and some suggestions on how you can *be a good animal* in responding to the instincts that will tell you how best to satisfy each of them.

Body Functions

Urination, defecation, menstruation, perspiration and other such basic body functions are obviously among the most natural and essential functions of human life. If you wake up one morning and realize you have not had a bowel movement in six weeks, it stands to reason that you are no longer alive and well on the planet Earth. You must have died and gone somewhere else. You may be sorry to learn this, if you rather liked your life as an animal, but the question is, are you relieved that you no longer have to do "those dirty animal things"? While you did inhabit your body, did you view these functions as somehow subhuman, as aspects of your life to be ashamed of, to be acknowledged as little as possible, even to be demeaned? Or did you see them for what they were, the evidence that you were still alive and well on earth, that your body was still happily running through its cycles of digestion and elimination, of reproductive capacity, of responding to heat or cold, and so on?

As absurd as it seems when you think about it, most of us have been conditioned to see defecation, for instance, not as that marvelous process by which our bodies, having broken our food down into what they can use to nourish us and what they can't, return the unusable portion to the biosphere—as "clean" a thing as we ever do—but as our "creating filth," and as evidence of how "dirty" we are!

Some people feel so squeamish about defecating, and see it as such a filthy part of their humanity, that their anxiety screws up their systems, creating nervous colitis—alternating sieges of constipation and diarrhea—or other difficulties in elimination, and they have to rely on laxatives and other medications to try to restore the natural cycles that their shame has destroyed. This of course is equivalent to "panic in the digestive tract."

In the same way, many women have come to view menstruation as a "curse," and to think of themselves as unclean during this time. They may cut themselves off from others unnecessarily, become defensive, withdraw to a corner in shame, waiting for it to be over, and by this means they may increase the intensity of their cramps or otherwise make their periods more miserable than they have to be.

Many people become so paranoid about perspiration and body odors that they worry about them constantly. They avoid activities that might make them sweat, and are forever spraying themselves with chemicals to stop them from perspiring naturally, or to make them smell like bowls of spices or pine trees.

Of course, these habits are heavily cultivated by the advertising industry, which will sell you any imaginable type of shame and guilt about your animal qualities so that they can sell you a product to get rid of those qualities. Since "natural" has become a big selling-word nowadays, the trick has become to convince people that they need at least a hundred chemicals to "get that natural look [smell, or whatever]," to "be their natural selves," and so on. And the pathetic thing is, it works! People accept that you just have to have a special scented disinfectant to turn the water in your toilet blue, a high-power exhaust fan in the bathroom that goes on automatically whenever you flush the toilet, three cans of aerosol air fresheners just in case, odor-eaters in your shoes, breath-freshening mints in your mouth, deodorant sprays in your vagina, and so on for every animal ill that Madison Avenue has created in order to destroy it with a product.

Surely you must recognize how all your judgments against the way your body functions work against you! A total acceptance of your perfect body and all it needs and wants to do is essential for you to be functional and effective in everything you do. Shame about your basic body functions inhibits you in *all* your functions. Guilt inhibits you. It keeps you from being happy.

To rid yourself of conflicts about your body functions, you must first recognize the extent to which your repugnance is the result of *learned evaluations*.

There is nothing natural about despising any part of your oganism! Why people have been taught to look at basic body functions in negative ways, and often have become dysfunctional in these very same body functions that are so necessary to their own survival, need not trouble you at this moment. The point to remember is that *you do not need to accept the attitude that anyone else, or society in general, wants you to take toward these functions!* If you do, you will be *choosing* to accept hand-me-down hangups.

Instead of taking other people's word on how unnatural your body functions are, you can choose to learn from other animals. They accept their total organisms and all they must do to survive as normal. The female cat may not know that her vagina is the cleanest part of her body, that her natural secretions and chemistry keep it to standards of sterility that put most hospital operating rooms to shame, but it has certainly never occurred to her to imagine that it is *dirty*. Nature keeps the human vagina in the same sterile condition, and yet many human females have come to the point of thinking of their vaginas as dirty. This in turn can lead to sexual problems: such women can view the sex act as loathsome because it involves revealing such vile parts of themselves. To make the parts less vile, they may saturate them with artificial chemicals, some of which may destroy the natural chemical balance and open the woman up to infections.

Take your cue from the cat, who never has to worry about any part of her body or its functions, and try the following exercises:

1. Make up your mind to recognize immediately all your attitudes of abhorrence toward your basic body functions, and convert them to attitudes of acceptance. Refuse to evaluate anything your

body does all by itself as negative, and don't communicate those kinds of judgments to others. You don't have to go into wild ecstasies about the perfections of nature every time you poop, but that would be far better than thinking of yourself as doing something disgusting.

2. For a few minutes of every day, while you are taking a shower or during a TV commercial break, take time out to become aware of your body and all it must do to survive and to *please you.*

How many times today have you put yourself down with critical judgments about your body and its basic functions? How much time have you spent learning to love your body and everything it does?

Have you ever thought to practice being more in touch with your body, for instance through Yoga or meditation?

When you become more knowledgeable about your body and how it works, when you appreciate more fully all that it miraculously does for you all by itself, you won't have any leftover feelings of aversion for your remarkable organism.

3. Remember that every negative attitude you have about your natural body functions is an attack on your basic animal instincts. Every time you catch yourself saying, "Ugh, I'm getting sweaty!" —stop. Do not run immediately for the towel, the shower or the antiperspirant. Take three seconds to think, "Some people would tell me that sweating is disgusting, but what is really happening here? The body's pores are opening to emit water that cools the skin as it evaporates. It is nature's skin-cooling system, and I have never yet had to have a refrigeration expert in to fix it. It works as designed every time."

After that you may still quite naturally crave the refreshment, cleansing and cooling of a shower, but you will not be running anxiously to the shower, shunning other people, thinking, "I've got to get this horrible sweat off me before anyone sees or smells me!"

4. The same kind of stop-and-think-for-three-seconds technique can be applied anytime you sit down on the toilet, change a sanitary napkin, anytime you have to blow your nose, cough, sneeze, vomit, change your sheets after a wet dream, or do anything else that comes under the heading of body functions.

To be a good animal, you always have to remember that individual people may do horrible things to themselves or others, but their basic body functions are never among the horrible things they do. On the contrary, if you accept your animal nature and appreciate your body's ability to keep you going and growing in every moment of your life, you can become *the No-Limit animal.*

Eating

How are your eating habits as compared with those of wild animals, who rely solely on their instincts to tell them what to eat and when?

The overwhelming chances are that your eating habits are far inferior to those of the average tuna fish.

As the tuna swims around in the ocean, how does it decide what to eat, and when?

The simple answer is, it doesn't decide at all, at least not in advance. The tuna just recognizes when it is hungry, looks at what's in the kitchen (or in its case the nearby ocean), eats what it wants at the time, and then goes on about its usual business, which may be something like swimming north for the summer.

Does the tuna fish ever get overweight? Or does its mother ever tell it, "Sweetheart, you're getting so skinny, I'm worried"? Does the tuna fish ever get vitamin deficiencies because it neglects its daily quota of this or that food?

It seems that somehow the tuna fish retains its perfect figure throughout life not by enrolling in expensive diet, exercise or other programs that promise to add years to its life, but simply by following its basic animal instincts as to what to eat and when, where to swim and how fast. Food intake is regulated strictly by its instincts as to what its tuna-fish body needs or wants now.

As far as eating is concerned, your body knows as well as the body of any tuna fish how to eat just the right things to keep your own normal weight and maintain your nutritional balance. It hates to be overfed, and it will tell you so in many different ways. If you overstuff yourself, your body will react with gas pains, indigestion, cramps, huffing and puffing when you walk up the stairs, with bloatedness and fat.

Your body pleads with you to let it eat just what it wants to be well nourished and be normal-weighted, but if you have a "fat mind" or a "skinny mind" you are going to let your thinking apparatus overrule your body's natural instincts toward health.

You may have overdosed your body with sugar despite its protests of tooth decay, pimples, greasy skin or layers of fat deposits. You may also have starved your body of needed vitamins, proteins, minerals and other nutrients by eating less wisely than the average animal. You may have spent a lifetime consuming products that have worked against your body, instead of letting your body tell you what it needs to keep you healthy. If you have done any of these things, and consequently have overfattened or starved your body or both (many overweight people are undernourished in vital protein, mineral, vitamin and other categories), I do not think you need to join any special diet program to correct your eating deficiencies. I think that if you just get back in touch with your eating instincts, your body will put you on the diet that is best for you. Of course you may be so far from your basic eating instincts now that you may need a trained nutritionist to tell you that you need so many carrots, leaves of spinach, potatoes, ounces of meat or pounds of salad to make it through the week, but as far as your eating habits are concerned—as with all your other self-destructive habits—*they are all in the past,* and if you'd like to become a healthy and good animal now in your eating habits, you might want to consider the following:

Eat only when you are hungry. Never eat by anyone else's timetable. Rid yourself of thoughts like "It's supper time, I guess I should eat." Consult your body. Is *it* hungry? Does it want to wait an hour, maybe take a bath first? *If you don't really feel like eating, then don't!* Listen to your body. It will never let you starve to death. Ask yourself, have you ever seen an overweight animal in nature?

Eat only until you are full—and no more, regardless of the circumstances. Rather than overloading your plate right away with food, try putting a little less food on your plate than you think you will eat. Eat that food and then consult your body for a few seconds. If it is satisfied, you won't need to go back for more.

Your body may prefer to eat fifteen times a day in small portions when you are hungry, rather than to overstuff itself a few times a day.

Be broad-minded about what foods you offer your body. Give it a wide range of healthy tastes to choose from. If it never tastes broccoli, carrots or other high-iron vegetables, it will not know what to get hungry for when it gets an iron deficiency. If you have the idea that you "just don't like" broccoli, carrots, liver or any other kind of nutritious food, it is probably because you were forced to eat those foods when your body didn't need them and when they did not *appetize* you.

"Tommy, eat your carrots!"

"But they make me gag!"

"Well, you have to eat them anyway. Your body needs them!"

"I *hate* carrots!"

This is the kind of situation that gives children nightmares about carrots and other "things that are good for you." Is it any wonder they turn to junk food for refuge?

But you as an adult know better. You know that if you are at a restaurant and your husband has ordered carrots, which you have hated and never tasted since you left home, and if he says, "Hey, these carrots in this sauce are great!" it will not kill you to say, "Can I have just a little taste?"

Those carrots are going to taste *completely different* from the ones that made you gag twenty years ago. You may go wild over them, or you may not care for them at all, but they will not hurt you, and at least you will get over your fear of carrots. At best, when your body needs the special qualities that carrots have, it will ask you, "Why don't you make up a recipe of those carrots for supper?"

Treat your children as you do yourself. Don't force them to eat when they don't want to, and don't make them swallow anything they have tasted and rejected. Just give them wide ranges of healthy foods to choose from. Stop making fusses about mealtimes, and let your children eat what their bodies tell them to. Forget the desserts, the processed-sugar rewards for their having eaten those horrible carrots. Stop filling the house with junk food and you'll soon see your children reaching for healthy foods, and eating regularly. When you reinforce noninstinctive, unhealthy eating habits, don't be surprised when your children don't want to eat healthy foods. When they are constantly tempted by food more healthy and appetizing than junk, they won't be consuming junk anymore.

Drinking

Think back to the hottest day of your childhood—that day when your throat was parched and you had to run another quarter of a mile in the blistering sun to get a drink. Maybe it was an old-fashioned hand pump at a nearby farmhouse. Your body tasted that well water before it got there. You couldn't wait as you and your friend worked the pump handle with all your might and heard the fresh well water gushing up out of the earth.

Your joy in drinking that water then, in savoring every particular mineral taste of the water from *that well* (or faucet, hose or fountain), was probably what you would call "the ultimate drinking experience" of your life. It was in response to your body's need, and because you responded to that need immediately you pleased your body *and* became immediately engrossed in savoring that water. You may never forget the taste of that water on that day.

Compare this with the way your body first reacted when you put alcohol into it. You probably got a violent reaction. You got dizzy, you got nauseous, perhaps you vomited. But you went ahead anyway, consuming substances that were poisonous to your body because others said it was "mature" or "sophisticated" behavior which somehow put you above "those animals who can't enjoy a drink."

I'm not saying you should become a teetotaler. There is even medical evidence that perhaps an occasional drink is good for you. What I am saying is, don't drink alcohol to be social. Don't automatically drink what everybody else is drinking when they are drinking it. Listen to your body.

The next time you drink anything, *ask yourself, Does my body really want this?* Will it receive this like well water on a hot day? Does it crave the vitamins in this drink? Why am I drinking this now? Would my body rather have something else?

Drink only when your body is thirsty, and drink only until your natural thirst is quenched. Be broad-minded in what you offer yourself to drink. If you are accustomed to drinking three cups of coffee, two sodas, one scotch and three beers every day, make it a point to try at least one different thing to drink every day: papaya juice, a dairy milk shake, apple cider—anything that represents a *change that your body may want from its present routine.* If your body craves any of those other drinks you've tried, indulge it! You may not be able to force yourself off the three-martini lunch by "sheer willpower," but if you give yourself permission to try different things and let your body decide which of them it wants and when, the three-martini lunch will just naturally become a thing of the past.

Breathing

What do you remember from your childhood about breathing? Probably there was a time when you suddenly realized that your lungs were working every single minute of every day and night, and were astounded by this miracle that kept you alive. Probably you remember one bright spring morning when you were on your way to school and the air was so crisp and clear and fragrant that it was ecstasy just to take a deep breath of it. You may remember times when you ran until you were out of breath, then stopped and thrilled to the steady rhythm of your lungs as they rapidly restored your oxygen balance.

Compare these simple animal joys with the excruciating reaction of your body when you first introduced it to tobacco. You coughed, your eyes watered, you got dizzy. Maybe you vomited. Did you force yourself to ignore those signals and retrain your body to accept tobacco? Are you now "addicted" to it? If so, I don't need to tell you what it is doing to your health or the health of those around you, or how important it is for you to stop. But I do want to emphasize the internal conflict you have created between yourself and your body. Your body *now no longer trusts you* and in some way is fighting back at you all the time.

Animals know better than this. Wave your cigarette under your cat's nose. In one motion she will flinch and grimace and close her eyes and shake her head and be off like a shot across the room, looking back at you resentfully as though you were the Marquis de Sade.

No animal will voluntarily inhale tobacco smoke or any other noxious fumes. In fact, the only smoking animals I know of are dogs that are forced to smoke—to provide experimental data on the dangers of smoking to humans! Not only do we override and abuse our own animal instincts, but we abuse other animals as well, which strikes me as a hideous practice and one which nobody ever would have thought of if humans hadn't violated their own animal instincts in the first place.

I am not here going to offer a short course in how to quit smoking. There are plenty of programs around, and if you need one, get into one. But whether you smoke or not, here are a couple of suggestions for getting back in touch with your breathing instincts:

Once or twice every day, stop for a moment and just savor the air. How does it taste? Can you smell the pines or the flowers or the freshly cut grass? Do your lungs *want* to take deep, relaxing, "inspiring" breaths? Or do you just smell fumes from automobile exhausts or a nearby factory? Do your lungs say, "I want as little of this as possible," and automatically throttle down? Simply by doing this, you will learn once more to appreciate and respect what your lungs do for you every moment of your life, all by themselves.

If you are about to light your first cigarette or your ten thousandth, remember the cat: do not block out the fact that your animal self is flinching, grimacing, springing up and taking off across the room. Ask yourself when you are going to let it come back.

Whether you exercise regularly or not, make it a point to do something every day that makes you breathe hard. Then sit back and notice the way your lungs automatically regulate your oxygen intake.

Yoga, meditation and other Eastern disciplines provide marvelous ways of getting back in touch with your breathing. If you really want to get "deeply into it," try them out.

As a summary to this whole section:

If you know that anything you eat, drink or inhale is unhealthy, stop using it, one day at a time. Simply refuse to put booze, drugs, tobacco, sugars or other questionable substances into your body today, for this one day, hour, minute or second, for as long as your animal body continues to reject them, which may well be forever. One day at a time: when you get into the instinctive habit of letting your body *become healthy,* you'll soon shed those bad habits, those excess pounds, those three martinis, those cigarettes. Never forget that being healthy is natural. It is instinctive. The only time you can make your animal self unhealthy is when you stop listening to your body and give in to cultural pressures.

Sleeping

You know how to sleep. Your body knows exactly how much rest it wants, and how to pack you off to dreamland in nothing flat, completely leaving the cares and troubles of the world behind while it repairs itself and refreshes your mind with peak efficiency.

Still, you may sleep too much, because you don't know how to fill all your waking hours, or have been overcome by dull routines, boredom or inertia.

Most people actually spend much more time sleeping or trying to sleep than they need to. The rigid eight-to-ten-hours-of-sleep routine is a sluggish habit your body doesn't even like. Your body reacts to too much sleep with grogginess, back pains, stiffness or even dizziness. If you insist on going to bed every night at eleven and getting up at eight every morning (except on weekends, when you may sleep until noon), you are forcing your body into an artificial routine that will actually interfere with your sleep.

Insomnia becomes a problem only when you don't trust your body. If you go to bed before your body wants to sleep, you will lie there stewing about all your troubles, or *trying* to go to sleep. Your body simply won't cooperate with your trying to sleep. When your body is ready, it will relax, quiet your mind, and you will be able to enjoy falling asleep without putting any pressure on yourself at all.

In addition to most of us who spend too much time getting low-quality or disturbed sleep, there are of course those who deny themselves enough sleep—the student who stays up for forty-eight hours studying for an exam, the trucker who just has to make it to Des Moines in the morning no matter how tired he is, the advertising executive who has to work around the clock to get the commercial done by deadline. Of course, all these people who try to deny that they as animals *simply must sleep* according to the needs of their bodies if they are to function at their optimal levels must rely on coffee, No-Doz, amphetamines or other artificial substances to suppress their sleep instincts. But nothing can suppress the effects of sleep starvation on your body: nervousness, irritability, churning guts, and a whole spectrum of psychosomatic effects which ultimately can lead to "crack up"—the student's mind breaks down and he scribbles gibberish on his exam, the trucker falls asleep and goes off the road, the advertising executive gets ulcers and nervous colitis, perhaps suffers a "nervous breakdown."

In fact, psychological research has demonstrated that you can drive animals insane very quickly by simply denying them sleep, by constantly interrupting their sleep patterns; by *inducing insomnia.*

By this time you may have gathered that *insomnia,* which is the prolonged and "abnormal" inability to obtain adequate sleep, has two faces. One is our tendency toward spending too much time trying to sleep, which is the result of inertia in our overall lives. It's a fact that busy people who are excited about and dedicated to life don't seem to "oversleep" the way people who have boring lives do. Oversleeping is insomnia in which your sleep is inadequate because it keeps your body in bed for more hours of the day than it wants to spend there. Maybe it would rather be running around in the park, but here it is stuck in bed. It rebels and disturbs what sleep you do get. It takes you twice the time you really need to get half the real rest.

The other side of the insomnia coin turns up when our anxiety about our life situations reaches the critical level (always on the edge of panic), and we deny ourselves the time to sleep. We take drugs, we press on. When we do sleep we awaken after four hours in a cold sweat of anxiety; we interrupt our sleep-and-dream patterns; ultimately, we crack up.

Your animal instincts, if you listen to them, will steer you unerringly between these two types of insomnia and toward the sleep patterns that are best for you at any time, in any situation. To get back in touch with those instincts and be a good animal in your sleeping habits, consider the following:

Trust your inner clock. You know you have a timepiece somewhere in your brain that is as accurate as any Swiss watch, and it comes with a lifetime guarantee. It works like this. You know you have to get up at a certain time to keep this appointment or catch that train. When you go to sleep, your body is aware of the importance of your not oversleeping, and it sets an alarm for you to awaken when you need to. Sure enough, five minutes before your alarm clock goes off, you wake up.

This isn't a coincidence. It happens every time. And yet you continue to set your alarm clock every night. Why? Because you are afraid you aren't allowing your body enough time to sleep, and maybe it will oversleep on you! The next step is that you forget about your inner clock and rely instead on the alarm clock to enforce your rigid sleeping habits. Pretty soon you find yourself saying, "I really felt like going to bed two hours ago. I'll have to set the alarm to make sure I don't miss the train."

The next time you catch yourself setting an alarm clock, stop. Consult your inner clock. If it knows you have to get up at 6 A.M., it will tell you exactly when to go to bed so that you can sleep in peace and awaken refreshed at precisely 6 A.M. You will feel sleepy not a moment too soon or a moment too late. If you appreciate the magnificent precision of this inner clock, you will go to bed exactly when it tells you, and you will sleep "like a baby."

Whenever you find yourself trying *to go to sleep—stop.* Are you tossing and turning about how tired you'll be tomorrow if you don't get to sleep right away, about how much trouble you are having in going to sleep?

Just relax for a second. If you stop trying so hard, you'll find insomnia disappearing. If you can't sleep, get up. Read a book, put your favorite record on the stereo, wash the dishes. Have enough confidence in your body to believe that even if you don't go to sleep for another two hours, you can still function effectively the next day—but also leave open the possibility that your body will want to go to sleep in another fifteen minutes.

The next time you feel tired—*stop.* Being tired has nothing in common with being naturally sleepy. "To tire" means to exhaust your physical strength and/or your patience, or to become completely bored.

Have you ever noticed how tired you get when you have something unpleasant to do? *Tiredness* basically comes from boredom, impatience and anxiety rather than from physical exhaustion. If you are mentally tired, insomnia is likely to be both a cause and a symptom. To cure it you may have to restructure your life along the lines I am suggesting in this book as a whole. But as far as learning to sleep according to your basic animal instincts is concerned, *learn to distinguish between when you are tired* (fatigued with worrying about things, usually what you have to do tomorrow or next year) *and when you are sleepy* (when your inner clock is ready to shut you down for a nap or for the night).

Remember: when you are *tired but not sleepy*, the solution is not to go to bed and try to escape your concerns by trying to sleep! Is the source of your insomnia the fact that you feel you have been procrastinating about what you have seen as unpleasant future tasks? Attack the tasks and get them done! Your tiredness will disappear as you pay the bills, wash the dishes, write those letters, or whatever it is that is keeping you awake. If at the same time you are prepared to stop writing a letter in the middle and take a nap whenever you get sleepy—whenever your body's inner clock signals you—you will be well on your way to reintegrating sleep into your nature as a good animal.

Healing

Your body has natural healing capacities that nobody in the field of medicine can pretend ultimately to understand. If you break a bone, it will heal itself. All the doctor does is make sure the pieces of bone are properly set back together so that the healing can pursue its natural course. If you cut yourself, your body will bleed, the blood will coagulate and congeal to form a scab, and under that scab your wound will disappear.

Watch a sick or injured animal. Notice how it will rest, drink water and stay away from too much exertion. Somehow it knows how to take care of itself. But you may not be as clever as those "inferior" beings. Perhaps when you know you are sick or injured, you push yourself beyond tolerable limits. You refuse to rest or eat properly, or you just can't allow your body the time it needs to recover from a major disease or injury.

You may even have talked yourself into being sick to begin with. Perhaps you have become a *hypochondriac*, focusing on your own imagined illnesses, worrying so much about your own physical health that you have made yourself sick.

Are you always telling everyone about this or that medical problem that you have now, and expecting things to get worse? Are you just waiting to catch that latest influenza bug that's going around? Are you constantly worried about your physical health *because you secretly know you have been abusing your body for a long time and wonder how long it can hold out?*

If you are constantly concerned about your health, or the capacity of your body to heal itself and continue your life, given just about any crisis it is confronted with short of a fatal injury or terminal disease, you are *thinking sick*—expecting your health problems to get worse, and ignoring the signals from your body that will allow you to heal whatever sicknesses or injuries you may have. If you want to trust your body to be healthy, forget about being a "sickly person," and listen to it whenever it tries to tell you what it needs to make itself "whole again." Try some of these suggestions:

The next time you are sick or injured, give your body credit for being able to heal. Rely on its instincts. Do not rely exclusively on doctors or drugs. Try to avoid becoming dependent on any chemicals just because you want to get through this healing process without interrupting your scheduled life. If you are sick or injured, you can trust your body to recover in its own sweet time, given the proper care *by you*—which may well include your seeking treatment by a doctor. If you do, go to a physician who is not exclusively drug-oriented, who believes in helping your body to help itself. By all means, seek out medical help when you need it—but don't fall in love with your medicine, or believe that drugs can cure your ailments. All of medicine relies on the ability of your body to heal itself, and any doctor worth his salt will tell you that the best thing you can do to help him help you is respect your own animal healing instincts.

Stop thinking sick! Forget about expectations that your health is only going to get worse. Start believing that you can avoid most of your illnesses if only you turn your attitude around! If you think only that you'll get sicker, if you constantly talk about your illness, you are setting yourself up to be your own victim. If you *think healthy*—that is, respect your body's needs for *healing* in certain situations and for *being healthy* for as much of its life as possible —you will experience fewer of the "normal human illnesses" such as headaches, colds, body aches, cramps or hypertension.

Remembering what I said in Chapter 1 about superhealth, do not confine your idea of your body's healing capacities to those that can restore you to normal health following injury or illness. Look also at what "healing" can do in *promoting superhealth.* Look not only at how the wound vanishes under the scab, but at how you can heal every deficiency you have caused in your body, from vitamin deficiencies to overweight or flabby muscle tone to tension-induced headaches or stomachaches by following your animal instincts—how you can become a No-Limit person with respect to your total physical and mental health by just asking your body, "Am I in conflict with you right now? Am I giving you the time and care you want to heal and ripen to your own perfection?"

Your body's miraculous ability to *heal itself* is the *master key* to your being a good animal. If you fully appreciate it, trust it, have confidence in it, this natural healing ability of yours will guide you in meeting all your animal needs, and lead you to a life full of more vitality than you have felt since you were a child.

Exercising and Playing

You know that you have instincts to exercise, that your body craves activity. It wants to be in top physical shape. You have inherited these instincts from your most "primitive" ancestors, from hunters who had to run to catch food or to avoid being eaten themselves, whose very lives depended on their strength and endurance and coordination. Our life styles and environments have changed radically over the past few thousand years, but our basic nature as animals has not: every human infant is born with the strong instinct to exercise, and from the time it first starts clenching and unclenching its fists, finding out how its fingers work and building up their strength, through the time it pushes itself up on its knees and starts to crawl, to the time when it is chasing madly around the house or the schoolyard, it follows these instincts unerringly. Exercise is play, play is exercise. Children run, climb, wrestle until they don't feel like it anymore. When they feel like it again, they do it again.

But then what happens? The child "grows up," gets a nine-to-five job, sits at a desk or repeats the same actions all day, and suddenly is too busy or too tired to exercise or play. The body deteriorates, gets out of shape. The adult has trouble catching his breath. He gets the idea that "playing" is for children, that "adult" exercises like thirty sit-ups every morning are boring. His muscles ache inexplicably, he gets headaches—all mere excuses to keep him from following his instincts to exercise.

The instincts never go away. The body sits there at the bar or in front of the TV getting angrier by the minute at its artificial enslavement.

Finally perhaps the adult's doctor says, "You have got to get some exercise," and puts him on a regimen. Perhaps he follows it, resenting it all the while. Perhaps he gives it up after a time. Or perhaps, at best, he recognizes how much better he feels, opens himself fully to his exercise-and-play instincts, and indulges his craving for more exercise in different forms until finally he is truly *in shape* again, and on his way to superhealth.

When you are physically fit, everything works better. You don't feel like overeating when you exercise regularly. You are constantly energized, rather than fatigued. Your digestive processes work more efficiently. Your heart is healthier. Your spleen, liver, lungs, arteries, all benefit, and so of course does your mind: your brain gets more oxygen, better circulation, and you are in harmony with your instincts, rather than in constant conflict with them. Exercise prolongs your life, it gives you the physical equipment to ward off diseases more readily, it provides you with stamina for fighting exhaustion. In fact, it is the essence of your survival, and that is precisely the function of instincts; to help the organism to survive in as healthy a fashion as possible.

When you *trust your body to choose its own exercise-play activities,* it will perform miracles. When you let it walk, run, swim, play golf or volley ball or tennis when it wants to, it will build itself into a model of strength, endurance, coordination and, yes, physical attractiveness, "in its own sweet time." If you just let it go at its own pace, trusting it to stop when it has had enough, and letting it have some exercise every day, then before long you will be in top physical condition. Your body will monitor itself. It will soon want to walk or run farther distances all by itself, increase the speed by itself, practice this shot, build up those muscles, get rid of that extra fat all by itself. Just follow it! It will take you where it is going without ever boring or injuring you.

On the other hand, if you go into a predetermined exercise regimen with your usual performance-oriented attitude, put stop-watches on yourself, decide beforehand how many pushups you "have to do" or how many miles you must run, forcing yourself to do better each succeeding day, before long you will be sick and tired of the regimen. It will be "work and not play" and almost as much of an imposition on your instincts as neglecting exercise and play entirely. You'll experience unnecessary pain and frustration. You are likely to exceed your body's capacities and injure yourself —which of course will keep you from exercising anymore for a while, and perhaps give you an excuse to say, "Exercising is more trouble than it's worth, it just gets you hurt."

If you want to get back in touch with your body's natural, instinctive approaches to being physically fit, try the following:

Set aside time for yourself to get some exercise every day, but do not decide beforehand what to do (unless you have to arrange it with someone else). Never exercise to the point of becoming so weary that you are turned off to it before you even get close to being in shape. Just run (or whatever) until you feel that you've had enough, and then go a little bit farther when your second wind catches up with you. If you resolve to do this same thing every day for two weeks, without trying to beat your previous records, *without any kind of timing pressure*, you'll be on your way.

When you run, for instance, remember, *nobody is chasing you!* Maybe your primitive ancestors had to run to avoid being eaten, but you don't. You are running strictly for pleasure, *as play.* You do not have to run in a straight line at a constant speed. Imagine that you are in a big open field, watching children chasing each other, maybe playing tag. They run here, they swerve there, they run somewhere else, they sit down on their haunches and rest. You can run like that if you want to!

Or imagine yourself just touring the countryside, moving at a fast trot, like an Indian scout, running down a road you don't know so well, through a section of town or a stretch of woods you've never seen, taking turns when something you want to see up close catches your eye, stopping when you want to rest and appreciate this piece of architecture or that old oak tree. You can run like that too if you so choose.

Look on your exercise as adventure and as play, not as a tiresome chore you have to complete to the satisfaction of any external authority. Remember, running is *not boring*. You wouldn't say that going for a walk or a swim is boring. You simply use boredom as an excuse to keep you from running in the beginning, because it is a painful process to overcome your years of inactivity.

Recognize that all your negative attitudes about exercise and play come from your need to defend your "normal" adult life of inactivity, and recognize how abnormal *that life is from your body's point of view.* Allow for the real truth, that *being in physical shape feels good,* that you will have more vigor and strength, more energy and less sickness when you let yourself become physically fit. Trust your body, go with it instead of against it, and give yourself enough time to go past the pains, aches and fatigue that are there because of your lifetime of ignoring your instincts.

When you are exercising, practice letting your mind wander to your body. Watch your legs going step after step. Tune in to the magnificence of your breathing, your heartbeat. Become joyful and at one with your body, and you will soon be marveling so much at what a fantastic organism you own that you won't have time for agonizing over your everyday worries or being bored.

You know that you have the power to think as you want to. Part of the rejuvenating purpose of exercise and play is to let your thoughts turn for a while from "the cares of the world" back to the basics of human existence. If you cannot stop worrying about other things when exercising or playing, you are still a slave to the beliefs or "normalities" of society, still letting someone other than yourself be in charge of your thinking center. But if you let your own animal instincts take charge, you will soon be enjoying superhealth and No-Limit living.

Sex

Look at all the people around you. Think of all the billions of people now on this planet. None of us would be here if nature hadn't made sex so good!

Everyone does it. Everyone instinctively knows how to do it.

No one has to go to school to learn it. It is natural, sensational, exciting, beautiful—unless we repress or put external restraints on our sexuality, unless we fall into the trap of pretending that we are "above" being sexual.

Human beings naturally love to copulate. We love to kiss, touch, feel, lick, caress. The only time we can stop our bodies from functioning in sexually perfect ways is when we start judging our sexual performance by "normal" social standards, worrying about it, creating needless conflicts with our instincts.

When you first enter a sexual relationship it may be perfect. If you are totally caught up in it, your bodies react normally because you let them. If you freely feel love and passion for each other, your bodies automatically do what they know how to do. They get moist without your prodding. They get sensations—goose bumps, heavy breathing, erections, plateaus and peaks and orgasms and ejaculations—all by themselves.

Your body is a perfect sexual instrument "in the beginning," because you are not interfering with it in any way. But after you have been in a relationship for some time, you may allow outside thoughts or worries to intrude. You may worry about the business deal you have to sew up tomorrow. You may worry that the children are listening, or think about the party next Friday, another person you'd rather be making love to, the fact that you haven't had an orgasm, or anything else, including the cracks in the ceiling.

When your mind is alienated from your body's sexual activities, your body stops behaving perfectly in sexual situations.

At worst you may feel ashamed of your sexuality, of your "private parts," to begin with. You may see sex as "dirty" (the same way you may have come to see urination, defecation, sweating, etc.). You may then become impotent, "sexually inactive." You will no longer get goose bumps, heavy breathing, orgasms. Instead you will get frustrated. You will get into the habit of shunning the very things your body craves: being touched and loved sexually. Of course, you will pay for this frustration of your sexual instincts, this "sexual inertia," in overall increases in tension, depression, perhaps in all kinds of psychosomatic illnesses.

If you find your sex life in this state of panic or inertia, there is only one thing to do. Wake up! Begin by accepting your sexuality like a good animal.

Have you ever seen an animal copulating with its mind on anything else? Of course not. Animals are right there, enjoying themselves *now*. They don't worry about the dog down the street being jealous. They don't worry about inflation or mortgage interest rates. They don't get headaches. They never feel that they are doing it out of obligation. They get totally lost in what they are doing. They don't even care if you watch. They are not ashamed of themselves. If you are ashamed of them, break them up and chase them away; they may resent it, but they will just run off somewhere else and do it.

We can all learn from the animals. We do not have to copulate in the streets; certainly there are more comfortable and romantic places. But if we cultivate in ourselves the same animal instincts they rely on to let them be completely engaged in The Act while they are doing it, we will get around a lot of interference that society has placed in the way of our natural human sexual responses.

Of course, humans seem *naturally* to want to linger more over sexual experiences than other animals, to make more of an art out of making love. Perhaps this is because humans are among the very few animals with a seeming instinct to "mate for life"—to see their children through their years of dependency and growth, to see each other through their old ages, together. So, along with the human's capacity to repress the natural sexuality as no other animal can comes the capacity to appreciate the wonder of sex as perhaps no other animal can: to *take it to the limit* of its unique potential for inspiration, intimacy and *meaning right now*.

Perhaps the high *Muga* art of making love is available above all to humans because of their high capacities to care for one another over long periods of time. Maybe that is why humans are capable of spending hours making contact, playing, going up, lingering on plateaus, hitting peaks, reaching orgasms together, drifting down again, and walking down out of the mountains hand-in-hand—because their instincts tell them that every sexual experience is an image of their whole life together, an affirmation of what they have been and will be to each other, a celebration of the fact that they as animals are *forever mated*.

Or perhaps people who have no desire to mate for life can just as easily satisfy their sexual instincts by simply responding to them when they are genuinely and freely aroused, when no moral or ethical considerations *they* can understand get in the way of their living-and-loving now.

But whether the incredible human capacity for making love/sex into an artwork of present-moment living comes from the human institution of marriage (meaning lifetime commitments to caring for each other) or simply from the innate human capacity for incredible care and sensitivity (*thoughtfulness*) in all situations, *No-Limit loving is available to any human being who seeks it through his or her own basic animal instincts.*

Whether you want to get back into your original erotic relationship with your mate of forty years or are twenty years old and still "playing the field," whether you are "straight" or "gay," upper, lower or middle class, you can gain peace of mind about your sexuality and cultivate your sexual experiences to the maximum of your potential as a human by keeping these thoughts in mind:

Get rid of your rigid ideas of when, where or how erotic encounters are supposed to happen. Stop trying to plan them. Realize that any place, any time, or any condition is all right if you are turned on to each other and agree this is a good time and place. If you have to ritualize your sex, making sure to do it only when the children are asleep, only at night or only in a certain room, you are limiting your free and spontaneous urges.

Do it in the car, the kitchen, anywhere you feel like it! If you demand absolute privacy, trust your instincts not to get your body ready until your body knows it has the privacy you want! Don't judge anything you feel like doing as bad as long as your instincts tell you that no one else is being hurt.

Any time you find yourself talking to yourself or others about your sexual prowess or exploits—stop. By constantly talking and bragging about sex, you are putting pressure on yourself to live up to your imaginary sexual status, or your sexual image as you are trying to project it to others, instead of satisfying your own internal sexual instincts according to your own best idea of what kind of animal you are.

If you keep any kind of mental scorecard of how many men or women you have "conquered"—get rid of it right now. Instead, look at your past love life as a series of paintings you have had a hand in. Keep the works you like in your memory; savor and cherish them. Learn from them. As for the discards—forget them now, period.

There is only one scorecard of your sexual life on this planet, and I think it is your own accounting of whether, when and how much you have enjoyed your animal sexuality.

Review your own taboos about sex. Are you hesitant to do a lot of touching of others? Touching is an instinct, nothing to be ashamed about. Do you hesitate to show sexual affection for your husband when the children are around? Are you afraid for them to see you kissing, touching, embracing him? How else are they going to learn?

What other taboos do you have?

A taboo is *an attitude you have adopted* that says that some areas of your possible experience have been forbidden to you just because some other, "higher" group of people (the high priests, medicine men or whoever) have decided that this ground is sacred —it is imbued with some supernatural, *evil* power that only they can lead you through if you want to enjoy its forbidden fruits.

If you let the advertising men, the psychiatrists or anyone else dictate to you what your own sexual taboos ("don't do's") are going to be, you will forget that in your own private sexual world there is no acceptable or correct thing to do. Anything that feels good, that both you and your lover enjoy, is perfect.

As you are entering any sexual encounter, make sure that you stop thinking *and* stop trying! Start just *doing!* If your mind is on nothing other than your pure sexual love for this person at this moment, you will find no limits to the heights of sexual experience you can attain together.

Just let your bodies be. Let them do what they know how to do.

Wandering, Traveling, Exploring

It may surprise you to see these needs grouped with the other eight I have listed. It may be obvious why the others, fundamental biological needs, are answered by instinctive behavior—but, you may be asking, is there really any basic human need to wander, travel, explore? Surely taking vacations, for instance, is pleasant, but isn't it more a luxury than a necessity, and do our *instincts* really tell us to do it?

Think again. Consider the entire history of the evolution of life on this planet. It is one long, unbroken story of living things on the move—venturing out into new environments, exploring them, adapting to them, moving out again. The bear went over the mountain to see what he could see; the milkweed seed blew five hundred miles before it dropped to earth and put down roots; Columbus set sail even though some thought he would sail off the edge of the earth.

There has seldom, if ever, been a culture of living things that simply drew a circle around its current habitat and said, "This is it, we don't care what's out there beyond this circle, we're going to stay here forever." And, if anything, homo sapiens is endowed with more natural curiosity and wanderlust than any other species.

You do know that we humans love to travel, to wander all over the map, to explore our environment, our planet, and even the planets beyond us. We are instinctive explorers! Exploration is natural and exciting. It makes for good and exciting and more fully alive animals.

Most everyone dreams at one time or another about "just taking off," about "hitting the road," for an indefinite period simply to travel; about backpacking through the mountains, or just driving away with no particular destination; about visiting new cities and countries, checking out new cultures; about simply wandering aimlessly, "to see what you can see."

Talk to children about exploring, and they immediately become fascinated. Tell them that you'd like to take them into the wilderness to see what is there, and their eyes get wide with excitement. Notice how if you take a child camping you can barely get the tent set up before he or she is wandering off to the edge of the site to check out the new turf, gazing up the trail, down the stream, off into the hills, full of wonder and itching to get going.

I have never met a person who wasn't at least secretly excited about the prospects of wandering, traveling, exploring. But unfortunately I have met a great many who squelch or deny their wandering instincts. At worst, you see adults who stick so rigidly to the routines of their home-and-work lives, driving the same way straight to and from every place they have to go, and always going to the same places, that they literally never see anything new or unfamiliar. If they take vacations (rather than just sticking around at home), they go to the same places year after year—places that are as much as possible "just like home." Needless to say, these types tend to be arch-authoritarians, among the dullest, least tolerant of people, and among the most depressed and miserable.

You hear it often from "grown children" in their twenties or thirties: "I don't know how my parents stand it. They never go anywhere! They have the money to take a nice vacation, but, you know, they have that Depression mentality: they think traveling is such a frivolous luxury, and there's no place like home, and all that. I'm afraid they're going to get crabbier and crabbier as they get older."

John Steinbeck put his finger on the way so many of us repress our wandering and traveling instincts, in *Travels With Charley,* his account of packing up and taking off with his dog to see what he could see of this country.

> And then I saw what I came to see so many times on the journey . . . A look of longing . . .
> "Lord, I wish I could go."
> "Don't you like it here?"
> "Sure it's all right, but I wish I could go."
> "You don't even know where I'm going."
> "I don't care, I'd like to go anywhere."

If you find that you have been fighting your nomadic instincts, perhaps because you have irrational fears of the unknown, perhaps because you equate *any* indulgence of them with irresponsibility, you are cutting off that one set of instincts for which all the others may have been made—your opportunity to move out into the world and discover it in all its limitless glory and mystery.

There are many ways in which you can wander, travel, explore. You can do it on foot or in a scuba-diving outfit, through a microscope or a telescope, a history book or a natural-history magazine. You can do it in your own town, in the jungles of Africa, on the surface of the moon. It can lead you to discover the lost city of Knossos or a great Hungarian restaurant in the next block. But however you do it, *do it!* If you have become accustomed to turning off that voice of intrigued curiosity when it tries to ask, "I wonder what's down that path, I've never been that way before," think about changing your attitudes and behaviors toward fulfilling this instinct in the following ways:

Take a few minutes of every day to fantasize about how you would wander, travel or explore if you could. If you find this hard to do because you are telling yourself that it is irresponsible to want to wander around on this planet, stop! Remind yourself that heeding these instincts is important for your own personal fulfillment, as vital as eating or sleeping. You need new places. You need to sniff around in new territory. If others want to label you "whacky" because you seem to be "straying off" all the time, that is their problem. Your solution is to take your exploring fantasies seriously. Which of them can you follow up on? Maybe you can't take a spaceship around the sun just yet, but you can go camping, or you can drive down a country lane until you run across a barn where they're pressing cider from a new crop of apples and selling it in jugs by the roadside. You can watch the presses in action, see the cider being made the old-fashioned way, smell the heavy scent of crushed apples and juice, talk with the farmer awhile about apples or cider or anything else.

You can make up your mind to take another ten minutes and drive a different way home from work, to take a vacation at a different place this year, someplace you'd like to explore.

Whatever your fantasies are, indulge them. Whenever you can. If you use your imagination, you will find that your fantasies of exploration and your possible experiences of it are literally endless.

Remember that exploration doesn't just mean traveling; it means being open to all kinds of variety in your life as a whole. No animal wants to do the same things day in and day out! New foods, new friends, new hobbies, athletic pursuits, music, art or whatever, all will indulge your basic animal instincts for wandering, traveling, exploring. Constantly changing environments in all areas of your life will not make you unstable! On the contrary, by giving you the variety and excitement you naturally crave, they will give you an even more well-rounded and full idea of what human life is about—fuller almost than you can imagine.

If you have seriously considered your attitude toward these nine of your most basic animal needs and the instincts that go with them, how you can *make them work for you,* by simply being open to them and letting your body be the animal that it wants to be—by ridding yourself of *trying too hard* and of all negative judgments about your body—you are now ready to let your body operate in the perfect ways that are natural to it in every life situation. When you learn the secret of respecting your body and trusting it to do the right things, then you will find yourself tuned in to one of the primary joys of being a No-Limit person, that of simply being a good animal.

5 / Be a Child Again

There was a time when meadow, grove, and stream,
The earth, and every common sight,
  To me did seem
 Apparelled in celestial light,
The glory and the freshness of a dream.
It is not now as it hath been of yore;—
 Turn whereso'er I may,
  By night or day,
The things which I have seen I now can see no more.

—WILLIAM WORDSWORTH,
Intimations of Immortality from Recollections of Early Childhood (1807)

The poet here speaks of a time all of us have known: those magic moments of childhood when life seemed purely good and wonderful, when we were totally fascinated by our worlds, completely engaged in the exploration of them, unmindful of the tragedies or hard work that might befall us tomorrow.

I share Wordsworth's enthusiasm for the way children live. I think children are, on the whole, better animals than most of the rest of us. I often look back with fondness and wonder at the most intense "living now" experiences of my own childhood. But in view of my own thoughts and life experiences, I know that the human adult does not have to idealize the child, or wish (hopelessly) that he could be a child again *in age,* in order to achieve a childlike state of existence—to gain a state of consciousness in which the earth and every common sight seems "apparelled in celestial light."

Few of us will pretend that we don't envy children in many things. You walk by a schoolyard, see and hear the children playing, and you feel how they are totally involved in what they are doing, how they scrap and run and laugh and banter back and forth, oblivious to future problems that are just as real to them as yours are to you. They have to go back to classes soon, they have tests to take, grades to make, friends they are concerned about, teachers who bug them, and many, many more difficulties to confront in their young lives. But somehow they have that magic ability to suspend their troubles and simply let loose; to give themselves permission to be free, and to become totally absorbed in their play. In sum, they have not yet had *futurizing* pounded into them so completely that they are unable to become totally involved in their present moments. They have not yet lost the knack of *living now*. Yet somehow you may suspect that you have lost that knack, and, just because you are an adult now, perhaps you believe that you can never get it back. So you walk past the schoolyard, perhaps mumbling to yourself, " 'When I was a child, I spoke like a child, I reasoned like a child; when I became a man, I gave up childish ways' "* or some other bit of wisdom that rationalizes your resignation to never having fun. You are jealous of the children, perhaps even resentful of them. But what do you do about it?

For many years I have been observing children and their parents in restaurants. It seems to be widely agreed among parents that restaurants are places where children should not be children, but rather "act grown up." Most likely the children have been sternly warned about "not being a child" before they've entered the restaurant. Because this is somewhat like telling a dog not to be a dog when you take it to the park, it never works, of course. Consequently, the parents cannot enjoy their meals because they feel they must spend so much of their time monitoring every aspect of their children's behavior. "Put your napkin back in your lap. Stop fidgeting! Don't laugh so loud. Stop bothering those people. Eat your spinach or you won't get any dessert. Cut one or two bites of meat, put down your knife, shift your fork to the other hand. How many times do I have to tell you?" By constantly reprimanding, the

* I Corinthians 11.

parents often unwittingly encourage the children to "get out of line" in order to get even more attention. In any case, one of several things eventually happens.

If the parents are extremely rigid and force the children to behave like robots, there comes a time when the children just can't take it anymore and "get out of line" once too often. This typically causes the parents to throw their napkins on the table and haul the kids out of the restaurant, perhaps with spankings, sometimes with everyone's dinner half eaten. As they make huge spectacles of themselves and what perfect little adults they demand their children be, you can often hear them tell the children, "That's the last time we're taking *you* to a restaurant!" To which you can almost hear the child thinking in reply, "Thank God for that. I *hate* restaurants!"

On the other hand, some parents are considerably less rigid in public eating places. After half a meal's "trying," when they are satisfied that the kids have eaten all they're going to and can't be restrained anymore, they may let the children wander around a little, go to the bathroom, whatever. The children are able to make new friends, explore the restaurant as much as they are allowed. They will talk to congenial customers, kibitz with affable waiters or waitresses, peek into the kitchen, and may even get the idea that restaurants can be pretty fascinating places, once you get past all the rules that go with them. Meanwhile, the parents sit back at the table drinking booze, smoking cigarettes, overeating and often engaging in superficial conversation, still keeping close eyes on their wandering kids to make sure they're not really bothering anybody, still thinking of their children's behavior as immature (and their own sophisticated), but resigned to the fact that you can't make kids act like adults *all* the time.

If the parents are much less rigid, they will certainly not let their children run so wild they disturb other people, but they are able to treat the restaurant much as they would a dinner party in their own dining room—a situation with which the children are already familiar. The eating rules do not suddenly become more strict; it is not suddenly necessary for the children to sit still when they would usually be allowed to leave the table. To such an attitude, children generally react calmly—or at least as calmly as they ever do at home, which is the most you can expect from them in public. They mind the best manners they know. If they wander off down the aisle, they sense quite clearly which adults are worth stopping for and which to make wide circles around. They find the adults who like and understand children and who are happy to stop eating or drinking for a moment to say, "Well, hello! Whom do we have here? Are you going to visit us for a bit?" This happens the same way it does in your home: the child-lovers end up taking some time with the children, and those who have little tolerance for children generally get left alone.

If the parents are of a NEZ mind, they will not be bothered by any authoritarian notions that children can be forced to act "grown up" in every situation and will recognize that if they themselves were to think otherwise they, not the children, would be the ones out of touch with reality. The NEZ parent knows that children do what they know best, namely, to be children, but that adults who expect children to be adults need to reexamine their own ideas so as to be adults and children again as well. The NEZ person recognizes that if he could learn from the child and adopt some of these childlike qualities for himself—learn to be exploratory, make new friends, shun dull conversations, avoid overeating and overconsumption of poisonous substances—perhaps he would find going out to eat a much more pleasant experience himself.

The No-Limit person is, quite simply, the NEZ person who follows up on those childlike instincts he has so admired in children. In restaurants you occasionally see parents who are totally engaged in both their meals and their children, distracted by nothing else. The children stay at the table and eat and banter back and forth with their parents or nearby receptive people just as they would at home. When the children are done eating and want to wander off, the parents may stroll behind them, making the acquaintance of the child-loving people who reach out to them. Maybe they run across a waitress who will end up taking them in for a quick look around the kitchen. Whatever they do, they are obviously contented to let their children be children, and happy to be able to be kids again themselves for a while.

On a recent trip to Denver I took a walk to the State Capitol building and noticed a group of parents with their children on a tour. While the tour guide was rattling off a lot of dull facts and statistics in his monotonous, canned speech, obviously packaged for adults, and even then without any sense of the historic dramas that must have gone on here or any spontaneity or excitement about the subject, most of the children gave up on him and took to rolling down a nearby grassy knoll and playing a game of tag. The adults, obviously all bored silly, continued through the ritual. Not one of them thought to break off and join the children.

The children have no trouble knowing how to have a good time, how to make even the worst of situations into fun. But the adult in us won't let us roll down a hill or play tag because—why?

Inside each of us is still a wonderful child who would love to roll over and over in the grass, not worrying about getting clothes dirty or about what everyone else will think.

You don't have to roll down a hill in your evening gown to get the message. In fact, James Kavanaugh, with his beautiful poem "Little Boy, I Miss You," may put you back in touch with your feelings for that child that still lives within you:

> Little boy, I miss you, with your sudden smile and
> Your ignorance of pain.
> You walked in life and devoured it—without anything
> But misty goals to keep you company.
> Your heart beat mightily when you chased frogs
> And captured one too big for a single hand.
> You wandered with friends in quiet woods and were
> Startled by a shuffling porcupine.
> Matches were a mystery that lighted fires and
> Chewed up leaves in savage hunger.
> There was no time for meaning—a marshmallow gave it
> On a sharpened stick,
> A jackknife in your pocket provided comfort when your
> Friends were gone,
> A flower in the woods hidden by an aging,
> Shriveled log,
> A dog who danced and licked at your fingers and
> Chewed your jeans,
> A game of football you didn't expect,
> A glass of cider, a cricket's cry.
>
> When did you lose your eyes and ears, when did taste
> Buds cease to tremble;
> Whence this sullenness, this mounting fear, this quarrel
> With life—demanding meaning?
> The maddening search is leisure's bonus—the
> Pain that forbids you be a boy!

If you find yourself missing that child inside you, perhaps you can begin to get back in touch with him by recognizing that he is not very far away at all. In fact, all that inhibits you is your own unwillingness to recognize and accept that child.

Notice how much fun it is to be around people who can act like children. These are usually the happiest, most fully functioning folks you know, who have not forgotten that it is possible to be happy and responsible at the same time, who know a little bit more than most people how to let the child within them go, who aren't afraid of what others think; people who can occasionally become totally immersed in fantasy, just as they did when they were children. They know that "real life" is not all work and no play, but the ability to grow through constantly combining growth with play as much as possible. They retain a kind of childlike innocence and curiosity about being alive, and consequently know how to be good adults while at the same time appreciating and cultivating the children within them. These are the people who I think are the best models for others to follow, or the adults I would call No-Limit people.

HOW DO YOU LIKE CHILDREN?

> Let the children come to me, and do not hinder them; for to such belongs the kingdom of heaven.
>
> —Matthew 19:14

> Any man who hates kids and small dogs can't be all bad.
>
> —W. C. FIELDS

How do you feel about children? *Any* children—your own, the children of others, or, most important, the child who always dwells within you? Do you like to be around children? Do they inspire you about the limitless possibilities of life? Or do you find yourself irritated, resentful, or even jealous around them?

We all know people who say they just don't like kids; who cannot put up with the constant exuberance, the boundless energy of kids. We all know about the old man who sits at his window all day just waiting to chase the neighborhood kids out of his back yard or off his lawn; the young couple whose house you don't dare take kids into because it is so meticulously and elaborately decorated, home owners so uptight about their furnishings that any normal child would be hard pressed to avoid breaking something valuable. You may have heard such people say, "The first thing any kid will do is pick out the most valuable thing around and destroy it," or "The problem with kids is that they don't have volume controls on them," or similar wisecracks emphasizing how superior they feel to children. The ultimate may have been coined by W. C. Fields, that great satirizer of child-haters, who, when he was asked, "How do you like children?" replied, "Parbroiled."

On the other hand, we all know people who love and understand children, who have an immediate rapport with them, who can enter into their world in an instant and make them comfortable, fascinated, at their best. We all know the old man who sits on his porch and waves at the kids on their way to school, who answers small knocks at his door, who takes the kids through his garden and tells them, "That's a tomato plant. You know what a tomato is? Well, those buds, in another month or so they're going to turn into tomatoes!" We all know the young couple who say, "Please, bring the kids! Really, it will take us ten minutes to put everything we care about out of reach, don't worry about that. We haven't seen Ginny in six months. How she must have grown!"

If you review your acquaintances and look into your own attitudes toward children, you will find that people who like children, who accept and enjoy them, who are "good with children," are also generally those who are most at peace with themselves—while those who don't like children are typically the sourpusses of the world, the chronic complainers, the pessimists about everything, generally the more unhappy people you know.

You will recall from Chapter 1 that I strongly reject the "sickness" model of the human psyche, which says it is somehow "natural" for people to be at least somewhat neurotic and unhappy, that instead I believe it is essentially natural for people to be happy, strong, healthy and creatively alive. I believe that we are all born in perfect mental health, and that we learn how to become unhappy and unsound only through cultural pressures, through actually coming to believe the nonsense that it is normal to be anxious, depressed and unhappy on a regular basis.

Assuming the premise that happiness is *instinctive,* if you will, it follows that all the miserable, neurotic, depressed and dysfunctional people we know (or have become) can find their way back to happiness *only* by looking at unspoiled children, who haven't yet had an opportunity to learn how to be unhappy and neurotic, and by learning how to become more childlike themselves. People who insist that they don't like children are displaying an erroneous zone that cuts them off from the realm of NEZ/No-Limit living before they even have a chance to recapture what it is like. They refuse to look at young children who *act naturally,* those who have yet to be spoiled or taught how to be unhappy, who do what seems right for themselves without consulting manuals or checking it out with experts, who rely solely on their own instincts and drives to make them *happy now*—in short, those who have not fallen under the influences of the neurotic models of "adulthood" they see in their families, in their schools, on television and virtually everywhere else in society.

Before those influences take over completely, a child is a wonder to behold, just naturally among the most fully evolved, highly functioning human beings around, personifying in many ways what it means to be a No-Limit person. Regardless of your own age or experience, I hope you understand that you have a child within you who is just waiting to escape from the prison you have built for it, and if you don't like it or other children, that's tough for you: that child is not going to go away. You cannot abort it. You cannot offer it up for adoption. You can neglect it, to be sure. You can refuse to respond when it cries, never let it outside to play, never answer any of its "naïve" questions ("Why is the sky blue? What's down that path?"). But if you do, you are going to be, and secretly feel, as guilty of child neglect as the parent who just leaves his or her two-year-old at home alone and goes out to a bar—forever.

If you don't like children—or, more properly, don't *love* them, even if you don't like everything they do—the chances are that you don't like genuinely happy and healthy adults either. They appear threatening to you because you are not that way yourself. It is easier to accept people when you know they are carrying around some weaknesses, when some unhappinesses or vulnerabilities are evident for you to gossip about, when you can exploit their frailties and enjoy feeling superior to them, than it is to accept fully functioning people, by whom you feel threatened because it is hard to find ways in which they are inferior to you. Not surprisingly, the usual way for "child neglecters" to gain feelings of superiority over childlike people is to label them "irresponsible," "immature," or even "too happy." The childlike qualities that make for healthy adults are essentially scorned out of jealousy by those who must resort to maturity comparisons to feel secure in themselves. The "silly" playfulness, the spontaneity, the ability to laugh and have fun, and other similar "childish" qualities of No-Limit adults represent something which all adults would like to have for themselves, but which few know how to obtain. Consequently, it becomes easier to mock and ridicule than to learn from children or childlike adults.

From here, you can see how the destructive cycles of child neglect perpetuate themselves in society. If being childlike is consistently met with scorn, it may seem easier to behave "maturely" all the time. The parent who constantly admonishes his or her child with sentences like "Why don't you act your age? When are you going to grow up? Stop being so immature!" is actively teaching that young person to abandon the child within himself. When those "grown-up" attitudes he has been forced to adopt turn out to come from and lead to the authoritarian attitudes and behaviors described in Chapter 2, the child becomes overly controlled, unaccepting, rigid, judgmental, humorless—*unnatural.* The child becomes contemptuous of his own innate desire to stay young and spontaneous. He begins to demand artificial maturity from his younger brothers and sisters and his playmates and schoolmates, and the cycle continues.

All my life people have been saying to me things like "Wayne, you've never grown up; you're just a little boy!" "Wayne, you are crazy; why don't you act your age? How can anyone with your education and experience be so silly? I can't believe you're going to play ball with the kids when we have all these *important* things to do!"

As long as I continue to hear "normal" people telling me I am too childish, I know I'm doing just fine. I enjoy being a child whenever I can. I love to be around children, any children, anytime. If you put me in a room full of adults, I am always looking for a child or an animal to be around. I love to tease, to play, to be "crazy," to explore, to do anything that is typical of little children. I don't try to analyze it. I can't even tell you why I like to be that way, except that it's instinctive, but I sure do know that it makes life a lot more fun for me. Quite simply, I find young children so honest and uncontrolled, so free from the need to impress anyone, so able to play freely without being cocky or trying to act superior, that they are like cool well water on a hot day. I also know that every one of my clients, readers or acquaintances whom I've helped to become more childlike feels better about himself and has more fulfillment in his life because of it, and that the whole process begins when you determine that you *really love* that child within you.

CHILDLIKE OR CHILDISH?

In the previous section I mentioned that the usual way to put down "childlike" adults *and* children is to label them "childish."

There is all the difference in the world between being *childish* and being *childlike,* even though these two words are sometimes used interchangeably. To be *childish* means to me either to be a child and act like one, which is perfectly all right, or to be an adult and act like a child in ways which indicate that your growth was somehow halted years ago, and that you have been stagnating ever since, which of course is not healthy for you or anyone else. What I am saying is that for adults "childish" and "childlike" are *opposites,* not synonyms, that in the two quotes at the beginning of this section, W. C. Fields was satirizing a *childish* attitude toward children (and most of all toward the child in yourself), and Jesus was displaying a genuinely mature and *childlike* attitude toward children. To be childlike means basically to be *innocent* of all the strange, authoritarian ideas of what adulthood ought to be, of what others have tried to thrust upon us; to be *trusting,* in the sense of not developing authoritarian paranoia that leads us to mistrust others with no good reason; and to be *ingenuous,* or straightforward, and "unsophisticated" in our dealings with others and in the way we view the world.

The central message here is that you should not think of yourself as having to give up being an adult in order to become more childlike. You do not have to become infantile or in the least irresponsible to become a child again in the sense I am talking about. The fully integrated person is capable of being an adult and a child at the same time. To accomplish this, you need to learn how to *regress voluntarily in a positive way* to your own childhood. The emphasis here is on "voluntarily," since people who regress to their childhoods without knowing why they are doing it, without mastery of their adult lives, are subject to being institutionalized in rubber rooms.

Voluntary, positive regression to a childlike state of being is not as difficult as it may sound. It just implies letting loose a bit, letting yourself be silly sometimes, laughing, making jokes, cultivating your own sense of humor about yourself, being nutty, knowing how to play. It means giving up the masks of adulthood for fun and enjoyment, not *always* having to be solemn, orderly, serious and dignified. It means remembering your original wide-eyed excitement and spontaneous appreciation of the world and everything and everyone in it, feeling awe and wonder at this magnificent universe in which we live, indulging your natural, childlike curiosity *to the limit,* and finding out there is no limit to what it will uncover. The French philosopher Maurice Merleau-Ponty applied a name to the essence of the childlike attitude I am talking about: he called it "wonder in the face of the world." He considered it that primitive state of mind that gives rise to the greatest, most human, and most truly mature and adult way of thinking. I consider it that, too, but first of all I consider childlike "wonder in the face of the world" just plain fun.

After having read this far, you may be saying to yourself, "Sure, I'd like to be a child again in the ways he's talking about, but it's got to be a lot easier to talk about than to do." You may find yourself defending your current "adult" position with thoughts like "Sure, I'd love to be a child again and have nothing to worry about. But I've got a family to feed, hundreds of responsibilities to consider, financial worries and many other problems. How can I justify taking time out to be a child, and still be a responsible adult? It's unrealistic."

Arguments like these mean you are not really interested in No-Limit living. When you argue with yourself like this, you argue *for* your problems, and the only things you will get from the effort are your problems. *One of the most responsible things you can do as an adult is become more of a child!* If you decide that you can and must be both child and adult at once—overcome the dichotomous, authoritarian thinking patterns that have artificially divorced the child from the adult in you, in favor of *holistic* thinking that recognizes the original child-and-adult at once—you can enjoy all your everyday tasks rather than be defeated by them. You can attack *all* of your problems more directly and with less seriousness, with a less somber attitude; and you can make all of your responsibilities more fun without ignoring any of them. Only if you choose to defend your position of always having to be "an adult," having to be forever grim and serious, will your problems always remain the same, and multiply.

If you find that you have become the obsessive adult who, in the name of being "grown up" and dignified, always gives up his or her ability to be childlike and fun-loving, that you have lost the ability to be creative and take social risks which will ultimately help you to become a better problem-solver, then you will find that you need to adopt a willingness to give up some of those artificial "adult" controls which have kept you from being a child again for all these years. To my mind, two of the *key controls* you must give up are *postponing your gratification* and *the destructive influences of your formal education.*

THE ABSURDITY OF POSTPONING YOUR GRATIFICATION

When beginning college students are introduced to "child psychology," one of the first things they are taught is that children have not yet learned to *postpone their gratifications,* whereas adults are people who have learned this invaluable skill. Professors the world around will tell you that the child who is offered one lollipop today or three lollipops tomorrow will take the one-lollipop-now option every time. Generations of elementary-psychology students have "graduated" to feel how superior they are to children because they have the good, adult sense to choose the three lollipops tomorrow (which, for many adults, literally means never enjoying a lollipop). This *childish* idea of "child psychology" has alienated countless millions of us from our own childlike selves.

During the years when I was a practicing therapist, I received countless referrals of "disturbed" or "disruptive" children from well-intentioned social workers, school counselors, psychologists and teachers. Inevitably the referral write-ups would follow the "postponing-gratification" formula for adult development: "Johnny must learn how to stop treating everything so frivolously, stop acting so impulsively. His basic problem is that he can't postpone his gratification. He does not seem to understand that he can't do everything he wants to exactly when he wants to. . . ."

Imagine sending a young child to a therapist to teach him how to rid himself of the very quality that distinguishes him from so many unhappy adults!

Predictably, the children who were referred to me for "gratification-postponement indoctrination" tended to be "behind" others in their age groups in conventional "maturity" categories, such as wearing makeup and padded bras and forgetting how to run. They tended to be the pranksters, the "class clowns," the ones who found it all but impossible to "sit still like adults" for hours at a stretch. But to me they were the most refreshing children in their age groups, often the most genuinely mature. Perhaps they weren't always paying attention when the teacher called on them. Perhaps they were making paper airplanes to throw across the room when the teacher turned her back, or they were passing notes to one another. But they were often also the best students, the "brightest" in their class, because when they did turn their attention to their schoolwork, they approached it not as an onerous task, to be procrastinated over and grumbled about the way they had heard adults grumbling about their jobs, but as a challenge to their "naïve" curiosity, which afforded them far greater concentration than their more "mature" counterparts could match. They were often the ones who made all the other kids mad because, sitting on the school steps with all kinds of chaos around them, they could do in the fifteen minutes before school started the same homework that had taken the others two painful hours at home. They were the ones who raced through tests, getting all the answers right, and then sat tapping their pencils or making paper airplanes while the others still slaved. For this they were labeled "show-offs," another way of saying "immature."

I always treated the "Johnnys" who arrived in my office as referrals from rigid adults who wanted me to help extinguish their sparks of life, with the greatest respect. I wanted to learn from them, and to help them become even more attuned to the idea of enjoying their lives now rather than postponing enjoyment forever. I would sometimes tell them that this "postponing gratification" business was a lot of nonsense, a smokescreen sent up by adults who planned out their entire lives in advance only to find they didn't know how to enjoy anything when their plans finally materialized. I tried to steer them away from the vicious cycles of extreme idealizing and planning that are bred by the "adult" syndromes of compulsive futurizing. At the same time, because many of them were in intense conflict about "not being able to control themselves," and genuinely suffering under the condemnation of their parents, peers, teachers and all other kinds of authority figures, I tried to help them find ways around "the system" that would preserve their childlike qualities while leaving them open to less condemnation. A typical example for a child in the fifth-to-eighth-grade range would be:

ME: Do you like to read?

JOHNNY: Some things. Adventure novels, frontier stories. There are a few authors that I really love . . .

ME: When you get bored in class, instead of throwing paper airplanes, why don't you just open up one of those books in your lap and read?

JOHNNY: I'd love to, but the teacher would never let me.

ME: Because it would be a bad example for the other kids, or because you wouldn't know what she was talking about when she called on you?

JOHNNY: I don't know. She just wouldn't let me.

A follow-up conversation with the teacher:

ME: There's nothing wrong with Johnny; he's just bored most of the time. Instead of trying to get him to postpone his gratification, why don't you just let him have some gratification? When the class doesn't interest him, let him read his favorite novel.

TEACHER: I can't do that. It would set a horrible example. Pretty soon all the other kids would be reading, too, instead of paying attention. I'd never be able to teach them anything. It would be making Johnny a special case, a privileged character.

ME: But Johnny was sent to me because he's already a special case. Your report says he's constantly disrupting the class, cracking jokes, shouting out answers to questions before you have time to call on anyone else. Do you think his reading quietly by himself would disrupt the class more than he does now?

TEACHER: It might. His desk is right up in the front of the room, because I have to keep an eye on him every minute, and the whole class would notice.

ME: So move his desk to the back of the room. Make a deal with him: he can read when he gets bored; you won't bother him if he won't bother you.

TEACHER: But when I call on him he won't know what I'm talking about. He'll never learn anything! My duty as a teacher—

ME: I notice Johnny got all A's and B's on his last report card.

And his only "poor grades" were in self-control and attitude toward school.

TEACHER: Yes, he's a very good student when he puts his mind to it, but he hasn't learned how to control himself.

ME: In fact, one of his problems is that he knows all the answers before you ask the questions, and doesn't have the patience to wait for other kids—so he just blurts the answers out.

TEACHER: That's right. He's a hopeless show-off.

ME: He's not a hopeless anything. Put him in the back of the room and let him read when he wants to, and don't call on him when you see he's reading! Or, if you do, be prepared to rephrase the question when he looks up and says, "What?" And, if I were you, I wouldn't worry about the other kids. *If they can all get A's and B's while reading novels under their desks for half the school day,* then more power to them.

TEACHER: But suppose Johnny's grades go down? His parents . . .

ME: Make it part of the deal that you'll let him read novels during class only if his grades stay up. Make this an experiment! I'm sure Johnny will have no problem with that. If anything, the idea that he can do what he wants during class time will be positive reinforcement for his academic growth. And reading the novels won't hurt his language skills, either. I'll talk to his parents about it, tell them I think we should try it for this next report-card period. What they care about is that Johnny gets less disruptive and gets good grades. I bet they'll agree this is worth a try.

When techniques like these were allowed a chance to succeed, they usually worked pretty well, but the key lay in getting authority figures to concede that "Johnny's problem" was not that he couldn't postpone his gratification; his problem was that he knew all too well, *instinctively,* that somebody was trying to addict him to a kind of futurizing thinking which he was bound to resist. If the parents, teachers and social workers were willing to give the experiment a try, nine times out of ten Johnny read more books in school than he had read at home, got better grades on his report card, disrupted the class far less and, most important, was a hell of a lot happier and more secure in his life. (While it is true that many *poor* students are also chastized for not "postponing their gratification," the logic is still the same. If they are permitted to experience school in a way which involves them *now*, their grades and behavior most often improve as well.)

Let's take a closer look at where Johnny's "gratification postponement problems" come from. The fact that many adults view children as incomplete human beings, as still *on their way* toward becoming genuine human (adult) persons, as "apprentice people," is central. This absurd kind of thinking leads children to think of themselves as incomplete, only *on their way* into "real life," not really there. Such thinking can become habitual. Thus when the child becomes an adult in age and finds he does not feel any more complete than he ever did, he looks further into his life, toward his thirties, as the time when he can finally enjoy life. When the thirties arrive, the "age of completeness" becomes the forties, and on and on it goes. Finally, you see elderly people wondering where their lives have gone, why they never got that magic feeling of completeness as people.

It is the whole story of striving-but-never-arriving all over again, and the only solution is to admit that we are *always* complete and whole human beings, whatever our ages or supposed stages of maturity; *always* to think of ourselves as *having arrived*, and of our present moments as time to be lived and enjoyed to the fullest. Only if you free the child in you will you be able to beat the postponing-gratification game.

Virginia Woolf once wrote: "What could be more charming than a boy before he has begun to cultivate his intellect? He is beautiful to look at; he gives himself no airs; he understands the meaning of art and literature instinctively; he goes about enjoying his life and making other people enjoy theirs."

The adult in you, when it excludes the child's abilities to enjoy the present, is your *enemy*. Remember, those children you admire so much for their ability to enjoy life are not foreign creatures to you. You have one of those children inside you. The question is whether you are going to let him out or be threatened so much by him that you insist on trying to change the real children around you to be more like you, to postpone their gratification, to feel as incomplete as you may feel. In fact, becoming a No-Limit person means precisely what it says—which is that you rid yourself of the self-imposed limits which are inherent in postponing your gratification. Living fully now means No-Limits, while endlessly postponing your enjoyment is a severe limitation to your fullest humanity.

Ironically, a number of the teachers who sent children to me to be taught how to postpone gratification at the same time were "teaching" Robert Frost:

> Oh, give us pleasure in the flowers today;
> And give us not to think so far away
> As the uncertain harvest; keep us here
> All simply in the springing of the year.*

OVERCOMING YOUR MIS-EDUCATION

Your formal education was hardly designed to help you become a No-Limit person. In fact, unless you were very lucky, you were carefully trained to be just the opposite, an authoritarian. The emphasis should have been on real intellectual development, your ability to ask questions that fascinated you and find or deduce your best answers. But the methods you were subjected to were often the least effective ways to help anyone learn anything. You were drilled to memorize lists of facts so that you could spill them back for future tests, even though you could not see what meaning these facts had for your life or anyone else's. The result was that, as soon as the examinations were over, you forgot the facts and moved on to new ones which were equally meaningless. (Do you think you could pass an algebra test today? A world history examination?) Your education did not follow the lines of your natural, childlike curiosity. If it had—if you had been introduced to the history of the American Revolution or the circulatory system of the frog and then left to ask *your own questions* about them, for instance—you would *naturally* remember what you'd learned to this day.

But the sad truth is most likely that most of your formal education was spent learning how to please teachers and administrators. You were seldom if ever encouraged to think for yourself, to write creatively, to draw outside the lines, to attack problems from your own unique perspective. You were put into a program, and you were taught that, above all, you were to conform to the rules of that program—or be "thrown out" as a hopeless troublemaker. You were taught that conformity yielded more long-term gratification than creativity, that pleasing the teacher was the surest way to

* "A Prayer in Spring," from *Country Things and Other Things*.

success in your school and your life. You were chided for thinking independently, for being different, or for challenging any authority. You learned how to adjust to the system rather than create your own system or ask why the system couldn't shift just a little so that it could better meet the needs of individuals. You were carefully weaned on being a *good* child. You were weaned away from your natural, spontaneous "wonder in the face of the world" by worries about failure to get into college ten years from now, and other erroneous-zone behavior. You learned that getting good grades was more important than acquiring genuine understanding of a learning principle. Your quests for approval by passing examinations, getting certain grades on transcripts, winning teachers' approbation and other externals probably became the "moving forces" of your student life. But, because the hollowness of all this caused the child inside you to resist your formal education all the more strongly, because somehow you knew that many of your teachers were phony, really didn't like you or accept you as you were, or feel committed to *their* work, you found sitting in a classroom and being treated "just like everyone else" a degrading experience.

As a child, you knew that once you had mastered long division it was a waste of your time to sit and wait until the teacher was ready to move on to something else for the entire class. You were aware that some things came easier to you than others, and that expecting everyone to be at the same place in mastering subject material just because all were exposed to the same lectures was ludicrous. You were "ahead" of your classmates in some subjects, "behind" in others, but you were always treated as "a part of the class," one of those "apprentice persons" whom the teachers thought of as all the same rather than as a person with your own special interests, instincts, potentials, desires. You knew that the artificial competition the educational system had forced on you and your classmates was just a huge indignity that teachers wielded like a whip to keep you in line. You *all* knew how terrible you felt when your grades were posted or read aloud and some got C-minus in a subject just because they weren't as ready, or as interested, as others were in that subject at that time. You may have wondered why, despite the fact that the C-minus student would master the material in a few months because everyone does not learn at the same speed, that same C-minus would stay with him *forever*.

You resented those rigid comparisons and competitions of your formal education. You knew that you and all your friends were individuals, and that any sensible person or system would treat you that way, rather than as soldiers to be regimented into uniform authoritarian ranks, with no individuality allowed to any of you. But in all likelihood you plodded along because "the system" seemed to be the only way. As a result, you may well have learned to hate "education," and may have become an authoritarian anti-intellectual.

The child in you knew better then, and it still knows better today. Overcoming the destructive influences of your formal education means reawakening your natural, childlike curiosity about things and following it wherever it leads. It means recognizing that you do not have to compete for grades with others anymore, that you are perfectly free to find out more about what your childlike curiosity wants to know about—whether it is the history of the American or Russian Revolution, or how to fix your car—without anyone (especially the authoritarian adult in you) standing over your shoulder and regulating your learning or growth activities.

If you want to transcend your formal education and become a No-Limit person, you will do well to remember those few excellent, highly motivated teachers you had in school who really cared about you and wanted to make a difference in your life, who were dedicated to satisfying your natural, childlike curiosity as it developed. Forget that those teachers were but a small minority, and that they along with you were labeled system disrupters when they tried to respond to individual students' needs in their teaching and their classroom "routines"! Just remember the way those special teachers helped *you,* and that *you are now perfectly free* to pursue *their* ideals and examples of what education can be if you want to!

As a school teacher and administrator for many years, I came into contact with thousands of educators of every description. Without exception, those teachers who were able to reach just about all of their students and cultivate their natural intellectual curiosity, who were most professional about their duties and who were popular with everyone in the school were those who rated lowest on all authoritarian traits. Especially, they tended to do the least *dichotomizing* of their classes along "conventional" lines. I never heard one of these highly functioning teachers categorize students as good or bad, bright or stupid, mature or immature, troublemakers or well adjusted, underachievers or overachievers, or any other classification devised for the convenience of teachers. These superior educators were unique, and admittedly very rare in my own experience, but they were there, and every student who has spent some time in our country's educational system must have had at least a few teachers who were more or less like them. They were the ones who were never viewed as favoring any one group of students over another. Rather these "No-Limit" teachers seemed to be available to all students at all levels of their development. The minority-group students and those who were continually afoul of the system saw these teachers as friendly to their cause. The attendance-problem students saw them as their advocates. So did the straight-A students. The student council members would chat with these teachers after school, and so would the "tough kids." In other words, these outstanding teachers seemed somehow to have the childlike quality of being open to everyone. Consequently all students, regardless of their interests, affiliations or cliques, would flock to these teachers and view them as their special friends.

Their childlike quality of being open to different viewpoints, being tolerant of the differences of others, adults or children, and refusing to lump people into categories, of course meant that these exceptional teachers had transcended dichotomous, authoritarian thinking and basically viewed the world in a holistic, open fashion.

You may have gone through a "standard" education system without particular trouble, but even if you were very "successful" I bet that you never really believed in it; that you were often bored and afraid of being a "troublemaker," unable to be heard, and abused day in and day out by a system that rewarded conformity and punished individuality. Still, out of your formal school experience you must have acquired *some* idea of the joy of learning and thinking for yourself, probably from your few No-Limit teachers. From them you must have learned, if you think about it, that becoming a No-Limit person involves *overcoming* much of your formal education and looking honestly at *what really matters in your life.* It means accepting that schools simply are not geared to teaching children how to be as fully human as they can possibly become. It means recognizing that in the ideal school system there would be no grades, transcripts, credits and cheating! How could you possibly cheat when you are learning for yourself instead of competing with others? How could you cheat on becoming as educated and healthy as it is possible for you to be? Nobody who could help you learn, nothing you might do to make yourself a better-educated person, could make you a "cheater." The grades, exams, credits and other external measures of "success" would have no place in a humanistically oriented system in which people were concerned to learn how to become happy, creatively alive and fully functioning in their lives. The course work in an ideal school would be designed to teach people how to think independently, how not to fear failure, how to become capable of doing anything rather than being rigidly specialized into doing one thing or another, how to be neurosis-free; in short, how to be a happy human being. Ideal schools would see the total education of the child as their mission. Their teachers would encourage children to become all that they are capable of becoming, rather than force them to be restricted, conforming or "adult" in nature.

Schools need not be permissive places with complete laissez-faire attitudes or atmospheres, but they must become concerned and caring places full of teachers who understand that teaching people to love themselves, to feel positive about their natural curiosities and in control of their own lives, ought to be given at least as much attention as geometry, grammar or anything else that tradition places exclusively on the intellectual or *academic* side of education.

"But," you may be saying to yourself, "there is no ideal school like the one he's talking about anywhere in the world, and probably never will be. Those No-Limit teachers—I remember some like that, but it was a long time ago."

Stop. That ideal school I am talking about is in your own head! You are *now* fully human. You have *arrived* as a whole person in this world, *whoever* you are and whatever age you are! Whether you are still in any kind of school or not, you can start to transcend the destructive efforts of your formal education *today*, by recognizing that it won't help you one bit now to sit around resenting what "the system" did to you when you were a child. What you *can* do now is resolve not to let yourself continue to be abused by those early negative experiences, overcome the cumulative effects beginning *today*, and recall those few No-Limit teachers and the kind of education *they* stood for. Remind yourself that there is still a child within you who *did survive* the hardships, abusive tactics and artificial restrictions imposed on you by that system. Because that surviving child is now aware of the pitfalls as well as the benefits of formal education, it will be stronger than ever in resisting them and in insisting that it *wants to learn*, but only along the lines of its own natural curiosity, and in its own sweet time. The child knows you can't change the past; you can only resolve not to continue to abuse yourself in the way you were once trained to. If you work at being that child again, only this time letting it operate from strength rather than weakness, it will teach you how to manage your emotions, to think for yourself, to ask and answer questions that are important or fascinating to *you,* so that you can live effectively in any situation, think and feel positively in your life. You will then be able to spend the rest of your life being truly and happily educated.

THE FOUNTAIN OF YOUTH LIES WITHIN

Mythology has always had it that there is somewhere on earth a magic fountain, spring or pool whose waters will restore your youth, keep you young forever. Common sense, however, has it that "you are as young as you think," and that the eighty-year-old grandmother who has cultivated and knows how to enjoy her childlike qualities can essentially be much younger, more vital and more alive than the twenty-five-year-old humorlessly battling his way through law school toward the top of his class, on his way through possible nervous breakdowns and ulcers to a partnership in a major firm in ten or fifteen years, and perhaps to a profound hatred of life.

The real meaning of the fountain-of-youth myths may be to point out the superstitious absurdity of searching for your lost youth under rocks, on "the other side of the mountain," in a drink of water, in a cosmetic jar, in a corporate board room—in *anything* external to yourself. It may be to remind you of your common sense, which says that you have a boundless fountain of youth within you, which you can tap anytime, all the time, by simply letting yourself be a child again.

SEVEN PATHS TO THE FOUNTAIN

An old religious song says there are "twelve gates to the city." There are many more paths to the fountain of youth than that; in fact, there are as many as the child within you can imagine exploring in a lifetime. But here are seven you might want to explore to get you started:

Laugh!

The child in you, like all children, loves to laugh, to be around people who can laugh at themselves and life. Children instinctively know that the more laughter we have in our lives, the better. They will go out of their way to linger with anyone who makes them laugh, who can go along with their jokes. They will laugh hysterically at things the serious, plodding, always-grim adult says "just aren't funny"; those silly "immature" grade-school jokes, even people who put lampshades on their heads. Sometimes they will laugh about "nothing at all," just out of their sheer joy in life, or because their instincts have told them, "Time to laugh now!"

Remember the teachers whose classes you really enjoyed and learned from the most? Weren't they the ones who had a lively sense of humor, whose classrooms had a less grim atmosphere than the rest of the school? Weren't they the ones who *kidded with you,* told you funny stories about history or the way the computer at the bank went crazy and sent all the depositors million-dollar checks? Weren't these the same teachers who had the ability to help you *learn for yourself?*

We all naturally seek out humor and laughter, because it is the one "natural cure" always available to us for eradicating depression, inertia or even panic. You simply cannot be depressed, anxious or nervous while you are laughing. A lively sense of humor and a hearty laugh a few dozen times a day are the best guarantee against neurosis and unhappiness. Furthermore, laughs are free, don't require a prescription from your doctor, and you don't have to go to the drugstore for them.

We all know people about whom we think, "His main trouble is that he takes himself so seriously." These are the most rigid, "uptight" people around. They cannot laugh at their own mistakes and, in fact, can seldom admit them, because they are so anxious about their personal futures they fear the slightest deviations from their preset life programs and despise exceptions to their fixed systems of values. The only group about whom true generalizations can be made, they typically come out at "the top of the class" in all authoritarian-personality traits, and are very frustrating to others because they may be very good at what they do for a living and have many endearing qualities. What is frustrating is that others see how much happier and more fun to be around they could be if only they would "lighten up" on themselves and the rest of the world. "It would make all the difference in the world," people say, "if only she could somehow get a sense of humor, some perspective on life."

Consider the people you know who do have a sense of humor and a perspective on life, and how happy they are as a result. Then ask yourself how you fit the pattern, and how happy *you* are. How many times today have you laughed, and at what? Can you recall the things that really struck you as funny this week, or last week? Have you laughed at "silly" mistakes of your own lately? Or have you just chuckled at how silly, immature or inferior others are—at snide gossip putting others down? Is your life one grim grind, or is it full of all the laughter you could ever wish? How many people have *you* made laugh lately?

If you find you are running low on laughter in your life and would like to get your childlike sense of humor back, you might try the following strategies:

Make someone else laugh today, tomorrow, every day. You will find that this does not involve *trying to be funny,* which is just another form of "striving"; it involves only relaxing for a second and seeing what "strikes you as funny" about whatever it is you're talking or thinking about, or letting yourself recall something that has struck you funny recently and sharing it with someone else. If you have always been serious, just give up your sober attitude once a day and see how much better life feels. Give yourself permission to laugh *once every hour* for a full day, by yourself or with others, and you'll soon discover that being a *creator of laughter,* of genuine humor, is a primary path to No-Limit living.

Find a child or group of children—the younger the better—to be with at least twice a week, with the idea of doing nothing but enjoying their company. Forget about monitoring their behavior, correcting them, educating them in the ways of "adult" behavior or telling them anything. Simply *be with them* for at least half an hour a few times a week. If you come to young children with an open, No-Limit mind-set, laughter and fun will soon become "the rule" of your life, rather than the rare exception in it. You will find it is very easy to make the children laugh, and for them to make you laugh. Whenever you leave them, ask yourself, "What was the real high point of my day: getting all that work done or laughing with those children?"

Every once in a while, make a point of recalling experiences in your childhood that were miserable then but are worth a laugh now. Laugh them off!

A friend of mine told me the following story:

"When I was in the eighth grade, I got kicked out of school for a few days for throwing peas in the cafeteria. I had been trying for a scholarship to a private high school I desperately wanted to go to, so I walked home in total depression and desperation, thinking, 'Well, I've blown it now. They'll never give a scholarship to an infant like me who throws peas in the cafeteria, even if Ricky threw peas at me first. Mom and Dad are really going to be crushed.' I felt as though my life was at a total dead end. I had just wrecked the whole vehicle, and that was it. Totaled.

"And then this funny little voice in me said, 'Who are you trying to kid? You're only thirteen years old, and you think getting suspended from school is the end of the world? And for throwing peas in the cafeteria, yet? Sure as hell, in another ten years you're going to have a good laugh over this—it's all just so ridiculous!' And I laughed right then and there, stopped crying inside and started laughing out loud, because I would have covered that whole school with peas if I could.

"Well, five years later I was a freshman at Yale, and one fine spring evening I was eating a peaceful supper in the cafeteria when suddenly the peas and potatoes and hamburgers became very thick in the air, and somebody yelled, 'Food fight,' and in five minutes more vegetables became airborne in that dining hall than I could ever have thrown in a hundred years of grade school.

"Now, let me ask you, did I laugh then? Behavior that got me thrown out of grade school couldn't get me thrown out of Yale! It was just accepted that once a year, usually in the spring, everybody got to indulge in a food fight. It was *an accepted ritual!* Students got to bury their school in peas if they wanted to—although they had to dig it out afterward, wipe the floors and so on, because nobody wanted to wade through a swamp of stale peas on the way to breakfast. Yes, I laughed. I launched my vegetables with the best of them, and got the first of many last laughs on that ridiculous public-school system that had once suspended me for throwing peas in the cafeteria. I was more than happy to spend an hour cleaning up for the joy of freely throwing that one helping of peas."

Just as you don't have to roll down a hill in evening dress to get my point about being a child again, you don't have to throw peas to recall those most miserable or embarassing moments of your childhood and laugh them off now. If you are willing to send your evening clothes to the cleaners or wipe the peas up off the floor, go ahead—roll down the hill, throw the peas. But, however you call up that neglected child within you, remember: it *can laugh* at many of those miserable experiences of the past, and it *wants* to laugh them off from your current perspective on life.

In the same spirit, the next time something happens that upsets you or makes you angry or makes you think, "This is the end of the world," stop and ask yourself, "Is this something I'm going to be able to laugh at in a while?" If so, maybe you can laugh it off now!

Let Fantasy Back into Your Life

Children love to dream, to make up stories, use their imaginations—and so would you if you'd let yourself. Remember, when you were young, how your room at night was filled with elves or pixies, the woods filled with Indians or pioneers in coonskin caps, how a twig became a magic wand, a broomstick a horse? Remember your imaginary playmates, who were just as real to you as anybody else? Remember when you played dressing up, and your father's hat made you a bank official, some play money made one playmate a teller, a pad turned into a checkbook and made another playmate a customer? Remember how you loved to draw, make up verses or songs, hear stories, make up your own games, wander aimlessly into your fantasy excursions with anyone who was willing to listen or participate?

That rich childhood fantasy life was not only great fun but also one of the healthiest aspects of your life as a whole. It provided much-needed escape from the hard business of growing up; it banished boredom in an instant; and chances are that the more you indulged in it and were encouraged in it, the more creative you are today.

As an adult you can allow yourself the same luxury of fantasizing and dreaming with the same fun and "mental-health" benefits. Moreover, you'll soon find that some of those dreams that started out as pure fantasies will ultimately become realities.

All of life's best realities start with "childlike" fantasies. All great vacation trips begin with fantasies. You must build your dream house in your dreamy mind before you can build it in reality. Getting a new job, moving to a new location, entering a new love relationship—everything that is valuable to you as a person begins first with a fantasy. The more you allow yourself to be dreamy-eyed and to fantasize, the more you will be able to change your life for the better. Of course, you must remember to enjoy your fantasizing while you are doing it, solely for its own sake, rather than let it become *futurizing*—in which you destroy your fantasies by confining them to things you plan to do or achieve someday—and then worry about whether your dreams will ever really come true. But when you steer clear of this pitfall, you will find that letting the child inside you escape now and then into its very own fantasy worlds will loosen up your negative and rigid attitudes about things, relieve a lot of the psychic pressures in your life, and open up whole new realms of possibilities for you.

To get back in touch with your fantasy life, you might try the following:

When you find some young children to laugh and play with, encourage them (and yourself) to fantasize as much as you all want, to be as creative and "absurd" as you want. If you are playing a game, let it get as far removed from reality as it wants to go. Don't impose "adult" rules or regulations; allow experimentation, exploration and imagination. Forget about having to nail down a set of rules. When the children discover that some rules are necessary, let them work them out; just stand back and admire as they figure out their solution. You will find that, even when making up rules, children are amazingly spontaneous and creative.

Whatever the children's fantasy game is—they are on a spaceship to the moon, they are fleeing from the wicked witch of the West—let *them* lead *you* into it. If they say this button is the zapofritzer which gets the starflunkies out of your way so you can land on the moon, don't stop them and ask what or who the starflunkies are or how the zapofritzer takes care of them! Do what the children do: go with your own fantastic images of what these things may be. Maybe they'll tell you their ideas, or maybe they'll just hit the button. Maybe the zapofritzer doesn't work, and now you're in real starflunky trouble!

In addition to getting the starflunkies out of the way of your spaceship, you might make a point every so often of going to the classic children's movies or plays, to a puppet show or a circus or a reading of children's stories at the local library. A whole generation of alienated Vietnam War–era youths helped keep their sanity and renew their belief in life by flocking to see Walt Disney's World War II–era "cornerstone classic" in this field, which could have been named nothing but *Fantasia.* Local theaters could bring that film back every year in the late sixties and early seventies and fill their houses for weeks with college and high-school "kids" who the day before might have been demonstrating in front of a draft board office, and the day after might be going to jail for draft resistance. You would hear these "flower children" saying, "*Fantasia*'s back! I've seen it four times, but I'm going again. Want to come?"

To the extent that *Fantasia* and other such "kid stuff" helped that generation of young adults keep the children inside them alive, they are all the healthier today. For you, it might be *Peter Pan, The Wizard of Oz, Winnie the Pooh,* the rodeo, the state fair—any of those "great spectacles" that over the years have brought the most delight to "children of all ages." The next time you get wind of one of these "classic chances," get up and go! (And take as many kids with you as you can.)

The next time you pass a playground—stop. Fantasize that you are a child again. Ask yourself what you could do then that you can't do now, as far as your body is concerned.

Go into the playground. Does your body want to swing on the swing? Anybody of *any* age can do that. If you're eighty years old, maybe you want to swing only a few inches each way—but you can still swing, still be as much of a kid as you were when your mother first put you on the swing and pushed it a few inches forward, a few inches back.

If you are thirty-five, maybe your body still wants to swing as high as it will go, still wants to weasel up and down through the jungle gym. Whatever your body really wants to do it *can* do, if only you forget how childish some people might think it is for a person of *your* age to be sliding down a playground slide. If you think of yourself as aged and creaky, just walking into a playground and asking yourself how much older *the child inside you* is than *it* was when you were ten years old can take as many years off your life as you can imagine.

If you have a family with children of any age still at home, try having occasional family meetings in which you all talk openly about what you would like to do most in the world, or simply spin out your favorite fantasies of the week as you experienced them. You'll soon discover that your fantasies aren't far out, impossible dreams at all! They are the free, creative outputs of your childlike imagination—the very stuff of life. Once those fantasies are out in the open, you may discover that you really can act out many of them, and that taking a few risks regardless of the way other "adults" might judge you will help you and your whole family to realize as many as possible of those fantasies that really deserve to be transferred into reality. For those fantasies that are just stories of the dream you had last night or the daydream you had this afternoon, free flights of the imagination about the imaginary friend who occupied the empty seat next to you on the bus—whatever they are, sharing them with your family will enrich your whole family life immeasurably.

Make up your mind to act out some of your fantasies. If you've always wanted to go river-rafting, to wander alone in the woods for a day, run in a marathon, bicycle to the next state, visit Bulgaria, climb a mountain in Canada, grow a beard, run for Congress, be on television, anything at all, do it.

Sit down right now and make a list of twenty things you have long dreamed of doing. Cross them out in the order of how impractical they are for you to do *immediately*. You should end up with at least one that you can do today! Now take active steps toward doing that one thing—but keep the list, so that you can get an idea of what you might do next to realize your "most realistic" fantasies.

I have enjoyed doing many things in my life that have made absolutely no sense to anyone but me. For instance, I once saw some people parasailing. I fantasized myself doing it, asked myself, "Why not?" and simply did it. I checked it off my list of "Fantasies That Can Be Acted On," and felt better about myself for accomplishing a *personal* objective rather than the objective of any crochety old "adult" within me. I had to remember, consciously or instinctively, that I did not need to explain my behavior to anyone, and that if someone else thought I was silly, not acting my age, then all I could do was wish them well and let them think what they wanted. Acting out my own fantasies has given me many inspirations for accomplishing things I might never have attempted otherwise, and I know that if I hadn't allowed myself to have those childlike fantasies in the first place, I certainly would never have been able to act out so many of my dreams.

Give yourself all the dreams you can get!

Be a Little Crazy!

There is no doubt about it: all children, including the one inside you, are a little bit crazy. They act "dumb" or "silly" a great deal of the time.

All children remember that what adults condemn as "crazy" in children is a terrific way to be. The child in you will tell you that you may have banished all those "crazy" moments from your life in favor of being more "mature and sensible" all the time, and the idea of being a bit zany and unpredictable now and then may sound foolish to you—but the child really enjoys wearing funny clothes at parties, going swimming at four in the morning, playing cops and robbers, or anything else that might make others say, "He's really crazy!"

Of course, there's a kind of "crazy" that nobody wants to be, the kind whereby you completely lose control of your life, panic, and end up in an institution. But that is not the kind of crazy I am talking about. Rather, I mean the kind of crazy you occasionally see on a vase, the pattern of small cracks, or crazes, describing the way its veneer has "cracked up." The kind of "crazy" I am talking about is the kind you can indulge in if you let yourself "crack up" with "weird behavior" and laughter now and then "like a kid."

Being "crazy" in this sense means letting go of some of the controls that restrict your life. You can be serious on the job, mature about how you face your responsibilities, earnest in attacking problems that call for straightforward, no-nonsense approaches, and still loosen up and let yourself go now and then. Not only will you have more fun; the whole office will loosen up, and everybody will be more effective when it is time for solemnity.

You might try a few of these suggestions if being a child by being "crazy" now and then appeals to you:

Ask your family members who their favorite people are "just to be around." See if their favorites (especially the children's) aren't those who can be a bit sillier and more fun-loving than most. Ask if they see you that way, or if they'd like you to be more that way. When you see how much others honestly enjoy being around "crazy" people, you'll find it a lot easier to let craziness become a regular part of your life—to throw snowballs, play tag in the pool, bring home a birthday cake when it's nobody's birthday, perform whatever craziness you can dream up.

The next time you hear yourself or anyone else judging someone's behavior as "crazy," stop and think what kind of "crazy" is meant. Is the person really "out of control" and consequently making himself and others unhappy? If so, the solution is to help him, not condemn him. Or is he simply open to the kind of childlike zaniness I've been talking about here, and a happier person because of it? If so, forget about condemning him, and try to emulate him. You have as much right to your freedom as he does to his, and if you stop doing the judging in the first place, you'll be more inclined to be fun-loving yourself. When you are upset about others' having fun and behaving in crazy ways, you are really upset about something in yourself. If it were just a matter of not approving of their behavior, you'd simply ignore it, but when you choose to be upset about it, then you are fighting something that reminds you of what you'd really like to be yourself. And rather than admitting it and changing, you simply resort to judging *them* as bad, and "let yourself off the hook" of being happy.

Make up your mind to do one "crazy" thing every day for a week—once or twice at home, once or twice at work, the rest of the times wherever the mood strikes you. Trust yourself to have the good sense not to be a practical joker or do anything that's going to hurt or inconvenience anyone else, and see how others react. If anyone condemns you just because they see you as "childish"—that's their tough luck. But nine times out of ten you'll find that people react with more enthusiasm than you could have expected, and that all your reservations were in your own mind to begin with.

Be Spontaneous

Notice how children are willing to try anything on a moment's notice. The child inside you wants to be impulsive and adventuresome, without always having to plan things in advance. Spontaneity is in many ways the key to all childlike behavior. That ability to stop suddenly by the roadside when something interesting catches your eye, and to have that same wide-eyed excitement about the new things you run across that you had when you were much younger, leads directly to childlike immediacy and "wonder in the face of the world." It is also one of the easiest things for desensitized "big people" to squelch in themselves and their children, by constantly reminding the children to *be careful* or always *be prepared*, by yelling at the kids to "get back here!" when they stray up an unfamiliar path instead of following the adult's "walking plan," and by all other kinds of tactics adults use to instill fear of the unknown in children and take away their natural curiosity about life.

Some children, of course, never lose their quality of personal freedom; regardless of how hard you may try, you will never stultify their creative, spontaneous urges. If they want to explore some new path, they will run away from you in one way or another (mentally, physically or both) as soon as they can run faster than you can.

These children may be spontaneous collectors of anything and everything. They may come home with snails, caterpillars, lizards, flowers, old wrenches, nails, coins and anything else that piques their curiosity. If you pound away enough at this kind of instinctive, impetuous collecting that gives these particular children so much joy, eventually you may teach them to *pretend* to believe that having a clean and orderly house is better than "having all that dirty junk around," but the childlike curiosity and spontaneous urge to collect curious things will always be alive inside them. And if someday they become happy archaeologists or museum curators or art collectors or botanists or antique or "junk" dealers, they will always have had to overcome the adult who once tried to tell them, "No, I don't want that in the house!"

The spontaneity of the child within you is such that it knows how to amuse you with anything at any time. It can pick up spools, rocks, pieces of chalk or old baseballs and fascinate you with them for hours. You may have learned to repress those urges to pull off the road and read the historical plaque under that two-hundred-year-old oak tree, but the urges are still there. If you have a totally planned-out life, with all your goals spelled out and knowing where you are headed every minute, if you are obsessed with organization, cleanliness and orderliness in everything you do—stop. You have forgotten how to be a child.

To reactivate your childlike spontaneity, you might try the following:

Look at your calendar of commitments for the next few weeks. Is your time so booked up that you would *never* have ten minutes to go spontaneously off "the beaten track"? If so, how many of those planned activities can you eliminate in favor of just giving yourself time to wander around "all over the map"? Schedule the time to get into your car and head north, without a road map, just deciding to go whichever way seems appropriate. Or, if you want to, play the game a child I know invented for himself: whenever you have any doubt about which way you feel like going, stop and flip a coin. (This child laughed the loudest when the coin took him around the same block four times. He says he found that block a little more fascinating every time, and was always "of two minds" when the coin took him off it.)

Stop imposing rigid demands for organization and planning on the lives of others. Instead, encourage *their* childlike spontaneity. Remember that what you call an orderly room or house is not "better than" your child's "disorganized room," which is "cluttered" with what you think of as "junk." The next time a friend calls you up with a suggestion for doing something together "on the spur of the moment" and you find yourself starting to say, "Oh, I can't"—stop. Ask yourself whether you can afford to keep saying, "I can't" to yourself and others forever. As much as it may "hurt" to tell yourself, "Well, I just won't mow the lawn today as I'd planned"—forget about your plans for one Saturday morning! Go to the flea market with your spontaneous friend! If you respond to one spur-of-the-moment call and see how much fun it can be, you'll soon be getting more calls—and making some yourself.

Give yourself a chance to get spontaneously excited about the things you do. Just because you've seen ball games before, you may find yourself thinking that you will be bored if you go to another one. Get rid of this attitude by taking each new ball game as a unique experience, which it is; you've never seen *this* game on *this* day. Likewise, if you are going to a party or other social function primarily to accompany your spouse or out of some sense of social obligation, you may find yourself telling your spouse, "I know this is going to be a boring party, and I want to leave after one hour no matter what." This kind of advance planning for being unhappy will, of course, turn into a self-fulfilling prophecy unless you eradicate it by allowing yourself to decide *after* you get to the party how much you are enjoying it—by giving yourself a chance to enjoy it, and trusting yourself to decide to leave at the moment when you are ready.

On the whole, learn to distinguish between things you need to or can best decide now and things you can just as well, or better, decide later. For instance, suppose there is a ball game you might want to go to next Saturday, but, then again, you're thinking you might like to go fishing, or to a local art show. Even if none of these things requires advance planning, the authoritarian in you might want to decide now which one you will do, just to get the uncertainty out of the way. The child in you, on the other hand, will say, "I don't have to decide that now. I'll just see what I feel like on Saturday morning. Maybe something even better will come up between now and then."

Whenever you can, listen to the child, in serious as well as playful things. If you find yourself agonizing over a decision about changing jobs, getting married or whatever, it may just be because the child in you knows that you don't really have to decide this now, you are artificially trying to rush it, ignoring the fact that you will have more information and/or clearer feelings later on, by the time the decision actually has to be made (if there is any deadline for it at all), and that a spontaneous decision later will be a lot better than a forced one now. You can waste a lot of time and cause a lot of needless anxiety for yourself and others by essentially trying to outguess your feelings, trying to predict how you are going to feel in the future with insufficient data now. If you don't *have* to decide now, don't! Leave room for your childlike spontaneity to work.

Don't Be Afraid to Make Mistakes

As a young child, you were not intimidated by making mistakes. You were willing to try anything, and if you weren't very good at it at first you were like the kitten that missed its first fifty mice: you just got a little smarter and a little quicker with every try, until finally you mastered ice skating, sewing or making soup. In fact, if you learned to ice-skate, the first thing your body figured out was how to *fall down* on the ice without getting hurt: how to relax and tuck your legs under you or roll or slide so that you just couldn't crack your head or break a leg, so that you could come up laughing every time, anxious to try again. "Failure" was nothing to be ashamed of or avoided; in fact, you welcomed it because you instinctively knew that you couldn't learn anything unless you were willing to fail at it first. Thus as a child you were a natural *experimenter,* accepting that nobody knows how to throw a ball, swim in deep water, ride a bicycle, or anything else, until they give it a try, make an error and give it another try. If children were made in such a way that they were afraid to try new things because they feared failure, they would never get out of their cribs! Likewise, adults who fear failure simply vegetate. Fear of failure becomes fear of success for those who never try anything new.

Children stop trying anything and everything only when they learn the neurotic idea that they are somehow inferior if they fail at anything, or that they should compare their performance with that of people who already have gone through the trial and error of mastering what the "novice" is just approaching for the first time.

Why is it that so few adults who never learned to swim as children ever learn *as adults?* Because they think it is somehow humiliating to be "classed with beginners" in *anything,* to show the awkwardness of the first stages of learning in public. Now, the adult, if he lets the child in him take over, can as easily or more easily learn to swim than the child, because his body has the advantage of full adult coordination to begin with. It is just the performance anxiety, the feeling that he is there to look as good as he can in front of everybody else, rather than get the feel of the water and learn how to propel himself through it, that makes him, and even those adults who go to beginning classes, far more awkward than most children, and makes them take much longer than they need to learn to swim.

Ask yourself whether, as you have grown older, you have learned to avoid more and more things that might involve "failures" on your part; whether you have learned to seek out "good grades" in everything all the time, to evaluate yourself as a *bad person* if you are in "the bottom half of your class" in anything. Have you accepted that you shouldn't do anything unless you already can do it well, and so eroded your natural childish impulses to try anything that strikes your fancy? If so, if you still fear making mistakes, you can overcome this fear by recognizing that you are avoiding the only thing that can teach you anything, namely failure! If you would like to regain a childlike acceptance of your own mistakes, you might want to:

Make yourself a list of activities you've avoided because you might "look bad" while learning. Have you never tried bowling, golf, singing, playing the guitar, painting, doing crossword puzzles —anything—because you are afraid your friends who are really good at these things will look down on you? *Go ahead and try one of them!* If any of your friends looks down on your novice efforts —if the good singer and guitar player says, "Oh, that sounds awful," and discourages you by asserting his own superiority—it stands to reason he wasn't much of a friend anyway. Reject the opinion of anyone who cares whether you fail or not! If you do, the very thing that you've feared, that is, other people's negative opinions and judgments, will turn out to be meaningless, and the only "masters" you'll care about are those genuinely willing to help you learn.

Remember that you can fail at anything *in life without being a failure as a person!* Don't confuse what you do, or how well you do it, with your worth as a human being. Your worth as a person comes from within—from the very fact that you are just as much a person as anyone else, and have what I call self-worth, which is as much a part of you as your heart or your brain. Your self-worth does not come from your scorecard for any activity.

At the same time, *don't be afraid to admit to others* when you've made a mistake! Whether you've balanced the checkbook wrong or misjudged a person, don't try to cover it up, deny it or rationalize it (a typical authoritarian response). Just say, "I goofed," and go on to rectify the situation. You will find that a great deal of respect comes to those childlike people who most readily admit their mistakes.

Stop placing such a high premium on being a success *at everything you or your children try.* Allow the child inside you and its children to "fail completely" at certain things.

For instance, suppose you try to do a repair job on your car, and you just can't seem to get it right; or suppose your child flunks high-school French. You may not want to spend any more time on the car, and your child may have flunked French because he was not interested in it as it was presented to him, but if you are a hopeless "perfectionist" you will never take the car to a mechanic or let the child decide he doesn't feel like repeating French 1 next term; he'd rather take other courses. You will keep fighting your own and the child's spontaneous impulses to "call this a bust" and forget it for now.

"If at first you don't succeed, try, try again" is a good motto only if you still care about what you originally set out to try! If you've tried it and you don't care for it—whether it's broccoli, opera, poker, car repairing or French—then what's the sense of insisting that you succeed at it?

The irony is, of course, that if you press yourself to "succeed at everything you try," you will end up in the same old bind of *trying only what you know you can succeed at!*

Who knows? If you give up your car-repairing attempts by saying, "I'm persisting in this only because I can't stand failure, which is no good reason at all," maybe in the future you will want to *try* car repairing again, with the same understanding: if you "fail" again, you take it to a mechanic again, and so what?

But if you continue to persist in something that no longer gives you pleasure just because you've *undertaken* it, and feel a compulsion to *succeed at whatever you undertake*—you will end up attempting fewer and fewer activities that the child within you would have enjoyed.

Accept the World as It Is

When the infant comes into the world, it has no thought that the world can or should be any different from what it is. The infant just opens its eyes in wonder and fascination at what is out there and makes its way in that world as best it can.

As the child develops, it gradually learns how to control certain things: how to drink from a cup, mow the lawn, win certain friends or influence certain people; and that is when the trouble is likely to start. The "young adult" who develops an authoritarian rigidity about *the way things should be* is likely to get mad at the world for not conforming to his expectations or demands, which leads to the angry-young-man syndrome, in which people *get frustrated at their inability to control things that no one human being can possibly control.*

Take people's attitudes toward the weather, for instance, a prime example of a natural phenomenon we cannot at all control. Children accept that the weather *just happens* in its own mysterious ways, and that no amount of carping about it is going to make the weather change in a particular way. Children accept snowstorms as natural conditions of winter and, in fact, welcome them, revel in them, enjoy them, while adults are busy telling each other, "Lousy weather!" and getting upset that their plans have been interrupted.

If you find yourself thinking, "Sure, children don't have to earn their living, they can enjoy snowstorms because they're not losing a day's work," that means you are ignoring the obvious fact that, no matter how upset you get about it, the snowstorm is not going to reverse itself and vacuum all the snow back into the sky for you. Your anger is not going to make up for your lost day's work; it is just going to ruin your day off. The child inside you would like just to go out and enjoy the snow, but the adult may insist on thinking neurotically about it and keeping you inside cursing the heavens.

Certainly, as far as your own immediate world is concerned, you can do your best to change things that you dislike: you can help combat racism in your town, your state, your country; you can make your contribution toward stopping the global arms race, feeding the hungry, caring for the orphaned or the infirm, saving the lovely old landmark building on the corner, or whatever else you care about. *The trick is to do it without getting angry at the world for having problems in it,* and having that anger make you upset or miserable.

An old saying goes, "Lord, give me the strength to change those things that can be changed, the *patience* to accept those things that cannot be changed, and the wisdom to know the difference."

That child inside you knows how to accept whatever cannot be changed, without judging the world to be fundamentally bad because of it; how not to be immobilized by striving to do what nobody can do and then lapsing into inertia or panic because it can't be done. In sum, it knows instinctively and immediately the wisdom of "how to tell the difference," which is therefore not a new wisdom you have to learn but a forgotten wisdom you have only to recall by calling up the lost child within you.

Consider children's attitudes toward people who have done things that have hurt or offended them. Children are prepared to accept that, people being people, they will hurt one another now and then, just as the weather, being the weather, will occasionally drench them in freezing rain on their way home from school. Consequently, they are prepared to forgive and forget in a few hours, while self-defeating adults may hang on to lingering grudges for a lifetime. Your inner child knows without thinking that holding grudges is painful and self-destructive, and so it will automatically forgive and forget—unless the judgmental adult in you wins out, in which case you will go on hating forever, regardless of how hard it is on you.

That accepting child in you can help you through all your human experiences. It will simply "take things as they come" and deal with them according to what seems to make the most sense at the time. As a child, you first simply accepted all things and people at "face value," without blaming the clouds for snowing, your blocks for not standing up the way you wanted them to, your mother for stopping you from falling into the river, or inflation for keeping you from buying a new TV this year. Being able to return at will to that wonderfully naïve, accepting state would help to eliminate many sources of unhappiness in your life. If you'd like to regain some of that childlike acceptance of the world as it is, and only on that basis to see what you might be able to help change for the better (while accepting inevitable failures along the way), perhaps you will want to:

Make a list of things that habitually irritate you, or that you have recently found yourself complaining about. Start with the first few that come immediately to mind. Maybe the furnace broke down yesterday, or a tree in the yard is dying and will have to be cut down, or gas prices have just gone up again, or your three-year-old just spread soap flakes all over the living room and he's *always* doing things like that; or maybe you love to ski but there's been almost no snow this year, and you're sitting around gnashing your teeth about it. Whatever it is, just write it down and put the list aside. Then make a point over the next few days of adding one or two things that most bug you each day. Keep your ears open to yourself, and whenever you hear yourself bitching make the subject a candidate for inclusion on your list. Maybe you want to put the list by the television and catch your own reaction to the evening news. Maybe you want to ask others what they most often hear you complaining about.

However you do it, after you have twenty or thirty items, run down the list and check off for each one (a) whether there's anything you could do to *change the original condition* if you wanted to (you can't help the fact that the furnace broke, the tree is dying, gas prices are going up; you *might* be able to find less destructive things to occupy your three-year-old; you can't make it snow); and (b) whether there's anything you have to do or can do to *rectify the condition now* (you have to get the furnace fixed and cut the tree down, maybe plant another one; there's nothing you can do about gas prices except to support long-term solutions to the energy crisis, but you can resolve to conserve gas, use your car more efficiently and/or get a more fuel-efficient one, walk or use public transportation whenever you can, etc.; you'll do your best with your three-year-old until he "grows out of it"; and, as for the snow, *forget it*—find some other way to get this winter's fun).

Now look over your list. How many "Forget Its" do you have? However many it is, forget them! The next time you find yourself getting upset over these or similar things, just stop yourself and laugh it off: that's just the way the world turns.

For those things you *might* be able to do something about, choose those you care enough about to devote some time and thought to, and act on them when and if you get the chance and the inspiration. As for the others—add them to the "Forget It" column, for now at least.

For those you definitely can and want to do something about, either by way of changing the original condition or rectifying the present situation (fixing it), by all means do so; but, as for getting upset that the furnace broke, the tree is dying, etc., *forget it!* Those things are also just the way the world turns!

As a matter of fact, if you look down your list and ask what you *should* be depressed or immobilized about, you'll find the answer is—nothing! This is not to say you won't ever, just naturally, choose to be angry or frustrated about things now and then. You would be a robot if you didn't. But the question is, how long are you going to stay in that condition, and how often do you needlessly put yourself in it just because you can't accept the world as it is?

Forget about social status and external measures of success when you are judging your *world and how much of it you want to accept and what you want to change about it.* Allow yourself to enjoy more things for what they are rather than worry about how they measure up to culturally imposed standards. Try to suspend *all* negative judgments about yourself for at least a short period of every day, by relying on your acceptance of the world as it is (with you in it!) to banish all those ideas of how others say you should be. If you carefully run through all the lack of self-acceptance that you have for yourself and your own personal world, you will find that virtually all of it has come from external, cultural sources! (Ask yourself how many of these feelings of guilt and inadequacy you had when you were two years old.) Those things you want to change about yourself for your own internal gratification will turn out to be things you *want to change back* to the childlike way they need to be!

Where judging other people is concerned, approach them just as children do. Children know nothing about prejudice because they are totally accepting of everyone until and unless people are just persistently nasty to them. They have no negative expectations about anyone, and until they are old enough to be influenced by stereotypes or the prejudgments and gossip of "more mature" people, they simply accept everyone for what he or she is, not caring whether the individual is black or white, "cultured" or "crude," Democrat or Republican, rich or poor, powerful or powerless, or anything else. All they care about is, how much fun, how interesting and understanding and sympathetic is this person now? They don't bother themselves with thinking that black people ought to be white, or women shouldn't "act like men," or any other such ridiculous "adult" hangups. Trust your childlike impulses, *whoever* crosses your path, and you'll find yourself a much more accepting and happy person.

Be Trusting

The next time you get a chance, closely observe small children meeting for the first time. They may or may not start out somewhat shyly, until they get the feel of each other, but if the feel is right (and with small kids it's almost never wrong), in five minutes they will be relating to each other as adults relate only to lifelong friends. They trust each other completely *to begin with,* and even if one of them does turn out to be a little pushy, the other just accepts that this kid is just this way and quickly learns to "forget it," or to resist it until the pushy one understands where the other is coming from (nonpushiness), or to deal with it in whatever other way ensures that all kids are going to have as much fun as they can now. As a result, children just about always get closer to each other and get more out of each other in an hour than most adults could in a month of Sundays.

Now compare this with your own approach toward the new people you meet. How long is your period of "initial shyness"? With children, it usually takes a few glances and a few words before they run off and turn a corner of the bedroom into a spaceship, and not more than three minutes before they activate the zapofritzer. But when you meet new people, you may be afraid of "coming on too strong," or of starting "a relationship" when you've already got too many relationships, too many ongoing interdependencies, to worry about. Or you may be suspicious of the other person's motives for any reason at all. Consequently you may be "cool" (a word with very many meanings), or standoffish, preferring to kill time with typical adult small talk rather than learning quickly how to treat this new person as you would your best friend and enjoy him or her just as much.

If your reaction to new people you encounter (even if it's just the gas station attendant who fills your tank and exchanges a few words with you) is typically "cool," it means that you are probably suffering from a touch of authoritarian paranoia that has turned your naturally trusting, childlike instincts around and made you suspicious of people *to begin with.* Of course, if you are suspicious of *all* people to begin with, *you are suspicious of yourself to begin with* (as you are, after all, one of "all people"), so that most of your mistrust of others is probably rooted in mistrust of yourself, which is a painful source of internal conflict.

But if you take your cue from the child in you and trust your animal instincts to tell you (in light of all your life's experience) when your ingenuousness may be leading you toward "real trouble" (which will probably turn out to be never), you can get rid of that painful conflict spot *and* learn to enjoy just about *all* the people you meet.

I am talking first about meeting *new people* in the context of becoming more trusting because comparing your reactions on meeting new people with those of young children (or of the child within you) is one of the quickest and surest ways for you to tell how much of your childlike ingenuousness, or *natural trust,* you have retained, and how much has been eroded by authoritarian paranoia. Conversely, your attitude toward old friends or acquaintances, your family or business associates is equally important, and, if anything, mistrust of them should signal you even more strongly to ask whether you fundamentally mistrust yourself, or have very greatly abused, neglected and alienated the child within you.

You may find yourself thinking, "Sure, I'd love to be as trusting as a child again. I don't *like* to be suspicious. But the attitude he's talking about is what leads childlike people to lose their life savings to con artists, pay for repairs on their cars that weren't needed or were never made, and a thousand other things."

If you think this way, I'm here to tell you it's just not the case. Any bunco-squad detective will tell you that "blind trust of strangers" (which I am not advocating anyway—you should never be blind about anything) is not enough to allow the con artist to separate you from your money, because con games depend fundamentally on *the greed of the victim,* who deceives himself into thinking he really can double his money overnight, get something for nothing, "make a killing." If you know better than that to begin with, no amount of trusting people is going to make you pour your savings into any fly-by-night get-rich-quick scheme. In fact, the kind of childlike trust I'm talking about will make you *better* prepared to spot con artists, for the simple reason that if you mistrust most people automatically, if you think everybody is something of a rat, you have screwed up your instinctive ability to smell a *real* rat when it comes along. Even if your instincts try to warn you, you may dismiss them in your greed by saying, "There's no reason to believe this guy is more of a rat than anyone else," and turn your life savings over to him. And the same goes for the auto mechanic, the door-to-door salesman or anybody else.

The ability to trust yourself and to trust others is really a matter of attitude development. If you think the world is a rotten place, and that most people really are out to get you, not only will you be more likely to be "gotten" by the real rats; you will already have "gotten" yourself by needlessly cutting yourself off from all the honest and straightforward people around. If you let your childlike trust take over, and you feel positive about being able to handle virtually anything that comes along, your very attitude of positiveness will most often see you through. To release this trusting mentality and to practice it, you might try these strategies:

The next time you meet a new person, monitor your reactions. Do you find yourself being cool, standoffish, keeping the person at arm's length with small talk? Are you a little uncomfortable, unsure whether you want to "get involved" with this person, even suspicious about what he "really might be after"?

If so, drop your guard, and trust it to come up again if it's really needed. Ask yourself, "What have I got to lose here?" If you are afraid of "getting involved," remember that your involvement need extend no further than this one meeting if you don't want it to. Take your cue from kids, who can have a ball with each other even if they *know* they're never going to see each other again, who are not afraid of gaining anything for fear of losing it. Set right out to find this new person's funny bone, or to find some other way to put him at ease. Once he finds that you immediately trust and respect him, that you take him at face value, you will see his guard drop, too. Remember, it should be no more than three minutes to the zapofritzer!

Go out of your way to meet at least one new person this week who is substantially different from you. If you are a professor, introduce yourself to a truck driver, or stop to chat with the guy who sells newspapers on the corner—anybody who strikes you as appealing. Trust him and yourself to make the best of the situation. If you are met with initial suspicion, if you sense that a person is thinking, "What does this guy want from me?," you have a perfect example of the needless mistrust I've been talking about, because you know you don't have any ulterior motive, you are not trying to take this person for anything. But, at the same time, there will be a child in that other person who will sense your honest ingenuousness (as long as you are comfortable with yourself). The trick, then, is not to let the fact that the child in you became a professor and the child in the other became a truck driver keep the kids from trusting each other.

The next time you suspect that you've been ripped off, or are going into a situation where you fear you might be, think only about the best practical way to find out whether you really have been ripped off, or whether you really are about to be and what you can do to prevent it.

Every year millions of us take our cars to mechanics. Especially if we don't know much about cars, we are likely to drop the cars off, get an estimate, have the work done, pay the bill—even when it comes to fifty percent more than the estimate (because the car had these other, additional problems)—and drive away with some technical explanation we don't understand rattling around in our heads, grumbling to ourselves, "I bet I was ripped off."

In cases like this, studies and investigations show that people who believe they have been ripped off for car repairs are right about half the time. But *this does not mean that you have to approach your next bout with Sammy the auto mechanic with suspicion or mistrust!*

After all, the chances are at least fifty-fifty that Sammy is as honest as you are (however honest that may be!). So start out by giving him the same benefit of the doubt you give yourself. If you are anxious about being ripped off, try being frank with him about your fears. You might say something like "I really have a fear of auto mechanics and taking the car anyplace to be repaired. You hear all these things about so many people being overcharged. I assume you're honest, just the way you assume I am, because you're trusting me to pay for the work you do. But I wonder whether you could help me get over this fear of mechanics by taking a couple of extra minutes to explain to me how to tell, for this job, for instance, how I could *know* I hadn't been ripped off. For instance, say this was your car, and it had this same problem in a strange town, and you took it to the nearest mechanic to be fixed. How would you know what was a fair price, or whether you were being charged for work that hadn't been done, or whatever?"

If Sammy never intended to rip you off in the first place, he undoubtedly also is furious at those other mechanics who rip people off and give all mechanics, himself included, a bad name. In that case, he may be so enthusiastic about your sincere desire to starve the crooks out of business that you get more than you bargained for—the half-hour cram course in valve jobs, camshaft replacements, radiator repairs or whatever your specific problem is, complete with references to diagrams in the manual, lists of the prices of replacement parts, why it takes three hours to do it, some time watching the guy do it, and—when you pay the bill—a handful or a trunkful of defective parts removed from your vehicle which are yours if you want to take them, along with a show-and-tell of what was wrong with each one, and the suggestion that if you have any doubt they needed to be replaced, you should show them to someone else who really knows cars, get a second opinion.

Whether your mechanic can afford to take this much time with you or not, *assuming that he's honest,* he'll take all the care he can in helping you know how to tell the honest people from the crooks in his field—just as you would do (assuming that you're honest) in your field. He will respond to your childlike question with a childlike pride in his own honesty and welcome the chance to introduce you to his world of valves, camshafts and radiators. After half an hour you may be relating to each other like lifelong friends.

If the mechanic evades your concerns, however, tries to brush you off, you will immediately sense that he does not like customers who ask too many questions, or who don't trust "the experts" without question, and you will then know it is time to take your repair business elsewhere.

The point here is that if you regain your childlike ability to trust others to begin with and be frank with them about your own concerns, you can always find a way to determine whether they really are "out to get you" or not, in case your instincts tell you they might be. The worst thing you can do is drive into the service station or anywhere else thinking, "I bet I'm going to get ripped off," and drive away thinking, "I bet I *was* ripped off." If you do that, you are *choosing* to maintain your unfounded, paranoid suspiciousness, rather than finding out for yourself whether distrust is really justified in this instance. The more you "*bet*" without *knowing* that others are out to get you, the more you see them as guilty until proven innocent. The child within you has a much better idea of justice than that: "Innocent unless proven guilty" is the only way for a No-Limit person to go.

The above "Seven Paths to the Fountain" seem to me to be among the most obvious and easily accessible ways to initiate your quest for your long-overdue reunion with that lost child within you —but I want to emphasize that there are countless ways for you to recapture that joyous youth. The child inside you knows exactly how to deal most effectively and happily with everything and everyone it encounters on this planet, because it is unfettered by cultural impositions, learned behaviors or paranoid judgments about how to "fit in" all the time. Perhaps the basic message of this whole chapter is that by letting yourself recapture that childlike essence of your being you can stay "forever young at heart."

Those glorious childlike qualities that can help you enjoy your life each and every day are no further from you than your fingers are from your hands. They are an inalienable part of you. If you try to repress them, if you insist on neglecting the child within you, you will be putting more chains on your legs than any slavemaster ever could. But if you really love that child within you, and really care to *be a child again* in the ways I'm talking about, you cannot help but be at peace with yourself.

When you have inner peace, you can do just about anything. Give yourself more of that childlike inner peace today, by letting yourself be that good old silly, fun-loving child again, and you will no longer miss that lost child. Or, as Friedrich Schiller put it, "Keep true to the dreams of thy youth."

6 Trust Your Inner Signals

One of the major concerns of this book so far has been the extent to which people's natural drives for happiness, growth and creativity, drives toward what I call No-Limit living, are systematically repressed and often perverted by the rampant authoritarianism in our society. A characteristic of authoritarianism is its insidious ability to addict people to the endless pursuit of external rewards: wealth, prestige, promotions, approval of life style by others, ceremonial honors, and status symbols of all kinds. To keep you "successfully" in pursuit of these carrots, you have etiquette guides, rules, customs, traditions and the like. In fact, you are continuously bombarded by propaganda and directives from a bewildering host of *external sources* which are designed to make you pursue these rewards "to the limit" in order to feel fulfilled. The self-defeating lesson is that the more external rewards you accumulate, the more satisfied with life you *should be.*

Part of the attraction of these external rewards and signals for people who demand quantitative or numerical ways to evaluate everything is that such symbols make it easier for them to gauge their worth as people and their relative position in the social pecking order. For instance, if you follow Emily Post to the letter, you can feel assured that you have "good manners," and feel superior to all those boors who don't know Emily Post and so don't know how to be "polite" to people. If you have three cars, nobody is going to say *you're* not a success.

As opposed to the external signals that are constantly encouraging you to run harder and faster after whatever it is that those messages are meant to sell you, however, you have within you numerous sources of *inner signals* which are competing with the external ones for control over your life. These inner signals strike you as thoughts or feelings, and among their sources are your animal instincts and the voice of the child within you, to which I would add the call of your "higher needs" as a human being (by which I mean those needs whose satisfaction can "make you the highest") and your own sense of purpose or mission in your life, to be presented in the next two chapters.

But before going on to think in depth about those higher needs, as well as that purpose or mission, it is crucial for you to stop and appreciate how much your ability to know yourself comes from learning how to consult your inner signals, rather than relying primarily on all those directions others are trying to give you. This is one of the most difficult steps toward No-Limit living for most people, because all of us have been so heavily conditioned to respond to those external orders and may have bought so many security blankets that we are literally buried under them. But trusting your inner signals may also be *the most important* step you can take toward your own personal goal of becoming as fully functioning and creatively alive as you can be.

Some researchers have used the term "locus of control" to differentiate "internal" from "external" types of people. When your life is predominantly controlled by signals coming from outside yourself, you are said to have an *external locus of control.* Psychologists have estimated that seventy-five percent of people in Western cultures are primarily *externally controlled,* so it's obvious that a lot of us have a lot of work to do to shift our centers of control from being mostly external to being essentially internal. But then, each of us is *perfectly free* to choose how much control we wish to exercise over our own destinies, and how much we want to let outside signal systems maneuver us through our life paces. If you do something as minor as buying a piece of clothing because you think someone else with better taste or a better "eye for fashion" than you have would approve of it (rather than because it is comfortable, affordable, and *you* like the way you look in it), then you are making others into dictators over how you will dress. The same is true if you decide that your warmest coat is too shabby to wear to a fancy party on a freezing night and you end up freezing just so that you can give others an "unshabby" impression.

When external controls dictate more serious decisions for you, such as how you are going to raise your children, what you are going to do for a living, where you are going to live and, most important, how you are going to enjoy your own life, the effects can result in devastating conflicts with those inner signals your own mind is constantly repressing. You can literally make yourself a slave to any manipulator you choose—and you know that there is really no such thing as a well-adjusted slave.

On the other hand, becoming attuned to the constant interplay of all your inner signals can give you real security, peace of mind and joy. The more you operate from a perspective of trusting your inner signals and relying less and less on those ever present external cues, the more you will be learning to put the locus of control over your life in your own hands, where it belongs.

Before looking deeper into the ways to become more trusting of your inner signals, it will help you to remember that each of us has some inner and some outer "locus of control" all the time, and that on some days or in some circumstances we may be more external than internal or vice versa. You may be far more sensitive to your boss's externally oriented signals than you are to those of your neighbor or your spouse. You certainly should not see yourself as either internally or externally controlled in everything you do, every single day of your life, or make an effort to categorize yourself or others as "external" or "internal" people, which is another one of those useless exercises in dichotomizing that really get you nowhere. The point is to keep those external signals from blocking out your inner impulses in situations in which you are apt to react in an external fashion, so that you can assume as much control of your own life, be as independent of other people's opinions and make as many important decisions for yourself as possible.

To be sure, it is not possible to eliminate the need for *some* external centers of control over all of our lives. We all live in this culture together, and we must have some systems which all of us can respect in order to make our society work at all, let alone at its maximum level. A prime example of a necessary and legitimate "external control" is a traffic light. Nobody in his right mind is going to say, "That external traffic light is red, but my internal light is green," and run the light just to prove how independent of all external controls he is. Certainly you will have to make some concessions to legitimate external controls in your life, and you'll have to learn how to suppress your own internal impulses on occasion. But if you trust your inner signals, you know they would never tell you to run a red light without good reason. They might tell you to run one in an emergency, but not before checking to ensure that you are not endangering yourself or others, at which time your inner controls can "give you the green light."

One more hurdle to be jumped on the way to becoming more internally directed is to *overcome those external signals that will tell you that you are being selfish if you take too much control over your own life.*

Certainly we all know what selfishness is. Selfish people are excessively or exclusively concerned with themselves, constantly seeking advantages over others with no regard to anyone else's well-being, typically trampling on the rights or freedoms of others. The "selfish" kid was the one who, when the bag of jelly beans was opened at the party, crammed as many of them as he could into his mouth, got mad when anybody else wanted some, rationed two out to each other kid, and then put the rest in his pocket.

Of all the criticisms I have had of my previous books and my thinking, the one that has stood out the strongest is that I am a promoter of selfishness. I certainly never have said or written that I think people should be selfish at the expense of others, and in fact have gone out of my way to try to say just the opposite. But it seems that when many people hear that I want people to think for themselves, to consult their inner resources and to become the captains of their own souls, they cannot help interpreting my words as encouraging widespread selfishness.

Let me take my own advice in the previous chapter and assume that you, the reader, and I, the writer, are approaching this wide-open world I've called No-Limit living with an honest, childlike desire to understand each other. If so, I should start by saying that perhaps half or more of this misunderstanding between me and those of my critics who have accused me of promoting selfishness is my fault. Perhaps in my previous writings I failed to make myself clear, to express myself so that no one could interpret what I said as promoting selfishness.

On the other hand, perhaps my critics will do me the favor of reading back through *Your Erroneous Zones* and *Pulling Your Own Strings* and ask themselves whether they might have "read in" things I never wrote. I particularly would like you, the reader of this book, to ask yourself whether you have yet read anything in this book that has made you think, "He's saying I should be more selfish." If so, I certainly did not mean that, and now I have a question for you: Do you use the word "selfish" to describe anyone who follows his inner signals more than you do, and is perhaps a great deal happier as a result, *even if he never takes advantage of anyone else?* If so, you may be abusing the word "selfish" to condemn people who don't conform to your authoritarian idea of what they should be like, using name-calling to dominate them just as you let others dominate you.

However you answer the above question for yourself, let me make my views on selfishness absolutely clear. It is not my intention to encourage anyone ever to be inconsiderate or abusive of others. On the contrary, I conceive of the No-Limit person as precisely that person who instinctively loves and/or accepts others as he does himself and consequently is *most considerate* of others, simply because not to be so would be to disregard his own inner signals, which are constantly trying to guide him toward the childlike joy of relating to others as equals, "lifelong friends" or "playmates."

At the same time, I cannot accept the judgment of anyone who tells me that it is selfish for you or me to run our lives on our own terms. I do not believe it is selfish to love yourself and treat yourself as a person of independent worth and natural dignity, nor is it selfish to want the kind of life that is most important and enjoyable to you.

To get over the hurdle of allowing others to make you feel bad by calling you selfish when your inner signals—in this case *your conscience*—tell you that your behavior is perfectly all right, you have only to remember that if you know that your own conscience is clear, and that you have in no way hurt or abused anyone else, the person who calls your behavior "selfish" must be trying for some reason to make you conform to some set of external, authoritarian values, to get you *below him* in the social pecking order.

The point I am making is that trusting your inner signals has nothing to do with selfishness *per se*, but with choice. If someone accuses you of being selfish, you have a choice: take his word for it and alter your behavior to suit him without thinking any more about it, or stop and review your behavior in light of your own conscience, and change it only if you decide he is right after all. I leave it to you to decide which approach is inner-directed and makes more sense.

With these three understandings, that we are all partly externally and partly internally controlled all the time, that some external controls are necessary and legitimate (but only your internal signals can tell you which ones), and that trusting your inner signals has nothing to do with selfishness, I strongly believe that the more decisions you can make based on your inner signals, and the more you learn how to ignore those external pressures which constantly try to manipulate or immobilize you, the better *all* our lives will be. The entire culture will benefit by having strong, inner-directed people as leaders and everyday citizens. A citizenry that thinks for itself, a country in which people know and trust themselves as individuals, would be virtually immune to manipulation by unscrupulous leaders. In families in which the individuals know and trust their own and one another's inner signals, mutual respect, rather than hierarchies of authority, is the binding that holds them together. And in one-to-one relationships, when both individuals are able to trust their own inner voices, you have the best insurance available that neither will try to manipulate the other, and consequently the greatest opportunity for a loving and lasting relationship.

FROM EXTERNAL TO INTERNAL

The first step toward trusting your internal signals is to examine your thinking and behavior to determine the areas of your life in which you have "gone too far" in submitting to external controls. Below is a chart that I think may help. It is revised from a chart I used in a book I coauthored some years ago, called *Counseling Techniques That Work.*

EMOTIONAL STATES AND THE DIMENSIONS OF INTERNAL AND EXTERNAL CONTROL

HAPPINESS	*Statements Identifying External Causes of Emotional States*	*Statements Identifying Internal Causes of Emotional States*
Mastery		
	1. The world is a great place.	1. I make the world a great place.
	2. My parents are good to me.	2. I love and respect my parents.
	3. My friends treat me well.	3. I enjoy my friends.
	4. Things are going well.	4. I have worked out a good life for myself.
Coping	5. Nobody is bugging me.	5. I don't let anybody bug me.
EMOTIONAL NEUTRALITY		
Striving	1. My parents mistreat me.	1. I allow my parents to upset me.
	2. My friends treat me bad.	2. I don't have any good friends.
	3. Everything is going against me.	3. I am messing up everything.
Inertia	4. Everybody is out to get me.	4. I keep allowing other people to get me.
Panic	5. The world is a lousy place.	5. I can't cope with the world.
UNHAPPINESS		

Now, obviously, each of us uses explanations of both these types to explain why we feel the way we do, and often there is an intimate connection between them. For instance, if your parents aren't good to you, if you feel they don't really love you but only use you as someone to dominate and boss around so that they can feed their own illusions of power, you are going to be hard pressed to say you respect them (whether you can say you love them or not).

If you are a predominantly external thinker, however, you will say to yourself, "Well, my parents mistreat me, they just make me unhappy, that's all," and stay unhappy. *There is no way out of the box of externally caused unhappiness that you can open for yourself other than through the internal route.* If you blame your parents, your friends, the world or anything else for your miseries, if you insist that *they* are solely responsible for the way *you* feel, you are going to have to wait until *they* decide to change their behavior before *you* can feel better.

Only by looking over to the *internal causes* for your feelings, or by "translating" external-cause statements into internal-cause statements, can you find anything *you can do* to improve your situation. Obviously, internally directed people will experience some negative emotions, but they will take as much responsibility for those feelings and for changing them as they can, and consequently they will have a chance to rid themselves of those emotions much more successfully than will people who sit around hoping that the world will change and make them happier.

If you find yourself consistently in the externally-caused-unhappiness frame of mind, therefore, your first step out is to your right. You may start by saying, "*I hate* my parents *because* they mistreat me." Now you are focusing on your own hatred as at least in part what is making you miserable. Of course, if your father gets drunk all the time and beats you black and blue for no reason except his own nastiness, you cannot do anything about the physical misery without getting rid of the external cause, by finding some way to avoid getting beaten up. This may mean running away from home, getting somebody who can control him to protect you, or any of a number of things. But notice: you may never get to internally caused happiness by being able to say, "I love and respect my father because he is good to me," but you may be able to get there by a combination of "I don't let anybody bug [or abuse] me," "I'm not going to let my hatred of my father immobilize me," and "I am doing my best to help my father overcome his problem so I *can* love and respect him."

If you find that you are habitually ending up in the external column, if you can always find twenty reasons why you are unhappy, but find it hard to come up with even a few things that "make you happy," I will bet you dollars to doughnuts that most of the reasons you have listed for your miseries are on the "external" side. Whether or not I am right, I hope you will seriously consider using *some* method to determine whether you have gone too far in giving up control over your own happiness by getting yourself trapped in "externally caused unhappiness," and think how you can get out of that frame of mind by becoming a more internally controlled person, which I believe is *the only way* to mastery over your life.

ACHIEVING GENUINE SELF-HONESTY

> This above all: to thine own self be true,
> And it must follow, as the night the day,
> Thou canst not then be false to any man.
>
> Polonious to Laertes,
> *Hamlet,* Act I, Scene III.

To thine own self . . . The second step toward trusting your internal signals is to *assure yourself that they are trustworthy,* or to *cultivate your own conscience,* to the point where you can trust your own moral judgments (when it comes to how *you personally* are going to act) over all the external signals that are bombarding you and trying to influence you in this or that way.

It may seem to you that "to thine own self be true" ensures only that "thou canst not then be false to any man," or that you *cannot* do anything immoral, inconsiderate or abusive to anyone else *if you have a conscience to begin with.* You may be saying to yourself something like "The Mafia hit man is being perfectly true to himself. His problem is that his particular self has no conscience."

But I would say just the opposite: that the Mafia hit man and every other human being on this planet is *born with* a conscience, whose "seed" is perhaps the childlike perception that peace with oneself lies in doing unto others as you would have them do unto you. The hit man's problem is that he has *repressed and alienated his conscience,* squelched his internal signals, by allowing his behavior to be determined by "the Mob," one of the most rigidly hierarchical and authoritarian "societies" imaginable—i.e., he is being false, first of all, to himself.

Being true to yourself primarily means being *totally honest with yourself.* It means getting back in touch with your basic human instincts for justice and fairness to yourself and everyone else. It means identifying the defenses you have erected against your conscience and all your other internal-signal sources that have kept you from being all you can become, and ridding yourself of all the defensive (or paranoid) thinking and excuse-making you have come to rely on to explain why you are so unhappy.

The point I am making, as far as conscience is concerned, is that a "good" or "clear" conscience can come only from the *harmony of your internal and external signals,* or, in other words, *personal integrity:* the *integration* of your whole self, in all areas from your animal instincts to your sense of purpose in life. Remember: *only you can be the creator of your own integrity. Only you* can conduct your own internal symphony.

But keep in mind: if you accept full responsibility for conducting the symphony of *all* your signals (thoughts and feelings), you will have to *listen to the whole orchestra.* You cannot just march to the drumbeat of external orders. You have also to listen to the strings of your conscience, to the voice of the child within you and to all the other voices of *internal* origin that you are privileged to conduct.

One of the greatest folk images of conscience is contained in the classic children's story *Pinocchio,* perhaps known to most people in the Walt Disney movie version. Pinocchio was a marionette-turned-boy with the particular burden that his nose grew longer every time he lied. However, to offset this huge handicap to entering the adult world, he was given a nice, clear, audible conscience (in Disney's version in the form of Jiminy Cricket, a cricket who followed him around and sounded off whenever he was about to violate his conscience). The point of the story is that if you aren't true to yourself, if you don't listen to your own private Jiminy Cricket and operate "above all" from your own internal locus of control, you'll be and secretly feel like just one more artificial, perhaps monstrous, robot.

As the seventeenth-century French moralist La Rochefoucauld said, "If we have not peace within ourselves, it is in vain to seek it from outward sources."

The Origins of Self-Deception

I believe that the self-deception that alienates so many of us from our internal signals actually begins with attempts to deceive others.

The infant, of course, has no capacity to deceive itself or anyone else. Knowing virtually nothing of external impulses, it operates solely on its inner signals. Only when the external signal-and-reward system becomes evident is there a temptation to try to "cheat" on it, to engage in self-crippling thinking and behavior by trying to fool others into thinking we are something we are not—

specifically, to send out "false signals" in order to manipulate others, to make ourselves feel superior by "external" standards. These self-defeating thoughts and behaviors then come to include prejudices with no basis in reality, false pride, pretentiousness and phoniness, hypocrisy (especially condemning others for doing the same sort of things we habitually do ourselves), and often using anger, mock humility, feigned embarrassment, quickness to take offense, arrogance and so on in our attempts to bend the external-signals system to our own advantage.

Our honesty with ourselves can largely be measured by how far we are willing to go out of our way to convince others that we are something which we are not. All of us know of people who will hire limousines and chauffeurs to impress others with their wealth when in fact they can't afford them, or go to similar extremes in making "external displays" of themselves. We know people who will pretend to be open and unprejudiced when external circumstances tell them it is politic to do so, and then turn around and talk in more private situations about the Italians or Jews who are ruining their lives. Others will rant and rave about the evils of the younger generation's pot-smoking while they pop their Quaaludes or "diet pills" or get themselves high.

When you wonder, "Whom are these people trying to kid?" you recognize that they started out trying to fool others like you, but before long ended up deluding themselves, leading themselves astray. They found they had to defend the false signals they had sent out, or live up to the false images of themselves they had projected. And, as the "false images" had been provided by the external-signal system to begin with, trying to live up to them led inevitably to more dependence on external signals for life guidance, more repression of internal signals.

To fool yourself basically means to convince yourself and others that you are something you are not, to *mistrust* the internal signals that are trying to tell you who you really are. It really means to make a fool of yourself to yourself, and the more you fool yourself, the more self-contempt you'll be creating, whether you have the self-honesty to own up to it or not.

A very real example of the internal consequences of this kind of self-deception comes from my own life. The experience led me to resolve to be different, and it suggests that you may have to go through some experiences of being dishonest before you can feel what it is like and then vow to eliminate it from your life.

I was playing a tennis match with an opponent who was actually much better than I—meaning I would have to play "over my head" to beat him. But I wanted to beat him in the worst way, and it was a very close match when he hit a lob over my head that I knew I couldn't return. I suppose what went through my head as the ball came down was something like "That ball *has* to be out!" I yelled "Out!" a fraction of a second before my inner signals told me, "It was very close to being out, but, replaying the image, it just nicked the edge of the baseline."

In a split second I had to decide whether to reverse my call and give up the point, or whether to let it stand. My opponent had no idea whether the shot had been out or in, because I had been blocking his view as I chased it.

I let myself stay with my dishonest call. I took the point and the game, but I was feeling lousy about it, and because of my lowered self-esteem my game fell apart. I lost the next three games, the set and eventually the match, even though I had been in a position to go ahead and win.

I felt exactly like Pinocchio, with my nose growing longer by the minute, and made a decision then and there that I would never let myself make a bad call again, regardless of the "external" importance of the match or any other circumstances.

I didn't feel a need to tell my opponent why my game had fallen apart. My own inner sense of disgust at myself was enough to teach me all the lesson I needed: that, for me, personal integrity and being honest with myself had to be far more important than winning any tennis match.

In fact, I have been in that same situation many times since that important day, and a few times I've even caught myself calling "Out!" when shots have nicked the lines. But now I always say immediately, "No, wait a minute, it was in, it just nicked the line —great shot!" When I do, I find that I can continue to play effectively afterward, because I am at peace with myself.

Being honest with others and true to yourself not only will help you feel better about yourself as a human being but will increase your ability to "play well" at whatever you do; really to *enjoy yourself* and your own internal personal integrity. I firmly believe that if you just make up your mind to catch yourself whenever your internal signals are trying to warn you that you are being dishonest with yourself *or* others, you can cut off self-deception *at its point of origin* by stopping and asking yourself, "Whom am I trying to kid?"

Toward Self-Honesty

If you have determined to ask yourself whom you are trying to deceive with all your externally controlled thinking and behavior, and have concluded that it is a mistake to try to fool *anybody* about who you are, you are on your way toward what I call *total self-honesty.* You may already have begun to identify some of the defensiveness and phoniness you've adopted for yourself up until now. If so, the next step toward self-honesty does not mean going to confession or feeling guilty about anything you have done in the past. It simply means accepting that you have been making some self-deceptive choices, and then coming to grips with them by working one day at a time on your ability to trust your internal signals.

Self-honesty means ridding yourself of the need to appraise your self-worth in external terms, and instead looking as objectively as possible at yourself, with an eye toward living more the way *you* want to live *now,* rather than primarily being true to "the way you've always been." It means facing yourself squarely in the mirror and feeling good about yourself because *today* you were willing to be honest with yourself and everyone else, and even though it may have been *externally* costly (maybe it even cost you your job, your marriage, your best friend), it gave you more internal peace than giving in to external pressure to be something that you aren't.

Self-honesty will require you to assess your strengths and weaknesses realistically, to identify those defenses you have erected against your internal signals and work at eliminating them from your daily life.

You need not make any public declarations or make anyone else aware of your program if you want to pursue self-honesty. You only have to make an internal commitment to being all you can be, and to recognize that *no one else can hand you truth or self-honesty.* You must confront yourself and discover truth from within yourself, by your own lights, because you believe it to be important. You may decide to continue sending false external signals to deceive others about you, but, even if you do, at least you can get started *now* in being totally honest *with yourself.* If you have appreciated what I've said so far, you know what I am talking about. You know that you have your own Jiminy Crickets, your own internal voices, that will interrupt you for brief dialogues with yourself whenever you are about to succumb to self-deception. "Why am I doing this? When am I going to stop trying to pretend I'm something that I'm not? I know I find it easier to be arrogant than I do to be honest, but I'm going to try to change that."

Such dialogues with yourself are the internal question-and-answer sessions you will engage in on the way to becoming more honest with yourself, shedding all the masks you have put on to disguise you from yourself and the world. If you want to continue to wear the masks before others for a while, go right ahead; but if you face yourself with an honest appraisal of what you are and why you behave as you do, and with a determination to change the things about yourself that are phony, before long you won't need to wear the masks for others at all. The point is that you do it for yourself, because living peacefully with yourself is what self-honesty is all about, and if you can trust your internal signals in guiding you as best they can in *your* life it will come naturally for you to trust them in dealing with others as well.

Another example from my own life perhaps best illustrates for me how trusting my internal signals is essential to my peace of mind *and* my honest dealings with others.

When I submitted the manuscript for my first book, I received some criticisms from the publisher's editorial staff, along with demands that I make many changes which would essentially have altered the message of the book. While I was certainly willing to make changes that would improve the quality of the manuscript, my inner signals told me very clearly to refuse any changes that would violate my original intentions in writing it.

I was told by the publisher, by editors, agents and even many good friends, that I should "just go along with" the suggested changes, because, if I refused, the publishing house would refuse to publish the manuscript, and I wouldn't have a book at all. But in that instance I had made up my mind, and no amount of persuasion, gentle or threatening, was going to change it. My book was going to say what I wanted it to say. I would go someplace else, even publish it myself, before I would give in on this principle.

With every external appeal for me to come to my senses, to take the money and run, to go along and get along, or whatever, I became more adamant in my stance. I sent the publisher a long letter detailing my position, and after he understood where I stood the book was published the way I wanted, saying just what I wanted to say.

Very few people understood my hard-nosed stand on this issue. Most would rather have seen me give in to the external demands. But my internal signals told me, "There's only so far you can go, and these changes are simply impossible for you to consider." In this case, as opposed to the time when I tried to make myself live with a bad call on the tennis court, I knew immediately that I had to live with myself, and I wasn't about to compromise with external pressures even if others were trying to assure me that "going along" would have been the easier path.

And, in fact, it was obvious that "going along" in this case would not have been easier in the long run; it would have been disastrous. How was I supposed to talk about this book with colleagues, use it with clients, speak about it in public, if it had been made to say things I just didn't agree with?

But, absurd as it seems, publishers and authors go through this very kind of argument all the time, most often with publishers saying things like "It'll never sell if you do it like that," and referring to various tried-and-true formulas for book writing, or pointing to last month's best seller and saying, "You should do it like *that*," or showing you the latest market-research report telling what readers are buying now and what they *want to hear*, so that you can tell it back to them—and often, in the process, reminding you what a dumb and shallow person the average book reader is, so you should always write for the lowest common denominator and never challenge the reader too much.

At this point you may be wondering what good a book is supposed to be if it just copies last month's best seller, tells you what you already think, and challenges you as little as possible—which is exactly my point. Fortunately, after that first experience I knew enough to make myself clear to publishers at the outset, and go only with those who agreed at the outset that no external rules or formulas were going to dictate how my books would turn out. Certainly I have always been grateful for editorial help that has made my books clearer, and for constructive suggestions of all kinds—but with the specific understanding that I would not accept any changes that would violate my own personal integrity, and that my inner signals alone would determine which ones those were, with no questions or arguments about it. I firmly believe that the only reason my books have climbed to the top of the best-seller lists is because I have rejected all external directives about how to get there, and instead relied solely on my own inner directives in taking full control over what my books are going to say.

CREATIVITY AND YOUR INNER SIGNALS

The example above brings me to my last point about trusting your inner signals, which is that what has come to be called "creativity" is obviously *completely* dependent on your willingness to consult your own inner resources—specifically, *your imagination*—and to undertake any task from your own uniquely individual standpoint.

You will remember my saying earlier that there is and can be no formula for creating *original* works, thoughts or anything else, and no way of predicting when, where or from whom they are going to originate. The great artists, musicians, writers, poets, architects, scientists, inventors—all the true innovators in our world—have without exception been those who, above all, not only learned how to trust their inner signals when it came to telling them what their life's work was going to be and exactly how they were going to go about it, but refused to allow anyone else to dictate to them on their own original thoughts and projects. In other words, the Fountain of Inspiration (or Creativity), just like the Fountain of Youth, lies within.

Mythology has it that "the Muse" is responsible for visiting people, for example, with bursts of brilliant poetic inspiration. That myth is fine as long as you know that "the Muse" does not represent some external being who has to "fly into you" before you can create anything (which will leave you sitting around scanning the skies and muttering, "I wish that Muse would show up so that I can create something"), but rather represents *your uncapping the well of your own internal creativity signals.*

True, only those who find the well so fascinating they can never bring themselves to put the cap back on are likely to get sufficiently carried away to pour their whole lives into it and end up building Parthenons or creating mathematical theories of relativity. But *each of us has a well of infinite depth within us,* which contains more potential for creativity than we can ever imagine. The only reason many of us keep our own wells capped is, as discussed earlier, that we fear failure by comparison with those whom external others, "society" or "history" have judged "the greatest." For instance, you will often hear people say things like "I'd love to write songs, but, really, I'm not very creative. I don't get those bursts of inspiration the great songwriters do."

Nonsense! How do you think the great songwriters do it? They can't afford to worry, "Would someone else say this is great?" They just never lost the childlike inner signals that somehow make up songs, poems, whatever, on all kinds of occasions. They never lost confidence in their own taste, because all they cared about was whether they liked their own songs, and they would want to recall and sing many of them *for themselves,* for or with their closest friends, or for whoever else might want to listen to them, in the future.

Surely you can recall when as a child you made up songs for yourself. "Silly little songs," you may be saying. But I say, "So what?" Get back into touch with those signals within you that want to make up new songs, inventions, recipes, scientific theories or whatever, and just let them loose! And, furthermore, remember that if what you are doing *makes good sense to you,* if all your inner signals, from your animal instincts and your conscience to your imagination and your reasoning powers, are telling you in twelve- or twenty-four- or forty-eight-part harmony that *you love what you are doing now,* that you really feel you are creating a beautiful, No-Limit life for yourself, how can they be wrong? (And if you want to make up a song to express and commemorate how you feel about life now, how can you make up a wrong song?)

The whole message of this chapter comes down to this: You and everyone else on this planet were "born free" to cultivate all the creative potential within you *and* live in peace with your own conscience. But you can claim your birthright as a person only if you are willing to take the social or "external" risks involved in ignoring all outside pressures to do things the way others say you "should."

Internally directed people have no respect for any external reward or signal system when it means having to compromise what they really believe in. No-Limit people may be rare on earth primarily because *internal directedness* is so rare. The ancient Greek philosopher Pythagoras said this to his students and followers some twenty-five hundred years ago: "Above all things, reverence yourself." If you choose to follow that sage advice, you will have taken a giant step toward No-Limit living.

STRATEGIES FOR TRUSTING YOUR INTERNAL SIGNALS

You—yes, you and anyone else—can begin to develop a more internally directed personality without going into therapy for years or arguing with yourself that you can't really change because you've been the same externally controlled person all these years. If you want the real inner joy of knowing that you are genuinely your own person, if you are willing to make your inner peace more important to you than how you are judged by others or how you measure up to any external standards, and if the external rewards you have been chasing for all these years are getting more and more meaningless and stale by the moment, you can literally *turn the game around* by opting for new thinking and behavior that is internally rather than externally directed.

Below are some specific things you can try today, some attitude shifts you can implement right now, if *you* (not some *they* or *it*) decide to "make it happen" between you and your inner voice:

Make your objectives clear to yourself. Try to eliminate external explanations for your behavior, your life circumstances, your thoughts or feelings, as much as possible. For example, instead of saying, "I am having an anxiety attack," as though a flock of enemy airplanes had suddenly attacked you with anxiety bombs, try translating this statement to "I am reacting anxiously in this situation." Or instead of saying, "My wife gave me a persecution complex," which is ridiculous, say, "I let my wife's opinions of me become more important than my own opinions of myself." Rather than saying, "Heights scare me," try saying, "I scare myself when I find myself in high places, even when I know I'm perfectly safe." Then see what you can do to "translate" those statements to truths about yourself reflecting internally caused happiness:

"I was reacting anxiously in this situation because I was afraid the boss wouldn't like my work, but that was a useless reaction because he hasn't even seen it yet; I was scaring myself with the worst that could happen. So I decided not to worry about it. Even if he *doesn't* like it, how is anxiety on my part going to help? We'll just discuss it, decide what to do next, and maybe I'll learn something. The *worst* thing I can do is be defensive with him about it! If he wants to be aggressive and try to *make me* anxious, that's *his* problem, but I'm not going to fall for it. I do the best job I can by my own lights, and that's really all I can do!"

"I decided not to let my wife manipulate me by condemning me for things that my internal signals tell me are perfectly okay."

"I discovered I was afraid of heights because I imagined myself falling even when I was in no danger *except if I chose to jump.* But I was actually afraid I would lose control of myself and really jump! I resolved the problem by determining to *trust my animal instincts* and imagine myself a cat whenever I was in a high place. Will a cat look out over the edge? Certainly. *Will it ever take a flying leap over the edge?* Never. I tried being a cat in a number of places of increasing height, working up slowly from the top of a ladder to the top of the tallest building in town, and it worked. Now I no longer fear high places."

Look carefully at where and when others really *are* trying to control your life in illegitimate ways, and thus whom or what you may have to confront directly. If you feel that your parents are getting out of line in controlling your life, your best way out of the externally-caused-unhappiness box may be to sit them down and have a very specific talk with them detailing what your internal signals reject in their attempts to control you. Whether they are making you take piano lessons which you hate, telling you that you can't go camping by yourself when you're sixteen, or pushing you to become a doctor when you don't know *what* you want to be, after a few honest confrontations with them, or with any people you've allowed to become external manipulators, if you are at once firm and calm—even cheerful—you will find them easing off and respecting you more. Remember, any time you feel that external rewards or signals are controlling you and clashing painfully with your internal signals, *it is happening only because you have permitted it to happen.* No one can make a fool of you without your consent!

Perhaps the main thing you should be aware of is that *you should never be a responder to your environment when you can be an initiator;* that you don't have to take what "life" hands you if you are interested in something else. If you remind yourself that you are stuck in a rut in one or another area of your life solely because you are letting your past history, present job, family or whatever dictate that you must stay in that rut, and if, when all your inner signals are trying to show you the way out, you decide you just have to take some "external" risks to make a change, you will begin to *create your own environment* rather than just react to whatever you get from external sources. Once you decide to *depend on yourself* to get out of your ruts, you will find that the opportunities come at you as fast and furiously as taxicabs in New York City. You can see every single situation in your life as an opportunity for growth, if only you will vow to reach out to your inner signals and take the risks that go with following *them* toward new opportunities for happiness.

Run through the following checklist of external things our culture encourages us to depend on for our happiness. Ask yourself honestly how susceptible you are to relying on them, and how much you are letting them keep you from becoming internally directed.

Pills, Alcohol, Tobacco and "Social Drugs"

We are a nation of externally oriented people obsessed with the idea that we must depend on "commerical substances" to cure our ills or make us high.

How many times lately have you said to yourself, "I can't cure myself of this headache, so I'll rely on this little pill to do it for me"; "I can't go to sleep"; "I can't stay awake"; "I can't cope with the children"; "I can't relieve all this tension"; "I can't control this constipation/diarrhea, morning sickness, these menstrual cramps, this runny nose, that minor muscle ache, this annoyance, but I can take any one of these pills"? These are the commercials that invade your life every day on radio and television, and you've come to believe them.

The message you are sending yourself every time you take one of those "magic pills" is, "I can't do anything about this myself, so I'll rely on this product to do it for me." And every pill you swallow helps you to believe more in pills than you do in yourself.

I am not saying that you should never take pills. Obviously they are necessary for many kinds of medical treatment. What I *am* saying is: before you take that next pill, ask yourself what you could do, what your internal signals are trying to tell you to do, to cure the problem *without* a pill. Are they trying to say, "To cure that headache, take a hot bath, put on some soft music, go for a walk in the park" or anything else that your animal healing instincts or any of your other internal signals may want you to do? If so, *forget the pill!* Try what your internal signals want. You will be astonished how many everyday maladies *your internal signals already know how to eliminate;* how many backaches can be cured by proper exercises (although few doctors advertise that fact), how many cases of chronic diarrhea or constipation you can control through proper diet, sleep and exercise. As I mentioned earlier, when you do have to go to a doctor, make sure you find one who believes his or her job is to *help you master your problem,* with maximum respect for your body's natural healing powers and a minimum of reliance on external aids.

When it comes to external substances that are *never* medically necessary for you to take, the cocktail to relax you, the cigarette to help you relieve the tension, the marijuana to get you high so that you can enjoy yourself, these are *all* needless and poisonous products that you've chosen to take instead of taking full responsibility for your own personal highs. Every time you rely on one of these substances to "get you up," you are taking one more step toward removing control of your life from your own hands and placing it in some signal system external to yourself. Your inner signals, if you trust them, will never let you poison your life with pills, alcohol, tobacco or social drugs, no matter how many external pressures are trying to sell you these things.

Dress Codes for Prestige

How often have you spent money for clothes you really couldn't get excited about because you could not *feel prestigious* unless you were wearing the proper designer label, or unless you were conforming to "the current fashion"? However many times it has been, each time you have placed responsibility for your personal self-esteem in the hands of designers whose job it is to make people believe that their products of this season are "in" and all others are "out," whether you like this season's fashions or not, whether you really need any new clothes or not. You can give dress codes a fantastic amount of control over your life if you want to, and if you can't feel comfortable with yourself without *their* sanction (whoever *they* are), then *they* have you in their hands, even if you are unwilling to admit it.

Stop right now for a second and think about your wardrobe. How much of it have you bought to conform to dress codes, for "fashion status" purposes, and how much just because your inner signals told you, "Buy that, you'll enjoy wearing it?" What do your inner signals tell you to buy next? A new pair of shoes to replace an "old favorite" pair that's wearing out, or a new pair of shoes to replace the ones that are "out of fashion" now, even though there's still plenty of wear in them?

I am not saying you should go out of your way to violate dress codes. Wearing a purple wetsuit to the opera, as much fun as it may be to imagine, would be as inconvenient and unnecessary (perhaps) as having to buy four new suits to keep up with the fashions every spring, or with your "image" as a whatever-it-is-that-you-are. All I am saying is: consider how much external dress codes for prestige rule *your* life, and resolve to minimize that control by consulting your internal signals as to what you feel like wearing or buying, and when.

Etiquette Guides and Codes of Manners

To what extent do you let external signals dictate how you will conduct yourself in social situations? Do you rely on your inner signals to tell you how to be really polite or considerate to anyone you encounter, or do you feel you have to consult Amy Vanderbilt, Emily Post or any other "authority on manners" before you decide how you should pick up your fork, how you should respond to an invitation, how you should react when you next meet another person?

Remember the child I described wandering down the restaurant aisle in Chapter 5? That child, I said, *minds the best manners it knows* and trusts others to do the same. But, on the other hand, that child feels absolutely no need to consult etiquette books to determine how to be really polite to people.

If you, as an adult, have determined to take a *childlike* attitude toward true politeness, you may know every rule in every etiquette book ever published, or you may not know any of them, but *it doesn't matter.* What matters is whether you can be comfortable with yourself and make those with you comfortable in whatever situation you find yourself.

There are many classic stories illustrating how the most truly polite of people have "thrown away the rule book" when it has come to making others comfortable, but my favorite comes from a friend of mine:

"Not long ago I was an usher at a friend's wedding. The groom and bride were high-society types, and their families had planned the most elaborate and formal of occasions. The best man, however, the groom's college roommate, was a poor farm boy from Arkansas—a great guy, but really lost when it came to all those things you were supposed to do by the etiquette books. So at the rehearsal dinner, which happened to be braised chicken breasts in a cream sauce, he did what he always did at home—picked up the chicken with his fingers and ate it.

"Well, you could just see the horrified glances from around the table, and all those starched-stiff Emily Post fanatics snickering under their breath—until the bride's mother, who happened to be one of the town's leading ladies, caught onto what was happening and immediately picked up her own chicken in her fingers.

"The best man never even knew what had happened. He just kept on happily being himself, friendly to everybody, enjoying his chicken, while those other guests who caught onto what *real* manners were like also forgot their knives and forks, and those who still had their heads stuck in etiquette books sat around not knowing what to do or how to eat. They are probably still wondering to this day what Emily Post says to do when the mother of the bride picks her chicken up in her fingers at the rehearsal dinner."

The message here should be obvious: etiquette guides and other externally formulated codes of manners are useful only insofar as they tell you what the accepted standards of a given *externally oriented* segment of society are at a given time. You can know all about the "manners" of the Eskimos in the nineteenth century, or the "manners" of twentieth-century Americans, as they've been written down by this or that authority, but only your inner signals can tell you how to have eternally good manners, how to make yourself and those you are with comfortable at all times.

If you respect yourself and trust your inner signals to present to you your "best manners" *all the time,* you will find that your *natural manners* are far superior to any idea of human politeness you can ever get from any book or code.

External Standards of Taste

When you taste a glass of wine, react to a movie or a play or a TV show, or decide whether you like a song or not, are you primarily consulting your inner signals, independent of what external forces say you are "supposed" to think about it? Or are you evaluating the wine on the prestige of the label or the price of the bottle, or prejudging the performance on the basis of what "the critics" have already said about it?

The French have a saying: *chacun à son goût*—each to his own taste. What that essentially means is that in matters of taste *you alone* are and must be the sole judge of what pleases you. If you have blocked out your inner signals as far as your own taste is concerned in favor of saying what you are supposed to say or pretending you like something when you don't, you can get back in touch with your own, real personal tastes by trying some of the following experiments:

The next time you are about to order a name-brand liquor at a bar, have the bartender bring you one drink each of that and his regular cheap bar brand, without letting you see which is which. Taste them both and decide which one you like best. If you can't tell the difference, then go with the one that is less expensive! If you find you really prefer the more expensive name brand, then enjoy it for how it tastes, not for the status that buying it is supposed to bring you.

The next time you visit an art museum, the house of a friend who has paintings on the walls, or anyplace where there are artworks which you notice, *determine which artworks you enjoy,* based on your own internal evaluations of how pleasing the works appear to *you,* before you find out who the artists are or how much the pieces cost. If others dislike things you find appealing and rave over things that do nothing for you, or even call you gauche because you are not "in" with the things "the experts" say you are supposed to like, you can just ignore their judgments of you *and* the artworks, because you'll know that they themselves are only paying attention to what others think—and if that's the case, why should *you* pay attention to what *they* think? The irony of this exercise will turn out to be that those you were most concerned about pleasing by trying to conform to their external standards will inevitably respect you more for trusting yourself than they did when they secretly knew you were just blindly following the experts or critics and being as phony as they were.

Advertising Messages

Every time you are exposed to commercials or advertising messages of any kind, remind yourself that they are all propaganda designed to convince you that other people's opinions of you are more important than your own opinions of yourself; that those messages are trying above all to condition you to think externally rather than internally. Whatever the messages are selling, from perfumes that will make your husband flip over you to foot deodorants guaranteed to make your dog stop flipping over your smelly feet, advertising messages are all but universally designed to erode your self-confidence and addict you to any imaginable kind of external "reward" they can convince you will make you happy if only you will buy it. The universal message is that what others *might* think of you is so important that you ought to squelch your own inner opinion in favor of being sure to please others.

The next time you hear or read an advertisement, ask yourself, "What real information did I get out of that which might have helped me decide whether that product might really be good and useful for me to buy, and how much of it was just pure appeal (or demand) for me to buy that product because if I don't, *others might condemn me?*"

If you look at enough advertising messages in this light, your internal signals will soon tell you how to laugh almost all of them off—and how to tune in to those few that really do offer you a good deal on something you would find useful in your life.

Bureaucracies

Our bureaucracies are enough to permit us all to choose going crazy if we let them. Our multifarious levels of government, our big businesses, our public utilities, our big labor unions and all the other crusty old superorganizations which have evolved huge bureaucracies to run themselves over the years are, primarily, *established centers of external control* that are *always trying* to regulate us beyond reasonable limits. That is the nature of bureaucracy: to control the lives of masses of people through "the proper channels," to make people conform to as many rules as possible (so as to make life as "easy," painless and thoughtless as possible for the paper-pushers or the computers). So the more a bureaucracy can get you to stand in this line for an hour, spend half an hour filling out that form, pay the price it dictates, forget your special case because the computer can't deal with it, see the man down the hall (who will send you to another man down another hall), the more it can get the message through your thick head that you are not a person but an external object for the bureaucracy to manipulate, and the more the bureaucrats will try to overcontrol you and everybody else.

The question is, how are we going to deal with this?

Obviously the first trick is not to let our bureaucracies drive us crazy, and the second is to avoid bureaucratic hassles when we can and resist them when our internal signals tell us we must. Only when enough individuals decide "I'm not going to take it anymore" will our bureaucrats decide it is "easier" to treat people with dignity and individual respect rather than as so many cattle to be herded into this or that pen as "the system" dictates.

The next time you find yourself cursing your incomprehensible income tax forms, the long lines you must stand in to get your money out of the bank, or any other bureaucratic hassle that some great system of external regulations has imposed on you, ask yourself, "What do *my internal signals* tell me to do about this?"

You will find you have three alternatives: (1) endure the hassle and get through it with the best humor you can, (2) get out of the hassle somehow, or (3) put up a stink about the bureaucracy's subjecting you to this needless hassle—i.e., *resist*.

Your internal happiness now comes into play: how can you end up on the "happiness" side of the game board *whichever* alternative (or combination of alternatives) you choose?

In terms of your objective of filling in as many entries as possible in the internally-caused-happiness column of your life, you will quickly see that if you are waiting in a line of forty people to get your money out of the bank, for example, your three basic alternatives are:

1. Say to yourself, "I expected this kind of line at the bank and allowed enough time for it; good thing I brought a book along."
2. Say to yourself, "This line is ridiculous. I'll see if I can cash a check somewhere else."
3. Say to yourself, "This bank is really getting out of hand. They expect me to stand half an hour in line for the privilege of depositing my money with them and then getting it out again if I can afford

the time and trouble! I'm going to have a real confrontation with an officer of the bank about my rights as a depositor, take my business elsewhere if I can't get satisfaction, tear up my checkbook and throw the pieces all over the place," or whatever.

The ultimate trick is, whichever strategy you choose in this or any other "bureaucracy bind," make sure you have followed your internal signals so that *you can be happy with whatever strategy they've chosen for you at the moment.*

If your inner directives told you to accept a long line at the bank with the best humor you can, maybe you want to read Chapter Six of your book while waiting in line, or to joke with others (or the tellers) about the long lines and how the bank couldn't care less about its customers, but you can still come out of this "waste of time" by saying, "*I used that time* in line at the bank to my own best advantage, and enjoyed every minute of it."

If your inner signals have told you to take the second option and get out of this impossible situation as fast as you can, maybe you have said to yourself, "There's a quick way to beat this bank, and that's to cash a check at the grocery store." In that case you should be happy that you figured out that a quick walk to the store would be more pleasant than a wait in the bank, and whistle all the way to the store.

If, on the third hand, as it were, your internal signals have told you, "Enough already!" and have led you to take the third option, resistance, you should likewise resolve to enjoy yourself. Whether you choose to tear up your checkbook and run laughing out of the bank, or have an earnest talk with an officer about the lousy service the bank is giving and how you are going to take your business elsewhere if they don't shape up, or get all the other people who are waiting in line to chant in unison, "We're mad as hell and we're not going to take it anymore!," *you can find that even resistance can be fun!*

As long as *you know* you have a legitimate gripe against a bureaucracy that is making absurd demands on you and your precious time, and it will do your heart good to flaunt it and see how "the computers of the world" react, why not? After all, the bureaucrats may be trying to tell you that you "just have to live with" their absurd, overblown systems of external controls, but, if so, you have an equal right to tell them that they just have to live with irate individuals whipping monkey wrenches into the works now and then, and too bad for them if they can't take a joke.

Grades and Ranks

Kindergarten, first grade, second grade . . . A-B-C-D-E . . . tenderfoot, first class, Eagle . . . first string, second string, "scrub" . . . private, major, general . . . We are a culture obsessed with grades, ranks and hierarchies of all kinds—with external frameworks by which we can evaluate the "progress" or "status" of everyone, ourselves included, in just about any area of our lives imaginable.

If we stop to think about it, we will immediately recognize that, although we have been heavily conditioned to accept all these grades and ranks as necessary and to defend them by telling each other that society could not run without them, in fact there are many that are completely unnecessary, and, even with those that one feels are legitimate, we take them far too seriously, with destructive and sometimes devastating effects on our chances for happiness.

For instance, why in the world is it necessary to organize a group of boys into six classes of Boy Scouts, with uniforms and pins and badges and sashes and all other kinds of rank-indicating gewgaws and doodads, to divide them into "patrols" and make some of them "patrol leaders," in order to take them camping? Of course it's not, but some adults seem to think a boy will never learn to put up a tent if he isn't given a merit badge for it, while others maintain that, although none of this is necessary *now,* its purpose is to initiate the kids into the way the adult world works.

This second argument makes about as much sense to me as the idea of a training bra, but it is more insidious, because it admits that the purpose of the Boy Scouts, in this case, is to condition children to respond to external signal-and-reward systems, and to repress their own inner signals, which are trying to tell them that this is all silly. Pretty soon it leads to regimenting even younger children into ranks of Cub Scouts, which is necessary to initiate kids into the way the Boy Scouts work. At this rate, it is something of a miracle that we don't have six grades of Tot Scouts, with merit badges in toilet training pinned all over their diapers. After all, wouldn't that be a perfect way to initiate kids into the way the Cub Scouts work? (While the Boy Scouts provide an excellent training ground for becoming more self-reliant and I strongly endorse such efforts, the overemphasis on externals, if unchecked, can subvert the very purpose of the training itself.)

As ludicrous as the above example may seem, it is really the logic followed by our whole "educational" system, where just about everybody agrees that you have to start getting grades in the first grade (or how will they know whether to pass you to the second grade?), and so on up through eight or twelve or more grades of education, with grades necessary every step of the way (or how will the college know whether to admit you, the employer know whether to hire you?).

Certainly these grade systems have nothing to do with helping you learn, as we saw in Chapter 5 under "Overcoming Your Mis-Education." Their real, basic purpose is to make you into an externally oriented human being, to get you to accept that the most important part of your education is measured by the grades teachers give you and other external rewards. The entire educational system is designed to shuffle you through an external labyrinth of grade signals, rather than to teach you how to appreciate the intrinsic or *internal* joys of learning. And once you have been conditioned in school to accept the pursuit of A-plus in everything, and "being promoted to the next grade" (high school, college, graduate school) as a measure of your "success," you are then ready for initiation into "the adult world," where everybody who has been conditioned the same way you have conspires to make the long-heralded necessity of grades in society a self-fulfilling prophecy.

Look at it this way: the Boy Scout "patrol leader" is going to recruit other kids into the Boy Scouts, because he has invested heavily (and sacrificed a lot of things his inner signals were saying he'd rather be doing with his youth) to attain his really meaningless rank. He knows he can't even pretend that his rank means anything if there are no "scouts" in his "patrol." (He would be reduced once more to leading only himself, God forbid!) So he goes out and rounds up some tenderfeet, and the whole charade continues. The same thing can occur anywhere, from social societies (Are you a Third-Degree Mason yet?) to job classifications (Have you made GS-3? Lieutenant? Full professor?).

Now, there is nothing wrong with the rank of lieutenant, or of full professor, *per se*. The army in battle has to have clearly defined command networks, and a university faculty has to be organized at least enough to protect academic freedoms. The questions I think we must all ask ourselves when it comes to grades or ranks or our positions in hierarchies at any time are, "If I get an A-plus in this and then get promoted to that, is it going to be because external signals told me I just had to take the next step up that ladder? or, Did my internal signals tell me I would enjoy learning more about this and the external system gave me this grade or that promotion just because that's the weird way the system works—it gives you pieces of paper called 'degrees' and all kinds of other merit badges (including money) when you learn new things or really get good at them?"

In other words, did the grade or promotion really come "by accident" (you weren't bucking for it, but the system just offered it to you), or did it come because you worked hard *for it* (external)?

Make a list of all the ways you are externally "graded" nowadays. You may be a GS-3 at work, a Third-Degree Mason, a member of the first-place team in your bowling league, twelfth in your class. . . . Write down as many grades or ranks or positions in hierarchies as you can for yourself.

Now, next to each of them, being as honest with yourself as you can, write down an A if you have got these "grades" primarily as a result of pursuing something your internal signals said you wanted to do anyway, and an F if you have got them (and aspire to "higher grades" in the same area) just because you have been willing to suppress your internal signals and pursue these external grades or ranks at the cost of many present-moment sacrifices.

Your list should give you a clear idea of how much you have invested in external grade-and-rank systems, and of which ones are really not necessary to or conflict with your internal signals. Determine to resolve all those conflicts in favor of your internal signals by eliminating your "internal F's" in favor of "all A's."

If you want an extra laugh, go back through your list or your past experiences of "being graded" and *grade all those external systems that have graded your performance in the past on the basis of how well they have served you as a person.* For instance, how do you grade your grade-school education as far as making you excited about learning is concerned? If you can give it more than a C, I will be surprised.

Go back to your old report cards. How would you grade those teachers who gave you all those ABCDE's? If you are honest with yourself, you will give out as many E's as they did, or more.

Remember when your grades were posted on some bulletin board for everyone to see? Do you remember all those honor rolls, standardized test scores, awards and disgraces that were made a matter of public record "as a matter of course" by all those grade-givers? Maybe a fantasy exercise will help you laugh them off. For example, I have often fantasized about walking into a school and taking a poll of the students grading their teachers on *their* performance and posting the results at the entrance to the building. Of course the teachers who had C's, D's and E's posted for everyone to see would have a hundred reasons why this grading system was illegitimate: students don't like the "hard" teachers who are willing to *discipline* them (to get good grades); they don't have the "adult" judgment necessary to grade their own teachers; they just give A's to teachers who let them have fun; and, above all, "You can't grade all teachers by the same standard, because each individual teacher works differently."

If you fantasize "grading" all the people and institutions that grade or rank you in the same public way they treat you, you should definitely get a few laughs and a much better *internal* perspective on all external grades, ranks and hierarchies.

It might also help you to recognize that in learning or achievement systems in which grades are given according to artificial and arbitrary rules, the motivation really to excel, or "outdo yourself," goes down. For example, if getting an A is the reward for your participation in a physical-education class, and the teacher sets up an arbitrary schedule of A equals fifty pushups, B equals forty, C equals thirty, D equals twenty and E equals ten, most of the students will aspire to do the fifty pushups and then stop. Very few will be interested in doing a hundred pushups, or a hundred and fifty. What's the point? You will get the same A as those who can do fifty. The same "motivation-limiting" effect of grades applies to any learning or achievement environment. If your job goal is just a promotion, you are likely to do just enough to achieve that goal. *Only when your motivations are internal to begin with, and you are pursuing the intrinsic payoffs of finding an even better way to do what you do, of becoming a more talented, more appreciative person, or whatever it is you want for yourself, do the motivations for growth become unlimited.* Therefore, the No-Limit person, by definition, cannot be concerned with external grades and ranking systems, since those very systems impose limits on motivation and achievement.

Family Status

How are you ranked or graded in your family? Are you "the senior male," the father or grandfather figure? Or are you "just one of the kids"? Are you the "great success" or the "black sheep" of the family? How much do you care about your rank in your family, and how much do you let this aspect of your external status rule your life?

The family itself in our culture is most often organized along the lines of external grades and ranks, or authoritarian hierarchies, rather than along the lines best suited to the internal happiness of all the people involved. This is in line with the tradition that the family as a whole is supposed to (has been conditioned to) respond to external signal-and-reward systems above all, which makes the "authoritarian family" a cornerstone of the external signals system. This is why families so often discourage independent thinking and punish members who stray too far from what is expected, by external standards. "Belonging to the family" becomes more important than thinking for yourself, which is often construed as a violation of family responsibility. Those who rebel at the call of their internal signals must do so at the expense of familial criticism or even ostracism. Except in the most healthy families, trusting one's individual signals is seen as an act of treason. Each family member is thoroughly trained in suppressing his own views in favor of "family loyalty," and you often hear things like "Why can't you be more like your sister? How can you think of yourself when you have the whole family to consider? You are going to upset your father if you don't do this his way. Remember, as the oldest son you have certain obligations. Who else is going to take over the family business?"

When you consider how many of us are pressured to put aside our own individuality in deference to externally oriented family systems, and how much our "ranks" in our families can force us to abandon our own individualism in favor of "playing the roles" our family status has bequeathed to us, you may begin to see why the family as a traditional institution is falling apart. (Or at least many social scientists *say* the family is falling apart.)

If *your* family is under great strain, or even falling apart, it is vital for you to recognize that *it is only when individuals grade or rank one another according to external standards of family hierarchies*, only when somebody is "pulling rank" on others, trying to force others to stifle their own impulses and to adapt to some externally imposed set of values and behaviors in the name of the family, that resentment and hostility erupt.

If you find it impossible to "control" your teenager, it is probably because you continue to insist that your rank as her mother or his father should entitle you to dictate her/his internal signals as a budding adult, which she/he is bound to resent because she/he feels you are trying to stunt her/his growth. The solution is to forget your "family status" for a moment, whether you are the mother, the teenage daughter, the rich uncle, the poor cousin or the black sheep in any situation. Just treat all your other family members and yourself as being of equal status or rank, and you will soon find that the best way to foster respect, love and "internal" responsibility in a family is to encourage each individual member to think and act as independently as possible.

I have seen it over and over again: those families that are most concerned about their status in society as a unit, and most rigid about each member's rank and role, are those in which the children are most apt to take off running as soon as they are able to, and come back as seldom as possible. On the other hand, families in which the children are helped to climb out of the nest and to fly in their own chosen directions as soon as possible, in which *everybody* feels most free of externally imposed "family status" binds, are the ones in which the children most frequently come flying back around the homestead, and which pull together most tightly in times of emergencies.

Your Psychology

One of the saddest commentaries on academic and professional psychology today is the extent to which it encourages externally oriented thinking, in terms of psychological theories, to the exclusion of helping people get back in touch with their own internal signals and to learn to *trust themselves*. Psychotherapists often lead their clients to become even more dependent on them for approval than they have been on parents, spouses, children, bosses or whomever else, and convey the message to their clients that they are never quite ready to solve their own problems.

Therapists don't deliberately set out to do this, and, in fact, they often talk at length about problems of "transference" and dependency. In my opinion, they just do not recognize how much their theories, names and labels for their patients' conditions, the whole external apparatus of psychology as a research discipline, get in the way of their clients' reestablishing direct confidence in their own internal signals, attaining true integrity and mental health or super-health. Instead of learning to interpret their agitation, aspirations, fantasies and even dreams *for themselves,* clients are led to feel that they can find the *real* truth about themselves only if a psychological expert interprets their internal signals for them; or, through studying psychology for years, getting degrees in it, they become psychologists themselves. (And even those who take this route seldom claim that their discipline has helped *them* become truly happy people.)

In the extreme, this interposition of the theories of psychology between the client and his own internal signals can keep him returning to the therapist week after week for years on end, perhaps spending much more money than he can afford (another cause of anxiety), which should alone be ample evidence that the therapist is somehow fostering an unhealthy external dependency. If this is the case, when the patient thinks of leaving therapy, a conversation like this may result:

CLIENT: I think I would like to stop coming for therapy. I've been coming for years now.
THERAPIST: You sound angry and frustrated to me.
CLIENT: I am somewhat frustrated. All of these years and I really don't see what it is doing for me.
THERAPIST: You are angry at me, aren't you?
CLIENT: Yes, I guess I am. I really just want out. I'd like to try to resolve my problems on my own.
THERAPIST: That proves that you're not ready to leave, you still can't keep yourself from being angry. This transference problem should be worked out before you go out on your own.

This may sound ludicrous, but it is an actual transcript of a session in which a client was talking with her therapist about leaving after seven years of weekly therapy, a client who felt completely trapped, as she really felt she wanted to quit therapy and rely on her own internal signals but could not bring herself to do so without the permission of her therapist! When she talked to me about it, I told her I didn't see how she had *any* obligation to her therapist, and if she felt she didn't need therapy, that was plenty of reason to stop, with just a simple letter or phone call informing him of her decision.

She was reluctant, frightened, because inasmuch as her therapist didn't approve, he must know something about her that she didn't, which would come back to haunt her in the future if she left before he agreed she was "ready."

This kind of dependency-fostering therapy is so common in the "psychology" of our externally oriented culture, and the idea that the professional therapist is necessary to help us solve our problems is so dominant, that many people have no free will left when it comes to deciding whether they need a therapist or not, and come to feel that they *owe* their therapists something beyond the time and money they have spent with them up until now.

Therapists can encourage external thinking and behavior in all areas of their diagnostic and treatment procedures, often with excessive reliance on external psychological test data of highly questionable validity. If you are urged to believe that the causes of your problems are rooted in your birth order, your parents' behavior, your infancy or childhood, your social or economic status, your father's personality, your sibling rivalry or any other source external to yourself; if you are pushed in the direction of wallowing around in your past with the idea that only a trained therapist can lead you back through it and help you unravel the complex network of destructive influences "it" still exerts on you; then you are primarily being trained as an externally rather than an internally directed person, and primarily being addicted to therapy rather than being encouraged to take responsibility for all that is happening to you, and to take control over your own life.

It is important to recognize that you do not necessarily need a dependency-fostering therapist to make yourself a slave to your own "psychology." Externally oriented psychology is so prevalent in our culture that you can end up "shrinking yourself." You will be taught to look for external sources to blame for your difficulties or to analyze them in terms of Oedipus complexes, inferiority complexes, compulsions and so on. It is therefore vital for you to catch yourself *whenever* you start automatically looking for psychological salvation from any source other than your own internal signals. If you are in therapy, and if your therapist is not helping you to eradicate your dependence on those external "determinants" while working toward getting you out of therapy, off those pills, and so onto making new and inner-directed choices, then I recommend that you either give up therapy or look for a therapist who isn't going to become one more externally directing force in your world. And there are many therapists who *are* interested in helping you to become inner-directed—you just have to be persistent in seeking out inner- rather than outer-oriented professionals.

Authority Figures and Laws

What is your gut reaction when you see a policeman? Do you get a little twinge of fear that maybe he's going to catch you doing something wrong? Do you suddenly review everything about your behavior to make sure he won't notice you?

What do you do if a cop gives you a ticket that your internal signals are trying to tell you is really unfair and unjustified, and cites some obscure law like "No parking within fifteen feet of a fire hydrant," which you were "supposed to know" even though the yellow line on the curb was painted only eight feet on either side of the hydrant, and you thought (were misled by it to believe) you were parking legally?

What do you do if you have been the victim of a minor traffic accident and your lawyer wants you to blow your injuries all out of proportion to "get every cent you can out of it" (meanwhile telling you, "Everybody does it.")?

How would you react if you were a soldier, and a superior ordered you to shoot down a lot of unarmed civilians?

What if there was a law that said all Japanese Americans had to be put into concentration camps immediately? Would you go if you were an American of Japanese extraction, or help enforce the law if you weren't?

However you answer questions like these for yourself (we all know what we'd *say*, but how many of us really know what we'd *do*, given specific situations like these?), you already know from your own internal signals that externally directed people will tend to obey authority figures and laws just because the cop has a uniform, the lawyer knows better what they do about these things, it is treason to disobey a superior officer in wartime, and, if the President says all Japanese Americans are potential threats to our internal security, he must be right.

Clearly it is highly authoritarian to believe that anyone who wears a uniform, who has a high-sounding title or who is in a prestigious position deserves to be obeyed unquestioningly, and the "egalitarian antidote" is to accept that all people, yourself included, regardless of their positions or titles, can make mistakes and can give orders that deserve to be challenged or disobeyed. Blind obedience to laws, rules, regulations and authority figures is therefore at the crux of externally dictated authoritarianism.

Once more, this is not to say that internally directed people are compulsive law-breakers or habitually contemptuous of authority. Just the opposite: when internally directed people agree or sympathize with those in authority, they will instinctively pay their tickets or become the ace fighter pilots of the war or the intelligence agents who will gather the best evidence about who really *is* an enemy spy. But they can do this only because, if the authorities ask them to do anything that violates their own personal values, they have learned to ignore those orders and rules—and, as far as your own aspirations toward No-Limit living are concerned, you might want to practice ignoring pompous authority figures and absurd laws as much as you can so long as no one is being hurt.

The next time you are about to yield to authoritarians who happen also to be authority figures, or to laws just because they are laws, remind yourself that in Massachusetts there is still a law on the books that makes it illegal to sit on a round toilet seat.

Organized Religion (in Some Cases)

Most of us are well aware that formal or "organized" religions, when they demand that their members conform blindly to ethnocentric prejudices, rigid traditions or other extensive "codes" dictating how individuals should conduct their lives, when they teach people to ignore their own inner senses of morality, are strong external or authoritarian forces in our culture, sometimes catastrophically dangerous, as when they promote witch-hunts, religious wars or excessive cult loyalty.

The irony of this almost universal awareness is that the most authoritarian of Catholics will be saying about all Muslims that "they are a bunch of glassy-eyed fanatics who never think for themselves, they just blindly follow the dictates of their Ayatollahs," while the most authoritarian of Protestants will be saying the same thing about all Catholics, the most authoritarian of Jews will be saying the same thing about all Christians, and the most authoritarian of Muslims will be saying the same thing about everyone in the Judaeo-Christian tradition. At this rate perhaps only the Buddha can get the last laugh (unless he is too busy crying about how externally oriented many so-called Buddhists have become).

The point is that while you may legitimately see much external direction in other people's "organized religions," the more externally directed you are, the more blind you are likely to be to the external directions of your own church. As one man asked us all at a time when no religion following his teachings was yet very organized, "Why do you see the speck that is in your brother's eye, but do not notice the log that is in your own eye? Or how can you say to your brother, 'Brother, let me take out the speck that is in your eye,' when you yourself do not see the log that is in your own eye? You hypocrite, first take out the log that is in your own eye, and then you will see clearly to take out the speck that is in your brother's eye."*

In other words, those with the biggest externally placed "logs" in their own eyes will be the last to recognize that fact—and also among the first to see specks in other people's eyes. They will be the first to say, "Abortion is right" or "Abortion is wrong," depending on what their religious leaders tell them to think, and also the first to say, "Those people whose religions forbid [or allow] abortion are just like little Hitlers, blindly following their leaders."

As far as religion and your own internal psychological health are concerned, forget about the speck *or* the log that's in anybody else's eye, and just think about your own eyes. Does your religion help put you directly in touch with what your internal signals immediately recognize as your God? Does it encourage people to think for themselves, to consult their own consciences, to think freely in religious matters? Such religions and their members are fine and important parts of any culture. But when it comes to telling human beings that they *must* think the way the "religious authorities" tell them to think, that they must do it this way because God is telling them to do so (through the intermediaries of the church authorities), and essentially conveying the message that "good" church members are supposed to be robots with no free will, or "animals" or "children" who are to be punished severely if they don't do the Church's bidding, "organized religion" emerges as just another authoritarian bureaucracy peddling self-defeating reliance on external punishments and rewards.

The more people are encouraged by their religions to become

* Luke, 6:41–42.

self-directed and in charge of their own behavior, to be *moral* and *just* because they feel it to be correct within themselves, the greater likelihood there is that the mission of all truly great, No-Limit religious leaders will be fulfilled.

Think about your own religion, and ask yourself whether any truly kind and loving God would give people the illusion of having individual free will and then sit back and establish an organized religion with rules that made every important decision in life for those same people. Ask yourself whether *your* God (if you believe in one) *believes in you,* believes that *you* should be an independent thinker, behave in ways that are consistent with the highest morality because your God tells you directly and personally (through your internal signals) that you will have more inner peace if you do, and if your religion is a very beautiful and *personal* experience.

If you find that *you take your religion* as primarily external in its teaching and orientation, remind yourself that some of the worst injustices ever inflicted on human beings have been perpetrated *in the name of* religion, and that, still, your religion can be internally and personally one of the most meaningful forces in your life—as long as it enhances your appreciation and exercise of your own individual free will.

I trust that this chapter has given you a strong idea of the extent to which individuals in our culture have come to be manipulated by external signal-and-reward systems, and has excited you about your own potentials for happiness and growth once you decide to explore, express and, above all, trust those inner voices and impulses that are always trying to guide you by your own lights, without censorship or repression by you or anyone else.

Looking back at Diogenes telling Alexander the Great that the only thing the great conqueror could do for him was to stand out of his light, and John Gardner's recapitulation that "one of the best things we can do for creative men and women is to stand out of their light," perhaps the central message of this chapter is that, assuming we are *all* people of potentially limitless creativity, *the best thing we can do for ourselves is to stand out of our own internal light.*

Look at it this way: a bunch of people have been dropped into the wilderness in the middle of the night, each with a lantern. Assume they are in no danger, there is no particular reason for them to stay together, they are just there to enjoy wandering around until morning, when they will be picked up again wherever they have roamed to. Which ones hold their own lights up high in front of them and cast about for directions to explore that strike their own particular fancies? Which ones automatically fall in behind others, and let their lanterns swing by their sides, so that all that their own lights show is the ground beneath them and the backs of those they are following?

Which ones say, "The first thing we have to do is get organized. Joe has the most experience in the woods, so let's all follow him"? Which ones say, "Okay, everybody, follow me, single file, hup, two, three, four"? Which ones say, "What on earth for? I feel like going the other way, and if anybody wants to come along, let's walk abreast, spread out, so we can light up more of the forest, discover more, and if any one person finds something really fascinating he can call the rest of us to share it"? In sum, which ones want to follow their own lights, and which ones want to stand in their own lights, or block their own lights with the backs of others?

I leave it to you *to decide* which kind of person you want to be. Of course, that has always been up to you, but chances are you have never looked on that as something to be decided by you alone. Chances are that in many or most areas of your life you have fallen into line, on the assumption that the guy at the head of it knew best where everybody should go. If so, you might give thought to what a man said before the religion following his teachings "got organized": "You are the light of the world . . . Nor do men light a lamp and put it under a bushel, but on a stand, and it gives light to all in the house."*

We all claim to love and cherish freedom, but all too often we define freedom itself externally—for instance, as "what the American political system gives us." All too seldom are we engaged in lifelong pursuits of that glorious experience of personal freedom to which only our own lights can lead us.

Naturally we want to be good family members, contented lovers, concerned citizens, and engaged in meaningful work that will improve the quality of life for ourselves and everyone else. But enjoying "life, liberty and the pursuit of happiness" in these and all other areas begins with you, with learning to trust your internal

* Matthew 5:14–15

signals. As Plato wrote, "The man who makes everything that leads to happiness depend upon himself, and not upon other men, has adopted the very best plan for living happily." Plain and simple words a few thousand years ago, plain and simple today: trust yourself.

7 Respect Your Higher Needs

At the beginning of the last chapter I mentioned *the call of your higher needs as a human* as being among those internal signal sources you have to learn to trust on the road to No-Limit living. By "higher needs" I mean those which "go beyond" your biological basic survival needs for food, water, shelter, sleep and exercise to include your needs for love, truth, beauty, meaningful work and a host of others which have been recognized through the ages as providing humans with the impetus for becoming all they can become.

By calling these needs "higher," I do not mean to imply that they are to be placed "above" any of your fundamental needs as a human animal in any kind of priority arrangement. You could argue if you wanted that your animal needs are "higher" because they are the ones you must take care of first and always if you are to meet any of your other needs at all. In another way you could argue that your "higher needs," for love, beauty, truth and the like, should be placed "above" your biological needs, if you conceive of them, as I do, as those needs whose satisfaction can "make you the highest," or contribute most mightily to your happiness. Furthermore, there is every reason to believe that neglecting these higher needs can be just as destructive to you in the long run as not eating, drinking or sleeping can be in the short run.

But why try to rank your basic human needs at all? There is no conceivable reason, except that you tend to neglect some of those needs at the expense of others. So, fundamentally, calling some of your needs "higher" and some "lower" as a means of placing more emphasis on the "higher" ones or neglecting the "lower" ones is a dangerous exercise in dichotomizing that ignores your fundamental unity as a person, splits you in two and causes anxiety and conflict. I choose to call those needs beyond your biological survival needs "higher" because they will help to elevate you to higher and higher levels of No-Limit living, when you begin to see them as *genuine needs* which you must fulfill each day of your life.

To avoid any kind of misconception about the relation between what I call your "basic" and what I call your "higher" needs, it is essential to think of *all* your needs, the entire spectrum from the need to eat to the need for beauty, goodness and justice, as a *network*, sort of like a trampoline. If you are bouncing on a trampoline, it doesn't matter whether it is the legs that break or a cord or the fabric. If any part fails drastically, you are going to end up on the floor. By the same token, if the stand is solid, the cords are strong and the fabric is as elastic, resilient and bouncy as it can be, you are going to be able to bounce as high as you want and do as many tricks as you want with no fear that any part of the trampoline is going to give way under you. Your "basic" needs as a human may be the stand, your "higher" needs may be the fabric. But try bouncing on the fabric while it is lying on the floor, or jumping up and down in the middle of the stand when the fabric is missing, and you will get an idea of how interdependent all your needs really are.

YOUR HIGHER NEEDS AS INSTINCTS

There is growing evidence in psychological research that your higher needs give rise to instincts just as powerful and just as necessary to your survival and happiness as do your basic animal needs. You will recall my having said in Chapter 4 that instincts are responses to your environment which are hereditary and unalterable, that do not involve reason; that they are immediate responses of your body to relieve bodily tension created by those life situations that call for basic animal reactions. Now I am saying additionally that the thoughts and feelings that come with our immediate, instinctive reactions when our higher needs are violated, when we hear a lie or experience something that strikes us as extremely ugly, *are exactly on a par with our reactions when a punch is thrown at us.* Our bodies may not react so dramatically, but in the whole of our persons, bodies-and-minds, an immediate tension is created, and there is an instinctive urge to resolve it: to say to the lie, "Wait a minute, that's not true," or to the ugliness, "This confrontation is really turning ugly, I've got to try to turn it around," or "Lord, this block is really getting ugly. We've got to clean up that vacant lot, cut down that dead tree and plant a new one."

The difference between your animal instincts and the instincts generated by your higher needs is that if your basic animal needs are denied, you are going to get sick or die from physical causes, while if your higher needs are denied in equally extreme ways, your mind is going to come apart, and you will be all but dead mentally, totally unable to control yourself or your destiny (as when you end up in a mental institution or become a suicide of one type or another).

As a matter of fact, denial of higher needs is just what all extreme forms of brainwashing depend on to break apart and reform the minds of their victims. The political prisoner who is sentenced to solitary confinement, who is lied to every day and totally denied any hope for justice; the convert to the cult who is subjected to rituals designed to shame him out of all self-respect, or made to sit in a dark closet for two days, completely deprived of human companionship or any external stimuli; the victims of abuses of psychological "sensitivity training": all of them are having the deprivation-of-higher-needs game played on them to the ultimate. Whether they are able to withdraw enough into the present moment and retain their faith in the meaning and value of life to emerge with their sense of themselves intact, or whether they are successfully bent or broken to the extent that they may be led around by rings in their noses forever, *someone else has intervened between them and their ability to fulfill their higher needs,* in an attempt to gain control over their minds.

In this light, *the higher needs appear as giving basic orientation to life,* rather like the sun and the sky toward which plants grow. They show "which way is up" as far as No-Limit living is concerned, and if you as a human have no idea which way that is, you will be like the (nonexistent) rosebush that sends all its shoots into the darkest corner it can find and buries its buds in the dirt.

It's as simple as this: without the respect of your higher needs to guide you, you will disintegrate as a person. But you do not have to go anywhere or do anything to discover what your own highest needs are or how to go about satisfying them, except to recognize the ways in which they call to you just as clearly as your sexual or self-preservation or other basic instincts, if only you will tune in to them.

YOUR HIGHER NEEDS AND HOW TO MEET THEM

Because our higher needs demand to be recognized so *individually* by each of us, we have to *talk with each other about them* in very abstract or general terms; philosophical terms, really, indicating that while each of us has discovered/created his own idea of what the abstract ideal of love is, for example, we draw from very different experiences of how love has been realized for us. We are therefore likely to disagree with or question each other's "categorical" definitions of love in some way or another, and so we *need* vague and general terms like "love," subject by definition to all kinds of different interpretations, if we are to talk with each other about our higher needs at all.

Such vague, general or philosophical terms, however, do not mean much unless we find ways to make them meaningful for our own lives. The function that ideas like love, truth and beauty can really serve for you can best be demonstrated by my discussing a selected group of concepts that have pointed *me* most directly toward appreciation of what I identify as *my* higher needs, and how they might be of use to you in gaining renewed respect for your own higher needs. Keep in mind that No-Limit living means more and more permitting yourself to be motivated by these higher needs and recognizing them as absolute needs rather than luxuries or secondary rewards.

Individuality

The need to create one's own individuality is an instinct that rules in every aspect of life, and the more it is denied, as in societies oriented toward regimenting everyone to conform, to look, dress, think and behave "just like everyone else," the more a creeping sense of malaise, of boredom, of dullness, descends on the minds of individuals.

Individuality is not something that you want to express purely or originally for its own sake. Your higher needs are not trying to tell you that you have to wear a big green pompom on your nose just so that you will stand out in a crowd and demonstrate to everybody what an individual (or what a "character") you are. Rather, individuality comes about "by accident," in your pursuit of the way you feel like doing whatever you do—dressing, cooking, talking, thinking, playing golf or painting a picture. In the NEZ person, however, individuality as a whole ends up being cultivated when he respects his internal signals above all external signals that are trying to deprive him of his *basic human right to individuality*—to make him paint the same picture the same way everybody else is painting it, to answer a question exactly the way everybody else in the class is supposed to answer it, to wear the same hat everybody else wears at the "regulation angle."

In my own life I have found that many others have appreciated my individuality, the particular way I choose to do things, as much as they appreciate their own, while those who have tried hardest to condemn my individuality and curtail it have inevitably displayed the fewest signs of individuality themselves, have appeared the most robotlike.

Think about the elevator operator who gives you a snooty look when you come into "his" high-class hotel at seven in the evening in your sweatsuit and get on "his" elevator at the same time as a bunch of guests in formal evening dress. His look says to you, "Sir, *we* don't wear sweatsuits in the elevators after five P.M. in this hotel." Isn't he inevitably the one who is dressed in the most meticulously "proper" uniform, with *no individual touch* added to it —never a flower in *his* lapel—and one of the most grim-faced and humorless of people? If you greet him with a cheery "Hello," he may quietly and politely say, "Good day, sir," or he may just grunt.

But he won't respond to your friendly invitation to treat each other as individuals. He fears his own individuality and so fears yours.

On the other hand, the elevator operator who prizes his own individuality and appreciates others in the same way is the one who greets you as cheerily as you greet him, gets a kick out of people in sweatsuits mixing with people in evening dress, remembers you, tells you a joke, picks up a conversation where you left it last time—and he is the one who is most likely to have a flower in his lapel, a bandana around his neck, a picture of his new granddaughter sticking out of his lunchbox, or any other little touch of his individuality for the world to notice.

For most people, individuality is irrepressible and even in countries where individualism is heavily frowned on, or in organizations like the military where it is actively discouraged, the instinctive need for it proves so strong that it surfaces anyway, although in subtle ways. Perhaps it manifests itself in a piece of gold in the front tooth, or a tattoo, or the particular angle at which the soldier wears his hat. Perhaps it is in those bright-red flower-pattern curtains in that one window of that endless housing project in which all the apartments look the same, or in an individual's own special way of smiling, laughing or dancing. But wherever your individuality breaks out, in whatever part of this world, in whatever situation, *it is the mark of your own originality as a person who never has been before on this planet and who never will be again* (at least in *this* present moment), and *you must respect your higher need to be that one unique individual now*, or you will virtually "lose your life."

Look at it this way: you were not born in a test tube like a million other experimental animals in "your generation," destined to be kept under the most controlled of conditions in some laboratory so that some mad scientist could assign you to the "control" group, to be treated exactly the same way, subjected to exactly the same environment, schedule and stimuli as the members of the "experimental" group, merely for the sake of the experimental difference the scientist wants to introduce. You were not born as a lab rat, destined to have somebody say about you someday, "Well, this is a member of the control group, and you'll notice that he is normally healthy, whereas half of these rats over here, the ones we tested that new chemical on, are sick."

But *that is precisely the way you think of yourself when you deny your need for individuality!* You are assigning yourself to the "control group." At the same time you are essentially denying a fact that (I hope) no scientist can ever alter: that you were born at a certain time and place in human history where *nobody* else was born. You have grown in a way in which nobody else has ever grown before, and already you have created an individuality for yourself that is yours alone, that will never be duplicated by another living being no matter *how* long time goes on. *Your destiny to be born, to live and to die as a unique, incalculably complex individual human being is something you can deny only in your imagination; it is a reality you can never erase.*

On the other hand, it is by accepting your human destiny and appreciating your unique individuality and that of others to the fullest that you gain a holistic, No-Limit view of yourself and come to respond to all your life situations by thinking, "Nobody has ever faced *this particular situation* before. I as an individual am called upon to make the most *creative choices I can* in this situation, for the benefit of myself and everybody else. *My individuality*—my personal freedom of choice and my responsibility—is a reality I could not escape if I wanted to. I must respect my own individuality *now*, or I will lose it and become as externally controlled, as individuality-starved, as the test rat in the laboratory."

If you heed your instincts for individuality in all areas, I think you will find, as I have, that they will lead you to a feeling of creative enjoyment of all your activities.

Respect

"To respect" means to consider worthy of high regard, and also to refrain from interfering with, as when you respect someone's need for privacy. From this it should be clear that the need for self-respect and the need to respect others around you (at least those who respect you) is fundamental to the human being, because if you do not respect yourself you automatically categorize yourself as *un*worthy of high regard or deserving to be held in *low* esteem, and you virtually demand shabby treatment from everyone else.

I mentioned earlier that techniques of brainwashing and psychological control in general depend heavily on attacking the individual's sense of self-respect, and that if it is lost the individual virtually disintegrates. Few of us are subjected to such extreme attempts to deny us our self-respect during our lives, but we are all involved constantly in situations in which respect between people is "supposed" to be *unequal.* For instance, many parents demand unquestioning respect from their children all the time, but demand that their children *earn their* respect by doing what the parents define as respectable. Many teachers and other authority figures likewise demand respect for themselves solely because of their positions, yet make it quite clear that students and other subordinates as such are not entitled to respect. A perfect example was Richard Nixon, who demanded respect for the Presidency while feeling perfectly free to voice consummate disrespect for student protesters and other "bums" who didn't like the way he was running things (in fact, many commentators trace Nixon's problems to a fundamental confusion over whether he was really the President or the Presidency).

Certain types of policemen are prone to pull this you-respect-me-I-don't-respect-you game. They are the ones who, if they stop you for speeding, are not content simply to give you a ticket, but have to swagger up to the car, demand with a condescending sneer to see your license and registration, treat you as though you were the worst of hardened criminals—the cops who seem to be challenging you to show them the slightest bit of disrespect (so that, you assume, they can give you another ticket, arrest you or *something,* for "disrespecting a police officer"). They make it obvious that your horrible crime of going eight miles an hour over the speed limit has given them license to disrespect you completely as a person, and they expect you to grovel before them, apologize *to them* for speeding (although, really, you ought to be saying only to yourself, "I'm sorry I wasn't watching the speedometer more closely—I'll do better from now on").

By now it may have occurred to you that respect between people is *real* respect, in the healthy sense, only if it is equal or reciprocal. Otherwise, it is just homage of one person to another. And the idea of *demanding* respect from anybody is absurd. The parent who demands respect from his children feels he has to demand it precisely because he has not given his children fundamental respect as human beings to begin with. If he had, the children would have responded naturally, instinctively, with their own respect, and no demands on either side would have been necessary. What such parents will get in return for their demands will be "shows" of respect, but not real, heartfelt respect, which in the end, when the parent's dominance of the children starts to run out of gas, will be about as useful as a gasoline can full of water when it comes to starting the relationship up again on a truly equal basis.

And so it is with respect for yourself. If you find that you have to *demand* that you respect yourself, it is only because you have somehow forgotten the basic truth that all humans, yourself included, are *automatically entitled to the respect of everyone.* Perhaps if someone shows consistent disrespect for you, you may end up saying, "I have no respect for that person," but if you do, it should be in the context of "I started out automatically granting respect to that person just like everybody else, but it is clear that he has no idea himself of the meaning of real respect; *he doesn't respect everybody's equal need for respect,* doesn't understand that basic human respect is not something to be manipulated, withheld, denied."

Moreover, the difference between your sometimes (perhaps) saying of others, "I have no respect for them," and your *ever* saying to yourself, "*I have no respect for me,*" is that *you have complete control over your own thoughts about respect,* and if you accept it as a higher human need of yours and everybody else's along the lines I am suggesting, you will never have to say to yourself, "I don't respect myself."

You must have this self-respect if you are to be a healthy organism. If you are denied this respect, you will soon see yourself regressing in every way. First you won't eat properly, you won't take care of your body, you'll lose interest in life, and eventually you'll become a very sick person. The instinct for respect is so basic that it applies to all of us, and yet most really sick people (mentally and often physically as well) simply fail to respect themselves. They treat themselves in disrespectful ways, and consequently other people do the same. Having respect is a basic need, and if you don't believe it, then try going into a mental institution and seeing all of those people who live there permanently. Notice the effects of a lack of respect. Observe closely how they got to be so mentally depressed that they "broke down." It starts when they are very young and are treated disrespectfully by significant others; before long they begin to believe those messages, and they are no longer able to function as healthy people.

Belonging

The need for *belonging*, with a community of humans, with your own environment or with the world as a whole, in the sense that you feel "at home" in your world, is as vital to your life as food or sleep. Human beings do not function well without a feeling of belonging. Even in the case of the hermit or the mountain man who roams the Rockies alone for months or years on end, if his sense of belonging appears satisfied, it is because he feels he *belongs to* the woods, the mountains, a certain part of nature, and *it belongs to him*.

Most of us, however, prefer (or, as the planet becomes more crowded, are destined) to work out belonging for ourselves in increasingly complex societies. That this higher need can be as easily denied in complex societies as in simpler situations is easily seen in the derelicts, "bums," junkies and others who can find no sense of belonging in the streets of our largest cities, or in the elderly who languish in nursing homes, deteriorate and give up on themselves because they no longer feel they *belong with* anybody, or *belong in* the world.

The opposite of belonging is *alienation*, which, as any alien will tell you, may be an inevitable stage in most lives. Sometimes you just have to move away from, even alienate yourself from, some people, family communities or even countries.

But alienation is valuable only as a stage or step toward fulfilling your need for belonging better somewhere else, with someone else, in another country, another job or whatever. It is constructive only if it happens in response to the call of your own higher need for belonging and your "better idea" of how you might satisfy that need. In those for whom alienation from everything and everyone has become a way of life, you will note suffering from depression, anxiety, and even physical deterioration, which often results in institutionalization or death.

The first step toward fulfilling your need for belonging is to ask yourself whether you really feel you belong in the world in the first place. When you walk down your block, do you feel, "Yes, I am just where I belong; that bird is singing for me, and I belong here appreciating that bird's song; there is Joe—he belongs here, too"? Or do you think, "I don't belong here; I really should be at the office by now. I wish I were back in California. We don't belong in this neighborhood, we belong in that swankier neighborhood across town. Who is that guy? Does he belong here?" or other, similar thoughts that indicate chronic alienation from "your world"?

If you find yourself hurrying through your life *always* trying to find someplace or some community in which you can feel that you *really belong,* it is because you have not accepted the basic fact that *you belong right where you are now,* in the sense that nobody on earth has a better right to be in this world than you have.

Suppose you are a poor kid with tattered clothes trudging through an upper-class neighborhood, dragging your lawnmower behind you, looking to pick up a few bucks cutting lawns, and a guy in a Cadillac pulls up next to you and says, "Hey, kid, get out of here. You don't belong in this neighborhood."

As he drives off down the block, what is your reaction? Do you feel, "He's right, I really don't. I thought I could get away with it, at least enough to buy myself some decent clothes and get some regular jobs here, but I should never have assumed that I belonged here in the first place"? Or do you say, "What the hell does he mean, I don't belong here? Does he mean I don't belong on the face of the earth, that if I can't afford any better clothes than this, right now I should go kill myself? He just drove away down the road, which is a part of the face of the earth, and a public road to boot. Who is he to tell me I don't belong here? I have as much right to walk on this road as he does to drive on it. I belong in this world as much as he does"?

The point I am making is that unless you start out accepting that *you belong where you are right now,* in the sense that you have an inalienable right to be in this world as much as anyone else does, you are denying yourself the chance ever to satisfy your needs for belonging *wherever you are now.* If you find yourself constantly saying to yourself, "I don't belong here, I belong somewhere else," then the problem is not that others have rejected you or tried to deny your need for belonging, but that you have rejected yourself as far as "belonging in the world" is concerned.

If you are willing to admit that you just plain belong in your world, on earth where you are now *in the first place,* and have forgotten all ideas like "I was born in the wrong century—I really belong back in the seventeenth century," then you are open to meeting your own higher needs for belonging *as you sense them now for yourself.* You are ready to ask yourself questions like "Why don't I feel that I belong to this family, this community, this country?" You are ready to identify those areas of life in which your needs for belonging might be fulfilled, to sort out those you really want to cultivate, and to respond to your own belonging instincts when it comes to how to satisfy them.

We all have an instinct to belong, to feel important, to engage in significant relationships. And the denial of these things is just as devastating to your organism as the denial of food or sleep; the only difference is that the symptoms just take a little longer to surface.

Affection and Love

The overriding importance of affection and love to the human infant is well known to all parents who have cared in the slightest about their children, and the effects of extreme deprivation of affection on infants are well known to all. An infant who is fed and changed on time all the time, who has all his "basic animal needs" met, but who is never picked up, cuddled, kissed, fondled, played with—an infant subjected to total deprivation of human contact and affection—will quickly languish, show signs of rejecting the world, become cranky, lose appetite, reject food or drink, and ultimately he may starve himself to death. In less severe instances, in which parents treat infants perfunctorily, picking them up and playing with them now and then, for a few minutes here and a few minutes there, but always hurriedly and with some resentment, the infants will similarly show signs of life rejection, but they will live, and perhaps as they grow they will overcome their deprivation and recognize how important affection and love are to them and everybody else. If they retain the memory of how deeply deprived they felt, they may become the most loving and affectionate people in the world. But whether the child within you has been starved for affection up till now or not, you still have to decide that you can have love and affection today and that you are not going to postpone it any longer. You not only deserve love and affection, you absolutely need it for your own survival.

We all know people of whom we say, for instance, "He's a very conscientious husband and father, but he's not very affectionate." Perhaps we most often hear remarks like this from people talking about their own family members, and usually the subjects are men, because, according to the male/female dichotomy, women are supposed to be overtly affectionate, especially with their children, but men are not—they are supposed to be the breadwinners, the protectors, the disciplinarians, the "immovable rocks," and overt displays of affection and tenderness are regarded as signs of weakness or vulnerability. This, of course, is absurd, and the irony of it is that in my experience men who respect their own needs for affection and allow themselves to touch, hug, kiss, cuddle and the like more than traditional social customs dictate are inevitably stronger than the rigid followers of the *macho* image, at least in the sense that they are more at peace with themselves, more even-tempered, less irritable, less inclined to get rattled about little things or to come apart in crises.

Quite simply, the person who systematically denies his needs for affection artificially alienates himself from those he loves and, whether he admits it to himself or not, feels to some extent isolated in the world. As much as he tells himself or others, "My son knows I love him without my going around hugging him all the time," there is something irreplaceable about physical contact when it comes to "really feeling" like a part of your family, of humanity, of the world.

Animals know all about this. The cats who sleep curled up around one another don't do so just because they're physically cold and need one another's body heat, but because they like the emotional warmth, if you will, that comes from physically feeling like a part of life, or of catdom, as a whole. The dog who comes running up to be petted has no qualms that "the other dogs are really going to think I'm not very tough if I do this." But a funny thing about humans is that, while just about everybody respects the need of his dog, cat or canary for affection, by custom the father is not supposed to put his arm around his son's shoulder as they walk off the field after the ball game; he *is* supposed to pet his dog, and to get a kick out of how affectionate his dog is to him. Perhaps that's because everybody knows *dogs* need affection—after all, they're only animals!

The conclusion to be drawn is that all we have to do as animals is treat ourselves and our loved ones as well as we treat our dogs, and we will soon find everybody's needs for affection being well met.

The need to love and be loved is somewhat more problematical than the need to be affectionate. While affection is a way of expressing love for others and "comes naturally" once we love a person as a friend, a mate or whatever, love entails questions about the self:

"Can I find anybody to love, and to love me, in the first place?" "How do I know whether or not I really love this person, or whether this person really loves me?" It seems that your ability to fulfill your need to love and be loved depends half on you, and, further, that if nobody else chooses to love or be loved by you there is not a great deal you can do about it. Others are just going to starve you of love.

This kind of attitude will not do, because there is absolutely no profit in your *worrying* about finding people to love or getting others to love you. There is no point in your admitting that the fulfillment of any of your own higher needs depends on anyone but yourself; and all you do psychologically when you think that satisfaction of your love needs depends on the whims of others is set yourself up to blame others for the lack of love in your life, resign yourself to it and pretend there's nothing you can do about it.

Fortunately, if you just think about love a little bit, you will see that, as much as our society emphasizes your finding that perfect, one-in-a-million guy or girl whom you were "meant to love," as much as you were taught to pluck daisy petals and recite, "He loves me, he loves me not," as many popular songs as you've heard repeating, "Don't you want somebody to love? Don't you need somebody to love? Wouldn't you love somebody to love? You'd better find somebody to love," as many parents as you've heard tell their children, "Make sure he *really loves you* before you commit yourself," and as many people as there are who spend immense amounts of time and energy worrying about how to "get" others whom they imagine they love to love them in return, the fact is that *your ability to love and be loved depends completely on yourself.*

Consider the myth of the perfect mate, the idea that the man or woman whom the fates or God intended you to marry is lost somewhere out there in the world like a needle in a haystack, and that you have to be lucky enough to run across your destined mate, recognize and be recognized by him or her and agree that you love each other, before you can begin to love-and-be-loved in the romantic/erotic sense.

Even supposing it were true that there is out there just one perfect mate for everybody (which any widow or widower, for instance, who has married happily for the second time will tell you is absurd), if you do not know how to love and be loved when you meet that person and cannot learn, no love is going to be possible between you. And if that person does not sense that you know how to love and be loved or want to learn more about it with him, you are going to go your separate ways in a hurry. Afterward you may say, "That bastard, he rejected me," but *what really happened?* You went out looking for that "one special person," and all the time, instead of asking, "What can I learn about love now, with this person?" you have primarily been worrying about "Is he the one, or not? How do I know whether I really love him? If I do, how can I get him to love me? What if I love him and he doesn't love me? My heart will be broken!" You have been so anxious about getting to the last daisy petal and finding out whether (or deciding that) he loves you or he loves you not that you have neglected to water the flowers! You have worried so much about the status and future of "the relationship" that you have been mentally blocked from actively cultivating it.

By pretending that love is sort of like a flying saucer that may or may not swoop down out of the sky and spirit you away to some magic world of ecstasy at any moment, you have denied its essential nature as *an art of present-moment living, of working-and-playing-now,* an art like dancing, which, if you love it and practice it, you can do with just about any partner at any time. A person who can't find anybody to love and can't get anybody to love him is like someone who *says* he wants to dance but just can't seem to find the right partner (someone he will automatically whirl away with, magically and effortlessly doing all kinds of fancy steps he has never bothered to learn).

To understand more clearly what I am saying, it might help you to think of those people you have known about whom you have said or heard others say, "Everybody loves him." Could that possibly have happened because he was lucky enough to fall into an environment that just happened to have all the right people *for him* in it? Do you suppose that if he were plunked down in a foreign culture halfway around the world, there just might be all the wrong people for him there, and nobody might love him?

Of course not. Everybody loves that person because firstly he loves himself and then he knows how to love everybody in one way or another. He knows how to be thoughtful in any human interaction without worrying about it (and possibly worrying it to death with the endless doubts and futurizing that kill so many potential love relationships). He demonstrates how to be considerate, to make others feel immediately at home with him; how to "open up" himself without being defensive or afraid that others will reject him, which he couldn't care less about.

Of rejection and the fear of it, the No-Limit lover will ask, "Who wants to run after somebody who doesn't want to dance with you —and snaps at you when you ask—when there are so many others around who really would love to dance?" And he will conclude that the person who "rejects" him isn't doing anything *to him* at all; he is just admitting his own inability to love or be friendly and playful in this situation—primarily, rejecting himself.

The moral is that loving-and-being-loved is not something that "happens to" you, but a creative art you pursue with other people in an endless variety of ways, from friendships-for-a-day to lifetime romantic/erotic relationships. Whether your needs for love and affection are going to be met in your life (at least in your adult life) depends solely on whether or not you really want to "dance," and whether you are really willing to learn how.

Of course, you have to accept that no two partners can learn to dance together without stepping on each other's toes now and then, and that you occasionally may get a really bizarre partner who just seems to want to step on your toes (and who may blame you for getting your toes under his feet instead of trying not to make the same mistake again), whom you just do not feel like trying with anymore. But if you are game, you will definitely find that there are tons of people who feel like trying the friendship jig with you, and plenty who are willing to give the romantic/erotic tango a whirl, too. As long as you keep in mind that the dance has nothing to do with your "acquiring" a wife or husband, "nailing down" a bunch of friends, "leading" your children through all their paces; that it only involves your learning how to improvise some love, affection, friendship or whatever else seems to be appropriate with whomever you happen to be with at the moment; and recognize every dance as a chance for you to "get higher," dance more inspiringly than you ever have before; you will find that your needs for love and affection know pretty well how to satisfy themselves.

You must already know how important your need to love and be loved is to you. If you are saying to yourself, "Well, it isn't all *that* important, I can do without it if I have to," or "I've tried, but it's just more trouble than it's worth," or even, as the title of a satirical popular song shouts, "Love stinks!," you must secretly know you are rationalizing, mumbling fruitlessly about sour grapes, rejecting dancing because it sometimes involves toes getting stepped on. You must suspect that you really don't *know how to love yourself, in both senses:* you do not have self-love (which is almost the same as self-respect), and you yourself do not know how to go about loving others.

If this is so, and if you feel a palpable lack of love in your life (and consequently of affection, since one follows the other), forget about whether others love you or not, and about trying to decide whom you love and whom you don't, which is just another way of abusing the love/hate dichotomy. Think only about how you can have some fun of the highest kind now with a friend, a lover, your parents or your children, the stranger with whom you exchange a few words in the subway or the store, anyone you run across. Let your natural love for yourself and humanity just try working itself out wherever it wants to, and you will find that love really *is* everywhere, all the time, for anyone who really does want to dance, from the newborn infant in its mother's arms to the ninety-five-year-old in the nursing home whom "everybody just loves."

Meaningful Work

We all need to feel productive as human beings. This is not to say that we must have a job working for someone else in order to be fulfilled in life. But the feeling of being useful, of creatively making a difference, of pursuing some task and carrying it out to completion, is crucial. These are basic needs. The consequence of their neglect is boredom and the most painful and debilitating of all human experiences: *loss of interest.* People who lose interest in life are simply wasting away. They are without purpose and they become a burden to themselves and their society as a whole. They suffer severe depressions, self-pity and physical symptoms of every description, and they eventually can die from this malady. Yes indeed, it is an all-out instinct to be productive and engaged in meaningful work activity. To those who don't follow this instinct, there is the boring life style and the eventual immobilization that come from inaction.

In this sense, every human being alive wants to work, at least originally, and it is only if you get stuck for too long in a job that is too tedious, that puts too much pressure on you or that you do not feel within yourself is really doing anybody any good that you are likely to think, "I don't want to work anymore. I want to retire and just play and relax all the time." If you do think that, however, I firmly believe you are misjudging yourself, and you will find that out soon enough if you do try retiring completely. Life will start to feel empty; you will start to feel useless, and after a while you will find yourself looking for meaningful things to do, whether it's volunteer work at the hospital, taking the neighbors' kids to a ball game or the circus so that the parents can have some time off, or trying to get that junk-filled vacant lot down the street cleaned up.

Just how deep the need for meaningful work is can be seen in the physically and/or mentally handicapped. No matter how severe their handicaps may be, such individuals can all do *something;* they always *want* to do something, and the difference between those who are given chances to do something and those who are not is like night and day. Those who are denied the opportunity to work, or are given some trivial job of make-believe work that they know is just meant to keep them busy and out of other people's hair, are resentful, frustrated, depressed. Their handicaps are exaggerated, their physical conditions deteriorate, and, like anyone else denied the chance to work, they may eventually go insane or become inactive and chronically dependent.

Those who are offered or can figure out something to do, however, and are given the help they need to do it blossom as people in the most exciting ways, and they will almost universally tell you that it was not their handicap that they resented but the possibility that the handicap would be allowed to deny them the right to work, the pride and the self-respect that come from making a contribution to society and earning a living. In general, they appreciate the need to work far more deeply than anyone else and are astounded at the idea that anyone could ever regard the need for meaningful work as being less than absolutely fundamental to human beings. In addition, they are able to find meaning in just about whatever work they *can* do, and they are hard pressed to understand how able-bodied people can be carping about their jobs all the time, thinking, "You just wait until you have an accident or get sick or something and can't do that work anymore. You'll carp twice as long and loud about that."

Another group that deeply appreciates the need for meaningful work is the elderly, those who have been forced to retire at age sixty-five when they know they have many more years of work "in them." The Gray Panthers and other such "senior citizens' " groups have been saying more and more forcefully in recent years, "If you're going to deny us the right to work, why don't you just bury us at age sixty-five?" They have seen all too dramatically the difference between those in "forced-retirement" fields who have been unable to find meaningful work after they've been kicked out of their professions suddenly on their sixty-fifth birthdays and those who have their own businesses from which nobody can fire them, or who are in fields where forced retirement does not apply. They know perfectly well that the hardware store owner, the lawyer or whoever who is hale and hearty, alert and productive into his eighties might well be dead now if he had been forced to retire at sixty-five. To them (and to me) it is a matter of consummate hypocrisy that members of the Congress who pass forced-retirement legislation for others would never pass the same laws for themselves, and insist on their right to go on serving in Congress into *their* eighties and nineties if they want to.

Whether or not your work is meaningful to you in the sense I have been talking about is a question only you can answer, but first you have to ask it seriously, which far too few people do. If you are a teacher, a doctor, a full-time parent or are working in any area in which your service to society is or at least should be quite evident, you may not have much trouble saying, "Of course my work is meaningful." But if you are a factory worker turning out so many shock absorbers a day, if you are in advertising turning out so many jingles a week, if you are a blackjack dealer in a casino, the question may be a little more perplexing. The factory worker may say, "Well, it's meaningful in the sense that people need shock absorbers in their cars. I am definitely producing useful and necessary hardware. But the work itself is pretty tedious; it doesn't give me much chance to exercise creativity or ingenuity, so it's not all that meaningful to me." Or the factory worker may say, "Well, the work is pretty repetitive, but I find ways to exercise my ingenuity—for instance, when a machine breaks down and I find the best and quickest way to fix it, or when I make suggestions for improving the process or the product, creating better and safer working conditions. Yes, I'd say it's very meaningful all around."

The advertising man may say, "It's completely meaningless. Most of the crap we advertise is useless junk that we're just trying to create a demand for with these idiotic jingles. I'm doing it only for the money. Otherwise it's a complete waste of my time and talent." (I've heard some advertising people say this in just so many words.) Or he may say, "Well, I think advertising performs a valuable service in giving the public information about products, and even if some of the products aren't the greatest there are some we advertise that I think are excellent. I try to be as creative as I can in giving people solid information about the products, even if it's in a jingle and a few lines of accompanying copy. I think I'm making a positive difference in the business, and so it's very meaningful to me."

The blackjack dealer may say, "Of course it's meaningless. All I do is win people's money for the casino. It's very interesting to me, all the different people you see, the different ways their minds work, but as far as a contribution to society is concerned, it's zero." Or he may say, "It's very meaningful. I find it fascinating, and as far as a contribution to society is concerned, well, people are going to gamble anyway, and at least here the taxes on the casino pay a big part of the state's education budget."

As I said earlier, if you do not find your vocation meaningful, you have two choices: find a way to make it meaningful or get out of it and into something you know you *can* make meaningful. This latter course may involve some patience, some risks, some retraining or further education, some financial "sacrifice." Furthermore, you may encounter some disapproval by others who just cannot understand why you would give up what they consider security to pursue whatever it is you want to try, those critics who really seem to believe that if you're making enough money you can meet all your human needs in one way or another, and that whether you consider your job meaningful or not is not very important. But if you appreciate the central necessity for meaningful work in your life and everyone else's, you know that if your work is meaningless you don't have real security, and no amount of money is going to compensate you for the emptiness in your life.

Recreation and Relaxation

If you consider those people you know or know of who have had the most productive and constructive lives over long periods of time, you will find that they all respected their higher needs for the self-renewal, restoration and spiritual refreshment that come from recreation. Winston Churchill found painting the perfect way to turn his back on the troubles of the world for a while. Woody Allen plays the clarinet in a New York City pub once a week. Many leading academics, for some reason, are voracious devourers of murder mysteries. Whether it's chess or volleyball, camping or restoring antiques, whatever form of recreation you choose, it is essential for you to heed your basic biological need for regular recreation. If you think you can get away without it, especially if you have become a "workaholic," so driven—by your compulsion to start preparing your next court case the instant you finish your current one, for instance—that you never give yourself a break, your work is going to suffer because you will run into the law of diminishing returns. You may work twelve hours a day, but over the last few hours you are going to slow way down, lose your ability to think clearly, and be lucky to get one good hour of work out of four hours of beating your head against the wall. If you keep it up day after day, you will find that you are getting slower and duller all the time, and even your first working hours of the morning will not be as productive as they should be. Next you will find your mind starting to wander, trying to take the time off that you refuse to give it. You will find yourself staring out the window blankly. You will say, "Come on, snap out of it! Get back to work!" But minutes later you will find yourself staring out the window again.

If at this point you do not listen to those internal voices that are saying to you, "What the hell are you trying to do to me? I'm not a machine, you know, that's going to keep running the same way just because you keep leaning on the 'On' button! I want to go for a walk in the park or something *right now!*" you are just going to keep driving yourself in deeper and deeper, thinking, "Man, what an unproductive day I've had! Now I've got to work all night!" And eventually your mind will just start to unravel, your anxiety level will go through the roof, and you will have to be carted off to a hospital or a mental institution or a health spa or *someplace* where you stand a chance of putting the pieces back together.

In fact, there is evidence that much of the process of creative thinking goes on "unconsciously," if you will, during recreation. Henri Poincaré, the great French mathematician, had been racking his brains for days on a series of complex problems. Then, as he later wrote,

> Just at this time I left Caen, where I was then living, to go on a geologic excursion under the auspices of the school of mines. The changes of travel made me forget my mathematical work. Having reached Coutances, we entered an omnibus to go some place or other. At the moment

> when I put my foot on the step the idea came to me, without anything in my former thoughts seeming to have paved the way for it, that the transformations I had used to define the Fuchsian functions were identical with those of non-Euclidean geometry. I did not verify the idea; I should not have had time, as, upon taking my seat in the omnibus, I went on with a conversation already commenced, but I felt a perfect certainty. On my return to Caen, for conscience's sake I verified the result at my leisure.*

Even more famous examples include Newton under the apple tree and Archimedes in the bathtub. So if you think you are doing your work any favors by denying yourself recreation, think again. Whatever your work is, whether you are a housewife "stuck in" all day every day with five small children, or a construction worker obsessed with the idea that you have to take every minute of overtime you get, or a political candidate with a calendar booked solid for the next four months, your body and your mind are going to rebel if you don't give them a chance to "turn their backs" completely on whatever it is you are engaged in all the time, and to engage in something else purely for the fun of it.

Along with the basic need to work and feel productive comes the instinct to relax, slow down and be able to simply get away from pressure. Your instinct to relax is necessary in that you would simply kill yourself with pressure and fatigue if you didn't have it. Without the ability to relax, you leave yourself open to many forms of disease, including hypertension, ulcers, heart disease, rashes, cramps, nervous tics and so on. Your body knows that too much pressure is a killer, and so it is fully equipped with the ability and the desire to get away from pressure situations and enjoy leisure. If you don't believe this is an instinct, try to imagine how you could survive if you didn't have an internal mechanism to tell you when you were exhausted. You'd just go on working until you collapsed. Unfortunately, many people have ignored this internal instinct and destroyed themselves in the process. You can become much more tuned in to your absolute need to have recreation and relaxation if you trust your instinct when you feel that you are just too harried. Whatever you do, your instinct to relax will stay with you, even if you push it away and ignore it.

* Henri Poincaré, "Mathematical Creation," in *The Creative Process*, ed. Brewster Ghiselin (Mentor, 1955).

Creativity

Many people, if asked to think about what the higher needs of humans are, might come up with certain things I have mentioned, such as love or meaningful work, but my guess is that few would list creativity, primarily because the creative/uncreative dichotomy is so pervasive in our culture. You hear it constantly in phrases like "Jimmy's very creative; I'll bet he grows up to be an artist. I'm not very creative. Creative people are different from most people. You have to be a little crazy to be creative." From thinking this way it is only a short step to concluding that just a few select "creative geniuses" should even *try* to be creative, thinking that creativity manifests itself only on museum walls, between the covers of books and so on, and that it would be pretentious and even foolish for you to aspire to creativity. How could creativity be a universal human need if so few people are equipped to fulfill it for themselves?

Naturally this will not do, because if everybody got to categorizing himself as uncreative all originality would cease and we would end up watching reruns of movies forever, building things the way we now do forever, thinking, talking, teaching, doing everything we do the same way forever, which would cause the human race to be bored to death in six months.

Fortunately, because creativity *is* such a deeply rooted instinct, this is not about to happen, and if you open your eyes wide and just look at all the things around you that people have created, from today's newspaper to the slides in the playground to the United Nations to the Apollo spacecraft and every other human-made thing, you will be awestruck by how creative we humans are. In fact, the opposite of creativity is simply imitation, so that the only way you can *avoid* being creative is slavishly to imitate others all the time—in the extreme, following another person around all the time and imitating everything he does.

In another sense the opposite of creativity is destructiveness, wantonly tearing down good, valuable and beautiful things people have made, or acting destructively in human relationships. In order to avoid destructiveness, you have to be creative in doing your own original thinking about yourself and the whole world, and to get that process started you have to avoid imitation of the thinking of self-destructive people (and there *is* no imitating the thought processes of really creative people, because there is no formula for originality). *So I consider the avoidance of blind imitation or thoughtless conformity to be the key to all of us meeting our needs for creativity and living up to the heights of our limitless creative potentials.*

The first thing for you to recognize about your native creativity is that it is the expression of your individuality, as ever present as your shadow, which will follow you everywhere. It oozes out in subtle ways even when you try to deny it; it rushes forward when you instinctively need it, when you don't have any chance to interfere with its response, as when you "automatically" add the right ingredients to your homemade soup or create a play in the huddle of a touch-football game, or come to the aid of an automobile accident victim. Some people might say, "That's not creativity, that's just good old Yankee ingenuity," but I would then ask, "Why do we talk about good old Yankee ingenuity all the time, and never about good new Yankee creativity? Ingenuity is *one type of creativity;* isn't it what inventors rely on, and wouldn't we call Thomas Edison, for instance, creative?"

The point is to forget how ingenuity and other talents you may pride yourself on having are "different from" creativity, because the distinction makes no sense, unless you need an explanation of how apples and oranges are different from fruit. Concentrate instead on looking at all the activities in your life in which creativity (as opposed to imitation) does surface or wants to surface, and I think you will find this is in *all* your activities. All you have to do to let it out anywhere—in cooking, playing with the children, fixing the car, in your vocation, in decorating your house or writing a letter, in absolutely anything *you choose*—is stop for a second and ask yourself, "How much of what I am doing here is just thoughtless imitation? If I let my imagination run wild on how this *might* be done better, more beautifully, and *think later* about which ones of my fantasies are practical and how, *who knows what I'm going to come up with?*"

That is the whole point about creativity, what makes it such a vital human instinct: the fascination and suspense of never knowing *what* on earth your mind is going to come up with next. What makes creativity work is accepting the offerings of your imagination as you accept the shells that your eye spots on the beach. Some among that vast sea of shells you will just want to glance at; others you may want to pick up and examine for a little bit; some you may have fun throwing as far as you can out into the ocean; some you take home and keep around for a few weeks; and some you may want to polish, make into a necklace, frame, even keep forever.

This is exactly the way "creative writers" work. They open the doors of their minds to suggestions from their imaginations. Because they have set their minds on forging their thoughts into works, their minds then sort out suggestions for particular works, and whether they are at their desks or off fishing somewhere, stepping onto a bus, even sleeping sometimes, if their imaginations come up with a shell that cries out to be picked up, it will immediately be brought front and center, looked at in the light for a moment, committed to memory, worked into the piece of writing.

This is not a process that is unfamiliar to you. You do the same thing whenever you open yourself to the creative possibilities in anything. Think for a moment about those areas of your life or those things you have done which you have considered *most creative*, and ask yourself whether your mind has not worked just this way.

Suppose you rate your cooking as highly creative. That means you don't just follow recipe books all the time, stick to the same menus repeated in two-week cycles or do anything else indicative of "compulsive imitation." Neither do you chuck a few hot dogs, some ice cream, pickles, lemon juice, hot red peppers, beer and graham crackers randomly into a casserole and cook it up just to see how it will taste. You may often use recipes—some old favorites and some new ones that look promising—but if you do, the recipes in your collection are likely to be scribbled over with variations and substitutions you have tried in the past, until the way you cook it now is a highly original variation on paella, beef Stroganoff, Kung Pau chicken, or whatever.

The more recipes you've tried and tasted, the more you've learned about what ingredients complement one another in what ways, and the more confidence you've gained when it comes to improvising, so that when you *set your mind to* "throwing something together" without a recipe and open your imagination up to suggestions, you may run through the entire inventory of ingredients and spices in the house, make some tentative selections, start with what you're positive you want, taste it and ask yourself what it wants or needs. Your mind will then make further suggestions, some of which you may laugh at (no, you don't put cream with lemon juice unless you want curdled cream!), some of which you may sniff and compare with the current aroma of the dish, reject, decide to try a little of something else, and so on through the process of bringing inspirations front and center, picking the ones that you want to work into the dish, getting them in the right proportions, cooking it until it's done, giving it the final taste and putting it on the table.

If countless cooks down through the ages had not exercised their creativity in this very way, if all of them had just followed the first recipes ever written, we would now all dutifully be following the instructions "Take one whole fresh-killed antelope and throw it into the middle of a hot bonfire."

If you have thought about your own life experiences in which *you* have been most creative, you probably have identified them not only as among the most intense living-now experiences of your life, but also as having produced those things, actions or interactions by which you most like to remember yourself, and by which you would most like to be remembered. At the same time, those experiences in which you have been most destructive have been those by which you would least like to be remembered, and those in which you have been the most imitative are the ones you've either already forgotten or don't care if you forget.

If you deny your basic higher need for creativity and instead opt for imitation and conformity, you are going to be an automaton, but with all the depression, anxiety, frustration and self-contempt that come from trying to beat down that "creative genius" within you.

On the other hand, if you take my advice in the first chapter and try to learn more from the way you have operated in the past *at your creative best,* instead of lingering on all the ways your creativity may have been stifled, how "sick" you may have been in the past; if you observe and learn about others at their creative best; and if you make up your mind to let your creative instincts loose *whenever* they suggest original ideas, you will soon find that in your own chosen ways you are as creative a No-Limit person as has ever lived on this planet.

Justice

Can you remember the first time you suffered what you now remember as a great injustice, or saw somebody else suffer one? Maybe somebody told your parents or a teacher a lie about you that got you a spanking or an hour after school. Maybe the neighborhood bully beat up your best friend for fun. Maybe your father couldn't get a job because he was black. Whatever it was, how instinctive was your reaction? How long did it take you to feel it? How strongly did you feel revulsion at it? How much did you wish you could right that wrong?

It seems very popular nowadays for people to deny their instinctive needs for justice for themselves and everyone else by saying, "Well, the world is unjust, and there's nothing anybody can do about it. Look at all the injustices that take place every day, everywhere!" From there they are likely to reason, whether in public or not, "Injustice is the rule of the world, and I'm just going to handicap myself in getting along by trying to be more just than everyone else. I'll get ripped off and stepped on all the time. I may not be able to keep from getting ripped off and stepped on *sometimes*, but I can gain equality with everybody else if I rip off or step on others to about the same tune that others do it to me."

This is the logic that the unscrupulous auto mechanic uses when he charges the loan company executive for $500 worth of repairs that were unnecessary or never done, the same logic the unscrupulous loan company executive uses when he approves the $5,000 loan to the auto mechanic knowing full well that the mechanic has not read that tricky clause in the fine print, and when he forecloses on the mechanic's garage. Under this logic, everybody decides it's justified to take a little more out of the next person to make up for what the last person did to you, to take your own resentment of injustice out on innocent others. If you decide further that you can *really get ahead* by playing this competitive game of life by the "real rules," and ripping other people off in advance for what they would surely do to you if they could, by ripping off *more* people than you get ripped off by, you will surely lose all touch with your basic instincts for justice, and your runaway chains of paranoid-aggressive reactions may lead you to complete lawlessness and criminality; to fraud, embezzlement, robbery, or worse.

It is absolutely true that the world is full of injustices, and that they all are instinctively offensive to the person who respects his own needs for justice. But the No-Limit person, first, does not blame the world for having injustice in it; second, will not accept that the world "naturally" has this amount of injustice in it, and that he is somehow being unnatural or handicapping himself if he doesn't want to participate in "his share" of dealing with it; third, does not believe that the world *has* to be this way if enough people decide they want to change it; and, fourth, does not let his instinctive distaste for injustices upset, confuse or immobilize him, because he knows that after the instant gut reaction of offense at the situation his creative sense of justice is going to suggest what if anything he can do about it. If the answer is *something* (anything), he cannot spare time or energy from doing it to curse the world for having injustice in it. Neither is he going to curse the world or himself if there's just nothing he can do about it.

The best way to lose your native instinct for justice is to think of justice as what the courts, the police, your boss or any other authority figures hand out. Your reaction may then be, "If they call *that* justice, there *is* no real justice." But the greatest jurists, police and bosses in the world will tell you that justice is just something they are *trying to get* as best they can within their own limits. The greatest or most creative jurists in the world will also tell you that when it comes down to writing a decision, there is and can be no higher authority than their own consciences, as informed by their own experiences in trying to make justice work in the past. In other words, those who have heeded the call of their own internal sense of justice so deeply that they have devoted their lives to the pursuit of it are the first to admit that in the end you have to go back to the original source, your childlike, instinctive need for justice and your gut responses to the equities of any particular situation.

Your need for justice is not a need to have justice done to you and everybody else all the time. If it were, you would be right in concluding that the world is such that nobody's need for justice could ever be fulfilled. Rather it is a need for you to *respect your own sense of justice,* cultivate it and bring it to bear in situations where you may now say, "Hell, there is no such thing as justice anyway, so I'll just let this ride."

For instance, perhaps you have found yourself in situations similar to one I was faced with several years ago, when a computer error by the Internal Revenue Service resulted in my being billed for a small amount of money I clearly did not owe. After numerous phone calls and letters, I finally got the clerks to admit it was an error, but they just couldn't seem to get the computer to stop sending me bills (or maybe they just couldn't get around to stopping it). My accountant, the IRS clerks, my family, my attorney, all advised me to pay the bill for this trivial amount of money, get the computer off my back and forget it. I was told that if I alienated the IRS I would invite a very strict audit, in which they would try to find any way they could to assure that my obstinacy would cost me more money in the long run and certainly make the whole thing more hassle than it was worth.

Surely anyone in this kind of situation is going to recognize the injustice in it. The question is, do you fight it or forget it? Which is going to make you feel better in the long run—saying, "Fighting this is just going to be a waste of my valuable time," or saying, "Standing on a principle and getting justice out of this is one of the most valuable uses I can make of my time, and it is going to give me tons of satisfaction when I win"?

I chose to fight it. I couldn't even imagine giving in; I didn't like being told to abandon my position just because it would be "easier" for everyone concerned, and I made it clear to my accountant and my attorney that they were not being paid to advise me to give up my own need for justice, that if they thought that was their job I would soon have a new accountant and a new attorney.

After many further trials and tribulations, somebody at IRS set the computer straight and I finally got the matter corrected. I was in fact given a more careful audit, and nothing terrible ensued. Since I knew I had nothing to hide, I welcomed any careful look at what I was doing. I do not fear careful scrutiny, because I am an honest human being. And I certainly will not abandon my very important principles, even if those principles are going to be costly to me. It is the principle, not the money, that I live by. I did not, moreover, consider the whole thing a waste of my time at all. In fact, I got a big kick out of it.

This is just one minor example of fulfilling your need for justice, nothing at all like the situation in which a witness to a major crime, for instance, who knows that the wrong person is about to be convicted has to decide whether to come forth even if he or his family have been threatened by the guilty parties—except that *the principle* is the same. You can respect your sense of justice or you can try to ignore or repress it. But, believe me, if you choose not to respect it, you choose not to respect yourself, and you will soon end up wondering how much your life is really worth.

To the No-Limit person, there is nothing quite so central and meaningful in life as the quest for justice. He can happily dedicate himself to getting a new law passed to prohibit some kind of common injustice, or work tirelessly in the name of civil rights, election reform, nuclear disarmament, human rights, the ERA or any cause he believes will bring more justice, peace and harmony to the world—not because he is under the illusion that he is going to solve all the world's problems or eradicate injustice, but simply because he gets joy out of responding fully and faithfully to one of his own very highest needs as a human.

Truth

Whether you recognize it or not, your mind originally and naturally functions on one basic principle, which is to present to you truths relevant to any situation in which you find yourself. "Truth" as your own mind interprets it does not mean never making a mistake, which is impossible, nor does it mean never telling a lie, which is sometimes unavoidable. It does, however, mean always operating on your best "information and belief." What your mind is looking for are contradictions within the entire body of your thought. It is the fastest, most thorough computer in existence (and much, much more), and if you just "let it run" with a given problem, you will see the green lights of "True" (or "assumed to be true"), the flashing orange lights of "Contradiction: Resolve Inconsistency," and the red lights of "False" (or "assumed to be false"), flashing at you with incomprehensible speed and precision.

To take an extreme example, imagine spending a week in the company of people who lied about everything. "Where's the toilet paper?" "It's in the closet." "I don't see it." "That's because I was lying. It's not there at all." "Well, where is it?" "It's in the cupboard." "I don't see it." "That's because I was lying. It's not really in the cupboard." "Well, where is it?" "We don't really have any toilet paper." "Is that true?" "No, I'm lying."

You may laugh now, but after a week of this you would surely conclude that you were not in the company of human beings, and in real life it does not take long in the company of chronic liars, cheats or frauds to develop chronic mistrust of humanity, including yourself, leading to paranoia, depression, inertia, panic. You will find yourself angry all the time, unable to communicate with anyone, and soon you will even doubt yourself. With excessive exposure to liars, you will come to hate them and yourself; your own health will disintegrate; you'll lose interest in living. People who have spent years in antiquated prisons, in which they were surrounded by liars and cheats, found it exceedingly difficult to regain any semblance of trust in mankind or even in themselves. The constant exposure to this kind of activity acts just like unchecked bacteria, slowly eroding the organism until it is no longer able to function. Yes, truth is absolutely necessary for survival; it is an instinctive higher need.

Thus, a No-Limit person is first and foremost an honest person. He confronts dishonesty; he is up front with his interactions, never trying to be evasive or to con another person. This honest approach to life comes from his strong attachment to truth and the need for it in order for us all to survive. What do you dislike about many politicians, bureaucrats, big-business or big-labor executives, fast-talking salesmen and so on? The fact that they appear to be dishonest, and that truth is so very unimportant to them in their regular dealings with the public. When an institution comes to the point where all truth has been abandoned, then chaos is the inevitable result. Our social structures, as well as our individuals, need truth in order to survive.

The No-Limit person pursues truth in all of his undertakings. The need for truth is so strong that he will go to great lengths to have it for himself. He is not motivated by power; he is motivated by the need for truth to be the cornerstone upon which his culture thrives. In the most insignificant conversations, the No-Limit person is unwilling to abandon the truth. He will not make up excuses or explain himself to the satisfaction of others, because he is unwilling to compromise the truth as he sees it. When he knows that he is being true to himself, and that his motivations are in the direction of bringing about truth in any area, then the No-Limit person feels content with himself.

The No-Limit person will respect his instinctive needs and natural abilities to find the truth of any matter for himself. He will accept that he will make mistakes, but will not accept that anybody or anything else knows better than he instinctively does about the way his own search for truth should proceed. The net result of his search for truth in all things will be his *fundamental honesty as a human being,* because if he never has to lie to himself, he never has to lie to anybody else (except where basic morality overrides the instinct not to lie, as when you tell the potential thief that you have no money, when in fact you have it hidden in another room). In sum, the No-Limit person will let loose his natural tendency to seek the truth *for himself* in all things.

Beauty

The need for beauty is perhaps the most overarching of your higher needs, because it encompasses all the others. Individuality is beautiful. So is respect for yourself and others, and feeling that you belong in the world and to the human race. So are affection and love, meaningful work, recreation, creativity, justice, truth and even physical beauty itself.

We are inclined to think of beauty very narrowly. When we say, "She's really beautiful," we may be commenting only on her appearance. But if we say, "She's really a *beautiful person*," we mean much more: that she brings beauty, grace, humor, love, respect or whatever else into her own life and the lives of others. Similarly, if we say, "What a beautiful day," we may just mean that it's sunny and warm outside. But if we say, "It's a beautiful day" because a gorgeous thunderstorm has just passed and it inspired us to make beautiful love in the hayloft, we mean much more: that this day has ushered beauty, grace, humor, love, respect or whatever else into our lives.

Try immersing yourself within a repugnant environment for a lengthy period. Take away all of the beauty in your life and surround yourself with the hideous and the unpleasant. The results will astound you. You will soon discover how very important it is to have beauty and appreciation for attractiveness in your life. Without beauty at all, you will soon become callous and indifferent to your surroundings. You will become spiteful, angry, upset, remorseful and even sick if you are denied access to the beauty of this planet. Many people think that beauty is a luxury, and that one can do very nicely without it if one has to. But this is not the case. The need for beauty is just that, a need, and without it the organism suffers just as much as if it is denied sleep or shelter, even though the results of the deficiency take longer to manifest themselves. Look at the people who must live in some of the most horrible surroundings imaginable, urban slums where there is little to experience in the way of environmental beauty. Look at the effects that just being in this kind of an atmosphere have on those who live there for long periods. People living in a world of rats, broken glass, rampaging disease, malnutrition, drugs, prostitution, garbage in the streets and poverty everywhere become people who give up on themselves. They soon lose their appreciation for living, begin to hate, to feel persecuted, to become sickly, and eventually to die long before their time.

People need to have beauty in their lives, if for no other reason than to feel positive about their world. Music, paintings, books, high-level discussions, theater, sunsets, flowers, animals, rivers, smiling faces and fresh air are absolute necessities if we are going to have people who are healthy and excited about being alive. A No-Limit person seeks out beauty and is instrumental in making it available for others. Almost without exception, No-Limit people are involved heavily in tasks that serve to make the world a better, more beautiful place for others to be. They want to make beauty appreciation available to everyone. Beauty provides hope. Watch the refugees who've lived in deprivation all their early lives. When they are exposed to a concert or a picnic or anything beautiful for the first time, it is like giving them a direct injection of happiness. They thrive on it; they savor it all and drink it in. One exposure to beauty is enough to give them renewed strength and hope for years to come. Make no mistake about it, the more you can learn to become an appreciator of beauty, *and to help make it available for others as well,* the more you will be working toward being a No-Limit person, and simultaneously fulfilling your own highest need instincts as well.

HIGHER AND LOWER NEEDS: PUTTING IT ALL INTO PERSPECTIVE

Almost everything No-Limit people do, they do to fulfill higher needs. The search for truth, justice for everyone, beauty, perfection and goodness is uppermost in their lives. They are not interested in power, materialism or exploitation for themselves. Their basic biological needs, while the same as everyone else's, are essentially filled by their capacity to thrive as living organisms in their environment. The No-Limit person loves his body, takes care of it and is not always trying to prove himself with it and its physical prowess. He is at peace with his body, and it is simply an accepted part of his life.

Thus the No-Limit person is free to attend to the higher values. He seems always to be aware of them, and his life revolves around cherishing them within himself, as well as helping others to appreciate them. He is not an evangelist for higher values, but seems to be put together in such a way that he suffers physically if his higher values are not met. He needs truth and seeks it out. He avoids being with phonies because he knows he will be dragged down by them. He avoids liars, thieves, even neurotics, because he wants to transcend their behaviors in his own life; he doesn't want to be affected negatively by their pathologies.

The No-Limit person is not as money-oriented as are people in general, because he doesn't work as much for money as for the internal satisfaction that comes from being in tune with higher goals. He is quite willing to sacrifice money accumulation in favor of performing his life mission. He is almost obsessed with wanting the world to be a better place, and will behave in ways that are difficult for ordinary people to understand. He will leave a well-paying job if he feels he is being compromised, without ever looking back with regret. He will put his life on the line if necessary, in order to make his attitudes toward truth and goodness known to others. The No-Limit person is strongly under the influence of these higher needs and views them as the most important part of his life. He is passionately involved in improving the quality of life for those less fortunate. He will risk reprisals in defending justice, and many people will never understand how he could be so foolish and so obsessed with what he believes to be right. He will chain himself to a fence in protest against social injustice—in fact, do almost anything to correct an injustice. He will be oblivious to the fact that many people see him as foolish. He knows what he must do; he is in touch with his inner signals, and no one will deter him from his mission.

In summary, all of our needs, from those which are basic to our biological survival to those which elevate our ability to live a No-Limit life, are *needs* in the truest sense. Deprive a person of truth and he will become just as sick as if he were deprived of adequate nutriment. The same is true for beauty, goodness, justice, self-sufficiency, uniqueness and all of the higher needs. The No-Limit person, whatever his occupation, cannot function without working toward these objectives for himself and for others. The No-Limit person will shun external values if he feels victimized by them, and no amount of salary or other compensation will work very long in corralling him.

Remember, if you lack inner peace and feel you are going nowhere in your life, it probably has nothing to do with money or the basic needs money can meet. You are probably just feeling that you have no truth in your life, that you are not being true to yourself. Your anxiety and depression, or your illnesses, are very likely the result of not having your very own higher needs met. Actively work at meeting those higher needs (all of them) and you will find yourself feeling more contentment than you ever did before.

8 Cultivating a Sense of Purpose and Meaning

Having a sense of purpose in your life is the most important element of becoming a fully functioning, No-Limit person! This is a very strong statement, and yet I make it with a genuine appreciation of how significant it is for you that you become a person who puts *a sense of purpose* at the very top of your personal commitment list. Without a feeling of purpose, your life will be empty, you will feel unfulfilled, and when these feelings become extreme you will find yourself experiencing frustration, anxiety, depression and other symptoms that are a facet of living an externally directed life.

For many people, their feelings of *purpose* are unclear largely because they are attempting to follow the rules for living that have been imposed on them by other people, who also lack their own sense of personal mission. The large majority of people become bogged down in their daily routines of trying to pay their bills, raising their families, commuting back and forth to work, attempting to save a few dollars in order to purchase more material objects, and generally living the kind of external life style that keeps them functioning yet internally unfulfilled. While there is certainly nothing unhealthy about making a living and paying your bills, there is something very unfulfilling and frustrating about them if the activities that lead to these results are meaningless to you, as the human being who is using up the precious moments of your life in behaviors that are not giving you a sense of inner contentment and peace. A sense of purpose is achieved by matching up your own daily schedule of work, play and everything else that you do with a feeling of importance and personal mission. If your life choices are not providing you with those personal feelings of peace and fulfillment, then you must reconsider why you are making the choice to live out your life in ways that are simply permitting you to exist rather than to feel a sense of mission and purpose.

A person does not necessarily have to change jobs, end relationships or do anything drastic in order to have a sense of purpose. The most important ingredient in the feeling of having personal meaning is the *attitude* that you bring to anything that you elect to do. But if you are simply going along with the routine of your life, performing duties that you find distasteful and having internal feelings of emptiness, then you have a huge void to fill. Until you start filling that void, you will never be acquainted with your potential for No-Limit living. Not now or ever, unless you are willing to say to yourself, and follow it up with constructive action, "I am going to feel complete and fulfilled in my life because I am worth it. Life is just plain too short for me to be going through someone else's motions. I am going to be the captain of my life, and if I make mistakes, or suffer hardships, then I am willing to pay the price, but at least I will have a feeling of self-satisfaction, that I am making the choices about how my life is going to be run." This kind of a crucial personal statement is vital to achieving a sense of purpose in your life.

A sense of purpose is a very personal thing. Some people can feel that sense of meaning and mission by working on the land, others by writing, and others by being with their own family members. Some people feel fulfilled in the role of raising their children, and they are completely submerged in all that is involved in this important undertaking. Some people feel excitedly alive when they are engineering a train, filling prescriptions or training fighter pilots. A sense of purpose has nothing to do with fitting neatly into any specific occupational slot. The feeling of purpose is very much an internal commodity. It comes from within you, and only you can know whether you have it or not. I can only report my own experiences in counseling thousands of people. I learned very early as a therapist that the biggest causes of self-defeating feelings and behaviors were all tied up in this lack of a feeling of purpose in life. Very few of the people I've known, be they clients, family members, friends or acquaintances, feel a really strong sense of purpose and mission in their lives.

Back in Chapter 3, where I described in detail the qualities of becoming a No-Limit person, I alluded to my own sense of mission. I have found that when I can get people to stop thinking in stereotypical ways about themselves and instead allow themselves the fantasy of thinking about what they would really enjoy doing, they start talking about things which would be personally rewarding and meaningful for them.

The sad part of this little exercise is that so many people simply refuse to take the steps that would lead to their own feelings of purpose. They use the same old tired cop-outs that I've heard from non-risk-takers a zillion times: "I'm afraid I'd fail." "But what about my family responsibilities?" "I surely can't just shift gears now, I'm too old to change." "It's easy to fantasize, but reality dictates that I have to make a buck in order to pay my bills." All of these and other sentiments of the kind are nothing more than excuses to keep you stuck in the place that you've chosen to be today.

A sense of purpose is achieved by ignoring these kinds of internal excuses and vowing to become the person that *you* want to become. The paying of your bills, your family responsibilities and everything else will work themselves out if you give yourself permission to have a sense of purpose in your life. If you have always been a responsible, bill-paying, conscientious human being, then you are not going to abandon these values and suddenly become a hermit living in a cave in the wilderness. You can make the choice to be fulfilled *and responsible,* and to meet all of your personal-choice obligations, if you are willing to eradicate those fears of change and failure that are the major deterrents to becoming your own No-Limit person. If you use excuses or argue for your own current status as something which you are stuck with by virtue of your earlier life decisions, then you will end up with precisely what you are defending: a life of met obligations, but no inner peace. And, to me, there is nothing more important than feeling a sense of significance and purpose about yourself as a human being. You just cannot give up on this if you are going to stay healthy and creatively alive.

The importance of having a sense of meaning cannot be over-emphasized. Nothing is more important for your survival as well as your emotional stability. When meaning goes out of your life, you become susceptible to depression, illness, stress and even death. I can think of many examples of people who, having said, "My husband [wife] is my reason for living; he [she] is all I have or care about," have taken on the symptoms of illness and died shortly after the loss of that spouse. *The danger in putting your own sense of meaning in anyone else is that you have no control over your own destiny.* If someone else gives your life meaning and then disappears, then your life no longer has any purpose. The sense of meaning and mission must by definition come from you.

Many people are literally kept alive by their sense of personal mission. Some people become so engrossed in a project that they simply cannot allow themselves to become ill or to die. When the project is completed, and the meaning in their lives also terminates, the individual will allow himself to become sick, and often death is the result. Victor Frankl, writing in *Man's Search for Meaning*, describes how some of his fellow inmates in a Nazi concentration camp literally lost their lives when they lost their sense of meaning and purpose. A companion in the prison camp had related a dream to Dr. Frankl, that he would be liberated from the camp on March 31, 1945. This became his singular reason for existence, his very purpose for life. Victor Frankl tells of the liberation this way:

> On March 29, he suddenly became ill and ran a high temperature. On March 30th, the day his prophecy had told him that the war and suffering would be over for him, he became delirious and lost consciousness. On March 31st, he was dead. To all outward appearances, he had died of typhus . . . The ultimate cause of my friend's death was that the expected liberation did not come and he was severely disappointed. This suddenly lowered his body's resistance against the latent typhus infection. His faith in the future and his will to live had become paralyzed and his body fell victim to illness—and thus the voice of his dream was right after all.

Frankl talks over and over of prisoners dying when they no longer had a sense of purpose. He felt that his own survival was the direct result of his purpose, which was to tell his story to all mankind. He knew that he must survive in order to fulfill his personal purpose. This *will* gave him strength he had not known he possessed.

While his is a dramatic example, it serves to illustrate how powerful a thing the sense of purpose can be in a human being. Your own personal survival in life-and-death terms may not be at stake, but I can guarantee you that your emotional stability, your feelings of worthiness and happiness, along with your sense of contentment, are definitely linked to your having a feeling of value, meaning and purpose in your own life. And this sense of purpose must be something that you feel from within, rather than having it connected to someone or something external to yourself.

WHY MOST PEOPLE HAVE NO REAL SENSE OF PURPOSE: THE "CRITICAL INCH"

If you think of life as having fixed boundaries between birth and death, with the total distance between these two points being exactly one mile in length, you will have a visual image of your entire life. That mile is traveled in many ways, but at the very end of the mile you will be met by death, just like every human being who has ever lived on this planet. Your life mile has 5,280 feet in it. All of your training, experience, goals and educational objectives are designed to help you with the first 5,279 feet and 11 inches of your life. This is the big hunk of your life, and the rules for this part of your life are very, very different from those for the critical one inch.

In the major part (5,279 feet and 11 inches) of your life mile, the rules are related to getting ahead, being competitive with the other guy, making money, raising a family, saving for the future, striving, upward mobility, promotions, getting an education, learning the ropes and generally mastering the skills of functioning in our externally oriented culture. The remaining inch, that tiny fraction that is left over, represents a completely different kind of reality, in which the rules are totally different. The critical inch is a very important segment of your life, as it symbolizes your life's meaning, but it is virtually ignored by your trainers and by you yourself. That last inch represents your *sense of purpose*, your feelings of worthiness, aliveness and significance as a unique human being, and your real reason for being here in the first place. In order to achieve fulfillment in this critical inch, you need a different set of guidelines, rules that simply don't apply in the larger portion of your life mile.

This entire book is written about that last crucial inch, the portion of your life that is largely ignored by you and your mentors. In this critical inch, the rules are internal, they are not about striving and upward mobility; they are about your sense of self-esteem, rather than looking over your shoulder at the other guy to see how you stack up. They are about personal fulfillment from within and trusting your inner signals, rather than accumulating external things.

Your sense of purpose and meaning in life that leads to mastering the critical inch has been largely ignored in favor of learning the rules for the bigger part. But the bigger part becomes almost totally worthless unless you can shift the emphasis in your life from those rules for making it in our culture to those rules which are going to help you to feel positive about yourself, while you still handle all of the things that our external culture throws at you, on a daily basis.

You cannot get competent at something you ignore. And if you shun the behaviors and thinking processes which are going to lead you to that sense of purpose, then you will continue to wallow around in the large chunk of your life, which may make you externally "successful," but leaves you unfulfilled. Having a sense of purpose is inextricably related to becoming a No-Limit person, taking risks, going after your own fulfillment and refusing to be someone who behaves just like everybody else. If you try to conform, fit in, measure yourself by external standards or behave in any other self-defeating way, you will never feel the sense of purpose that is vital to your own NEZ/No-Limit status. You will be acting in a way that will win you some approval, help you to get promoted and maybe even to get rich, but you won't be able to send away that inner turmoil until *you*, as a unique human being, have a feeling of being active in your own life mission. The critical inch is the most important part of your life mile, and you are going to have to master a completely different set of rules in order to feel fulfilled in this final inch.

Why do you suppose we in the Western world are so suspicious and uninformed about Zen, Taoism, Transcendental Meditation and all of the Eastern philosophies? Because the large part of our lives has nothing to do with what these philosophies offer. We don't even have words to describe certain conditions which are taken for granted in a Zen approach to life. We have no terms to describe total concentration or intense living-in-the-present-moment behavior. We have never needed a word to describe having our minds completely at rest with no outside interference.

It is difficult to describe the concept of total fulfillment in the languages of the Western world, largely because we have ignored these concepts in our hurry-up, competitive, assembly-line, ulcer-producing desire to build better mousetraps. You have had almost zero training in developing your own inner sense of purpose and peace. You have been schooled in externals for so long that it is hard for you to even think in transcendent terms. You've been conditioned to think in local terms, in boundaries, rather than in global, humanistic ways.

For those who have been able to articulate their own sense of purpose, the goal has always been achieved via the avenue of transcending self, reaching out to all of humanity, and in making this planet a superior place for all to live on. The feelings that you get from being kind to another person, from making a difference in the world, from improving the quality of all life—these are most often the sources of a sense of purpose. We are not very good as individuals at achieving our sense of purpose, because we have bypassed the real source of meaning and, instead, focused almost exclusively on the narrow, rigid and unfulfilling road of being external and adjusting to a pressure-packed, fast-paced world.

GOING AFTER A SENSE OF PURPOSE

The very first thing you must do in order to achieve a sense of purpose in your life is to reverse the priorities of the critical inch and the first 5,279 feet and 11 inches. It is time to give precedence to making your own sense of purpose the goal of the larger chunk of your life, and to reduce all of the external thinking and behavior to an insignificant although necessary inch of your life. The more emphasis you personally place on the new rules, on becoming a No-Limit person with all that it encompasses, the more you will begin to feel a real sense of mission and significance about your life. You, and only you, experience your inner self. No one can get behind your eyeballs and be you. You must feel good about yourself and what you are doing, or you will have those demoralizing feelings of boredom, routine and emptiness that result when you make the bigger portion of your life mile the external part and the remaining leftover inch the sole domain of your own inner self.

Repeatedly you read about a person who has had a close brush with death and then emerges with a totally new philosophy of life. He may be a busy executive who has suffered a heart attack, or a person who has escaped unharmed from a serious accident in which he was only a split second away from being killed. When people have experiences like these, they almost always shift their lives around so that the old "critical inch" now becomes the 5,279 feet, 11 inches. In other words, it takes a close call before most people will put the emphasis in their lives on the sense of purpose and meaning.

These reawakened people often leave their hustle-bustle life styles behind them. Often they look for ways to make a living that are less stressful, and they begin to spend more quality time with their loved ones. Often they redevote their lives to the things which will bring them fulfillment, and they elect to relax more, taking time to enjoy the real beauty of being alive. Their brush with death is the catalyst that permits them to reawaken themselves and to make their own lives into something which is more than what they had previously been willing to settle for.

You do not have to experience a close call before you work at developing a sense of purpose in your life. You can make the decision to live meaningfully each and every day for the simple reason that it will make you a happier, more effective and, most importantly, contented human being. It amounts to giving yourself permission to live your own life in the way that would provide the most gratification for you and those you love. To settle for anything else is to buy into the self-defeating logic that you can't change because you have invested so much of your time and effort in your old life style. In fact, you don't even have to reverse your life style in order to have more meaning in your life. What you have to do is vow to yourself (and follow it through with new behaviors) that you are going to make sure you personally shift your attitude around so that you will feel the substantial sense of purpose which eludes almost everyone in our culture.

If you build a house which has as its foundation only one support system, and that particular support collapses, your entire house will topple. The same thing is true for you! If you build your entire life around one person, one activity, one job or one support system of any kind, and that particular support vanishes, then you will topple just as your single-support-system house would. What you need to do in order to feel secure is have the ability to shift gears, to rely on yourself and to elicit meaning from a variety of activities. It is futile to attempt to gain all of your sense of meaning from any one single person or activity. The No-Limit person is one who can feel creatively alive in virtually any situation. He needn't be entrenched on familiar territory or doing only things that he is accustomed to doing. He does not have to be around his close friends in order to feel fulfilled. Anything a human being is capable of doing is a potential source of human gratification and purpose, provided he knows how to reverse those old thinking patterns which lock him into an unfulfilling life style.

You can be content while spending a few moments with your child in the living room, or you can use this time as an opportunity to feel bored, alienated and distant. The choice is always yours. You can find miracles anywhere, or you can search for them endlessly. Abraham Maslow once wrote these words about miracles: "*To be looking elsewhere for miracles is to me a sure sign of ignorance that everything is miraculous.*" Learning this fundamental truth is at the very heart of becoming a person who has a sense of purpose and meaning. When you stop the searching and the inclination to place the meaning for your life in people or events outside yourself, and instead look at the world with new eyes—that is, eyes which allow you to have purpose in *all* of your activities—you will have taken the first step toward a real sense of purpose for yourself.

ACCEPTING CHANGE AS A WAY OF LIFE

Most people fear change. They stay in the same place not because they wouldn't know how to function in a new milieu but because they are intimidated by the actual process of change. Nevertheless, you can be absolutely sure of one thing: you, and everyone else, will never remain the same. Change is the very stuff of life. If we didn't change, we would all stay precisely as we are. There would be no growth, no life, no death, nothing, if change were not built into the very fabric of our humanity. Like it or not, change is a big part of you. If you want to have that elusive sense of purpose in your life, you are going to have to get very comfortable with the entire concept of change and learn to welcome rather than to fear it.

Learning to welcome change may be a big new step in your life. True, you gradually get comfortable with your own surroundings, and you know what to expect each day. You feel a kind of external security in having some predictability about your life. But when that predictability becomes too much a part of your life it creates that empty feeling of no purpose that is so enfeebling to your own fulfillment. Getting to a point where you can have a healthy dose of some predictability and stability with a built-in capacity for newness and change is the place where a sense of purpose will begin to take hold for you. Giving yourself the permission to try out new experiences, to take risks and, most importantly, to do the things which *you* feel are significant, regardless of how others view them, will give you more and more meaning in your everyday life.

Our world is a fast-changing place, requiring people who are not threatened by change. Many of the jobs that people have today didn't even exist ten years ago. What we need are human beings who can shift, who are comfortable with the unknown and who can try out anything, if we are going to make this world work at a level in which it meets the needs of all its inhabitants.

You are a part of this fast-changing world. You are not isolated from the rest of us in this place; you are very much a part of that changing process. In fact, even as you sit and read this book, you are changing. Your cells are shifting, you look different each day, you have different attitudes than you had a few years ago. You wear your hair differently; new clothes at which you once scoffed you now wear proudly as your best garments. You allow yourself to attend functions which you once thought to be inappropriate, and you speak with a different vocabulary from that which you used at an earlier time in your life.

You will also be different tomorrow. You will wear different styles, use new fad words, attend different functions, support different political views, and on and on. Once you recognize change as the inevitable condition of being human, you will be more inclined to welcome it in the significant parts of your own personal life. If you can get yourself used to the idea that change is wonderful rather than something to shun, you'll be on your way to new, exciting, risk-taking behaviors which will give purpose to your life before you even recognize it.

I am often approached by people who have these worries about me, expressed in these typical sentences: "Wayne, I hope you won't ever change just because you are well-known." "Don't let fame change you, Wayne." "You're just not the person I once knew; you used to come over and see me, but now that you're a celebrity you don't." These are people who are expressing an opinion about fearing change. Of course people change, and they are not going to do the same things that they once did. Certainly one isn't going to stay exactly as he is. Instead of being afraid of that change, I welcome it. While I don't want to become someone who is conceited, too big for his britches, or any other stereotype which people might apply to a successful author (or painter, or musician), I also am not interested in staying exactly as I was.

The well-known opera singer Beverly Sills wears a piece of jewelry with the initials "I.D.T.A." engraved on it. When she is asked about anything she is doing that represents change, such as leaving the opera stage in favor of producing, she shows her detractors the inscription, which translates to "I Did That Already." For a highly functioning person, having done something already is enough of a reason to move on. Rather than endlessly repeat what she has mastered and experienced, the person who feels a sense of purpose moves on to new, unexplored terrain. This kind of willingness to tolerate and even welcome change will assure you of having a renewed sense of purpose almost every day of your life.

Authoritarian people are threatened by change. No-Limit people welcome it! It is the difference between being able to function effectively in virtually any situation and being upset and immobilized whenever the outcome is uncertain. An attitude of being comfortable with change starts with being comfortable with one's self. When you begin to feel more at peace with yourself you are less and less threatened by new circumstances, because you trust yourself to be able to handle anything new. It is the insecure person who avoids change, always doubting himself and wondering if he will be able to handle something new that comes along. It is easier to stay with the familiar, where the territory has been previously explored, and to know precisely what to expect all of the time.

Being a No-Limit person means being willing to become an adventurer, to try out new behaviors, to meet new people, to explore the unknown and to not only be comfortable with a changing environment but actually welcome the mysterious and the unknown—to take delight in going to new places, to be excited about the prospect of being in new, unknown territory. No-Limit people are constantly seeking new challenges. They do not want everything to stay as it is. They are willing to change jobs without being internally afraid that things just won't work out. The No-Limit person somehow seems to have an attitude of internal confidence that he can handle anything that comes along, and that there is no special virtue in keeping things as they are.

To a No-Limit person, being comfortable with change is manifested not only in welcoming new and different environments but in allowing himself to adapt to them as well. He does not hang on to old beliefs when they are no longer applicable or useful. A No-Limit person is not interested in staying the same for his entire life. He is unthreatened by awareness that he now thinks quite differently from the way he did before. The No-Limit person is perfectly willing to admit that old values and attitudes no longer work. Those old ideas can be discarded forever once they no longer prove useful. The No-Limit person has an inherent capacity to simply declare to himself that a shift in opinion is called for, and he feels no remorse over the fact that the old attitudes are no longer useful.

Because fully functioning people are always exploring new areas and wandering around in the unknown, they are constantly bumping into new ideas and attitudes. When they approach anyone new, they do it from an open-minded position, having nothing in particular to gain or lose, only seeing the new for what it is. This open-mindedness makes them welcome change, because through change they are always encountering newness and innovation. By the same token, the closed-minded person resists change, because it threatens the very same things. You will often see NEZ/No-Limit people working toward reform, while authoritarians want to cling to the old, even when the old and familiar no longer work. You'll see many people who are afraid of change voting against introducing new equipment in a factory because they don't understand it, voting against revolutionary principles because they aren't sure they could handle the new, and even steadfastly continuing to perform tasks in old ways which are largely self-defeating, simply because it is all they know and they are fainthearted about doing it a new way.

The No-Limit person will take the risks that go with change, especially social change, and, while many will oppose him in the early stages, the end result is that most people eventually come around. Today's established practices, such as bathing suits rather than full clothing regalia at the beach, legal rights for the poor, voting rights, universal education, civil rights, air travel, satellite communications and almost every other practice we regard as normal were once viewed as radical and threatening. The reason we have accepted these practices is because someone who was comfortable with change, who wanted to see the world improve and who felt internally secure about wandering into unexplored turf was willing to take the risks and feel excited about innovation.

If you want more No-Limit internal attitudes, then you must be willing to work at becoming more comfortable with change in your life. Try on some of these new behaviors to help yourself get there faster.

• Do something that you've never done before. Don't evaluate it, don't analyze it to death, don't even ask yourself why, simply see if you can do something new and be comfortable about it. Try sailing a boat all alone if you've never done it. Make an attempt to run one mile without stopping. Visit the floor of the stock exchange, climb a mountain, eat an octopus, make love in your car, or do anything that would be new. Try on change and see if you like it. If you don't try it out, you'll stay safe but less fulfilled and you won't be able to handle the really important changes that are going to come, whether you are ready or not.

• Make it a point to talk to a stranger today. See if you can spend a few minutes in sharing with that person, just a few moments of your time. By opening yourself up to new people even for a few minutes at a time, you'll be gaining invaluable practice at shedding some of those groundless fears about the unknown. I have made it a practice in my life to meet at least one new person every day. In restaurants I will talk to a friendly waitress or a fellow customer for a short time and practice being open with them. It is always easier to just let strangers go by, but when you take a few minutes, share a bit of yourself and learn something about them, it is almost always an enriching experience.

• Stop defending things as they've always been, including yourself. The good old days are over; *these* are the good old days. By hanging on to old beliefs and reminding yourself and others about how things used to be, you simply detract from enjoying today, and you become more change-resistant. Carl Sandburg wrote these lines about the good old days: "Sometimes old men sitting near the exits of life say, 'There were giants in those days.' " Don't wait until you are near life's exit to live.

Accept change as inevitable even if you dislike it. Nothing stays the same on this ever-spinning planet. New ideas, attitudes, customs and values are not an indication that the world is falling apart; they are the very ingredients of what makes being alive so sensational. The changes are going to take place independent of your opinions about them, so why not become an individual who lets himself experience those changes in comfort rather than fighting them every day? The more you practice enjoying the unknown, checking out the unfamiliar and taking risks, the more enriched your life is going to be. Boredom comes from sameness and routine. A sense of purpose and mission stems from the new and different and acceptance of change. Take your pick!

THE IMPORTANCE OF PERSONAL HOPE AND TRUST

In the film version of a marvelous book titled *A Man Called Intrepid,* Nazi German officers are talking to a young woman who has been captured as a spy for the Allies in World War II. One of the officers, trying to convince the spy that she has absolutely no chance of escaping and that she ought to cooperate in order to save herself a great deal of unnecessary suffering, uses these words to attempt to dissuade her from her obstinate refusal to talk: "Without hope, we become warped and crippled creatures." But she has chosen protection of her fellow spies as her life mission, and thus she remains silent and hopeful.

When you lose sight of hope for yourself and begin to see yourself as trapped by your circumstances, you soon become warped and crippled internally. You begin to feel depressed, as if you were imprisoned by your life setting, and the more you stay in this condition, the more stifling it becomes. Ultimately, when all feelings of hope have been eroded, you begin to deteriorate, first mentally and then physically as well. But think about the word "hope." It is purely a mental process, which you can elect to send out of your life or welcome as a regular part of you. While I have encouraged you to become more of a present-moment person, you can still enjoy those present moments by feeling hopeful and positive about yourself. You can envision yourself as being able to escape from any self-imposed traps, and this exercise of feeling hopeful will make your present moments more purposeful.

Having hope for yourself is tantamount to saying you have confidence in yourself. They are both necessary in order to have either. Hope means the belief that you can use your own creative energies in order to improve the quality of your life. You will need confidence to act this out, and confidence comes only from behavior, not from wishing or meditating about anything. The hope is the mental part, the confidence the behavioral part, and you must start with the notion that nothing is hopeless. Regardless of your circumstances, you can still decide to think hopefully, and this will help you to elect confident behaviors. Prisoners of war who have survived affirm the importance of a willingness to always think hopefully. William Niehous, who was rescued from more than three years' imprisonment in a Venezuelan jungle where he was held by rebels in the most primitive conditions, attributed his survival to never abandoning hope and living one day at a time.

Hope is up to you and it comes from deciding to trust yourself and to never selling yourself short as a unique and significant human being. You get hope by deciding to have it. Period! There is no magic formula. There is no secret way to have it. You simply decide that you are not going to be beaten down by anything external to yourself—that you are going to take responsibility for changing your life if it is unsatisfactory, and that you are going to do it regardless of the risks involved. When you then carry out your resolve with behavior which is of your own purposeful choosing, you'll be doing the things which will lead to a sense of meaning and purpose. The things themselves are different for everyone, and you will discover what they are for you by experimenting rather than complaining and being inactive. Your neighbor might feel totally fulfilled by being a sheepherder, your sister might enjoy operating her own bookstore, your parents might love to travel, your brother might feel fulfilled as an attorney researching a particularly fascinating case, and all of these things might have absolutely no appeal to you. But you will find your activity when you stop searching and allow yourself the freedom to try new things. It won't come from any one single activity; it will be there when you allow yourself the opportunity to experiment, to take risks, to have hope and to never fear your own success. This attitude of fearing your own success is one of the biggest obstacles to having a sense of life mission and purpose.

NOT FEARING YOUR OWN GREATNESS

Many people fear their own potentiality and consequently settle for much less than what is satisfying and meaningful for them. They are willing to accept being mediocre because they can't seem to muster the internal sense of pride and purpose which would allow them to be great. Abraham Maslow called this the "Who? Me?" syndrome.

If you ask a child if he is going to be a great human being, he will often respond, "Who? Me?" When I talk to young people who are going into medicine, or law, or architecture, or any profession, I ask them about how great they are going to become. Will you be the doctor who comes up with the breakthrough for the cure of cancer? Will you become the attorney who fights for equal justice before the Supreme Court? Will you design the most important new building in the world? Will you end hunger on this planet? Will you be the greatest *you* which you can become in a certain chosen area? Almost always the answer is, "I just want to make a living; I don't want to change the world."

This very attitude is the thing which detracts from having a sense of purpose. If you are only making a living at what you do, going in to work because it is a job, it won't take very long before you'll feel empty inside and lack purpose in your life. If *you* are not going to solve the energy crisis, cure cancer, rid the world of hunger, eliminate injustice and generally contribute toward the resolution of our multitudinous social evils, then who is going to do it? I'll tell you who. It will be those people who have a sense of purpose in their lives. It will be the people who have transcended their own egos, their own need to be "fitting in," and have gone beyond what most people ever think about in their lives. Those people who are dedicated to making a difference, to making their own lives as well as those around them work at their highest levels, will be the doers with a sense of meaning in their lives. They will be busy, involved, excited and dedicated in what they are doing. Furthermore, they will operate on their inner signals, trusting themselves and conducting their lives from a perspective of importance rather than indifference and routine. These are the No-Limit people I've been writing about throughout this book.

You can choose to be a part of the social problem or a resolver of the issues. It is up to you. You can lower your vision, keep yourself from having a self-image of greatness and opt for the more "secure" road of just making a living—and I guarantee you that you will never experience that sense of purpose which you want so desperately. You do not have to be a social reformer in order to feel fulfilled; you have to have an inner sense of doing things which really matter. And the words "really matter" translate to your own sense of fulfillment in making this world a better place for at least one other if not large numbers of others as well.

All of us have a potential for greatness within ourselves. Most of us never allow ourselves to think about it. It becomes threatening to be reminded of the need to take risks and become a doer rather than a talker. Consequently, you see people running away from their own greatness. You see a lot of defenses, and you see a whole lot of just plain "settling for less." The more you are inclined to "settle for less," the more you allow yourself to evade that sense of purpose that this entire chapter—in fact, this entire book—is devoted to helping you achieve.

People look at other human beings who have achieved greatness, and they marvel at their superiority. They view a Leonardo da Vinci, a Copernicus, an Alexander the Great, a Joan of Arc, a Socrates, a Lincoln, a Jonas Salk or a Madame Curie as a person who is superhuman. What we tend to forget is that Socrates and Leonardo had to wrestle with the very same thoughts, doubts, anxieties and fears as you do. They were not superior people, they were human just like you, except that they were doers. They transcended their own "Who? Me?" attitudes and, instead, opted for being activists—for doing rather than carping. And eventually they became idolized.

It is useful for you to imagine yourself as Socrates, contemplating his philosophy as a human being and being willing to take the risks that went with going against the establishment. The times are different, but your humanity is the same as that of Socrates or any other human being who accomplished anything before you. The solution to your own lack of purpose is to allow yourself to feel and think in terms of your own personal greatness.

How do you feel around people whom you regard as superior? Do you choose to feel less than adequate around them? Do you quake at the thought of interacting with a great thinker? These kinds of attitudes are not uncommon when "average" people react to superachievers. But once again it gets back to your self-image, to how you elect to view yourself. If you compare yourself to a genius and see yourself as inferior, never allowing yourself to think in transcendent terms, then you will always stay inadequate in your own eyes. It's a vicious circle: any feelings of personal inadequacy which keep you immobilized are the ingredients which also keep you from feeling a sense of purpose in your own life.

Think big. Imagine yourself as great and fantastic, and you'll be giving yourself permission to achieve a sense of purpose that may have eluded you up until now. If you are running away from your own greatness and opting for routine and feelings of being a deficient person, then you are really fearing your own perfection as a human being. I discussed earlier the dynamic of allowing yourself to feel *perfect* and still be able to *grow*. It applies here as well. All of your personal putdowns, your feelings of inadequacy, your willingness to "settle" for what you've become—these are the components of your overall feelings of a lack of real purpose in your life. In order to rid yourself of these feelings and to surpass your own dreams of greatness, you must look carefully at how you personally view all of life, including your own, on this planet.

VIEWING ALL LIFE AS SACRED

Having a sense of purpose involves feeling purposeful about all of life. The individual who thinks and behaves in a No-Limit manner believes very strongly in the sacredness of all living things. The most important quality of life is the value of life itself, and No-Limit people find it exceedingly painful to see anyone or any animal dealt with disrespectfully. Each human being is seen as having intrinsic worth, and consequently you will seldom see NEZ/No-Limit people being critical or abusive toward anyone. When you talk to NEZ people, you will not observe them to be talking cruelly about others. They are not judges, and they do not spend their time watching others in order to have some juicy gossip to spread.

On the contrary, a NEZ/No-Limit person will usually talk about ideas. He does not focus on what his neighbors are doing, and he is almost oblivious to what they are wearing, buying, consuming and the like. He has a strong belief that people have dignity and are deserving of respect, and accordingly he expects others to treat him as dignified and important, because that is how he views himself and achieves his own sense of purpose. Because of his intense involvement in his life goals, he is typically a very busy person—always active and excited about what is happening in his life.

You will see that other people are buoyed by being around No-Limit people, who seem to have very special qualities that attract others to them. They are sought out because they are honest and willing to say exactly what they think, and consequently other people tend to lionize them, often giving them saintly attributes and treating them as very special people. They are motivators because their lives are an example, and their high esteem for life rubs off on those who tend to be less kind. Because NEZ/No-Limit people simply are not interested in being petty, those around them soon shift to more intelligent and humane behavior.

NEZ/No-Limit individuals treat everyone with special attention, and after having spent any time around this kind of person you will leave feeling very special and unique yourself. They enjoy being unusual and they treat others as if they were matchless, not because they are flatterers but because they really see the unique quality of each person they encounter. These people know that others in the world are trying to get everyone to conform and be just like everyone else, so they fight the battle of being individuals in everything they do. They resist being conformists for the sake of getting along, and they are willing to endure the outrage expressed by others because they have chosen to think and act as individuals.

Consequently, they naturally respect the individual dignity of everyone else. They don't judge people by surface qualities, nor do they evaluate any human being as bad simply because he may have behaved badly. They are quick to forgive those who have learned from their mistakes, not holding grudges, and are easily able to give others a second chance. The American poet e. e. cummings wrote this little poem which sums up how important the NEZ/No-Limit person feels about being an individual and resisting all efforts to simply fit in for the sake of conforming:

> to be nobody but yourself
> in a world which is doing
> its best day and night to
> make you like everybody else
> means to fight the hardest
> battle which any
> human being can
> fight and never
> stop fighting.

NEZ/No-Limit people will not be puppets in an audience who act just like everyone else. They cannot be persuaded to vote in blocs, or to behave in groupie ways. They have too much respect for themselves to be seen as belonging to any artificial category. They are not pro-management or pro-labor, but pro-humanity, and they express their opinions on any subject according to what they feel, not what they are expected to feel. They think for themselves on every issue and refuse to be treated as tiny parts of a big whole. They vote their consciences and respect others who do the same.

Don't try to compartmentalize a NEZ person; just when you think you've got him figured out, he'll turn around and behave in a totally unexpected way. But if you would emulate him, here are several ways to start.

Watch yourself in conversations. Try to avoid talking about anyone in negative terms, and don't let yourself get seduced into being catty and critical. Eliminate phrases from your vocabulary which are meant to cast aspersions, and remind yourself that you are not doing anything but fooling yourself into feeling superior by using others in a put-down fashion.

When you find your friends and relatives engaging in abusive talking-about-others behavior, remind them gently about what they are doing, and simply refuse to join the game. By teaching others that you aren't interested in focusing on what particular people do or don't do, and by not using sarcasm yourself, you'll be helping yourself to become more fully human, while simultaneously helping others to reduce their own negative behavior.

Practice respecting everything that is alive, and having the same reverence for other lives that you have for your own. If you see any creature in need of help, take time to help it. You'll soon see how much better you feel by being a person who protects life instead of destroying it. The reverence for life can extend throughout the animal kingdom. We are all here together, and when we help one another to become more independent and to stay more healthily alive *I believe we are fulfilling one of the major purposes for our being here in the first place—that is, our mission in life. When you adopt an attitude of sacredness for life, you will genuinely feel more purposeful, and consequently happier and more content as a human being.*

THE ULTIMATE SENSE OF MISSION

No-Limit people are different from almost everyone else in that they are involved in a personal cause that actually transcends the self. This kind of vigorous involvement is difficult for ordinary people to comprehend. What it means is being able to get excited about what you are doing, to feel vitally involved in your purpose here on earth and to feel within yourself that you are really *making a difference.* This sense of mission fulfills an inner need and yields an almost creative arrogance about the importance of what you are and why you are functioning as you do.

In talking to people who feel a sense of mission and purpose in life, I have discovered that virtually all of them receive their inner feelings of satisfaction from doing something for others. When you behave in a way that is going to help improve the quality of life for someone else, on any level, you will find your greatest source of fulfillment and the surest way to lead yourself in the direction of having more of a sense of mission. In talking with people who have made career changes late in their lives, I've found that those who shifted from something like selling insurance (for example) to counseling youngsters in trouble often express a strong sense of mission. (Of course, one can go into selling insurance late in life and feel the same sense of mission.) And when I've asked them why they feel different, they almost always reply, "I now feel as if I am doing something worthwhile."

Grasping a sense of mission in your life is almost like discovering your destiny without having to go on a massive search. It is a rare person who discovers that sense of mission in total isolation. Instead, it will come to you when you devote yourself to tasks, ideas and specific behaviors that are of some service to others. Notice how that special warm feeling of being appreciated comes to you when you hear that what you've done has been helpful to another human being—that feeling of having your spine tingle with a quiver of personal satisfaction when you know that you are doing things that are appreciated by someone else.

I experience this glow whenever I receive a letter from a reader who has been touched by something I've written. I know that my mission is right on target when people tell me they've changed for the better as a result of hearing me on a talk show or reading an article that I've labored over. I speak from a very personal place when I tell you that my mission in life is achieved most vividly when I know that I have made a difference in the life of another human being. It is all tied up for me in helping others to achieve their own sense of truth, beauty and justice. When they feel it, I feel it as well. And, despite the fact that I really don't believe I need that adulation or approval, because I would go right on writing and working without it, I also know that I love the knowledge that I am an instrument of help for others. When I get it, I feel better than at any other times in my life.

In many ways, my work is outside me. I do not have my ego tied into it. I know that what I do is of great importance and I put myself into it wholeheartedly, but I do not feel that I personally must do this in order to feel positive about myself. It is almost as if I have transcended myself and allowed myself to go out there and do what I love to do, and I can stand back and watch the results. I do not feel that I must do it in order to justify my existence; it is, in fact, the other way around. My existence is justified by the fact that I say it is, and I genuinely believe this to be true, regardless of what anyone else may decide to believe. Consequently I am free to function tirelessly without having anything to prove. When I get to this state of being able to just do what I do, and to do it well, without judging myself, I find I function at my very highest level. By transcending yourself and having your life mission outside yourself, you are most able to flow freely without interference from others or yourself.

As you approach the capacity for seeing your work or behavior as something that is outside yourself and that you are the instrument of delivery to the world, you will see your work as being inextricably tied up with higher and higher values. You will see that you work more for the value of being a contributor than for a paycheck, even though you will gladly accept your financial remuneration as well. You will find a kind of excitement in going after the truth inside you and sharing it with others. You will become motivated by your very highest values. You will love what you do for transcendent reasons.

That is what having a sense of mission is all about. And achieving that feeling of purpose can be accomplished right away if you start looking at yourself and your life with new eyes. You might want to take on a few of these specific behaviors and attitude shifts if you are really interested in feeling purposeful each day. There is nothing very magical about it. You simply make a decision that this day, *today,* is going to be one in which you practice more purposeful behaviors. That you are not going to be artificial, with yourself or with others, and that you are going to consult your own inner voice to determine what you are going to do with your life. Try a few of these behaviors on for a change and see if they lead to more intense feelings of purpose and meaning in your life.

SOME PERSONAL STRATEGIES FOR ACHIEVING A SENSE OF PURPOSE AND HONESTY

To be sure, a sense of purpose is not something you will feel automatically just because you try out a few new strategies. Developing a sense of meaning and purpose results from a general attitude that is itself the result of being your own person, consulting your inner signals, being enthusiastic about your work and behaving in the No-Limit ways I've described throughout this book. You can have a sense of purpose if you change around some behaviors and adopt an inner attitude of personal esteem and significance. While you will eventually reach that wonderful feeling of purpose if you work at becoming more of a No-Limit person, here are a few techniques which will help you to speed up the process:

Remind yourself that you can earn a living in many different ways. Also, that it is not necessary to stay at the same job or career slot simply because you have a great deal of time invested in what you are currently doing. Give yourself permission to be anything, and to wander onto new turf in your vocational decision-making. Don't buy the absurd belief that it is vocationally immature to change jobs or shift careers in midstream. It is foolish and neurotic to continue to do things that bring you no satisfaction when you have so many other options available to you. Keep remembering that anything in which you have an interest is a potential way of making a living and of feeling vitally involved in your work as well. If you enjoy doing something, but others evaluate you as immature or irresponsible, then you are going to have to ignore their protests if you are ever going to have a sense of mission and purpose. You can't always be sensible and please everyone else if you want to feel right with yourself; you must often take risks, the risks that lead to your own sense of purpose. Take those risks and invite your loved ones to join you, rather than resenting them for being obstacles to your growth.

Be enthusiastic about anything you elect to undertake. When you tackle any problem or deal with any personal task with a degree of enthusiasm for your work and yourself, you will feel more purposeful in what you are doing, and in your life in general. Enthusiastic people are those who have an attitude of fun and excitement toward life; they view life as a challenge, and they are not discouraged by having to do things over and over again. They accept the fact that they have made a choice, and they then take to that choice with zeal. The proper attitude directed at any task, no matter how unpleasant you may judge it to be, can make your time in the task worthwhile. I have spent many pleasant afternoons doing things that others see as boring and routine. Outlining a chapter can be exciting if one sees it in the proper perspective. Similarly, cleaning my house becomes enjoyable in direct proportion to my enjoyment of the results. I can feel great while baby-sitting or staying up all night at my typewriter meeting a deadline. This is true not because I am special, but because I choose to be genuinely enthusiastic about my life. And my *time* is the precious currency of my life, which I value immensely.

Be natural and trusting. Forget about being a person who has to impress anyone else. Practice stifling yourself when you are about to brag or to be phony in any way. Allow yourself to be as natural as you feel. If you want to cry in a place where others choose to suppress their tears, go ahead. Similarly, if you want to laugh out loud, practice doing it and you'll see that your naturalness is infectious. The more you work at just being yourself, the more likely you'll feel purposeful and significant in your life. When you put on airs or act unnaturally, you lose your sense of purpose, largely because you inwardly dislike yourself for being shallow. And when you dislike yourself you never feel a sense of genuine purpose in your life. You must be at peace with yourself before you can take that self out into the world to be productive and useful. When *you* feel good about you, and act naturally as a result, you'll take a worthy self out into the world, and that is when you'll feel a sense of purpose—when you are just being you, with no defenses or artificiality.

Be a busy person. People who are active are often much more at peace with themselves than those who are inactive and inert. When you have many different interests and things to do, and you balance relaxing and challenging time periods for yourself, you will feel much more useful and excited about living. The more you do without suffering from "hurry sickness," the more you want to do. And people who can do many things are much more inclined to be content than those who have severe limits in their lives.

Allow yourself to be guided by your highest values. A No-Limit person is most distinguishable from ordinary people in that he lives and is motivated by those highest values that I've talked about throughout the pages of this book. Seek out your own truth, go after beauty and justice in your world. Insist on being treated with dignity, and demand goodness instead of accepting evil in your life. The more you operate from within, upon those values which transcend all others, the more meaningful your life will be to you. Remember, an absence of truth, beauty, justice and dignity is just as harmful as an absence of oxygen and food; it just takes a little longer for the disease process to take hold and reveal itself.

Decide for yourself what you really love in your life. Then actively pursue that love, rather than trying to fit into a mold which leaves you feeling empty. You are entitled to love anything you choose, and no one thing or activity is any better than any other thing or activity unless you choose to judge it that way.

Become a doer in your life, and stifle your inclination to be a critic of other doers. The more you transcend your old tendencies to talk about people in petty ways, and the more you use that time in being a doer in *any* activity, the more likely you'll be to feel a real sense of purpose. Gossiping about others usually leaves you feeling cheap and inconsequential, and these are the kinds of feelings which you want to erase from your life completely if you are going to be acting with a feeling of purpose.

Give yourself permission to have some sacredness in your life. Your family, your lover, your religion, your feelings of being truthful, your love of the arts, or anything that you truly hold to be sacred is wonderfully helpful in building your own sense of purpose in your life. When you feel that certain people and ideas are sacred, you tend to act in a wondrous way toward them. The more of this kind of feeling you have about the important things and people in your life, the more purposeful you'll feel when you act on that sacredness. By holding people and certain things as precious, you inadvertently allow yourself to function at a higher level, and, of course, the higher the level on which you act out your life, the more purposeful and important your life will be.

Cultivate friendships that are meaningful for you. Allow yourself to have a confidential relationship with someone. Keep that friendship sacred and honest, allowing yourself to be free with someone whom you genuinely trust. This kind of relationship can become a treasure to you as you develop your own sense of purpose in life. Don't just say that you love this person, show that you do through your behavior. When you have a significant person to share your life with, one who you know will never judge you, and with whom you can be absolutely open and honest, you treasure the time you spend with this person. Having moments to treasure and value at the highest NEZ levels enhances your sense of purpose.

Be more growth-oriented in your life. Try to ignore the deficiencies in your life and instead shift to asking yourself what you would like to become. Remember the line I've used before, "You don't have to be sick to get better." Be more of a person who makes growth choices, and work at giving yourself permission to have some flaws. Those flaws don't have to be the source of your motivation. You don't have to be looking at your shortcomings in order to decide where you want to be. You can accept yourself where you are, but work regularly at growing each and every day. The more growth choices you make, the more you'll feel a real sense of purpose.

See how many of your defenses you can identify honestly. Stop kidding yourself—if you aren't true to yourself, you'll never develop a sense of purpose in your life. Acknowledge when you are being greedy, pretentious, prejudiced, arrogant, judgmental or even stupid. Chalk it up as a learning experience, but be aware of trying to reverse this trend the next time. All change starts with an acknowledgment to yourself that you are being defensive. Once you admit it, even if you have some trouble in changing right away, the actual admission process is a big step toward more self-honesty. And when you are really honest with yourself you are going to feel a lot better about your life, and you'll soon have that elusive feeling of purpose which so many people never experience in their lives.

Remember that you can't fail at being yourself. Go after whatever you want with a total anticipation of meeting some failure head on. While you can fail at certain activities—and, of course, you can never master any human skill without going along the failure path first—you cannot fail as a human being at being yourself, because you are complete as you live each moment. Learn to accept some failure and to quit evaluating yourself as a failure simply because you didn't succeed at some activity.

Come to grips with the real issues of life. Try to get rid of the drapery talk in favor of knowing your own position on the highest human values. You will find yourself feeling much more significant if you deal in your conversations with things which will make a difference in the world. While you will want to be able to be childlike and frivolous at times, that does not preclude your being aware of the highest values in our culture. When you are aware of these values and what they mean to you, and you share them with your confidants, you are likely to be working on a self-improvement package for yourself at the same time. If you ignore the key issues and remain ignorant about those highest values and concerns which engage mankind, you will be viewing your own contribution to the world in insignificant ways. How many times have you heard people say that they really don't count, that they are only the little guy, and so on? This kind of sentiment leads to do-nothingism and avoidance in life. It inhibits one from feeling a sense of purpose, because obviously a sense of purpose is impossible when you feel helpless. See yourself as someone who can change the world, who is informed and who really counts, and you'll also develop a sense of inner purpose as well.

Try to transcend the localism in your life. If you see yourself as belonging only to a tiny fragment of humanity and restrict yourself to that fragment, you will also feel insignificant as a result. Become a global person. View all of mankind as your brothers and sisters. If people are starving in Pakistan, a part of you is starving as well. And when you feel global you'll be more inclined to want to make a difference rather than save your reactions for your own back-yard local concerns. Unemployment, prostitution, drug abuse, poverty —these are as much a concern in Ohio as in Indonesia. The fact is that we all occupy this fragile planet together, and thinking larger rather than smaller will help you feel more of a sense of purpose in your life. It will also motivate you to corrective action if you see *their* problem as *our* problem.

Don't settle for less than you might become. You are as great as any human who has ever lived here before you. Don't fear your own greatness. Remind yourself that you can become anything you choose, and that greatness is yours for the taking if you really want it. You are not great because others say so; it is very much an inner thing. All of the major problems which face this earth are going to have to be resolved by great people. So why shouldn't you be one of them? If not you, then who? If everyone passes the buck, the problems will go unsolved. If you get active and feel important, you will gain a sense of purpose as a bonus spinoff.

Ask for the information you want to have about yourself. When you honestly seek out information about yourself from those who are significant in your life, you will take much of the guesswork out of your relationships. Be willing to take in what someone else has to say without defending your position. The more self-knowledge you acquire, the less you will have to wonder about yourself. You'll soon find it is quite easy to gain access to information about yourself, and you don't have to be guessing all the time. I know that I never spend any time wondering what people think of me. If I want to know, I simply ask. That way, I gain the information I seek, and I feel more knowledgeable about myself as well. The more self-awareness you have, the more you will feel a sense of purpose about your life.

NINE QUESTIONS TO HELP YOU GET AT YOUR OWN SELF-HONESTY

Ask yourself these questions and make an effort to answer them honestly without resorting to playing games with yourself. You may find it difficult to answer each of these questions without making a reference to what you believe to be true about yourself up until now, but if you can suspend your past history and simply react, particularly with someone whom you know and love, you'll be able to get an accurate handle on your ability to be totally honest.

1. *How would you change your life if you knew that you had only six months to live?* The answers to this question will be very revealing to you in helping you to become more candid and straightforward with yourself. If you would make some very drastic changes, then you are not living your current life with absolute personal integrity. The fact is that you have, compared to eternity, only a short time to live. Even if you have fifty or more years left of your lifetime, it is still equivalent to only a few seconds of eternity. Thinking in terms of six months is useful in that it gives you enough time to act on things which are important to you, and it isn't so short a span that it is over with the blink of an eye. If you say to yourself that, given the condition of having only six months left in your life, you would change many things, then I would suggest to you that making those changes is something you ought to do now.

Remind yourself of your terminal status. If you would change jobs, relationships, locations, friendships, life styles, means of communicating with your loved ones, or anything else, then why not get on with it while you still can? If you are not doing precisely what you would be doing if you knew that you had only a few months left, then you are living a lie, and your score on the total-personal-honesty scale is very low. You cannot have a sense of purpose and meaning in your life if you are merely going through the motions of your life rather than living as you would really like to. Regardless of how you justify it to yourself, you still lack a sense of purpose if you would drastically shift your life style in this adverse event. Because, in reality, given the perspective of eternity, you have only a few months left anyhow, and the "wait until later" people are gambling on there being a future. Don't gamble with your life—live it!

2. *Whom would you choose to live with if you could live with anyone in the world?* Suppose for a moment that you have no legal obligation to stay with your immediate family, assuming you have one, and that you know no reason why you could not legally live with anyone outside of your immediate family. Given this kind of situation, with whom would you choose to live? Who are your favorite people in all the world? Are you with them as much as you'd like to be? The point here is this: if you are living your life in relationships (family or otherwise) in which you feel obligated to be where you are rather than because you genuinely want to be there, then you should be asking yourself why you make these kinds of dishonest choices.

Are your close friends the people you really enjoy? Is your love relationship based on mutual love, or is it based on obligation? I believe that you can turn most relationships based on obligation into liaisons of choice by allowing yourself and the others who are important to you to have the freedom to be what you choose for yourselves. You need not establish your close relationships on something so undignified as duty, but, rather, be totally honest in asking yourself whether these relationships are what you (and they) really want them to be. If the answer is no, then you can resolve either to improve all of your relationships so that they are what each of you really desires or to get out of them and get on with being with people whom you really enjoy.

Thomas Hobbes once said, "Obligation is slavery, and slavery is hateful." If you are living out your life with people simply because you feel obliged to do so, then you are lacking in total personal honesty, and you've opted for some slavery instead. While you may justify your choices as representing your being a good responsible person, in fact you are stultifying your own sense of meaning and purpose by constantly being reminded of your inability to choose what you would genuinely want for yourself. Besides, who among those you spend your time with would really enjoy knowing that you do it out of obligation rather than your own personal choice? Would you want to have someone stick around you if you knew that he or she really didn't want to be there, but stayed only out of a sense of obligation? Any relationship based exclusively on obligation lacks dignity.

3. *Where would you choose to live if you could live anywhere in the world?* Suppose now that you had no commitment to where you've lived up until today. Where would you choose to live? Would you pick the neighborhood, city, state, country, hemisphere in which you currently live? If you are living in a place because you've always lived there and for no other reason, then you do not have a handle on total personal honesty. You may feel that it would be impossible for you to move, and that your roots are firmly established where you happen to be right now, but most of that kind of logic comes from a fear of trying out new activities and settling instead for staying where you are because it is easier, safer and less worrisome.

You can be wherever you would like to be. Period. You need not be rooted by your history, but can become involved in what you would really like for yourself. The fear of change, of moving to new places, of checking out your potential in any place that is personally appealing, is based only on not being honest with yourself. While you may defend your inertia and tell yourself that it is impossible for you to move at this stage of your life, the fact is, if you would like to be someplace else and you opt for staying where you are, for whatever reason (unless you are in prison) then you are not living your life from a *totally* honest perspective, regardless of how much you argue to the contrary.

4. *How much sleep do you think you would get if you had no clock or ability to measure your sleep time?* Do you go to bed at "bedtime"? Do you wake up when you are supposed to? Do you go to bed thinking that if you don't get eight hours' sleep you are really going to be tired tomorrow? Just give yourself a little fantasy for a few moments. Imagine that you have no clocks, and that you have no way of knowing how many hours of sleep you get. Imagine that someone else keeps track of your sleep time but you have no knowledge of it. How many hours a day do you imagine you would sleep? Do you think that you would go to bed at the same time if you had no idea of when "bedtime" arrived? Imagine yourself living underground in a bunker where you had no idea of day or night and you could go to sleep whenever the mood struck you.

Most people guide their sleep lives on externals such as clocks and calendars rather than on when they really want to sleep. Much of your sleep is done in reaction to what you've learned rather than for what you need or crave. You would very likely sleep a lot less if your life was filled with exciting, missionlike experiences and if you didn't keep track of what time you went to bed and how many hours of sleep you chalked up. A totally honest person is honest in all things, including why he sleeps when he does and whether he does so in response to boredom, unpleasant activities or habit. The more time you allow yourself for being awake and alive, and the more you conduct the natural affairs of your life according to choice rather than habit or fearful expectations, the more likely you are to have a totally honest assessment of yourself. Many studies have shown that when people are busy, unaware of time and excited about life they think less about sleep; fatigue is something they rarely experience, and they feel more purposeful as humans.

5. *How much, and when, would you eat if you had no mealtimes?* Suppose that you could eat only when you were hungry, and then only until your appetite was satisfied. Do you think you would have the same eating habits? Many people eat because they fear they will be hungry in only a few hours. Also, people eat by the clock rather than by consulting their own inner hunger clocks. Total honesty involves making your own decisions about when and what you will eat, according to your own needs rather than the dictates of some externally imposed schedule. The more you trust yourself to have good personal judgment and also permit others to do the same, the more likely you'll be to gain a sense of faith and trust in yourself.

Children will develop a very strong sense of proper nutrition if they are trusted to monitor their own eating habits. The more you permit yourself, and those you love, to have personal trust, the more you will be building a stronger sense of personal integrity. This goes for almost everything in life, but it is particularly relevant to eating. I have seen parents who literally force their children to eat, who make mealtime into a battleground, negotiating each vegetable for a promise of some reward. The process of healthful eating, a very natural process indeed, can be turned into a nightmare if you don't have trust in yourself and your loved ones. You really don't have to eat just because it is mealtime, or because everyone else is doing so, or because you will be hungry in a few hours if you don't. You can eat properly when you feel like it, and you don't need to follow any schedule unless you don't have the kind of faith in yourself to make proper judgments about your own personal health.

6. *What would you do if there were no such thing as money?* Just allow yourself to imagine doing anything that you would like to do. Forget about earning a living, and simply ask yourself what you would do if it didn't make any difference in terms of monetary reward. If you are spending your life struggling at something that has no meaning for you, and justifying it by saying that you must do it because it gives you the money you need to pay your bills, then you are opting for some personal dishonesty with yourself. You have made the money more important than your own sense of purpose, and as long as you keep the priority in that order *you will always be lacking in purpose and total self-honesty.*

Most people never fully come to grips with the idea of having money chase you rather than the other way around. You can be fulfilled in your life, doing the things that bring you pleasure and a sense of purpose, and money will chase after you in amounts large enough to keep you responsible and out of debt. But if you convince yourself that you will never be able to do the things you'd really like to because you would certainly fall on your face financially and end up on welfare, then you will make the choice to continue in the chasing-money syndrome that is its own psychological dead end. Whatever it is that you would really enjoy doing is a prime possibility for earning a living as well. There is a market for everything on this planet, with billions of people to benefit from your own personally fulfilling undertakings. The issue is whether you can be honest enough with yourself to take the risks to do the things that bring you a sense of purpose, rather than chase the money which will guarantee you a sense of external security. There is no substitute for risk-taking in this area. If you elect to avoid the risks, you can assume the posture that Jackson Browne sings about in "The Pretender" with these words: "I'm going to be a happy idiot and struggle for the legal tender."

7. *How old would you be if you didn't know how old you were?* If you simply didn't know your date of birth and you had no way of finding out, how old would you estimate yourself to be? Do you think in terms of being able to do only certain age-typical things and consequently rule out many of life's activities because of your age? Are younger people supposed to behave in one way and older people in quite another? If you think in age stereotypes, you are

not being completely honest with yourself. You can really do anything that suits your fancy, even if no one else in your particular age group condones what you are doing. In fact, a totally self-honest person does not even think in age-group terms.

You are as old as you decide you are, and any restrictions based upon age are pretty much self-imposed. You can swing on a swing, go disco dancing, enjoy Lawrence Welk or suck your thumb if you really want to. If you didn't know your age, you would estimate it to a great degree according to your attitudes toward life. You might see yourself as young and vibrant even if you had lived three quarters of a century; you wouldn't know the difference if you didn't have some external document, such as a birth certificate or other people's reminders, to keep you posted. The totally honest, purposeful person does not let his age have anything to do with the life choices he makes. He behaves according to what feels right for him, rather than by what he is supposed to be doing in a particular year in his life. Some people find themselves traumatized by birth anniversaries—thirty, forty, fifty, sixty . . . Others who are much more honest with themselves pay no attention to these artificial boundaries and go right on being what they choose for themselves, without considering their age.

8. *What kind of personality would you elect if you were starting today?* Imagine yourself as a person who can elect any personality you desire. What would you choose for yourself? Would you be more assertive, less shy, more outgoing, less guilty, more stable, more humorous, easier to talk to, less gullible? If you do not have the kind of personality you would like to have, you have chosen to be less than totally honest with yourself. Everything about yourself which you do not like is within your capacity to change if you make the decision to do so. Of course, the decision must be followed up with some hard work, but the point is that the choice is totally yours. Your personality is what you allow it to be. If you would elect different characteristics given the opportunity to choose a totally new personality, you are not understanding that you have that choice right now. No one forces you to stay shy, nervous, nonassertive or gullible. You make those life choices, and you can "unmake" them if you really want to. The totally honest person understands that he is responsible for his own personality and he doesn't blame anyone else for what he is, even if he knows that some of his earlier life experiences contributed to what he chooses to be today. Total honesty means no blame! It means that you don't

defend your lack of ability and willingness to be what you would like to be by blaming others for what you are today. The fact is that you can choose to have the kind of personality you would like.

9. *How would you describe yourself if you couldn't use any labels?* Suppose someone asked you to define yourself, but you were forbidden to use any of the traditional labels on which most people rely so heavily. Suppose you couldn't say how old you were, where you lived, what you studied in school, what ethnic background you came from, your job history, your family status, your economic status, your marital status, the color of your hair, your height or even your name. Instead, suppose you had to describe precisely what kind of human being you are. Could you do it?

Could you talk about yourself without resorting to the traditional labels that are used so frequently as a mask to hide what we are really all about? Could you talk openly about your feelings as a human being? Your personal sense of purpose and meaning in life? Could you describe your sensitivities, anxieties, defenses and desires? Could you talk openly about your ability to give and take love? To contribute and leave your own footprints here on this planet? If you would have to resort to labels and describe yourself as if you were filling out a résumé or a job application, then your sense of personal honesty and purpose may be tied up in things and accomplishments outside yourself. You may view yourself as a statistic sheet rather than as a special human being, and this very image may in fact be the reality that you have chosen for yourself. Total honesty demands being able to identify yourself, and your unique humanity. It means being able to answer the question "Who am I?" without having to use stereotypical labels and statistical information.

These nine hypothetical questions will help you to get a real handle on what you are all about as a human being. Total self-honesty is a big part of having a clear vision of your sense of purpose. Being honest with yourself has nothing to do with how many lies you tell in the course of a day. It has to do with how much you really know about yourself and how willing you are to admit to yourself all of your defenses and shortcomings—how well you can look in the mirror and face yourself and see yourself for what you are. The lowest form of self-deceit is to be pretending and then to pretend that you are not pretending. If you sell others a bill of goods about who you are, that is one thing, and it may even work for a while, but if you are deceiving yourself you will lack that sense of purpose and meaning that can literally turn your life into something genuinely worthwhile.

A real sense of purpose in life is not aligned with figuring out what you should be doing each day. Instead, it is aligned with being honestly involved in living out your days as you believe they should be lived. People are always asking me, "How can I find out what I really want to do?" The answer is something that eludes most people because they want to chase success rather than be successful according to their own inner feelings of purpose. While it may sound evasive and even metaphysical, I think Nietzsche provided the best answer to those searching people: "He who has a *why* to live for can bear with almost any *how*." It is not what you choose to do that will bring you total honesty; it is knowing that *why* you are doing it fits in with your own feelings of worthiness about yourself. It is immeasurably important for you to feel that sense of mission about your life if you are going to be a No-Limit person.

9 Winning One Hundred Percent of the Time

A No-Limit person is a winner one hundred percent of the time. To become a full-time winner, you must accept the notion that we don't need losers in order to have winners. Our culture is imbued with the idea of creating winners via the external route; that is, in an external world one must defeat someone else or achieve some external goal in order to be classified a winner. But a NEZ/No-Limit person does not operate on the system in which most people find themselves hopelessly trapped. *To a No-Limit person, winning is an internal process.* It is the ability to think of yourself as a winner (because you are operating on inner signals) in virtually all life situations. You do not have to beat someone else in order to be a winner if your self-worth is based on an inner rather than an external scale. If you must defeat an opponent to become a winner, then you are allowing that opponent to determine how you will view yourself as a human being. The inner-directed person refuses ever to label himself as a loser simply because someone else has greater skills than he on any given day.

The No-Limit person has a firm grip on the reality of winning and losing. The fact is that no one person is better than everyone else at anything for more than a few minutes in one single day. It is possible for the world champion at anything, on any given day, to be surpassed by many others around the world. If you accept this reality, you begin to understand that if we use the external definition of winning and losing (that is, you must defeat another person to be a winner, and if you don't you're a loser), then all of us are losers every day of our lives. This kind of win/lose dichotomy must be transcended if you are going to become a No-Limit person and stop thinking of yourself as a loser.

Keeping in mind that your inner attitude is always a matter of your own personal choice, you can begin to develop a winning philosophy about everything that you are without deluding yourself at all. The first step in developing your winning-one-hundred-percent-of-the-time attitude is to get rid of the idea that we can neatly label people winners and losers in specific competitions. The total winning attitude, on the contrary, is one which allows you to think of yourself as a winner all the time while still giving yourself room to grow. You never have to engage in self-flagellation simply because you've encountered an opponent who is more skillful than you are on a given day. You do not have to find fault with yourself because you fail to achieve a goal. You do not have to look at the other guy to see how well you stack up as a human being, nor do you ever have to use comparison in order to measure your own self-worth.

The point is that everything you do in life affords you an opportunity to think of yourself as a winner. You can learn from every single experience. And when you use your life experience to provide yourself with motivation for growth rather than as evidence of your deficiencies, you will be on the side of being a one-hundred-percent winner. Winning is really an attitude, whereas defeating an adversary is something that you will do on some days and fail to do on others. Once again, no one can ever defeat everyone else all of the time. This is simply impossible on a planet with billions and billions of people. But anyone can emerge from any activity as a winner, and also with the skills to become even more competent at any given activity, if he has his own internal attitude set on thinking of himself in winning ways. What you need to do most urgently is get yourself out of the self-defeating pattern that is so prevalent in our culture, the attitude that stresses winning as a result of defeating losers.

THE ABSURDITY OF HAVING WINNERS AT THE EXPENSE OF LOSERS

Our culture places an extremely high premium on winning at the expense of losers. In the business world the name of the game is upward mobility and always be wary of the other guy who is trying to get the job you want. In athletics, young people are force-fed a diet of winning at all costs, and the person who doesn't win considers himself a loser. Schools, with their heavy emphasis on grades and test scores, label students as winners and losers. Books are written about how to become a winner, how to outsell the other guy, how to be "number one," how to outpsych your opponent, and many other subjects which focus on the external concept of being a winner.

The No-Limit person operates on inner signals, as I've discussed in various other sections of this book. To a person who is organized on inner principles, the idea of having to defeat anyone else, or to compare himself to someone else, is a contradiction in terms. Consequently, the No-Limit person looks toward himself to determine if he is or isn't a winner in life. Winning, to a NEZ/No-Limit person, has nothing to do with defeating, outselling, comparison, upward mobility, competition or any other external means of self-evaluation. The NEZ/No-Limit person understands how futile it is to use anyone else as an index for measuring his own status. Thus he can undertake any activity and emerge from the experience as a winner. This is true because the individual, rather than some external criterion, is making the determination of whether he is a winner or not. Thus winning one hundred percent of the time is based on learning how to have a winning attitude about everything you undertake in life, rather than on evaluating yourself in any external performance manner.

The idea of never thinking of yourself as a loser is something to give a great deal of consideration to if you really want to become a No-Limit person. If we use any single standard of comparison or performance, then every person on this planet is a loser almost all the time. Why would you ever want to label yourself in a negative, self-deprecating manner and evaluate yourself with regard only to how you stack up to others? You are unique in all the world. You know that no other person looks, acts, thinks or feels exactly as you do. This being true, how can you possibly be a loser simply because you are not meeting some standardized norm that other people are supposed to use as a comparison guide?

There are no losers in life when you are a No-Limit person. There are people who have different skills, abilities, interests and instincts. Some people make choices to be in competition with others, but this doesn't mean that when you score fewer points, or hit a ball at a fielder instead of through a hole on the ball field, you are a loser. In reality, all it says is that you hit a ball at a fielder and were thrown out, or you hit the ball over the net fewer times than your opponent. You may want to work on being more effective at this business of hitting or kicking a ball, but you need not label yourself a loser in the interim training period. After all, when you lose a game, what have you really lost? Absolutely nothing. Your life still goes on; you still have those higher values and needs, the desire to create your own truth, and everything else that goes into being a fully functioning person. You simply had a lower score than your opponent on a given day. Period!

The same is true when you go after a goal that you set for yourself and fail to achieve. You are not a failure as a person simply because you failed to achieve a goal; you just have to learn from the experience and move on to other goals for yourself. You cannot learn without some failure. Everyone who has ever achieved anything has experienced a great deal of failure. But you need never label *yourself* as a failure in the process. Once you think of yourself as a failure, you set yourself up to view yourself in negative terms. When this takes place, you are doomed to believe the nonsense that you are a loser in life. The entire process of labeling yourself as a loser keeps you from growing; and to a NEZ person, operating from a position of being able to grow is what life is all about. Thomas Edison was once asked how it felt to be a failure after some twenty-five thousand futile attempts to invent a storage battery. His reply has significance for all of us. "Failure? I'm not a failure at all. I now know twenty-five thousand ways *not* to make a battery."

Anything that keeps you from growing is never worth defending, and thinking of yourself as a loser is the biggest deterrent to your ability to make growth choices. *Thus your ability to be a winner one hundred percent of the time is based upon giving up the notion that losing at anything is equivalent to being a loser.*

You can't invent anything if you view yourself as a loser simply because you haven't succeeded yet.

This is not simply a game I am asking you to play with yourself, much less an invitation to you to delude yourself into calling yourself a winner when you are not. I am asking you to shift around the entire concept of winning/losing in your mind, to transcend this vicious dichotomy and to think in terms of being what *you* choose for yourself, rather than having to measure up to any external standard. Everything you elect to do can be approached from a position of having a winning attitude. I mean everything! You need never think of yourself as a loser again, regardless of your intelligence, skill levels, hobbies, talents or anything else. Being internal and consulting yourself from a position of self-esteem is what really distinguishes winners from those who think of themselves as losers.

Reality tells us there is no such thing as number one. There is always another team, another individual, another goal beyond our current level. The four-minute mile was a barrier we thought would never be broken only twenty-five years ago, and now we are talking about three-minute miles in the future. Are all of the people who ran four-minute miles a few years ago losers today? No human being ought ever to think of himself as a loser, and any behavior that is directed at convincing others that they are losers is self-defeating for everyone concerned.

Hope, not frustration, is the key to improvement. Cooperation, not competition, increases performance levels in most human enterprises. Inner pride rather than self-flagellation is the key to inner success as well as outer success. Being relaxed, at peace with yourself, confident, emotionally neutral, loose and free-floating—these are the keys to successful performance in almost everything. Taking a test, playing a crucial ball game, giving a speech, anything at all that is thought of as tension-producing, is best accomplished in a spirit of inner peace. And any screaming, berating, needling, cajoling, punishment or derision is generally going to produce more tension, and consequently more "failure" under stress.

The more at peace you are with yourself, and the more you give yourself permission to just enjoy any activity, the more likely you'll be able to perform at a higher level; and, of course, with that kind of internal attitude, you'll never stoop so low as to tag yourself, or any other human being, with so undignified a label as "loser."

THE PROCESS OF BECOMING A ONE-HUNDRED-PERCENT WINNER

Becoming a full-time winner in life involves a process which will require you to transcend many of your normal ways of functioning. Before this time, you have been conditioned to thinking in dichotomies and to using the labeling technique to describe yourself. That is, you were taught to compartmentalize as a substitute for thinking. In school you were encouraged to put names, facts, ideas and problems into specific categories. You were encouraged to memorize data and to give it back. You were taught that there were right and wrong answers to everything that comes along in life. If you got a problem right you got a reward, and if you were *wrong* you were penalized.

Consequently, you were taught to avoid the kind of thinking that I have been supporting throughout the pages of this book. You were rarely taught that thinking internally was a valued ingredient in your life. In fact, you were told quite the opposite: get the facts straight and forget about thinking for yourself; life is divided into rights and wrongs, and your job is to find the rights and avoid the wrongs.

You were told that a poem could be interpreted only a certain way, or that Ernest Hemingway had something very specific in mind when he wrote his novels, and your purpose was to discover his hidden intentions. You were told in every subject area to look for the answer which would please the external authority, earn you the appropriate grade and transcript entry, and to forget about your own individualized thoughts about things. Getting educated meant conforming, behaving, memorizing, passing tests, forgetting and then cramming again for a final test, and then forgetting this information forever. This very kind of rigid approach to learning was applied in virtually all of your life experiences.

You were taught that life has winners and losers. That when you play a baseball game on the playground the winning team is the one with the most runs. You began to equate being a winner as a person with scoring runs, or some other external kind of activity. You were admonished by your coaches for not having integrity when you missed a play or performed poorly in comparison to others. You were weaned on being a superachiever and never permitting yourself the luxury of just enjoying an activity; instead you were told to always *do your best* at everything, even though this kind of mentality leads to ulcers, depression and self-reproach.

You were not encouraged to just *do,* to enjoy, to be pursuing your own truths. Instead, your upbringing focused on external reward systems such as school grades, competitive activities and learning how to earn money so that you would be happy. Almost all of your education was designed to teach you to compartmentalize yourself and to use external validators to determine how worthy and significant you were as a human being.

Winning one hundred percent of the time involves taking on some dramatic shifts in your life, shifts which are based exclusively on common sense and your own pursuit of your very highest values. Obviously, doing your very best at everything all the time will wear you down and keep you from achieving excellence in any area of your life. You know that you can't be better than everyone else, so why ever use anyone else as an index of your own worth or ability? You are aware that in any competitive activity, if you are keeping score, even the most talented of all individuals in a given area must still lose almost as often as he wins.

So why should anyone ever think of himself as a loser when he runs into the inevitable? You just can't beat everyone else all the time, and if this is true why not admit it and begin to run your life on inner- rather than outer-directed motivation? You know that nothing in life is ever all one thing or the other, that every problem has many potential solutions, and that nothing ever gets resolved by simply putting a label on it. You know that all people have dignity and value, regardless of the mistakes they make, and yet these very commonsense notions are forgotten by many people as they indefatigably chase after winning and label themselves and others as losers almost every day of their lives.

The new way of viewing yourself and all your activities is what this book is about. Your one-hundred-percent-of-the-time winning self will be achieved by your taking on (1) *new thinking,* leading to (2) *new feelings,* and concluding with (3) *new behaviors.* Anytime you are interested in changing anything about yourself, you must go through this three-part stepladder if the change is going to become a permanent part of your new No-Limit self. It works like this:

1. THINKING as a One-Hundred-Percent-of-the-Time Winner

You are responsible for the thoughts you have in your head. You have the capacity to think whatever you choose, and virtually all of your self-defeating attitudes and behaviors originate in the way you elect to think. Your thoughts are your very own personal responsibility, and once you accept this as a fundamental part of your total humanity you will be on the way toward changing anything about yourself that you feel displeased about. Emotions don't just happen. Actions don't simply take place. All of your feelings and behaviors are preceded by mental processes called thoughts, and no one can make you think something you don't want to think. Your corner of freedom, even when others are manipulating or even imprisoning you, is your ability to choose the thoughts which you have within your own mind. And once you understand that your emotions and behaviors come directly from your thoughts, you will simultaneously understand that the way to attack any personal problem is to attack the thoughts that support your negative emotions and self-defeating behaviors.

You know that you control your thoughts, and that if you really want to become a No-Limit person it is pretty much a job of learning how to think differently from the way you have trained yourself until now. Attitudes are nothing more than thoughts, and a reminder to yourself that you can choose any attitude that you would like to have, under virtually all circumstances, is the first step in the one-hundred-percent winning life style I am presenting to you.

Your ability to become a full-time winner is contingent on your willingness to decide to think in winning ways and to work at eradicating any loser images you may be carrying over from an earlier period of your life. Thinking like a winner means not always having to defeat someone else. It means being able to grow from a situation in which you fail to reach your goal. It involves not demanding perfection from yourself in every single thing you do, but, instead, thinking of yourself as perfect and thus capable of growing. It means reminding yourself that perfection doesn't mean staying the same; it means being able to allow yourself to grow. Thinking as a winner means not coming down on yourself; it means refusing to allow self-repudiating thoughts into your head. It involves pushing out the inclination to evaluate yourself in comparison with others, and giving yourself permission to be the unique person you are.

All the thoughts in your head that contribute to your thinking of yourself as a loser are easier to send away when you think of them as choices. Once you take responsibility for your losing thoughts, you can make the choice to convert them to winning thoughts. If you play a tennis match against a strong opponent and emerge defeated, you are a loser only if you think that way. Actually, every single defeat you experience is something which builds character and improves your ability. You could leave the match saying to yourself that you learned some things today, that you know what shots you have to work on, that you had a really terrific experience playing against such excellent competiton. The choice to be just the opposite is also readily available to you. You can pout and throw your racquet, become angry at yourself, call yourself worthless and become obsessed with the fact that you lost. Whichever choice you elect, reality will stay precisely as it is. You will not have hit the ball over the net and into the opposite court as many times as your opponent did, and that will always be true for all of your losing matches. But how you think, what you do with the loss and how you decide to place it in a sensible context in your life are all choices for you to make. A consistent winner knows that you grow just as much from defeats as from victories and that nothing in life is worth making yourself miserable over.

2. FEELING as a One-Hundred-Percent-of-the-Time Winner

If your feelings come directly from your thoughts, and you know that you can select your thoughts, it stands to reason that you can decide how you are going to feel as well. Emotions are no great secrets. They are the physiological results of your thoughts, and there is nothing robotlike in deciding how emotional you choose to be. Any emotion that is functional, helpful to you, pleasing and something you want to hang on to—you can have for yourself. It is absurd to pretend that we can't help the way we feel, that our emotions just happen to us and we have no control over them, that we really can't help the way we are emotionally.

A No-Limit person can be very emotional, but he is not someone who becomes immobilized by his emotions. Learning how to manage your emotions and take responsibility for them, rather than blaming some mysterious "unconscious" or long-past experience as the source of your emotions today, is the means to achieving personal autonomy and freedom in your life. To understand anger as a choice rather than as something that just happens to you gives you an opportunity to do something about it when it is immobilizing you or others. If you simply buy into the idea that you can't help the way you are and that your emotions just happen, then you obviously are incapable of doing anything about changing them when they interfere in your life. There is something very sensible about taking responsibility for how you are going to feel rather than just leaving it up to luck or to a genetic system based on random distribution of emotional traits.

A one-hundred-percent-of-the-time winner is one who elects to work at not becoming depressed, traumatized, angry, guilty, unnecessarily fearful, self-rejecting or anxious as a reaction to problems and life experiences. In a contest between you and an opponent, your emotional state will determine how effective you are going to be. The more uptight you are, the more you make this contest have a life-or-death consequence, the more you get angry at yourself, tense and just plain "tight," the less opportunity you will have for emerging from the experience with a victory.

These emotional reactions which lead to immobilization come directly from the way you are thinking at the moment. When you put pressure on yourself or relive something that is already over, when you get angry at yourself or your opponent and make yourself tense with mental threats to yourself, you are choosing to *feel* like a loser. The more tense you become as a result of those sentences in your head, the more likely you are to feel worse and worse, until ultimately you become so anguished that you give up on yourself.

The same kind of emotional reaction is possible when you go to take an examination in school, or go for a job interview, or any other test which may be rough for you to do. The more unnatural you are —the more you start thinking of yourself in self-forfeiting ways, and the more you are inclined to evaluate yourself at the time of the activity—the more likely you'll be to choose negative emotions that will get in your way and keep you from being effective. Moreover, if you then grade yourself on how well you did, rather than focusing on how well you've done and what you can learn from it, you will get right back into thinking of yourself as a loser and then *feeling* like a loser as well.

Feeling like a winner all the time is possible even in the worst of times, or in the most frustrating situations. Your emotional reaction to all of life's activities, and all of your own individual pursuits, is entirely up to you and the way that you decide to think. The NEZ/No-Limit person seems to understand that feeling bad and depressed is a waste of those precious moments that he has here in this life, and so no situation to him is worth being immobilized and full of agony. *Doing* something about a problem is the No-Limit approach, while sitting around and feeling bad is the self-defeating tactic. When you are busy doing, and not thinking and evaluating your performance all the time, especially in comparison with others, you are too involved in life to have negative emotional reactions. People who are inert, lazy or self-indulged are generally those who have the time for all of the mental self-denunciation and self-pity that lead to negative emotional reactions. The one-hundred-percent winner is so excited about doing, and being able to enjoy a present moment, that he just doesn't have the leftover time for the loser mentality. Determination, yes! Expressing quickly and painlessly one's frustration, yes! But wallowing around in the mire of self-reproach, anger, depression and the like—never for a one-hundred-percent-of-the-time winner.

3. *BEHAVING as a One-Hundred-Percent-of-the-Time Winner*

Your winning-one-hundred-percent-of-the-time behaviors will naturally fall into line once you have convinced yourself that you can in fact change your thinking to that of a total winning philosophy by being the sole determiner of what you elect to think. Then you will have accepted the notion that your emotions need not be barriers to your own No-Limit objectives, because you can be the manager of your own feelings as well. You will automatically begin to act in ways that are conducive to your own self-image as a one-hundred-percent winner. You will relax, stop trying so hard, allow your body to do what it knows how to do by virture of your experience and learning, and you will emerge from every single encounter in life as a winner.

The total preoccupation of our culture with winning is largely in the competitive, defeat-the-other-guy, accumulate-externals style of winning. Obviously this mode of winning is impossible one hundred percent of the time, since no one is ever going to be better than everyone else all of the time. In fact, pushing for this kind of winning at all costs will result in your not even being a winner five percent of the time. When you are always looking over your shoulder to see how the other guy is doing in order to assess whether you are a winner, or if you need another person to compare yourself to, or to defeat, or even to surpass, you are dependent on externals for your winning ways. Under those conditions you will rarely emerge as a winner. You'll spend almost all of your precious present moments chasing the other guy, and you'll be a "loser by definition" almost all the time.

Full-time winning behaviors can be practiced in virtually all of your life experiences and activities. They flow directly from your winning attitudes, and you can find yourself being a winner in situations where most others choose madness. Moreover, your attitude soon becomes infectious and overlaps to all areas. When you start becoming an appreciator of life, for example, you become someone who understands that you can grow from adversity. Thus, when you are going through a particularly tough time, such as a tax audit, a low point in income, an illness, a death in the family or even milder difficulties such as traffic jams or long lines, your ability to appreciate each moment and to live it fully allows you to transcend the losing attitude which previously caused you to become immobilized and upset for long periods. You begin to look for something beneficial in tight situations rather than let the circumstances defeat you. Before long, even in tough competitive games or on the job you look for something to learn rather than something to complain about. You begin to take risks and try out new behaviors that you previously shunned, because you no longer fear being a loser. The rewards for adopting a winning attitude are essentially one: the No-Limit status I have presented throughout this book.

Some examples of how a one-hundred-percent winner performs are shown in these typical situations from everyday life:

On the job. You do not have to get yourself cornered into the upward-mobility trap. In fact, the less you are concerned about trying to advance, the more likely you'll be able to function effectively in the present, and ironically the better your chance of being promoted. People who just do their work, enjoy what they are doing and live one day at a time are the most likely to be productive and considered for promotion. The more humanistic you are toward others and yourself, the greater the demand for your leadership services. But when you are always striving, apple-polishing and making yourself into a nervous wreck about your future, you'll never have the winning attitude of a NEZ person.

I have been interviewed for jobs many times in my life. In each of these interview settings my attitude was, "If I am just myself, and not phony in any way, along with demonstrating that I can positively survive without this job, then I will be coming across in the way I really want them to see me." The less concerned I was with trying to impress my interviewers, the more able I was to simply be myself. I always emerged a winner, even when I didn't get the job. As I look back at those jobs that I "almost" got, I realize that they weren't right for me then or now. I learned something very important from every interview, and I always left the interview situation feeling like a winner. Why? Because I didn't need a particular job in order to feel good about myself. I saw the experience as valuable; I tested myself in a tense situation, and I emerged having grown from the experience.

You can see yourself in winning ways in every interaction that you have with your bosses or co-workers. You can approach a supervisor from a position of knowing that you are a terrific person regardless of how this thing comes out. You can leave the encounter having learned how to be more effective in future interactions, and having your self-worth intact because you never placed it on the line in the first place. You can see your job as something *you* choose to do. If you are going to do it again today, then you are going to enjoy and grow from this occupational choice—*today!*

When you no longer want to make that choice, or when you are willing to take the risks involved in making new vocational choices, you can grow in a new occupational direction. The one-hundred-percent-of-the-time winning attitude on the job involves not placing your own personal worth or sense of purpose in the external mold of doing your job, but, instead, operating from a perspective of inner appreciation for yourself. When you reverse the process of validating your worth from your job to doing it from within, you stop the business of "needing" any particular job. Once you stop the *need,* you are free to do it from choice. When you are honest enough with yourself to admit that you no longer feel fulfilled by your work, and you've sent away that *need,* you will be able to do anything you choose and earn a living. The key ingredient in a No-Limit attitude on the job is your ability to attack any problem or task from the perspective of actualizing yourself. The creative person is involved in his work rather than simply performing tasks for a salary. If you aren't involved and actualizing yourself in what you do, then begin to do so with an attitude of being able to learn and grow each and every day.

In your personal relationships. You can have a winning-one-hundred-percent-of-the-time approach to all of your personal relationships if you decide to become more of a No-Limit person in this area. It involves forgetting about the history that you have with your loved ones and, instead, accepting them today for what they are. It means shedding those manipulative efforts to have them become more like you, and replacing them with a one-day-at-a-time acceptance of them. It means nonaltering efforts in your relationships.

Winning relationships work because each person in the alliance is willing to take the other person at face value, and they deal with each other from an appreciative viewpoint. If you simply look at your spouse, children, friends or acquaintances with the attitude of total appreciation for what they are, you will never be a loser in love again. You can't lose when you simply appreciate and grow from a relationship. When I am about to say something that might be unkind or to complain to my daughter, I constantly say to myself, "Do you really want the relationship to be based on petty squabbles and hostility? If you really appreciate her, you will not make those little discrepancies very important." Once I've reminded myself that this is a dignified, significant human being who has feelings of her own, and that I don't really want to take any of that dignity away, I generally find a more effective and productive way of airing my complaints.

The point is, when I really work on not being overly critical, abusive, complaining or anything else that creates hostility in a relationship, I usually put a stop to the behavior. Alternatively, when someone I love is being obnoxious, rather than engage in a long fight about the behavior I dislike I simply state my point of view and remove myself from the potential eruption. With a cooling-off period, virtually all human differences can be ended in a winning way.

By working at eliminating the tension points in a relationship, and by cultivating a strong sense of appreciation for the worth of the other person, your relationships can be one-hundred-percent winning ones, too. In a healthy unit, you do not have the same old family fights. You can eliminate all of that abuse by adopting a winning attitude toward all of the people who are important to you. By all means, you will never have total agreement about everything, but disagreement does not mean that you have to be disagreeable.

In academic activities. If your reasons for becoming educated are external rather than internal, you will always pursue the grade, the easy course, the approval of the teacher and the high examination score. The individual who is a winner all the time is one who knows that being educated is an internal matter completely—that learning for the sake of the pure joy it gives you, the fact that it brings you closer to your own truth, to beauty, to an appreciation for life, is reason enough for seeking out knowledge. When you are immune to the pressures that others place on you to get an education, and you go into any learning experience because you want it for yourself, you will have a handle on being an academic full-time winner.

Those grades are virtually meaningless, even if a lot of external people convince you that you must have them. In fact, you will advance and enjoy your life according to what you are able to do when you are out there in that external world, rather than on any entry on a school record. When it comes to excellence, your past grade reports are nothing more than unpolished merit badges, and you must either produce or get out of the way and let someone else do the performing. As many times as I've appeared on network television or spoken before large audiences around the world, I've never had any potential host or businessman ask me what I got in Psychology 101. People don't care, or, if they do, they shouldn't. *You get to be where you are according to how much you trust yourself and what you do, not on what you did to get a diploma.* Because many young people think of themselves as losers if they have mediocre academic records, it is important for them to understand that their worth has nothing to do with those records—that they can leave a course getting a C and be a winner, if they think in No-Limit terms. You learn from everything you do in life. Sometimes others will evaluate you in critical ways, and sometimes you won't be at the top, but if you are satisfied that you received something valuable from the experience, you are a winner.

In athletic competition. This is the place where most of the winner/loser mentality surfaces in our culture. I have written about this attitude in other sections of this book, and by now you know that I subscribe to the notion of approaching any athletic contest from the perspective of enjoyment, inner peace and fun. True, it is important to be competitive in any athletic contest, but it is never necessary to carry around "loser" images of yourself if you run into a superior opponent. Playing for yourself, to improve your skills, to achieve at the level that is satisfactory to *you,* to be relaxed and stress-free and to stop the incessant comparison with others, can make you into a winner one hundred percent of the time in any athletic endeavor. If you are an inner winner, with a firm grip on yourself and your reason for playing, then ironically you'll emerge with more victories than if you push, strive, demand, get angry and tense up. The relaxed, inner-peaceful person who simply lets his body function in the way he has trained it to perform is the kind of athlete who is a winner not only on the field of athletic competition but in all areas of his life.

All of these categories, along with others which have been touched on in this book, such as parenting, sexual partnering, travel, hobbies, management exercises and the like, are things in which *you* can be a one-hundred-percent winner. If you go into the encounter with a kind of self-knowledge and inner confidence, you can't emerge as a loser, regardless of what anyone else has to say. You may read about yourself in the paper as a "loser," or have all of your friends label you as a "loser," but in reality you will never be a loser unless you decide to put that label on yourself. And what you choose to label yourself is entirely up to you. Learning to ignore the opinions and criticisms of others, and to consult one's inner signals, is certainly at the core of being a one-hundred-percent winner. No one is ever going to convince such a person that he is a loser. He may make mistakes; he may appear foolish; he may be soundly defeated in any endeavor; he may never sell another book or appear on any best-seller list or even make another nickel in his life. But he will always be a winner because he chooses to think of himself that way. And every mistake he makes is simply another tool to help him carve out an even more effective life for himself. With that kind of attitude he can never be a loser to himself, and that is what this entire business of being alive in a No-Limit way is all about: being a winner in your own eyes.

I have talked at great length about No-Limit people, normal people and neurotic or self-defeating people throughout the pages of this book. I know that being more of a No-Limit person means being able to transcend the typical kinds of attitudes and behaviors for which many others are willing to settle. There is a king of *going beyond* that No-Limit people choose, which most others never even contemplate. If you begin to consider going beyond what you've always been, or thinking in new ways, ways which will give you a real sense of purpose and meaning in your life, then the real purpose for my writing this book will have been accomplished. Learning to transcend the *typical you* that you've accepted up until now, and to become your own tower of greatness, is a genuine possibility.

As a full-time winner you must see yourself as an end rather than a means to an end. Look at yourself as a whole person, as complete, as someone who has intrinsic value simply because you exist, rather than having to prove to yourself that you are worthy through achievements and acquisitions. While you can certainly grow and become someone different if you choose, you can still view yourself as whole and worthy where you are. It is not a contradiction to be able to grow and change in the future and still be whole and perfect now.

In addition, you can view others as they are, instead of as they "should" be. Instead of always reminding others of what they should become, try to view them as complete and whole now.

Your ability to be a No-Limit person and to go beyond even your most imaginative expectations for yourself is right in your own hands. I believe this as deeply and as sincerely as anything I've ever said or written. It is simply a matter of whether you are willing to make the growth choice more often than the self-defeating or even normal choice.

I have put it all down between the pages of this book. I can't say any more about it. Reading it won't make it happen; it will only give you a guide. What I can guarantee you is that you will feel more personal inner peace and human fulfillment if you opt for the No-Limit choices which I've described throughout the pages of this book. If you go for it, do it today, and if you see others going for their own No-Limit status, do as Diogenes asked of Alexander the Great: Stand out of their light.

Appendix

Neurotic to No Limits: Attitude and Behavior Chart

Below is a chart you can use to check out your own present attitudes and behavior according to the differences between the neurotic, "normal" and NEZ/No-Limit persons as I conceive them. This chart is based on my own observations of the way different people react to the same world. First, how neurotic or chronically unhappy people think and behave, and why their self-defeating attitudes make them miserable so much of the time. Second, how "normal" or "average" people think about the same areas of life, and why their attitudes so seldom lead to real happiness or fulfillment. Finally, how the NEZ person views the same areas of life in the transition to total No-Limit living as well as I know how to project those No-Limit attitudes at this time.

I want to point out that while I have listed thirty-seven entries in this chart, all of which are relevant to themes stressed throughout this book, the choice of entries has largely been arbitrary: I could have listed three or 3,700. I trust that as you read through this chart you will see how you think and behave in the three categories (or, more likely, will find aspects of yourself in all the categories) and decide for yourself whether you choose to adopt the NEZ/No Limit attitudes. In addition I trust that you will do some creative thinking about your own philosophy of life, that you will become more sensitive to your own attitudes and behavior in all your life situations, make your own "chart" showing where *you* want to convert your "neurotic" or "normal" attitudes toward life to No-Limit perspectives, and go on to re-create your life on your own original design.

Remember: the best that "authority figures," be they psychiatrists or politicians, can ever do for you is lead you toward being normal or average according to the accepted rules, to "cope with" standards of established society as *they* perceive them. To go beyond "normality," you have to strike out on your own, trust your own internal signals and cultivate your natural creativity, your inherent love of life. You have to enter the "forbidden paradise" of unlimited free will and original thought, letting no self-styled angels of authoritarianism bar your way or challenge your right to enter.

NEUROTIC to NO-LIMITS: ATTITUDE AND BEHAVIOR CHART

Panic — *Inertia* — *Striving* — *Coping* — *Mastery*

NEUROTIC	"NORMAL"	NEZ to NO LIMITS
1. *Fears and avoids the unknown;* stays with the familiar and is intimidated by new surroundings. Upset by *change* of any kind; defends staying the same himself.	Accepts the unknown, but does not seek it out. May adjust to changes as they come along, but generally will not initiate them. Little positive effort to change self.	Seeks out the unknown and loves the mysterious. Welcomes change and will experiment with almost anything in life. "The beauty of life is in its changes."
2. *Self-rejecting;* publicly or privately finds many things about himself to dislike; feels unattractive, unintelligent, "below average." Mistrusts self and others; little sense of belonging.	Self-accepting in most regards, but with more resignation than enthusiasm; feels as though he "fits in" about as well as others, is pretty much "where he belongs."	Self-fulfilling; has great enthusiasm for himself, with no regrets or reservations. No time or need to be conceited. Feels a strong sense of belonging in the world and to humanity.
3. Frequently *immobilized by irrational anger,* unable to control himself or "think straight" in many situations; characterized by bitter eruptions that create unpleasantness for everyone.	Often feels anger, but usually does not let it control him. Can express his anger or frustration and generally find a rational way to deal with its cause; seldom creates real unpleasantness.	Sometimes feels anger, especially at injustices, but is mobilized rather than immobilized by it; "keeps his cool" while fighting for a creative, constructive solution; a pleasure to work with.
4. *Externally motivated* in just about everything; constantly measuring people's worth in terms of "status symbols" of all kinds. Opinions highly controlled by *external signals.*	Aware of some internal motivations, but still primarily externally motivated, influenced by external rewards. Will sometimes override external signals in favor of own conscience or desires. Wants to "fit in."	Fully aware of external reward-and-signal system; gives it as much respect as his internal signals tell him it deserves, while pursuing his own individual destiny by his own best internal lights.

Panic *Inertia*	*Striving* *Coping*	*Mastery*
NEUROTIC	**"NORMAL"**	**NEZ to NO LIMITS**
5. A *chronic complainer* about the conditions of his own life and the state of the world; uses others primarily as "fenceposts" to which he can unburden himself. Would rather grumble about anything than be satisfied with or change it.	Finds many things to complain about, but seldom voices complaints or dwells on them for too long; can usually talk with others about resolving complaints. Does not go out looking for things to complain about.	Sees nothing in life to complain about except where the "complaints" can be addressed to those who can resolve the problem. Does not "complain" to himself; may *share* his complaints with others to enlist their support. A doer, not a critic.
6. *Feels unloved, unappreciated or disrespected* by others, and blames them for their callousness toward him; never looks inward to ask how much love, appreciation or respect he really gives to others.	Usually feels loved and respected to some degree by his family or special circle of friends, somewhat alienated from the rest of humanity; can give some love and respect to his "in group"; may be devastated if rejected.	Recognizes that love and respect come to the person who cultivates them; *is* genuinely loved and respected by all who can return his original openness to them; does not worry about others "rejecting" him.
7. *Worried constantly about performance* in all areas of life. Becomes depressed when others rate his performance poorly on the job, in bed, etc. Equates worth with job, money and acquisitions.	Has "the normal amount" of anxiety about performance in most areas of life, with some special areas of sensitivity (job, sex, sports, etc.). Able to accept "poor performance" sometimes, but badly upset by it at other times. Feels trapped by the need to acquire things and money.	Has no "performance anxiety" whatsoever; realizes that as much is learned from "failure" as from "success"; doesn't care how others or external standards rate his performance anywhere; knows that worrying only inhibits "performance." Unconcerned about acquisition.

8. *Shows signs of aimlessness* in life; finds little purpose or meaning in work, relationships, etc. Finds life a constant struggle; is frequently on the verge of panic about survival even when objectively "secure."	Finds purpose and meaning in some areas of life, but unable to integrate all areas into a unified, purposeful whole; frequently striving or struggling in one area or another, although on the whole outwardly "secure."	Displays a strong sense of purpose in most or all areas of life. His holistic world-view allows him to see meaning everywhere. Never wanders aimlessly or struggles fruitlessly. An unshakable sense of security comes from internal feeling of self-worth.
9. Motivated almost exclusively by need to fulfill basic animal needs and external expectations. Little or *no respect for his higher needs* or those of others.	Largely motivated by animal needs and external rewards and signals, but able to respect some higher needs of himself and others and meet them with some success.	Primarily motivated by higher human needs and values; recognizes basic animal needs as crucial, but meets them with little trouble. Search for truth, beauty, justice and peace always uppermost.
10. *Feels strong sense of ownership* toward family, friends and community. Views them as property he is always afraid of losing. Often subject to intense and irrational jealousy.	Has strong dictates about how others should behave, and may be devastated by jealousy in certain situations. Upset easily when disappointed in love.	No sense of ownership toward others or anything he is associated with; recognizes that the best way to lose anything is to try to hold too tightly to it; virtually immune to jealousy in any situation.
11. *A compulsively dichotomous thinker.* Can seldom see two sides to any issue; takes one side and sticks to it with a vengeance. Labels and forgets most people, things and ideas. Frequently upset by others as he has labeled them.	A dichotomous thinker in many respects, but can be reasonable on some issues if approached delicately; occasionally upset by others-as-labeled; usually has special prejudices (anti-minority, etc.) and intolerance of vague or unclear situations.	Seldom uses dichotomies except for specific purposes and with qualifications; sees the wholes behind them first; understands the truth in seeming opposites. Takes a cooperative approach toward thinking through any problem; never upset by labels people stick on him or others.

Panic — Inertia: NEUROTIC	Striving: "NORMAL"	Coping — Mastery: NEZ to NO LIMITS
12. Constantly *concerned with the past and the future*. Frequently dwells on injustices of the past and/or "the good old days"; governed by futurizing, usually with anxiety about what the future will bring and many plans for preventing "the worst."	Dwells sometimes on the past; is greatly taken up with futurizing, with some anxieties but usually pretending that "things will get much better when . . ." Is seldom immobilized by regrets, but equally seldom is able to live fully in the present moment.	Sees the past purely in terms of what it has taught him about how to *live now*, and the future purely as more present moments to be lived to the fullest when (and if) they come. Plans for the future only insofar as is necessary for fulfillment of personal life projects. Lives exclusively and fully in the present moment.
13. Highly *judgmental of "immature" behavior* of himself and others; governs his life by rigid, superficial standards of maturity; quick to condemn spontaneous or childlike behavior as "childish"; upset by "immaturity" of anyone at any age; cannot let children be children at all.	Fairly rigid in demanding "mature," sedate or stuffy behavior from himself in many circumstances; tolerant of childlike behavior only in children who have not yet "grown out of it." Often disapproving of "immature" behavior, but seldom greatly upset or angered by it.	Rejects trying to label his behavior or that of others as "mature" or "immature"; decides what pattern of growth he wants to pursue next for himself and lets others do the same; appreciates childlike behavior by people of all ages and cultivates it in himself.
14. *Experiences no emotional peaks* or intense moments of living now. Unable to block out external signals of futurizing and performance anxiety; incapable of genuine "natural highs"; feels emotionally "flat" or "low" most of the time.	Experiences some emotional peaks, but wonders why they are not higher and more frequent, why life is so often dull and flat; generally accepts that "life is just like that," without wondering what he can do to live "higher" for more of the time.	Able to make "peak experiences" out of almost all activities, because he has made them a primary part of his life, transcends futurizing and performance anxiety, and thinks creatively about how to get "more peaks now."

15. Feels and often expresses *revulsion for basic animal functions;* may see natural body odors, sex, etc., as disgusting, exercise as boring; does not accept aging as a natural process, but resents it and tries to deny or hide it.	Feels some shame about basic animal functions, but keeps it mostly to himself and copes with it discreetly, as "just the price you have to pay for being an animal"; will exercise, but mostly for external rewards; resents aging but knows he can't stop it.	Loves his basic animal nature and is in awe of how beautifully his body functions. Responds immediately to all its needs; exercises for the physical joy of it. Appreciates aging as the universal medium of life and growth; never hides or denies his age.
16. *Hypochondriac:* constantly afraid of all kinds of illnesses, ultimately of death; may often complain of mysterious aches and pains, become heavily dependent on doctors and pills; no thought that he can cure himself; complaining about his infirmities may come to dominate his life.	Generally accepting of "normal health" without undue worry, experiencing "fear of death" only occasionally, for some rational reason; but still heavily dependent on doctors and pills to "fix it" when anything goes wrong, and unaware of what he can do to promote his "superhealth."	Pursues physical "superhealth" with minimal reliance on doctors and pills, knowing it is all in his power to preserve and strengthen himself; fears death only when it is a real and present threat, and then trusts his animal instincts and his body to meet the threat if they can.
17. *Feels guilty* much of the time; feels judged, especially in family situations, when no judgment was intended; susceptible to manipulation by others because of irrational guilt; tries to make others feel guilty in return; constantly concerned with "who is really guilty."	Feels guilty about specific behaviors, but does not feel "judged" all the time; sometimes subject to manipulation by others "peddling guilt"; sometimes tries to use guilt to manipulate others; overly concerned with "who's guilty" but usually capable of forgiving and forgetting.	Feels guilty only when his conscience tells him he has done something wrong; responds immediately to the call of his conscience to make it right and erase the guilt feelings; never manipulates others with guilt or allows them to use it to manipulate him; doesn't care who's guilty, only about setting wrongs right.

Panic — *Inertia* — *Striving* — *Coping* — *Mastery*

NEUROTIC	"NORMAL"	NEZ to NO LIMITS
18. Has *strong feelings of dependency* on family, friends, job, and organizations to which he belongs. Clings tightly and timidly to them because so much of his ego depends on them; may "come apart" if any central dependency relationships are broken; represses own needs for independence.	Depends heavily on family and friends for identity, but also feels needs for personal independence (as in "typical adolescent rebellion"). Resents too many dependencies in his life; would like more independence but is seldom willing to take risks to get it.	Has resolved dependence/independence dichotomy into concept of *interdependence;* depends on nobody else for his own identity or self-worth, but appreciates the way all people "depend" on each other in this world to act as independent, compassionate human beings.
19. *Blames others* or "society" for his unhappiness; puts responsibility for his faults on his parents, his boss, his family, etc. Becomes angry and defensive when others confront him with what he can do about it himself. Is not interested in solutions to problems, only in blaming.	Seldom blames specific others for his own mistakes, but feels that most of his life is out of his control, and may blame the world for being the way it is. Often wastes time blaming others he sees as "at fault" in specific situations instead of working toward a good solution.	Never wastes time blaming anyone for his own faults or the woes of the world; realizes that all of his life that matters is what is under his control; may find fault with the actions of others or himself, but instead of attaching personal blame (or guilt) he works to eliminate the faults.
20. *Humorless* in most situations. May tell "canned jokes" or try to force humor (laughs loudly at his own jokes) now and then, but never in connection with what is "most serious" to him, usually his authoritarian beliefs, quest for status, etc. Cannot appreciate spontaneous humor; disapproves in most cases.	Generally able to enjoy a good laugh when it is "appropriate" (during coffee break, etc.), but often at the expense of others gossiped about, seldom at himself or in connection with what is "most serious" to him; can appreciate and engage in spontaneous humor only in selected circumstances.	Recognizes that a sense of humor is vital to all aspects of life; that it does not always involve laughing or being funny, but reflects an overall acceptance of life in all its eccentricities; loves a good laugh whenever he can get or create one; will laugh at himself above all; loves spontaneous humor in all life situations.

21. Very *local in values and self-identification;* very often highly chauvinistic about his family, neighborhood, closest friends or most prestigious acquaintances, favorite restaurant, brand of tires, or whatever. Feels called upon to defend those local values at all costs; is very personally threatened when they are questioned.	Some local chauvinism, but more inclined toward patriotism and nationalism as ultimate values; less threatened by local changes or questioning of things "close to home"; feels some overall concern with human problems, but still primarily motivated by localistic and nationalistic chauvinism more than by a genuine love of humanity.	Completely global and humanistic in values and self-identification; able to take pride in genuine local accomplishments when they contribute to the good of humanity, but equally able to oppose local and national chauvinism when they do not. Rejects all forms of ethnocentrism to put "the big picture" first and see himself as "a human" above all.
22. *Comparison-oriented.* Constantly aware of what others are doing and how he compares (or competes) with them in all areas of life; upset when others compare favorably to him by external standards; may denigrate accomplishments of others to make his own seem greater by comparison, even become a cheat or fraud.	Accepts comparison and competition as "facts of life" but seldom as matters of life and death; may often "suffer from comparisons" with others in sensitive areas (job, love relationships), but usually will not go out of his way to compare himself unfavorably with others; plays the comparison/competition game as fairly as he can.	Rejects the comparison/competition game as a whole. Usually so caught up in what he is doing now that he does not notice what others are doing except if they are working or playing with him. Takes joy in the successes of others as further contributions to the happiness of humanity now.
23. *Fears failure;* avoids activities in which he is unskilled or inexperienced; becomes angry at himself or others when he does fail at something; unable to learn from failures; often tries to hide or deny failures; may ridicule others for their failures.	Dislikes failure; works hard at being successful at everything; demands same emphasis on success from other family members; usually tolerates failures as the price of success; able to try some new things; "If at first you don't succeed, try, try again"; "Don't be a quitter."	Rejects success/failure dichotomy; welcomes failure as part of learning process; willing to try almost anything that interests him; no compulsion to "succeed" (compete) in everything he tries; "success" comes naturally in fulfillment of life projects and practice at things he deeply cares about.

Panic *Inertia*	*Striving*	*Coping* *Mastery*
NEUROTIC	**"NORMAL"**	**NEZ to NO LIMITS**
24. *Inclined to hero worship.* Puts forth famous people with whom he identifies as larger than life, lives vicariously through them; upset when his heroes "let him down"; argumentative with others about the greatness of his heroes, angry when others do not share his worship or question it.	Has heroes, may worship them to some degree, but accepts them as subject to human frailty; especially inclined to "great historical figures" as heroes (George Washington *et. al.*); identifies self with "what they stood for"; may be defensive about them, but seldom to the point of immobilizing anger.	Has no specific heroes. Recognizes that for every famous hero there are millions of unsung heroes; sees a hero in everyone; admires and learns from examples of those who have advanced humanistic causes, but too busy making his own contribution to live vicariously through anyone else.
25. *Conformist* in everything; constantly worried about whether he has "got it right" according to the majority and/or "the authorities"; constantly consulting etiquette guides, advice columns, etc., and watching "trendsetters." Will obey the most petty rules and regulations unthinkingly and demand that others do, too.	Obeys most cultural rules and conforms to most customs; sensitive to "fitting in," but allows himself some individuality; conformist mostly in "big things" such as choice of career, political attitudes, where to live, etc. Able to ignore petty rules and regulations and etiquette guides when they are plainly ridiculous.	Places no positive value on conforming for its own sake or for external rewards or approval, nor on nonconformity for its own sake. If he happens to conform, fine. If not, equally fine. Rejects blind conformity primarily in "big things"; will get around petty rules and customs as easily as possible; will challenge and fight to change really destructive rules or customs.
26. Afraid to be alone; *rejects his need* and the needs of others for *privacy,*	Usually prefers not to be alone, but able to appreciate some "private mo-	As happy alone as with anyone else; insists on his rights to privacy and

moments alone with self; dependent on constant external feedback for "sense of reality"; afraid others are trying to hide from him (or hide things from him) if they just want to be alone; frequently invades the privacy of others.	ments"; subject to severe "loneliness depression" if "left alone" for too long; respects others' need for privacy in most cases, but worries or wonders about those who like to be alone "too much"; may secretly want more privacy.	those of everyone else; his life is a productive alternation of alone-time and together-time of his own design; knows nothing of "loneliness depression" because he is at peace with himself and can always find people to be with if he wants.
27. *Dishonest with himself.* Constantly in internal turmoil caused by trying to pretend he is something he is not; cannot admit own errors; instead makes up defenses and excuses. Internal signals almost totally blocked. May lead to massive dishonesty with others.	Deludes himself or blocks his internal signals in many ways; puts on "petty" pretenses, but does not pretend to be anything radically different from what he is; can usually admit own errors, but with excuses or defenses; internal signals strong enough to prevent serious dishonesty with others.	Closely in tune with internal signals that warn of any dishonesty; makes peace with his conscience above all; catches himself every time he is about to be pretentious or put on a false identity; easily admits own errors, with a sense of humor but no excuses or defenses; approaches others with pure, childlike honesty.
28. *Lacks creativity* in approaches to life; thinks of himself as "uncreative"; never gives the creative genius within him an out. Imitates others in almost everything; secretly resents their domination over him; is intimidated by truly creative people or unconventional life styles.	Exercises creativity, or expressions of individuality, only in select and limited circumstances; finds little outlet for creativity at work (where it may be discouraged) or in key relationships or family situations, but may find outlets in "avocations," hobbies and "off hours."	Lets his own creative imagination loose in any situation it wants to address; approaches everything in life from a creative point of view; imitates others only when he can't find a better way to do it; applies creative urges above all to his vocation and key interpersonal relationships.

Panic *Inertia*	*Striving*	*Coping* *Mastery*
NEUROTIC	"NORMAL"	NEZ to NO LIMITS
29. *Intellectually stagnant,* often anti-intellectual; feels education "ended" with formal schooling; represses natural intellectual curiosity and suspects or envies others who indulge theirs; gives shallow or "canned" explanations for "what he thinks"; gets angry when others "embarrass" him with information he was unaware of.	Intellectually motivated in very limited ways. May indulge in a few areas of curiosity, mostly in spare time (the "history buff," the amateur horticulturalist or meteorologist), but will seldom apply full intellectual powers and curiosity to central problems-and-promise of life. Interested in education mostly for self-advancement or external success.	Intellectually motivated by his natural curiosity and instincts to seek the truth for himself in all possible life situations. Recognizes that all education, in school or out of school, is primarily self-education; able to apply concentrated intellectual powers to any area of curiosity, especially central areas of problems-and-promise in the life of humanity.
30. A *compulsive planner,* uncomfortable without a concrete schedule for everything and angry or peevish when all schedules are not precisely met. Spends more time worrying about "the program" than enjoying any occasion; can hardly wait to get on to worrying about the next schedule.	Often concerned with "regularity" in life (mealtimes, bedtimes, lovemaking times) and preferring to have a concrete plan in most cases, but able to enjoy a certain amount of spontaneity, seldom showing undue concern for plans and schedules, but still "overregulated" in life.	Makes up all plans as needed in concrete present-moment situations; honors commitments to others, but keeps commitments to a level he knows he wants to handle; prefers not to have "a plan" if possible to leave room for spontaneity.
31. A *follower,* but never a real leader. May attain "ceremonial posts" awarded by some authoritarian soci-	Primarily a follower, but able to exercise real leadership abilities in some areas of life, and responsive to	Recognizes no "leaders" and no "followers" in the world, except where people choose to label themselves as

	ety, but never follows his own lights in initiating new ideas or challenging authority. Constant denial of his needs to "lead himself" and secret resentment of his status as "a follower" create internal conflict and immobilization.	his own internal lights when deep matters of conscience or real bursts of inspiration are involved. Frequently denies his need to "lead himself," and feels some resentment at his fate, which he takes to be mostly that of a follower.	"followers." Follows his own internal lights in all things; is inspired when others agree he is right and want to work with him, but wants no thoughtless disciples, only co-workers who are as willing as he is to lead themselves.
32.	*Obsessed with money,* no matter how much he has; constantly worried about survival, long-term security or getting rich as the only "objective" measure of his worth; will take or keep a job he hates if it pays well; seldom able to enjoy the money he has; usually stingy; looks down on poor (even if he is poor) and up to super-rich. Secretly resents dependence on money; internal conflict.	Apt to be overly concerned with money even if he has enough, but more for material comforts and "independence" it can provide than for its own sake; seldom measures self-worth primarily by money; would love to be rich, but not willing to take a repugnant job to get there; able to enjoy money he has, although with some guilt in spending it; can be fairly generous. Frequent conflicts about money.	Couldn't care less about money *per se.* Pursues work that is meaningful to him, adjusts his life style to live happily on whatever money it happens to bring; never measures anyone's worth in terms of money; if he gets rich it will be "by accident" in pursuing his work; enjoys all experiences whether they cost money or not; spends money without guilt (although not carelessly); very generous to those in need; no conflicts.
33.	Virtually *incapable of relaxation or recreation;* sees it as "of no profit," a waste of "valuable working time." Consequently riddled with anxiety and bodily tension. So competitive and uptight in games that he cannot enjoy them; spends vacations worrying about petty details or schedules, about work left undone; can't unwind.	Neglects full needs for relaxation and recreation, but indulges in them enough to keep him "sane." Seldom attains full relaxation because of preoccupations; feels recreation is a luxury that must take second place to more important things ("Wait until vacation"). Can enjoy games and vacations more or less; unwinds infrequently.	Cultivates the arts of relaxation and recreation as vital to happiness, creativity and living now, being at ease in any situation. Expert at attaining total relaxation regularly, whether through Yoga, meditation or other avenues of his own discovery or invention. Looks on games as pure recreation; "vacations" several times a day, knows how to enjoy all vacations; never "wound up" in stressful sense.

Panic · Inertia	Striving	Coping · Mastery
NEUROTIC	**"NORMAL"**	**NEZ to NO LIMITS**
34. *Insensitive to beauty;* very narrow and rigid ideas of what it is or where it can be found (sunsets, magazine cover girls); sees ugliness everywhere ("That house down the block is an eyesore; it needs painting"); judges beauty of people on appearance or status and finds most people ugly; repression of needs to see much beauty in the world leads to dullness, "crabbiness."	Fairly standard ideas of what beauty is and where it can be found; frequent use of the word "beautiful" indicates a response to higher needs, but little thought is given to expanding "conventional vision," resulting in many "blind spots" in how beauty can be seen and/or created. Beauty judged by acceptable external cultural standards.	Sees the whole world as beautiful and wonderful to begin with; no limits to its varieties of beauty, no boundaries on how or where it can be discovered and/or created. "A child's smile can outshine any sunset." "That dilapidated house down the block would make a great picture if I caught the side where the lilacs are running wild." "All people are intrinsically beautiful, even if their actions or creations sometimes are not." Constantly fulfills an ever-expanding instinct to pursue beauty in life.
35. *Feels he has "no choice"* about how his life goes; resigned to the idea that life is predetermined, "you just get the luck of the draw"; a fatalist who often views things or people (himself included) as "hopeless," and who will fall into deep depression and despair unless he keeps himself busy pursuing externals.	Sees much of life as predetermined by externals like race, social class, upbringing and luck, but feels people can "better themselves" by intense personal ambition and making "the right choices" in playing society's "success games." A limited belief in personal choice keeps him from deep despair.	Feels every moment of life as one of free personal choice; rejects externals as limiting what he can become; ignores "ambition" and "the right choices" as defined by others when it comes to making his own personal choices; believes in unlimited free will.

36. *Has little respect for life* or for humanity as a whole. Believes most human lives are worthless (not worth living), as those of starving peoples halfway around the globe; accepts war and violence as in the nature of the species; cares only about the lives of those closest to him; may be paranoid with the idea that others care as little about his life as he does about theirs.	Has a fundamental respect for all human life, but focuses it narrowly on those closest to him; accepts that some starving people halfway around the world might be better off dead; hopes that war and violence can be eliminated someday, but is pessimistic; accepts competition between people and nations for the world's resources as inevitable, along with famines, plagues, etc.; hopes his loved ones will not be affected.	Sees all life as sacred, all human lives as intrinsically of equal worth. The devotion he shows every day to those closest to him is reflected in his concern for all people and the well-being of the race. He believes war, violence, famines and plagues can be eliminated if humanity chooses, and devotes his life to improving the lives of everyone and ending injustice.
37. *Always fighting life.* Feels forever struggling upstream, never able to stop and catch his breath, always about to be swept back or pulled under by the treacherous currents; in constant internal turmoil (whether well masked or not); dominated by cycles of panic, inertia and striving.	Not often fighting life to the point of panic, but feeling that it is an upstream struggle much of the time, and uncertain how much he really wants to risk to explore all this unknown territory; would rather wade in shallow water or sit on the bank when striving-time is done; cycles of inertia, striving and coping.	Goes with the flow; feels forever borne downstream; thrills to his mastery of the "white water," the beauty of the ever-changing life-world he swims through; appreciates quiet moments just lounging on the banks and resting or exploring the surrounding wilderness. Thinks, feels and behaves as a self-master.